In Loving Memory
of
Margaret Murphy Bernard '80
1962-1991

Patricia Dailey Hayes

The Class of 1980
Mayfield Senior School

Women in Waiting
in the
Westward Movement

Women in Waiting in the Westward Movement

Life on the Home Frontier

By **Linda Peavy** and **Ursula Smith**

Foreword by John Mack Faragher

University of Oklahoma Press : Norman and London

Library of Congress Cataloging-in-Publication Data

Peavy, Linda S.
    Women in waiting in the westward movement : life on the home
frontier / by Linda Peavy and Ursula Smith ; foreword by John Mack
Faragher.
        p.   cm.
    Includes bibliographical references and index.
    ISBN 0–8061–2616–7 (alk. paper).—ISBN 0–8061–2619–1 (pbk. :
alk. paper)
        1. Pioneers' spouses—United States—History—19th century.
2. Women—United States—History—19th century. 3. Frontier and
pioneer life—West (U.S.) 4. West (U.S.)—History. 5. United
States—Territorial expansion. I. Title.
F596.P43   1994
973.8'082—dc20   93–38832
                                                             CIP

Text design by Cathy Carney Imboden.

The paper in this book meets the guidelines for permanence and dura-
bility of the Committee on Production Guidelines for Book Longevity of
the Council on Library Resources, Inc. ♾

2   3   4   5   6   7   8   9   10

Contents

VI
Emma Stratton Christie
"If We Only Had a Place of Ourn and You Was with Us"

VII
Augusta Perham Shipman
"Do Have Your Visit or Exploration
or Whatever You Call It and Come Back"

Notes

Index

Illustrations

Foreword

Americans have always had itching feet. The unceasing movement of people from one place to another led the historian Frederick Jackson Turner to conclude in the 1890s that "for nearly three centuries the dominant fact in American life has been expansion." Even in colonial New England—that bastion of tight little communities—Puritan mobility drove the minister Increase Mather to preach against parishioners who "have forsaken Churches, and Ordinances, all for land and *elbow room*." By the time of the Revolution, in communities throughout America, four of ten families typically packed up and left every ten years. Movement has continued to characterize our national life. In our rates of mobility we Americans are exceeded only by New Zealanders. We have always been a people in search of *elbow room*, right up to the current shift of population toward the metropolitan centers of the Sunbelt.

Such movement was the motive force behind the settlement of the American West. In communities throughout the West, as well as those on its fringes, rates of mobility rose as high as they would climb in the American experience. In the past quarter-century historians have focused on the prominent place of families in this movement. Eight of ten persons who went overland to Oregon in the mid-nineteenth century, for example, moved within family groups.

The gold rush to California, on the other hand, was overwhelmingly male, and in the long history of American westering tens of thousands of migrating men were unaccompanied by women. But as Linda Peavy and Ursula Smith point out in this remarkable book, without both the work and support of "women in waiting" back home, few sons, brothers, or husbands could have gone west. Not only did women keep the home fires burning (and since men often came home broke and sometimes humiliated, they were sorely in need of those comforts) women also ran the farms and the businesses, paid the mortgages, and frequently sent off the money that men needed to pay their passage home. The record of women's achievement chronicled in these pages suggests that we must re-think the dynamics of expansion, for as Peavy and Smith argue, the westward movement was supported, to a degree few have appreciated, by the labor of women back east.

These "women in waiting" frequently expressed their frustration at the wanderlust of the men in their lives. "If you dont settle your mind on what you are going to do you can bea runing about all the rest of your days and never bea settled," wrote Emma Christie to her husband, David, in Montana. His defense—"Now Dear dont blame me for thinking this way"—suggests that this was a dispute they had rehearsed many times before. Their fascinating dialogue reminds me of a popular song of the mid-nineteenth century:

> Since times are so hard, I'll tell you, my wife,
> I've a mind for to shake off this trouble and strife,
> And to California my journey pursue
> To double my fortunes as other men do;
> For here we may labor each day in the field
> And the winters consume all that summers doth yield.
>
> Dear husband, I've noticed with sorrowful heart
> You've too long neglected your plow and your cart;
> Your horses, sheep, cattle, disorderly run,
> And your new Sunday waistcoat goes everyday on.
> Now stick to your farming; you'll suffer no loss,
> For the stone that keeps rolling can gather no moss.
>
> Dear wife, let us go, and don't let us wait.
> I long to be doing, I long to be great,
> And you some great lady, and who knows but I
> Will be some great Governor before we do die.
> For here we may labor each day in the field.
> And the winters consume all that summers doth yield.
>
> Dear husband, remember your land is to clear,
> It will cost you the labor of many a year.
> Your horses, sheep and cattle will all be to buy,
> And before you have got them you are ready to die.
> So stick to your farming; you'll suffer no loss,
> For the stone that keeps rolling can gather no moss.

With appeals such as these the wife of the song succeeds in dissuading her husband from moving. Many women were not so lucky. As one abandoned wife wrote: "My old man has left me & has gon to

Califona and took my wagon and left me and my children in a bad situation."

The stories in this book also document the agonizingly slow communication between husbands and wives separated by hundreds and thousands of miles. Two-way conversations required many months. It was nearly a year after his departure for California before William Hiller heard a single word from home. His wife, Abiah, suffered through an equally long period of silence before finally receiving a letter. "I was glad to hear that you are alive," she wrote back, "I had almost given you up for lost." Not knowing where her husband, Henry, had settled, Sarah Yesler spent hours making multiple copies of her letters, sending them to every conceivable Pacific port in the hopes that one would find him. These letters often chronicle a painful loneliness. "I have been Dreaming of you every night," David Christie wrote to his wife, Emma; "I have got the blues. I will be glad when I can get hom for I am sick of this knocking around."

Without discounting the troubles of the men "knocking around" the West, this book concentrates on the struggles of the "women in waiting." They have a deep and rich history. A century before the period in which this book is set, Rebecca Bryan Boone, wife of the legendary American pioneer Daniel Boone, endured months, even years of his absence hunting in the woods. Not only was there the cooking and cleaning, spinning and weaving, and washing and sewing, but there was also water to be fetched each day from the spring, wood to be chopped, gardens to be tended, and cows to be milked. And there were fields to be cultivated and crops to be harvested as well. In need of fresh meat for her stew pot, many was the time Rebecca hunted for small game in the woods near her cabin. She was a strong, intelligent, resourceful woman. Yet when a traveling preacher stopped at her isolated cabin during one of her husband's long absences, he recorded in his journal that "she told me of her trouble, and the frequent distress and fear in her heart."

Rebecca Boone's confession may stand for the fears of generations of American women. More than a century later, Montana pioneer Clark Shipman received a letter from his daughter. "I know that you have had a hard time to get started in a new country," she wrote sympathetically. But "it has been hard for mother too." As long as men have been moving, women have been waiting.

JOHN MACK FARAGHER

Yale University, New Haven, Connecticut

Preface

In researching the role played by women in the settling of a small canyon community near Bozeman, Montana, we came across a collection of letters written by a couple during an eighteen-month period of separation when he was out in Montana Territory searching for a homestead and she was back home in Minnesota looking after their children and the family farm. A short time later, during a presentation on our work in women's history, we shared our fascination with the letters we'd come across. After that presentation, a woman came forward to tell us of the uncanny similarity between the experiences of the Bridger Canyon couple and those of her own great grandparents—he a gold miner at Pikes Peak in 1860 and she a housewife and mother left at home in Little Falls, Minnesota, to tend children, farm, and business. And yes, this woman said, there were letters, lots of letters, housed in the archives at the University of Montana in Missoula.

Shortly thereafter we discovered that Daniel Tuttle, the first Episcopal bishop of Montana Territory, had left his wife and small son behind when he first went west to ride the circuit and that John Bozeman, the founder of our then hometown, had left his spouse and three young daughters in Georgia when he went west in search of gold.

As we came across more and more cases of families separated in the westward movement, we became increasingly convinced that the experiences of the women left behind—whom we were by now calling "women in waiting"—deserved to be explored, and that exploration has been our focus for the past ten years. We began our research by querying archives throughout the West and Midwest, looking for primary and secondary materials that would help us to reconstruct the experiences of women on the home frontier and to analyze the immediate and long-range effects of the absence of westering husbands and fathers. Through both dogged persistence and serendipitous good fortune, we were able to find materials relating to fifty-three different couples separated during the westward movement—but those materials were of varying quality and quantity.

In several cases, notably those concerning the six couples whose stories we've told in chapters 2 through 7, we found exactly what we had hoped to find: double sets of letters that described in varying detail the day-to-day activities and experiences of wives on the home front and husbands on the far frontier. For most of these couples we've also been able to find letters to and from family members, friends, and business associates; diaries and journals; photographs; business records; and genealogies, all of which helped us reconstruct these stories. In other cases, many of which became a part of the overview presented in chapter 1, we were able to find materials that gave us only a part of the story—most frequently the husband's part, since letters written by and describing the feelings and deeds of the husband were found far more often than letters and diaries revealing the thoughts and activities of the wife.

In the course of our research, we have traveled many miles, worked in many archives and courthouses, and been assisted by many persons and organizations. First and foremost, our gratitude goes to those who worked so patiently with us in reconstructing their family histories. These descendants of separated couples gave unstintingly of their resources, time, and energy to help us flesh out the stories that lay behind the materials found in the archives.

Jane Dunning Baldwin of Spokane, Washington, and Peter and Virginia Ashlock of Lawrence, Kansas, were most gracious in adding their personal memories, records, and artifacts to the material on Abiah and William Hiller with which we worked in the Eastern Washington State Historical Society archives in Spokane. We regret that neither Jane nor Peter has survived to see the results of their collaboration.

Personal interviews and extensive correspondence with Almira and Daniel Stearns's descendants, Robert and Louise Stearns, Jim and Opal Stearns, and Fay and Ruth Stearns, all of Oakland, Oregon, helped us gain a better understanding of the materials housed in Special Collections at the University of Oregon in Eugene and in the Douglas County Museum of History and Natural History in Roseburg, Oregon.

Gretchen Palen Peterson of Edina, Minnesota, great-granddaughter of Harriet and Ard Godfrey, provided family records and vintage photographs to supplement the documents we read in the Minnesota Historical Society library in Saint Paul and at the Hennepin History Museum in Minneapolis.

Lawrence Christie and Ina Christie Denton, both of Bozeman, Montana, were involved with this project from its beginnings, for their grandparents—homesteaders Emma and David Christie—wrote the letters that set us off on this quest. Lawrence and Ina not only alerted us to the Christie Family Papers in the Minnesota Historical Society in Saint Paul, but also provided us with records and reminiscences that added immeasurably to our understanding of this phenomenon of the separated family in the westward movement.

If the letters of David and Emma Christie helped us begin this project, then the letters of another homesteading couple, Clark and Augusta Shipman, helped bring the work to completion. Indeed, the Shipman Family Papers, which now reside at the Montana Historical Society in Helena, were brought to our attention by Susan Shipman Burnham of Lewistown, Montana, after a presentation in which we'd remarked that our research on women in waiting was finally completed. Although Susan Burnham's mention of the letters of her grandparents led to another two years of research, her candid discussions of family history deepened and broadened our understanding of westward migration and gave us new perspectives on the dynamics of separation.

We are equally indebted to the descendants of the families whose stories appear in chapter 1 of this book. The great-granddaughter of Pamelia and James Fergus—Charlotte Orr of Bozeman, Montana—has, along with other Fergus descendants, been given our thanks already in the preface to *The Gold Rush Widows of Little Falls,* a book that tells the Fergus story in full. Rivé N. Talbot Hoover of Lebanon, Oregon, shared letters and memorabilia of her great-grandparents, Mollie and Robert Kelley; Dr. Dick Warner of Montana City, Montana, gave us the letters of his great-grandparents, Mary and Leroy Warner; Melba Wickes of Kalispell, Montana, shared the story of her great-grandparents, Sarah and Ambrose Kiser; Shirley Bachini of Havre, Montana, gave us materials relating to her great-grandparents, Elizabeth and Peter Levengood; Beverly Jensen of Drayton, North Dakota, provided the background and letters of Mary Elizabeth and Granberry Rose; and Isabell Leaver of Birmingham, Alabama, contributed to our research on her great-grandparents, Mary Jane and Jack Swilling.

We owe our thanks not only to the descendants of our various subjects, but also to many other people who at various times pointed us toward new cases, answered a desperate query, provided an esoteric connection, or corrected a misconception. Many of these people are identified in the end notes; many others remain anonymous but appreciated.

For as long as we've been involved in researching women's history, we have been indebted to the archivists and librarians who have guided us in the use of their materials. Such professionals were no less helpful in this current work, a work so protracted that some of them are no longer at their posts as we conclude the project. Still, they deserve our thanks: Eileen Hurley Clark, formerly at the Washington State Historical Society in Tacoma; Edward Nolan, formerly at the Cheney Cowles Museum in Spokane; Hillary Cummings, formerly at the University of Oregon Special Collections in Eugene; and Minnie Paugh and Marlene Anderson, formerly at the Merrill G. Burlingame Special Collections, Montana State University Libraries, in Bozeman.

We thank as well those archivists and librarians who were with us from beginning to end: Bonnie Palmquist and Dallas Lindgren at the Minnesota Historical Society in Saint Paul; Terry Abraham at the University of Idaho Library in Moscow; Dale Johnson at the Mansfield Library, University of Montana in Missoula; Dave Walter at the Montana Historical Society in Helena; Rick Caldwell at the Museum of History and Industry in Seattle; and Carla Rickerson and Richard Engeman at the University of Washington Libraries in Seattle. And we thank those who came to their posts in the midst of our work, notably Glen Mason at the Cheney Cowles Museum in Spokane, Kathryn Otto at the Montana Historical Society in Helena, and Nathan Bender at the Montana State University Special Collections in Bozeman.

We're grateful to the countless, and largely anonymous, professional and volunteer staff in libraries, museums, archives, courthouses, and town halls across the country who helped us in the use of their resources, especially John Neal Hoover of the Saint Louis Mercantile Library Association, who led us to the *Haus and Herd* magazine that yielded our jacket/cover illustration.

We also extend our thanks to the individuals, organizations, and institutions who provided funds and facilities essential to the completion of this work: the National Endowment for the Humanities, which provided us with Travel to Collections grants; the American Association of University Women Educational Foundation, which provided Linda with a Career Development Grant; the Centrum Foundation of Port Townsend, Washington, which provided us with uninterrupted writing time during two nonfiction residencies; and Dorothy Boulton and Paul Conn, whose Gardiner, Montana, Depot became our haven and our refuge more than once during the development of this manuscript.

Over the past decade we have enjoyed the support of many scholars who in one way or another provided the inspiration that kept us believing in this work and the guidance we needed to bring it to completion. We wish to thank in particular Susan Armitage, Jeanie Attie, Merrill Burlingame, Elizabeth Hampsten, Elizabeth Jameson, Ruth Moynihan, the late Sandra Myres, Paula Petrik, Richard Roeder, and Lillian Schlissel, as well as all our colleagues in the Coalition for Western Women's History, whose work in the field inspires and informs our own.

In closing, we wish to extend our thanks to family members and personal friends who endured this decade-long project of ours with good cheer and quiet encouragement; to the staff at the University of Oklahoma Press—notably Mildred Logan, Patsy Willcox, and Cathy Imboden—who tolerated our countless queries and supported our many requests; and, of course, to John Drayton, who has displayed remarkable patience during his lengthy stint as editor in waiting.

LINDA PEAVY
URSULA SMITH

Women in Waiting
in the
Westward Movement

Families in Flux

The Dynamics of Separation
in the Westward Movement

In October of 1860, Pamelia Fergus of Little Falls, Minnesota, opened a letter from her husband, James, far distant in the goldfields of Pikes Peak. Filled with news of his adventures in the mountains, the letter contained but a single nugget concerning matters at home: "My going away has [been] and will be a great benefit to you, by throwing you on your own resources and learning you to do business for yourself." James's optimistic assessment of her situation must have engendered at least a bit of skepticism in Pamelia. She was, after all, facing the oncoming winter with few material resources to sustain herself and her four children and with little experience to call on as she juggled the affairs of a small farm and her husband's nearly bankrupt business.[1]

Trying as they were, the experiences of Pamelia Fergus were not unique. The separation of the Fergus family was representative of a fairly common pattern in the westward movement. Lured first by the promise of gold and later by the hope of debt-free homesteads, thousands of men went west. For any number of reasons, many of the married men among them made the journey alone, intending either to return with fortunes that would assure a comfortable future or to move their wives and children west once they had found employment or secured a homestead. While the experiences of these westering men have become a part of the legend of the American frontier, the stories of the wives they left behind have seldom been told.[2]

This fact is hardly surprising, for until the last quarter century the

American frontier experience was generally presented within a masculine context. Though this view has gradually been broadened, the experiences of women and children that *have* managed to make their way into the history of the westward movement have, by and large, been those most directly tied to the journey itself and the settling-in process.[3] Out of sight and out of mind, the women on the home frontier have remained a largely invisible sector, though their work directly supported a sizeable percentage of the men who explored and settled the American West.

Often carried out under adverse circumstances, the work these women undertook on behalf of their absent husbands was not necessarily confined to the home and frequently required venturing out into the world of commerce—in direct violation of the prevailing ideology of separate spheres.[4] Furthermore, since most of these women had had little or no prior experience in the business world, their dealings there were not always pleasant or successful. They were, however, essential to the survival of the household.

So completely were these women thrown upon their own resources that Pamelia Fergus of Little Falls came to refer to herself and her fellows as "the widows," an appropriate term, since only the death of a husband would normally have given a woman of that era such complete autonomy in business and personal affairs. But while true widows saw their situation as more or less permanent and could begin to adjust accordingly, the "widows" of Little Falls, and others like them, were women thrust into limbo by the departure of husbands with whom they would, presumably, be one day reunited. Even as they dutifully attended to all matters left in their charge, they were ever mindful that the world in which they operated was skewed, altered, and by no means permanent. They were women in waiting, women whose role and status in the home and the world beyond would not be decided until the return or death of their wandering husbands. Designated as surrogate heads of household, they assumed responsibilities and privileges they would be expected to relinquish upon reunion with their husbands.

Though they were waiting for the time when the return of their spouses would restore life to some semblance of normalcy, these were hardly "women in waiting" in the inactive sense of that phrase. Children had to be fed, clothed, housed, and educated; farms and businesses had to be managed; and creditors had to be paid or pacified—with or without a husband at hand. In one sense, then, the adventuring husbands were the ones "in waiting," in that they were standing someplace in the wings while the drama of everyday affairs back home went on without them, directed by the wives they had left behind.

Turning our attention to the drama being played out on the home frontier should not only deepen our appreciation for the indirect contributions women made to the settling of the American West but should also alter our stereotypical perceptions of the accomplishments of the men who were more directly involved in that settling. Granted, the idea of a westward movement supported by the paid and unpaid labor of women back east is inherently unsettling. How do we incorporate the idea of an "allowance" from home into our long-standing image of the frontiersman as rugged individualist? And how do we measure the heroism of the adventuring men who faced the unknowns of the far frontier against the heroism of their stay-at-home wives for whom even the knowns became unknowns as they coped with old problems in unorthodox ways?

The very invisibility of life on the home frontier has made it difficult to assess the significance of this particular aspect of the westward movement.[5] While women who crossed the plains and established homes in the West sometimes had enough awareness of being part of a major movement to feel compelled to record their activities and feelings in diaries, journals, and letters, those women who stayed in place and held life together for absent husbands had little or no sense of the historical importance of their contributions and were far less inclined to compile a written record of their day-to-day activities.

There were exceptions. Westering husbands often expected and sometimes received a fairly full accounting of the activities of wives left in charge of matters at home. Thus, though they are relatively difficult to locate and necessarily limited in their perspective and scope, the letters of wives left behind provide a means of examining life on the home frontier and of assessing the nature and extent of the impact the separation of families had on the women themselves, on their marriages, on family life as a whole, and on the westward movement.[6]

The letters of waiting wives not only give us a way of looking at such questions, but, taken together with the more readily obtainable letters, diaries, and journals of westering husbands, they also suggest that the separated family was a far more common phenomenon in the westward movement than has heretofore been supposed. While the great numbers of single men found in the mining camps and on the overland trails has led to the assumption that the westward movement was largely one of bold young bachelors, there is increasing evidence that many of these "single" men had left wives and children back home. Some fifteen years ago Andrew Rotter's study of Forty-niner diaries established the widespread presence of married men in the gold camps, and a careful reading of letters of westering husbands and waiting wives corroborates Rotter's findings, since such letters contain numerous references to other couples struggling to maintain their marriages under similar circumstances.[7]

For westering husbands, there was comfort in not being the only man who had left wife and children behind. From a winter camp eight miles above Sacramento, John Marsh Smith wrote home of the "consolation of having in the party two married men who have wives and little ones. It's an old saying—'Misery loves company.'" And for their wives, there was comfort in being with other women who knew, first-hand, what it was like to be left in responsible charge of a family. The letters Pamelia Fergus wrote to her husband over a four-year span in the early 1860s reveal the camaraderie that developed among a group of ten women, the previously mentioned "widows," who were left behind in Little Falls, Minnesota. At that same time, but across the country in the primitive settlement of Roseburg, Oregon, Almira Stearns was writing to her husband, Daniel, letters that detail the day-to-day activities of a coterie of women whose husbands had all "gone north" to the Salmon River mines.[8]

Pamelia and Almira—and thousands of other women left behind in villages throughout the country—were well aware of the pied-piper effect that was partly responsible for the situation in which they found themselves. With every report of success in the goldfields, more and more married men felt justified in following the example of others who had gone west without their families. So widespread was this practice that Mahala Rayner, one of a number of gold rush widows left in Noble County, Ohio, begged her spouse, Henry, not to set off yet another mass exodus of husbands and fathers by sending home exaggerated reports of his successes in California but rather to tell the truth about his experience, to "write [it] as bad as it is for I don't want any more wives left here to grieve after their husbands."[9] If the separation of families in the westward movement was as common as Mahala Rayner's comment would suggest, then this phenomenon might even have been the norm, rather than the exception, and deserves to be examined in light of what it can add to our knowledge of the westward movement as a gendered process.

Others have examined the male-female ratio in the gold camps and on the overland trail. John Mack Faragher observed "a strong and at times predominant male character to the emigrations of the fifties and sixties." In her study of women on the overland trail, Lillian Schlissel concluded that while "great numbers of men went west, leaving their wives and children at home," women who made the overland journey "almost always traveled within a family structure." This does not mean that women lacked the courage to set out alone, for deciding whether to go west was not so much a question of courage as of privilege—gender privilege. Mobility has long been a male prerogative, perhaps because men, both married and single, have traditionally been free to make their own decisions in such matters, while women have been obliged to operate within parameters set by their husbands.[10]

Thus, while Odysseus made a choice to leave home and informed Penelope of his intention, she would have been obliged to ask his permission for any such undertaking of her own. Indeed, she—like almost all wives in the centuries since her time—not only lacked the autonomy to choose the life of the adventurer for herself but also lacked the authority to keep her husband from choosing that life, no matter how strongly she might have opposed his mission or longed for his company at home. As Henry Jenkins admitted to his Quaker wife Abigail back in Jay County, Indiana, "The sacrifice of the comforts of home and all its endearing ties . . . has on my part been gone into voluntarily [but] thy case is different [for] submission has been thy part." This same letter reveals still more gender bias, for Henry Jenkins felt that no mother and wife worthy of those titles would ever willingly choose to abandon a family the way he had, and he told Abby, "Nothing this side of heaven could have induced thee to have left me and our dear children as I have done."[11]

If husbands were the actors, exercising freedom of choice by deciding to take the risks associated with going west, then wives were the reactors, assuming or refusing to assume the duties that fell to them by virtue of the departure of their spouses. Almost invariably, a wife accepted her new responsibilities, even when doing so meant placing herself under great stress, for open defiance of her husband's wishes meant endangering her marriage and thereby jeopardizing her future and that of her children as well as risking the loss of whatever support she might otherwise expect from the community.

She needed all the support she could muster, considering the challenges she faced as a "single" married woman without the company, guidance, and protection of a husband, yet still under legal restrictions that made it virtually impossible for her to be fully autonomous. Fair game for creditors and others who viewed them as vulnerable, these women surely harbored some resentment at being left in such circumstances, yet they seldom voiced that resentment. Elizabeth Cress, a rare exception, was sufficiently stunned by her husband's sudden departure from Illinois in 1851 to write her parents, "My old man has left me & has gon to Califona and took my wagon and left me and my children in a bad situation." Even rarer were those instances in which wives expressed their resentment directly to their spouses. Thus, while Augusta Shipman's blatant question to her westering husband, Clark—"What are you there for anyway?"—was hardly typical of the questions raised in letters sent west, Augusta might well have been expressing what other wives felt but dared not verbalize. Some chose to remain entirely silent. Left in Greenwood, Wisconsin, in 1898 with three children and a fourth on the way, Mary Warner was so embittered by her debt-ridden husband's departure for the goldfields of the Klondike that she pledged not to write him a single word.[12]

Whatever their wives' opinions of their actions, significant numbers of married men did, indeed, choose to go west alone—some because they were operating out of well-established patterns of setting off on their own in search of new opportunities, some because they were going for gold and expected to be back home in a short time, some because they felt the "untamed wilderness" was no place for women and children, some because they could not afford to transport their families, some because they wanted to find the perfect homestead before sending for wives and children, some because they were glad for an excuse to leave unpleasant family situations, and some because their wives declined to join them.[13]

Whatever their reasons for setting out alone, for these men, as well as for their unmarried counterparts, going west was a response to the pervasive idea that the frontier, with its promise of gold, land, and adventure, represented boundless opportunity. Many who eventually moved to the far West had already made at least one other move in that direction, and for their wives, being temporarily left behind was hardly a new experience. Left at Minnehaha Falls, just outside Minneapolis, when her husband, Ard, set out for Montana Territory, Harriet Godfrey could call upon experience gained during two earlier stints as woman in waiting. And though this time she lacked the support that parents, siblings, and in-laws had provided while she waited as a young woman in Maine, the children who had been but toddlers during Ard's previous forays were now young adults who provided help and companionship. Left behind first in the city of Dundee, Scotland, and then again on a farm in central Minnesota, Agnes Russell was one of many immigrant women married to men for whom crossing the Atlantic was but a prelude to a lifetime of seeking a better life ever farther west.[14]

Many women in waiting had married into families that had long operated out of the belief that better things lay to the west. For Emma Christie's husband, David, the decision to leave wife and children behind in Blue Earth County, Minnesota, and look for farmland in Montana Territory was part of a heritage passed down from an immigrant father who had moved from Scotland to Wisconsin to Minnesota, determined to leave his family a legacy of land. And when John Bozeman set out in 1861 in search of Colorado gold, both his wife, Catharine, and his mother, Delia, knew he carried with him the memories of a father who had left home when John was twelve and had died en route to California. Men like David Christie and John Bozeman were not only drawn west by the promise of opportunities abroad but also pushed there by problems at home. Christie battled ill health and huge mortgage payments; Bozeman chafed in an unhappy marriage.[15] Since the home-front experiences of Emma Christie and Catharine Bozeman and other women in waiting were directly and indirectly influenced by *all* the factors surrounding their husbands' decisions to go west, any analysis of separated families must take into account not only what men expected to gain in the West, but also what they sought to leave behind in the East.

Gold was, of course, what most expected to gain. Few gained it. Soon after his arrival at Pikes Peak, James Fergus realized what most miners eventually came to concede: "Some will make their fortunes, a great many more will only pay expenses, while the great mass will go home poorer than when they left." Fergus himself was one of the very few who found substantial amounts of gold. After a four-year separation, he brought his family to Montana Territory on the strength of the eight thousand dollars he had taken from his

Virginia City claim. Far more typical of the gold seekers was Joseph Kenney, who left his wife in Linn County, Iowa, and went west with the idea of making a quick profit and returning home in triumph. Instead, Kenney found that "a person [could] Shovel up [no more] money here . . . than they [could] any Place Else." Two years later, no more successful and even more jaded, he admitted to his father-in-law, "This countrys nothing but a lottery with five thousand blanks to one prize." The odds he quoted were close to accurate.[16]

Having boasted of the fortunes they would bring home, disappointed gold seekers were faced with the dilemma of either lingering on through a second or third season in hopes that their luck would change or else packing up and turning back, thereby admitting defeat and risking loss of status in the eyes of those back home. Having invested four years in his fruitless search, Joseph Kenney wrote his wife that he "would Rather be dead than to come home with out Some money." Such strength of purpose might be considered worthy of praise were it not for the fact that a man's refusal to admit defeat only prolonged the suffering of his wife and children back home. Even men like Henry Rayner, who realized early on that "no man that has a wife had ought to go to California," sometimes found it hard to get home. Having conceded to his own wife, Mahala, waiting back in Ohio, that wealth was, at best, "an idle name," he could still see no honorable way of going home: "How can I return and not bring back as much money as I started with for I have sold of[f] my property and what could we do. . . . I am worth nothing."[17]

While most of those who sought their fortunes in mountain streams fared no better than Henry Rayner, many men did manage to profit from their sojourns in the mining towns by relying on the trades and skills they brought with them. Thus while the wives of gold seekers could at best entertain only vague hopes that their husbands would be among the successful ones, the wives of those who went west as merchants, attorneys, or physicians had some basis for optimism. Almira Stearns at least knew that when her shopkeeper husband, Daniel, left her and two-year-old George behind in New Hampshire and set out for California, he went not to mine for gold but to sell his wares in the gold camps. And Sarah Yesler had every reason to believe in the soundness of her husband Henry's plan to set up a sawmill to meet the lumber demands of California's mining towns, since they had been well supported by a similar operation in Massillon, Ohio. Although Virginia Morley may have had concerns for her husband James's safety as he set off for the West, she had confidence in his plans to work as a mining engineer in Montana Territory. Equally sound were the plans of attorney William Wallace, who left his wife, Luzena, and son, Willie, in Iowa and set out to practice law in the lumber towns of Puget Sound. And when physician Charles Brown left his wife, Maggie, and daughter, Mattie, in Westview, Virginia, he knew he could make a living by practicing medicine in the mining camps of the Colorado Rockies.[18]

Even those men who had set out for the goldfields with no intention of falling back on their old trades were often enough glad to be able to do so. Thus, though the promise of gold drew Ard Godfrey west, the profits from sawmilling enabled him to return to the East with the funds he needed to rescue his failing business. When Fort Wayne, Indiana, printer Ambrose Kiser failed to find the gold he sought in Virginia City, Montana Territory, he turned to writing articles about his more successful peers, and his newspaper, The Madisonian, eventually gained him both professional and financial rewards.[19]

Gold was not the only thing that drew men west. The lure of land proved equally strong, and the Homestead Act of 1862 and subsequent land legislation drew thousands into what John Mack Faragher has called "the dominating social motif of the nineteenth-century West." Not all the homesteaders were young yeomen farmers. Fifty years old when he and his fifteen-year-old son set out for Montana Territory in December of 1881, Clark Shipman had already tried teaching, farming, and peddling in Vermont and New Jersey before he decided to look for a homestead in the West. Making claims in his own name and those of his adult daughters, who soon joined him on the plains of central Montana, he built a homestead shack on skids so that it could be moved from claim to claim to facilitate meeting residency requirements. Despite such ingenious finagling, Shipman met with little success until his wife, Augusta, came west ten years later to share—and secure—the family holdings.[20]

The dream of owning a farm that could be profitably operated by himself, his wife, and his children led stonecutter Frank Kirkaldie from Vermont to Iowa. But his ineptitude at farming soon had the family in financial difficulty, and in 1864 Kirkaldie traded plow for pick, setting out for Montana Territory and sending his wife, Elizabeth, and four children to live with her mother in Joliet, Illinois. But the gold eluded him, and his attempts to make a living at farming went equally badly. Like men disappointed in gold, Kirkaldie found it hard to give up his land and go home in defeat, admitting, "It seems as though every move I have made in the last ten years has been one from bad to worse." On the other hand, neither was he willing to "abandon this country poor & go back [home] to work by the day for our support it would look like the last term in the decreasing series."[21]

After a season of failure in the Montana goldfields, Joseph Kenney, still planning to get home to his wife, Susan, and their four children as soon as he could "make a Raise," fenced eighty acres in the Gallatin Valley on the eastern slopes of the Rockies and put in wheat and barley. Each year brought a new disaster, and when he lost his wheat to "Hopper Jumpers" in 1866, he wrote Susan that "the grasshoppers have done a more effective job than [she] ever could" of turning his thoughts toward home.[22]

Kenney's experience was hardly unique. Homesteaders failed at least as often as they succeeded.[23] Married men who went west ahead of their families usually had to decide whether or not to send for their wives and children long before they could be certain that their investments would pay off. Since, like finding substantial amounts of gold, finding good land was not always as easy as newspaper articles and promotional booklets implied, many men were obliged to linger on alone far longer than they had intended, forcing their wives and children to stretch their meager resources much farther than expected.

David Christie spent two summers looking for just the right place to set up his farming operation and managed to make up his mind on a site only after his normally patient wife, Emma, declared, "You can bea runing about all the rest of your days and never bea settled. . . . I don't think we can live this way much longer and I hope you will not ask me to." Eager as women like Emma were for the reunion they hoped would bring an end to their scrimping and scraping at home, life in the West rarely proved to be all that they had envisioned, especially if the journey out was made prematurely—as Emma herself discovered when she and her six children were obliged to spend their first Montana winter in a one-room cabin with a lean-to kitchen.[24]

While disappointment came often to men who went west for gold or land, those who made the journey solely for adventure could at least count on getting their fill of that commodity. Even for the most responsible of men, the promise of adventure played at least some part in the decision to go west. Though "excitement" was not always an openly acknowledged motivation before a husband's departure, it often crept into letters sent from the frontier. James Fergus, a man not usually given to whimsical pleasures, pointed out to Pamelia that even if he did not make any money out west, he would still "have seen the 'Elephant,'" and he noted that "the Rocky Mountains and the pains and pleasures of a camp life are all worth something." Some married men were neither so guarded nor so gallant about admitting to the lure of adventure that the West held for them. Jack Swilling of Wetumpka, Alabama, wrote his wife, Mary Jane, that even after "be[ing] with the wild Indins of Arizonia and at gal partes" and "fac[ing] the Shinny Bewey knifes of the gamblers," he was "still not satisfied."[25]

The promise of adventure, land, and gold would not, in and of itself, have been enough to trigger the massive westward migrations that characterized the last half of the nineteenth century. Other factors were at work. Men were as often repelled by things at home as they were attracted to things afar, and those caught up in unpleasant economic, political, and personal situations at home were especially likely to find going west an attractive possibility.[26] The wives these men left behind were in an especially precarious situation, since they were left to face alone the very situations their husbands had found intolerable.

Those women whose husbands went west because of financial difficulties were especially put upon. Often, despite years of frugal management of household monies, they had no understanding of their husbands' financial affairs. All they knew was that, at what seemed to be the most precarious moment of their lives—with creditors about to seize homes and farms and with cash reserves at an all-time low—their husbands were deciding to go west. Just getting together the money for the trip out sometimes meant going even further into debt, and once the supplies had been purchased and passage paid for, there was generally very little cash left for the wives who stayed behind. After Ard Godfrey had bought a new team to pull his wagon west and purchased enough supplies to last the crossing and the planned-for year in the goldfields, he had only sixty dollars to hand his wife, Harriet, who was left with seven children.[27]

For some women, financial worries had been a factor throughout their marriages, since husbands who went west in hopes of getting out of debt were often downwardly mobile men. Less than impressed with the many debt-dodging drifters he had met up with in the West, Joseph Kenney declared such men "no great credit to any country. They come here and lay around for a while and then go back and curse the country [itself when] . . . its their fault and the countrys all Right."[28]

But not every man who went west because of economic pressures had gotten into debt out of carelessness or laziness. Unpredictable economic events and unavoidable natural disasters could ruin even the most astute businessman. Ard Godfrey was a hard-working mill owner and family man who had to mortgage his property to survive the depression of the late 1850s and could find no other way out from under his burden than to look to the gold of Montana. Sometimes a single unwise investment pushed a struggling family over the edge. Having followed her husband, Henry, from Pennsylvania to Ohio and finally to Indiana, Abby Jenkins watched him sink most of his capital into what turned out to be a disastrous sawmill venture. Faced with mounting debts he saw no way to pay off, Henry put his hopes in the gold of California, leaving Abby to manage farm, children, grandchildren—and the creditors who pounded at her door.[29]

Despite the fact that going west to escape financial pressures at home nearly always meant leaving wives and children in untenable situations, thousands of indigent men took their leave, convincing themselves that they were doing their best to help their families by seeking the gold or land they needed to ensure economic recovery. Robert Russell of Little Falls, Minnesota, was convinced that any hardships his prolonged absence in Colorado was causing his family were more than justified in light of the luxuries they would enjoy once he had "made his pile." Even though he had received word that his wife, Agnes, might not have enough to feed their eight children through the winter of 1861–62, Robert continued to believe he belonged in the West, insisting, "As faur as i can see this is the place . . . for a man and the place that's good for a man is good for his famaly."[30]

Forty-niner Granberry Rose shared the same motivation—and expressed the same rationalization: "I will say now that I do not expect to make a fortune but I [do] hope I will better myself and you and the children," he wrote in his first letter to Mary Elizabeth, the wife he'd left back in Missouri. Four years later, having made considerable sums of money as a packer and freight agent, yet still not ready to come home, he wrote again to assure the wife who struggled with the care of his four children, "I am not staying in this country for the sake of good living or enjoyment but for the sake of helping the conditions of myself, you and the children."[31]

Granberry Rose at least sent home enough money to keep his creditors satisfied, but other miners either could not or would not send home the money needed to pay off old debts, and their wives were forced to expend considerable energy upholding their reputations in the face of rumors suggesting that they had taken the less-than-honorable way out. Nancy Boardman was left in Fond du Lac, Wisconsin, in the midst of angry creditors when her husband, Alonzo, went to the Colorado goldfields in the spring of 1863 in hopes of finding enough gold to clear up their sizeable debts. Well aware of the awkwardness of his wife's situation, Boardman advised her to "get along as well as you can" and to tell those "who are disposed to insinuate that I have left the country to avoid paying my debts [that they] may go ahead and make all they can out of it, for time will show them that I know my own business better than they do."[32] Nancy Boardman continued to defend her husband's reputation throughout his absence—and even after he returned home with nothing to show for his trip to the goldfields.

Not all wives found it so easy to defend the reputations of their westering men. Offering anonynimity, if not amnesty, the West attracted its share of criminals—men accused of everything from petty theft to murder—and the wives they left behind lived under the stigma of their misdeeds. Once these fugitives crossed the Mississippi, they often took on new names, a practice so common that a popular ballad of the day asked:

> Oh, what was your name in the States?
> Was it Thompson or Johnson or Bates?
> Did you murder your wife,
> And fly for your life?
> Say, what was your name in the States?[33]

While acquiring an alias and moving to a new locale gave an accused man a fresh start, the wife he left back home was not afforded an equal opportunity. In 1856, when Jack Swilling "got . . . into trouble" in Alabama, he left his wife, Mary Jane, and three-year-old daughter, Elizabeth, behind in Wetumpka and set out for the Southwest, essentially sentencing them to live out their lives under the stigma of his alleged misdeed.[34]

Kansas newspaper editor Robert Kelley was another man compelled to flee for his life. He was never accused of murder, though his "incendiary appeals" roused lethal mobs against abolitionists on more than one occasion. Retaliatory actions by antislavery forces in 1858 sent him to Wyoming and left his wife, Mollie, and infant daughter, Kate, to seek shelter with her parents in Doniphan, Kansas. Unlike other waiting wives who begged their husbands to come home, Mollie dared not ask Robert to return to Kansas and admitted, "I am afraid all the time you are here."[35]

In the case of Peter and Elizabeth Levengood, it was the wife's political leanings that made moving west expedient, though it was the husband who was forced to leave town. Unwilling to fight against his brothers in the Confederate army or against his friends serving the Union, Peter, a shopkeeper in Memphis, Missouri, a town about equally divided between Yankee and Rebel sympathizers, succeeded in maintaining a neutral stance until 1862, when Elizabeth openly voiced her support for Jefferson Davis, an act that landed Levengood himself in jail. Fearful lest he share the fate of his cellmate, a man with Confederate sympathies who was killed by a sniper's bullet, Levengood headed for the Iowa border immediately upon his release, leaving behind three children and the wife whose sentiments had caused the furor in the first place. Even after a band of Union soldiers shot her cow and seized her husband's dry goods store, Elizabeth Levengood refused to recant, though she did finally leave town, joining Peter in Vernon, Iowa, some sixty miles to the north, in time for the birth of their fourth child. With Elizabeth's sympathies still too firmly Confederate to make for a comfortable life in Iowa, Peter joined an 1864 wagon train bound for Idaho Territory. Left behind once more, Elizabeth took her five children home to her in-laws in Kentucky, where she waited three years for her husband's invitation to join him in Montana Territory.[36]

In late June 1864, sisters-in-law Martha and Nancy Friend of Poweshiek County, Iowa, bade farewell to their husbands Franklin and George. The Friend brothers were bound for Montana Territory, traveling in the company of several other Southern sympathizers unwilling to be drafted into Lincoln's army. Pleased to find a more tolerant atmosphere in the West than they had known back home, Franklin reported that "wee live peacibel . . . [and] have no war or politics" and advised Martha that he and George planned to stay where they were rather than "bee forsed in[to] this war."[37]

Another Southern sympathizer, Joseph Kenney, went west from Iowa at about the same time and for the same reason. "Keep a Stiff upper Lip and do the best you can till old Abe's infernal negro war is over," he wrote his wife, Susan, in 1864. Though he described the residents of the territory as "nearly all Southern People," others reported a more balanced populace. James Fergus wrote his wife, Pamelia, at home in Minnesota, that the gold camp of Bannack boasted two distinct settlements, Confederate Gulch and Yankee Flats, with "the Secesh whiskey rowdies on one side of . . . [Grass-hopper] creek and the civil quite Union men on the other."[38]

Conflicts on the battlefield were not the only ones that sent men west. Even though flight from domestic problems might not have been their primary motivation, tensions within households provided many men with the needed nudge west. Thus, though economic problems were the main impetus for Clark Shipman's homesteading venture, marital discord was likely the greatest single factor in his decision to take his fifteen-year-old son west to Montana Territory and leave the rest of the family back home in New Jersey. In response to her six-year-old daughter's oft-repeated questions as to why her father had left them, the embittered Augusta Shipman spoke the truth as she saw it: "To get rid of us I suppose."[39]

In a sense, the westward movement legitimized abandonment. In an 1866 letter to his mother, John Bozeman made it clear that he never intended to return to Georgia to live with the wife and three daughters he had left behind five years earlier. "I am a friend to Catharine and always will be," he wrote, "but the way we lived to gether my life was no plesure to me. We never lived a week to gether without quarling and I doo not think it right for us to live to gether that way." Noting that he had "bine a way long a nough" to allow Catharine to obtain a divorce on grounds of desertion and that she would "not be violating the law or hir plege to me by giting Maried," he wished her the best.[40]

However fortunate a wife might have felt to be free of an unhappy relationship, the absence of a husband posed problems of its own. Whatever freedom she might have felt at first, she soon realized that life in limbo was only another form of bondage. Left as a "single" married woman, she was far worse off than she would have been either as a spinster well accustomed to earning her own way in the world or as a true widow who could count on the support of her community. Instead, she often found herself without the financial resources needed to carry on family affairs, the legal authority required to finalize business matters, or the moral and legal imperatives needed to seek a new spouse.

Many of the frustrations of life on the home frontier can be traced to the fact that married women left behind to fend for themselves were expected to operate within certain cultural constraints and yet still carry out tasks that moved them into an uncomfortable corridor where gender roles were blurred. The letters of women in waiting provide a unique opportunity to observe the ways in which the ideology of separate spheres proved inoperable when circumstances brought an end to the gender division of labor on which it had been predicated.[41]

That division of labor worked well enough as long as a husband was on hand to take care of such worldly matters as earning a living in the world outside the home, but the husband who went west left his wife in an extremely awkward position. The prevailing ethos of the time maintained the importance of her staying within the confines of her home and attending to the labors considered to be "woman's work," yet the pressing reality of her situation required that she venture into the business world in order to obtain sufficient capital to run her household.

Women left on the home frontier dealt with this dilemma in any number of ways. Most began by expanding their endeavors in such acceptable areas as raising cows and chickens and selling butter and eggs. Pamelia Fergus, who sent James regular reports on her "fatten hog," milk cow, and chickens, rightly concluded, "So you see, if I had not of sold butter I would of done without a great many things." While Pamelia often had excess butter and eggs to sell, she raised only enough vegetables and grain to feed her family and her livestock. Other women sold their produce at a profit. When Sarah Oliver and her children decided to remain in Wood River Center, Nebraska, and allow Edward Oliver to continue his Mormon pilgrimage to Salt Lake City without them, Sarah sold fresh vegetables grown on her farm to residents of nearby Fort Kearney and to emigrants who passed by the thousands through Buffalo County. And the turkeys Augusta Shipman raised on Perham Hill in central Vermont graced holiday tables in Boston.[42]

Women found other socially acceptable ways of making money. When Jack Swilling fled Alabama, his wife, Mary Jane, supported herself and her daughter Elizabeth through her work as a tailor. Adept at housing and feeding their own families, many women earned extra income by opening their homes to travelers and schoolteachers, trading hospitality for cash or lessons. Sarah Oliver opened her home to "emigrants, eastward or westward bound," offering good beds and fine food to those on the overland trail.[43]

When Margaretha and John Ault lost the Northern Hotel in Little Falls, Minnesota, and John left for the goldfields, Margaretha found herself in an especially precarious position. With no hotel to run, no home in which to put up boarders, and no land on which to grow crops or keep livestock, she became a renter herself, paying her bills with money she made as washerwoman and midwife. "Find[ing] it very hard to be thrown upon [her] own resources so many years," she quickly availed herself of a chance to earn room, board, and income by serving as head cook for the "officers mess" at nearby Fort Ripley. Although she was merely putting to good use skills she had learned in her own kitchen and in that of the Northern Hotel, working outside the home and in the company of soldiers made her vulnerable to gossips who talked of supposed infidelities.[44]

Other women whose lack of property forced them to work outside the home also risked the disapproval of their neighbors. Finding herself "in a sufering condition without any thing to keep [her]self with" during her husband's stint at Pikes Peak, Minnesotan Mary Paul decided she could best help herself and her "sick and destitute" children by leaving her six offspring with relatives and moving into Saint Cloud to work as a maid—hardly an ideal solution to her problem, but one that kept the family solvent until her husband, Alexander, returned from Pikes Peak.[45]

Left in Windham, Vermont, in the fall of 1854, Jane Chandler waited in vain for her husband, Newton, to send home money from California. Hardly on the best of terms, the couple played a waiting game of sorts. Jane declined Newton's repeated invitations to come west, unwilling to settle "for life" anyplace so far from home. In return, Newton declined to send money east to support such insubordination, yet objected strenuously when Jane left their two children with relatives, moved into a boardinghouse in Lowell, Massachusetts, and took a job in the textile mills. Whether or not Newton had intended to force his wife into the workplace, he did not "like the idea of [her] working . . . in them mills." Pride played no small part in his stance, for he argued, "A washer woman in Cal[ifornia] is a Lady while the factory girls are servants." When she continued her work, he issued the ultimate threat: "I think you had Better not go to Lowell any more Except you wish to get married again."[46]

Teaching generally was held in higher regard than millwork, but it was looked upon by many as a profession a woman followed only until she married. However, a number of women left behind by westering husbands supported themselves by their work in the classroom. When her husband, William Ransom, joined her father, Henry Jenkins, on a trip to California in 1851, Ann Jenkins Ransom returned to teaching, leaving her mother, Abby, to care for little Cordelia and boarding out all week with a family in the district in which she taught. As the men in the Jenkins family extended their stay in California and money became more scarce, Abby herself mused, "If I thought I could stand it I would teach this winter [myself]," though she soon gave up on that idea because "the family are all against it they do not like mother to be away so long."[47]

Like Abby Jenkins, some waiting wives were helped in their economic struggles by older children. Agnes Russell's eldest son not only worked her fields but also hired out to neighbors, and her eldest daughter taught school and contributed all her earnings to the family budget. Though he was still a schoolboy when his father left for the mines of Idaho's Salmon River country, young George Stearns worked in a bookstore and shared his wages with his mother until he finished his schooling, then became completely self-sufficient by taking a clerking job that included room and board. After his father's departure for Montana Territory, seventeen-year-old Abner Godfrey plowed the family's fields, tended their livestock, handled Ard's business dealings, and hired out to haul government freight. His sister Helen gave up her teaching job, purchased a sewing machine, and did piecework for hire so that she could provide her mother, Harriet, with company and household help as well as income.[48] In all such activities Helen was, like her mother, performing traditional tasks in an effort to meet nontraditional needs.

Even those women who restricted their income-producing activities to traditional work done in the home were often obliged to transgress traditional boundaries in order to handle such business transactions as renegotiating mortgages, collecting delinquent notes, taking legal action against debtors, and paying taxes. As inexperienced as they were in handling matters out of their realm, they were bound to be less than successful in some endeavors, and their bungling of business affairs could draw disapproving letters from their husbands. When Nancy Boardman, eager to avoid going farther into debt, promptly paid the dollar she had been assessed by the postmaster, husband Alonzo wrote from Colorado that she should not have done so without asking his advice—but "never mind it now." Forced to make a major decision concerning assessments for the repair of the dam that powered James's temporarily defunct mill, Pamelia Fergus found her first action as a surrogate stockholder in the Little Falls Manufacturing Company so unnerving that she wrote to James, "I feel very unseasy or afraid I have done wrong." Her decision was, indeed, different from what his would have been, but James assured her, "only do the best you can & I will be satisfied."[49]

Pamelia's misjudgment was partly a result of advice given her by several board members eager to take advantage of her inexperience. She learned quickly not to accept advice from every man who offered it and soon grew to distrust even the counsel of her husband's lawyer, whom she condemned out of hand for his treatment of her friends. "Hall is working at his old traid cheating the widows," she informed James, then she denounced the man's behavior as "a mean action . . . to do such a thing to a lone woman when her husband was gone." Lawyer James Hall was not the only man ready to prey on "a lone woman." From her mother's farm in Vermont, twenty-year-old Rebecca Shipman wrote her father, Clark, that "there are two or three mean despicable men in Bethel and Royalton, but they have not succeeded in doing us much harm so far but they failed principally from lack of brains."[50]

Some of the men who went west sought to buffer their wives from dealings with such "despicable men" by asking trusted friends or relatives to act as advisors in business matters. There were times when such help was invaluable. Abiah Hiller was able to leave the unfamiliar city of Richmond and go home to McDonough, New York, soon after William's departure for California only because she could depend upon his former partner, Martin Daniels, to close out her family's business affairs in Virginia. But there were times when the women were hindered by the "help" of others. Almira Stearns was at first relieved to know that her brother-in-law, John Stearns, would assist her with business dealings during Daniel's packing expeditions in Idaho, but she soon found that John managed her affairs as ineptly as he handled his own.[51]

There were other cases in which well-intentioned men actually caused as much trouble as they prevented. Although Pamelia Fergus had always liked and respected Charles Freeman, the man James had asked to assist her in business dealings, she soon had reason to complain of his haphazard managerial skills, his secretive dealings with her debtors, and his negligence in paying taxes. Finally moved to take action, though reluctant to interfere in what she called "mans bussiness," Pamelia gathered her courage and walked into the Morrison County Courthouse—where she found herself quite capable of understanding and settling tax matters. "I only had to regret I had not went before," she wrote James, and more and more she bypassed Freeman's "assistance," explaining that "Most of my little afairs I prefer to do my self."[52]

Whether or not they preferred to handle their business affairs on their own and whatever their occupations during their years of "widowhood," what little cash women in waiting were able to earn was crucial to the survival of their families, for those who waited for the gold their husbands had promised to send might find themselves and their children without shoes, clothes, food, and shelter. Money was needed to sustain a household in the absence of a visible provider, and though friends and neighbors might assume that westering husbands must surely be sending a living allowance to their families, in most cases this was not so. Most of the home-front widows received no money at all from their far-distant husbands, and others received only occasional gold pieces or sporadic bank notes.

From the first, Harriet Godfrey knew that her husband Ard would be sending no money home and that she and the children would be sustaining themselves on the food produced on their farm, the income generated by the older children, and whatever proceeds she might obtain from the sale of a mill and millstones that Ard had not been able to sell before his departure. Almira Stearns was also expected to count on income-producing property—a hotel and a ranch that had been leased out when Daniel left for the Salmon River mines. But when the family who rented the ranch fell behind on payments and the man who rented the hotel turned it back to Almira and bought a competing property, she found herself very short on cash and was reduced to writing Daniel for funds, reminding him, "We cannot live without money."[53]

If Mary Elizabeth Rose had expected to receive bags of gold from her Forty-niner husband, she was to be disappointed. At one point Granberry boasted of having earned two thousand dollars a month as a packer and merchant in northern California, but he sent little, if any, of that money directly to his wife and four children, although he did send funds to his brother to invest in a farm back home in Greene

County, Missouri. To Mary Elizabeth's complaint that she could hardly manage much longer without him, Granberry admonished her to "remember your task is nothing to what mine is." He then moved to stifle further complaints by sending his brother seven hundred dollars with which to "buy a black girl" to help his wife with childcare and chores.[54]

Alonzo Boardman's letters from Colorado to his wife in Fond du Lac encouraged her to "try and get along until I can send you money." That vague promise was his only contribution to the family income over the course of a year's absence, at the end of which he admitted to Nancy, "I ought to have sent you money and should have done so but expected to start home soon and neglected it." Joseph Kenney sent similar regrets home to his wife in Iowa. Having spent four years in Montana mining, farming, hauling freight, threshing, and building Mackinaw riverboats—all without turning a profit—he conceded, "If we [just] had all the money we put in our farm [out here] and [in] them boats we could come home now with a pretty good Raise but as it is I do not know as we will Ever Realize a dollar."[55]

Soon after Edward Oliver arrived in Davis County, Utah, he was doing well enough to send fifty dollars to his wife Sarah in Nebraska. But when that money was stolen before it reached her, he decided that he would send no more money to be lost in the mails—although he assured her that he had plenty to share if she and the children would only come out and join him. Leroy Warner confessed to feeling "very blue" whenever he thought about his wife, Mary, and his three little children in Greenwood, Wisconsin, and "the shape that [he] left [Mary] in," but his belated apology did little to brighten the mood of his pregnant wife or to alter the damage his ill-timed departure had done to their relationship. Indeed, though Leroy eventually sent home nearly twenty-six hundred dollars over the fourteen years he spent mining in the Klondike, working in Washington state, and logging in British Columbia, Mary applied almost all of that money toward debts he owed her mother and continued to rely on her own earnings as a seamstress to sustain herself and her children.[56]

If Mary Warner's earnings were meager, they were at least steady, which was more than could be said for those of her husband and of most of the men out on the frontier. Indeed, given their frugality and loyalty to their spouses, wives at home sent butter and egg money west about as often as husbands on the frontier sent gold east. David DeWolf had no compunctions about asking for money outright, writing his wife, Matilda, to send cash "as soon as you can as I cannot get along without it." Requests from men like Henry Rayner were more oblique but no less persuasive: "If I had had one hundred dollars . . . I would have left and tried to . . . work my passage home." And still others were too proud to take a penny. When Susan Kenney offered to send Joseph money for his trip home, he declared, "If I cant make enough here to come home on I will leave my bones in the mountains so you see at once you need not send it."[57]

Other men were not so proud. Rather than sending money home to his wife, Augusta—who was back on her family's farm in Vermont "losing more dollars than she ma[de] cents"—Clark Shipman asked *her* to send *him* money to invest in some cattle in Montana. Augusta had some savings from an inheritance from her father and a final payment from the sale of their New Jersey farm, but she was disinclined to put her husband's interests ahead of those of her children. "You had better help me get to a place where the childre[n] who want to can be schooled sufficiently . . . & then you may have the $800," she wrote Clark. "I can not do all the hard work & then hand over the money."[58]

Those wives who failed to take such a stand sometimes found themselves in difficult straits. When Amanda Smith's husband Timothy wrote asking her to sell their home and send him the cash out in Colorado, she did so, taking out a six-month lease on a rental house, confident that she would soon be leaving Little Falls, Minnesota, and heading west herself. Even her subsequent eviction for nonpayment of rent did not shake her faith in her alcoholic spouse, though his profligacy meant she and the children had to rely on the charity of others for their own survival.[59]

Although other women in waiting did not support their husbands as directly as did Amanda Smith, without the work women did to maintain family holdings back east, married men could hardly have afforded to go west in the first place. Often a woman's managerial skills were her greatest contribution to the family economy, and ingenuity was a particularly valuable asset. When Abiah Hiller's potatoes rotted before harvest time, she used them to fatten her hog, then substituted turnips for potatoes in family meals that winter. And when Pamelia Fergus's cow went dry "in the time of the Indian excitement"—when "nearly every lady's cows went dry"—she killed the animal for beef. Pamelia also became adept at barter, taking turnips, coffee, flour, wheat, a yoke of oxen, and a pony in exchange for money townspeople owed James.[60]

Women sometimes ensured a family's survival almost solely on the basis of their frugality. Emma Christie's careful husbanding meant more to her family's well-being than did the cash she earned through the sale of butter. Willing to do everything in her power to avoid signing any more of the hated "notes" that had made her life so miserable, Emma vowed, "As to our running [further] in det we have not or wod not if we had to do with out grocers." Although she had "a family of 9 to provide for," Abby Jenkins blamed herself for not being able to make ends meet and confessed to Henry that she felt "ashamed of the manner we use up thy hard earnings, while trying to be [as] economical we think as possible."[61]

The effort that Abby Jenkins expended in being as "economical . . . as possible" was every bit as important to maintaining a family as Mary Warner's labor as a seamstress or Ann Ransom's work in the classroom, yet Abby's labors within the home, like those of countless other women, tended to be devalued as "women's work," subsistence labor that sustained the family but generated no real income. Nonetheless, such labor represented a significant contribution to the westward movement—and to the capitalist system as well—though it remained essentially invisible and unremarked by a society that recognized only the wage earner as a contributor to the economy.

In one sense, the work of women on the home frontier became even more invisible when their husbands were not at home to observe it, but in another sense, as Andrew Rotter discovered in his study of Forty-niner diaries, the work of far-distant wives became newly conspicuous by its very absence in the lives of westering men. Realizing, perhaps for the first time, the amount of work that went into cooking, cleaning, washing, and mending, men on the frontier either hired the work done—and thereby learned the market value of the labors they had so long taken for granted—or did it themselves while longing for the day when their wives would once again take over the niggling chores associated with comfortable day-to-day living. "It is right funny to see the boys washing," Granberry Rose reported to his wife, Mary Elizabeth. "I have heard some of them say they did not know . . . their women were as good property as they are."[62] Despite such moments of insight, there is no indication that westering husbands attached any greater value to women's work once they got back home—other than to be glad they had wives to handle tasks they themselves found to be always tedious and sometimes odious.

Nor is there any indication that undertaking some of the labors normally assumed by their wives did anything to offset the prevalent idea that such work was easier for the women because it came so naturally to them—that the washing, ironing, sewing, cooking, and gardening that filled a woman's day could not be real work, not only because it brought in no wages but also because it was simply the natural overflow of the love a wife and mother had for her family. So pervasive was this attitude that James Fergus wrote urging his wife Pamelia "not to be making up foolish things now that [she had] leisure." Resentful of that statement, Pamelia replied, "I do not seam to have much leisure . . . yet," an answer easy to appreciate in light of the fact that she was, at that time, presiding over a household of eight, "and four of them children to make wash and mend for." As Pamelia herself well knew and made note of, "it all takes time," yet society had little, if any, appreciation for that fact.[63]

Difficult as her situation was, Pamelia Fergus considered herself lucky when she compared her lot with that of her fellow "widows." Although left with very little cash, Pamelia was nonetheless fairly self-sufficient, for owning even a few acres of land and a house could give a woman the edge she needed to survive the absence of her husband. In the spring of 1861, when Sarah Oliver chose to have her husband Edward continue his Mormon pilgrimage without her, she and her seven children were left in a sod-roofed log home on the banks of the Wood River. She undertook her voluntary widowhood in the belief that she could turn rolling prairie into a productive farm. Agnes Russell's farm kitchen may have lacked enough chairs for all eight of her children to sit down to a meal together, but she survived because she had fields to work and a roof over her head.[64]

Those women who were uprooted from their homes upon the departure of their husbands did not fare nearly as well. Sarah Yesler was living in her own house at the time of Henry's departure, and within a year she had followed his instructions to sell off her furniture and rent out her house in order to be ready to join him the moment he sent for her. Six years later, she and her son George were still drifting about among friends and relatives, waiting for the promised call to reunion. Similarly, Maggie Brown and her daughter, Mattie, were obliged to "board around" among friends and relatives in Virginia for more than two years before joining Charles in Colorado.[65]

Women left without homes of their own frequently moved in with parents or in-laws, who provided financial and emotional support as well as shelter. Susan Kenney moved in with her parents when her husband, Joseph, set out for Montana Territory. That arrangement provided her with company and good care during the final months of her pregnancy and the birth of her fourth child. Two years later, when tensions built within the household and Susan began to talk of moving to a place of her own, Joseph rejected that "absurd Idea," but admitted, "I Presume your folks are getting tired [of] keeping you and I cant Blame them."[66]

Long estranged from her own family, Almira Stearns welcomed the opportunity to be with her husband's parents and siblings during his 1849 voyage to California. Since she had but one child at the time of Daniel's departure, her presence in the Stearns home was hardly an imposition. The same could not be said about the impact of Emma Christie's move into the James Christie home, for she brought along five lively little boys, and her living conditions soon prompted her to write David, "If we only had a place of ourn and you was with us."[67]

Emma, like other women in waiting fortunate enough to have family members close at hand, depended on them in many other ways. Abiah Hiller looked to her mother for child care and housework as well as for good company and sound advice. When Jane Chandler's husband, Newton, berated her for balking at his invitation to come to California, she had the support of her parents and his in refusing to take her children on what she viewed as an extremely dangerous journey.[68]

Sometimes relatives who willingly provided food, shelter, and financial support were unable or unwilling to offer emotional support. In 1867, Polly Dalman welcomed Sarah Kiser and her three children into her home in Fort Wayne, Indiana, yet did everything in her power to persuade her sister that she was well rid of Ambrose Kiser and would be better off if he never came back from the goldfields of Montana Territory. Mary Hommel Warner was reluctant to accept the financial assistance offered by her mother, since every such gesture was accompanied by the accusation that Leroy Warner had gone off to the Klondike specifically to avoid repaying substantial sums of money he had borrowed from the Hommels.[69]

While women in waiting could not always depend upon the understanding of family members and friends, they could almost always depend on that of others left in the same situation. There was usually plenty of company, since gold fever was notoriously contagious and tended to strike entire communities at once. "California widows" abounded in Quincy, Illinois, where "a majority of the males" became Forty-niners. Pamelia Fergus and the circle of widows left in Little Falls, Minnesota, and Almira Stearns and the women in waiting of Roseburg, Oregon, drew together to share their troubles, their triumphs, and their letters from absent husbands. Such sharing was invaluable, since not all the men who went west could or would write letters home, and communities devised plans similar to the one Henry Jenkins reiterated for his wife, Abby, whereby "each family on the receipt of letters [was] to communicate to the others as far as practicable."[70]

Women in waiting shared more than their letters. They were present for one another in the birthing of babies, the care of sick children, and the burial of parents, and they could be counted on to share provisions and housing in time of crisis. The widows of Little Falls opened their homes to Amanda Smith and her children after their eviction, took food to Agnes Russell and her eight children in the winter months, and commiserated with Mary Paul in her need to leave her children behind and go into Saint Cloud to seek work.[71]

Mary Paul missed her children, for she, like other women in waiting, was frequently buoyed by interactions with them. With her husband, Robert, away in the West and her faith in their future faltering, Mollie Kelley received comfort from the four-month old who nursed at her breast, noting, "Little Kates bright eyes will tell [me] there is something to live for and . . . cheer [me] in . . . moments of sunshine and sorrow."[72] Even while taking solace in the bright eyes of a baby, women like Mollie Kelley wondered how their little ones would ever come to love and appreciate a father they had seldom—perhaps never—seen. Fearing that even older children would not remember their long-absent fathers, most women in waiting went to great lengths to keep memories fresh, reading aloud letters as they arrived, urging their husbands to write a few lines to the children, and asking the little ones whether they could remember what Papa looked like.

Even so, as months stretched into years, many children lost all memory of their wandering fathers. When William Jenkins sent his picture home to his five-year-old daughter, his mother, Abby, wrote him that though little Livvy would "doubtless prize it highly" in future years, the picture meant nothing to her now, for she had apparently "lost all recollections" of the father who had gone off to California before her first birthday. Some men were more successful in maintaining ties with their children than were others. Leroy Warner was a caring father who addressed each of his children by name in almost every letter home, and David Christie was equally careful to sustain a personal relationship with each one of the five sons he left behind in Blue Earth County, Minnesota. Frank Kirkaldie's interest in his little ones was expressed in almost every letter. He pressed Elizabeth, who had taken their four children to live with her mother back in Joliet, Illinois, for "a word about our babies," twins Nellie and Willie, wondering how they were "getting along with their teeth and with their walking," and he reminded nine-year-old Fanny to "keep her shoulders straight and her teeth clean."[73]

The letters of most absent fathers tended to reflect the authoritarian nature of the roles they played in person. Although Papa was absent, his admonitions to good behavior and hard work were not, and Granberry Rose's injunction to "be a good girl and mind your mother" is typical of the generic advice offered by distant fathers. Sometimes the interest fathers took in their children was clearly superficial, more good intention than reality. While Alonzo Boardman's first letter home asked Nancy to "tell Franky to be a good boy and I will pay him for it sometime," as he became more and more preoccupied with problems with his Colorado sawmill, Alonzo ceased to mention the boy at all—except to send him one brief note containing five dollars. Soon after his departure from home, Joseph Kenney urged his wife, Susan, to "tell Gilford to be a good boy and I will fetch him something pretty when I come home," a line he repeated verbatim some four months later, after which time his letters never again mentioned the child.[74]

Newton Chandler, like many other men in the goldfields, heightened his children's interest in his endeavors in the West by sending them gold dust and nuggets, but he failed to keep the promises he made to them. In the spring of 1859, Chandler wrote, "If Siss May will have her Ears Bored I will send her some little Earrings." A year later, in response to a letter indicating that the child's ears had been duly pierced but that the earrings had not yet arrived, he reiterated his promise to send them soon. But by the time Newton Chandler got around to mailing the long-anticipated "Ear Drops," his daughter was dead. "I will not attempt to Describe my feelings," he wrote his wife upon receipt of the news, "You can Imagine better than my pen can describe." This was not the first child the Chandlers had lost, though Newton had at least been at Jane's side when their first had died some ten years earlier. Now his words of compassion took months to reach the wife who grieved her daughter's passing alone in Massachusetts.[75]

Since the postal service was no respecter of circumstances, a mother's letter describing the death of a child and a father's letter conveying his great sense of loss took just as long in their journeys west and east as did letters carrying news of such mundane affairs as turning out a wash or working a claim. Well aware of that fact, Abiah Hiller waited weeks before writing William the news that their home had burned to the ground, preferring to delay until she could tell him the steps she had taken to replace it. And though Rosanna Sturgis wrote her husband at once concerning the dangers she and the children faced during the Indian uprising of 1862, William read newspaper accounts of the crisis long before he received his wife's letter assuring him that his family in Minnesota was unharmed.[76]

Because months, even years, might pass between the writing of a letter and the reading of a response, only the most devoted and diligent couples managed to maintain communication. After two and one-half years of letter writing, Abby Jenkins confessed, "It takes such a long time to hear from each other I long to be done with it, I would much rather use tongue than pen." The most successful correspondents were those who kept writing letters, even when they were receiving none. Even though he was disappointed in not getting his wife's "expected letter," Alonzo Boardman kept his resolution to "write every Sunday," noting, "I have no doubt you write as you promised and I will get them in time." Other men were neither so persistent nor so trusting. While Daniel Bosworth himself was hardly a model correspondent, he expected his wife to be, and James Fergus reported to Pamelia, "Mr. Bosworth . . . says tell his wife for God sake to send him a letter."[77]

Caroline Bosworth insisted that she was indeed writing, but like all the others in her position, she had to rely on an unreliable postal system. Mail steamers sank in the Atlantic and Pacific, steamboats ran aground on the Missouri, and stages carrying letters from the goldfields were prime targets for highwaymen. Many miners worked in mountainous areas with no service, and even after a settlement grew stable enough or large enough to warrant the establishment of a post office, winter storms could close off communication for weeks or months. Incomplete or incorrect addresses posed problems for wives whose husbands were working in gold camps located in areas whose territorial status was constantly changing. [78]

For men living in such isolated outposts, even finding paper and pen could pose problems. David Christie once borrowed a pencil and scrawled out a letter to Emma on the paper lining his can of pipe tobacco. Henry Rayner frequently used "the Pocket Letter Book," one of several booklets "Designed to Facilitate Correspondence Between Cities and Towns and the Mining Districts of California." Other husbands sometimes wrote on embossed paper featuring scenes from the mining camps. Frugal wives back home tended to write on plain white paper and often used up every inch of space, scribbling all around the edges of a letter and enclosing the exact number of completely filled sheets that could be mailed for the minimum charge.[79]

Sometimes wives were self-conscious about the appearance or content of their letters. Mahala Rayner confessed to her Henry, "You must excuse my awkwardness in putting my letters together for when I go to write I keep thinking about you and forget what to write next." Intolerant of such "awkwardness," James Fergus advised his wife Pamelia: "Write your letter first out on your slate, rub out alter and correct untill you think the spelling is all right, and [the letter] is as good . . . as you can get it. Then write it on paper with a pencil, correcting any further errors you may see, then copy it in ink, and your letters will certainly look better than they do now."[80]

Whether or not she made every letter "as good . . . as [she] could get it," Pamelia continued to write James every Monday morning, hoping he would get at least some of the letters she sent. Like other women in waiting, she devised creative ways of coping with the problems posed by unreliable or slow mail service. Since it was impossible to know which letters would or would not reach her husband, she formed the habit of repeating those items of greatest interest or concern. Abiah and William Hiller numbered their notes to one another, and when Sarah Yesler needed to convey crucial information to her husband, Henry, she not only repeated that information in several different letters but sent the letters to several different locations.[81]

Sometimes the news a man waited for most anxiously was word of the safe delivery of a healthy baby. Pregnancy was such a delicate subject that an expectant father's letters home usually contained only the vaguest allusions to his wife's condition. When David Christie failed to hear from Emma for a span of several weeks, he expressed the fear that she might be "sick," a euphemistic reference to the fact that she was in the last weeks of pregnancy. Leroy Warner's frequent allusions to the "shape" in which he had left his wife are clarified only by Mary's announcement of the birth of a son.[82]

Unaccustomed to taking the lead in choosing names for their children, new mothers often asked absent fathers to suggest or approve a name for the baby. The process had its limitations. When Susan Kenney asked her husband, Joseph, to "send a name for [her] big fat girl," he suggested that she ask his mother's help, since girls' names were "mighty scarce" in his part of the country. After waiting three and one-half years for Leroy to come up with a name for their new son, Mary Warner finally named the boy herself.[83]

Glad as many women were to have long-awaited letters from the West, some of those letters brought less-than-welcome news. Mahala Rayner read with great anxiety Henry's description of a life in which he was obliged "to wade in the mud to the croch and water to the neck and up and down mountains where a goat could hardly go without nothing to eat." Henry Jenkins sent Abby a description of his bed—"some weeds strewn on the ground my dirty clothes spread on them . . . on top of them a piece of muslin (left from my tent) then two small but tolerably good blankets and my valese for a pillow"— but he added that Abby need not "scold [him] for sleeping on the ground," since the air and ground were "so dry that there [was] not the least danger of dampness."[84]

Abby Jenkins was always "truly glad to hear" that her husband was being careful of his health, for like most women in waiting, she feared that he would fall ill while so far from home. Henry's letters concerning his journey to California had been filled with accounts of shipboard cases of cholera and yellow fever, and as the time for his return drew near, Abby wrote, "I fear much for thee on thy journey home particularly in crossing the isthmus try to come in the healthiest time with every precaution."[85].

Concern for the health of a far-distant loved one was not a female prerogative. While Charles Brown was enjoying a Fourth of July celebration in Hayden Creek, Colorado, his wife, Maggie, was "sitting over the cradle" of three-year-old Mattie, who had "commenced passing blood and slime" and was not expected to live. Physician that he was, Charles had first thought Maggie's account of the situation exaggerated and dismissed Mattie's sickness as "some attack of indigestion." But upon learning that the ultimate diagnosis had been "typhoid dysentery" and that his beloved Maggie also showed symptoms of the disease, Charles grew most "uneasy" and anxiously watched the mails for word of the recovery of his wife and daughter. The health of parents, as well as children, was of concern to westering men. Henry Jenkins urged his eighty-two-year-old mother to "take courage" and avoid "dwell[ing] too much" on his absence, so that they might "see each other again in the flesh."[86]

While wives were quick to write in great detail of the illnesses of children and parents, they tended to minimize their own health problems, many and varied though they were. Foil to the stoics was Augusta Shipman, who mentioned her assorted ailments in almost every letter.[87] Pamelia Fergus wrote in some detail of a "draining breast," a topic few women of her day would have felt free to discuss with a husband—absent or present—and, like Almira Stearns, Emma Christie, and Augusta Shipman, she also mentioned feelings of depression. James's disdain for any display of emotional weakness later led her to deny that she had ever had "the blues," though she had already confessed, "Just as often as I sit down to drop a few lines to you [the tears] . . . . come right along."[88]

If James Fergus himself ever felt lonely enough to shed a tear, he never expressed such feelings in letters to his wife. Indeed, many women in waiting were reduced to reading between the lines to find any expression of a husband's love. All too often, the only evidence of a man's devotion had to be deduced from his assertions that he was working in the mines exclusively for her good and that of her children. When Mary Elizabeth Rose pressed the point, her thirty-one-year-old husband Granberry responded, "I am too old to write a love letter." Yet the letters of forty-two-year-old Henry Jenkins regularly assured his "much beloved wife" that "thee is uppermost in my thoughts and my love is unabated by distance but rather the contrary." Robert Kelley wrote ardent notes to his wife Mollie, who "love[d] such letters" and responded in kind: "How I wish 'my Robert' was here, then I would have a pair of loving arms to encircle me, and a heart to beat 'responsive to my own.'"[89]

Like other men away from their wives, Henry Rayner was given to dreams of reunion, such as the one in which he met Mahala "on the isthmus [and] soon my arms around thy waist I flung and pressed my lips to thine but lo it was all a dream." He wrote of "gaz[ing] upon thy beauteous face and snatch[ing] the nectar kiss from thy sweet lips." Mahala matched him sigh for sigh: "My love for my dear loveing henry is so intinse that language falls short to express it send me all the love you can for that is better than your gold."[90]

As amorous as Henry and Mahala Rayner's letters might seem when set against typical letters between couples separated during the westward movement, they pale by comparison with the letters of Charles and Maggie Brown, a passionate pair who spared no words in expressing their longing for one another—even in sexually explicit terms: "I feel that I could kiss that little 'tater hole if . . . . [I had] it back with me," Charles wrote to Maggie, "and I think I will kiss the other when I get to, for it is so sweet." Maggie met his frankness with her own: "So you have not gotten out of the old way of 'wanting it' at night. Never mind you wont have to suffer much longer." Having expressed more than once concern about her husband's faithfulness—"Have you kissed anyone since you did me? I tell you you had better not"—she received his answer, plainly writ: "[Knowing yours is] the best in the world . . . I am satisfied to think of how nice it will be and go and jack off." Aware that this might shock even his Maggie, he begged, "Now don't blame me for I do get awful hard up some times."[91]

Other men resorted to other means of satisfying their sexual urges. Having left his wife and two sons behind in Little Falls, Minnesota, in 1864, Johnny Johnson worked as a bartender in several Montana Territory saloons, eventually becoming involved with a prostitute in Blackfoot. When he was killed in an altercation over the woman's favors, Ellen Johnson learned of his infidelity only through newpaper accounts of the ensuing trial. John Ault was another Little Falls resident who gave in to temptation out in Montana Territory. When James Fergus heard of Ault's death thirteen years after the two of them had gone west together in 1862, he mused, "Poor John he has made a great deal of money in this country, he ought to have had his wife [Margaretha] here and been well off but he has lived fast, been always in debt, spent his money in eating, drinking, and with women. I think he thought a great deal of his wife, but with him it was out of sight out of mind."[92]

That phrase struck fear into the heart of many a wife back home. When Mary Jane Swilling confessed similar anxieties to her husband, Jack, who was working in the mines of the Southwest, he insisted that she need not worry, for he was "bound to go back to gods country where I can see American women ever day instid of the Mexican women. . . . [No] white man could live long in such A country." Apparently Swilling lingered on long enough to change his racist perceptions, for although his wife and daughter never knew it, early in 1864, nearly eight years after he had left them behind in Alabama, he was married to Trinidad Escalante in Saint Augustine's Cathedral in Tucson, Arizona—obviously without having mentioned his first marriage to the officiating priest or anyone else out west.[93]

Other men were equally reticent about mentioning wives back home. Alexander Kissell "played him Self . . . for a Single man" while out in Montana Territory, leading his friend Joseph Kenney to comment, "It is none of my business, but I dont like to See a man forget . . . his wife as Soon as he gits out of Sight of her." William Hiller teased his wife, Abiah, about the issue of fidelity, writing, "I sle[e]p alone and I suppose you do too," but infidelity was no joking matter to Leroy Warner, who warned his wife, Mary, "Dont have any thing to do with any one else for if you do I will kill them quicker than I would a snake."[94]

Sarah Kiser of Fort Wayne, Indiana, was equally serious about the subject of marital fidelity, for despite her determination not to believe her sister Polly's repeated assertions that Ambrose Kiser had gone west primarily to get away from her and the children, she grew more and more worried as month after month passed without a single letter from the West. Certain that Ambrose had deserted her, she broke under the strain. When the doctor theorized that Sarah's physical illness was caused by mental anguish, a contrite Polly— who had never liked her brother-in-law and had thought his departure a blessing—drew from their hiding place a stack of unopened letters from Montana Territory. The letters were promptly read aloud to Sarah, but it was too late. Weakened by dysentery as well as depression, she died before Ambrose could be notified of her illness. Friends and relatives raised the couple's son and two daughters, and Ambrose stayed on in Virginia City, eventually remarrying.[95]

Another instance of remarriage occurred under vastly different circumstances. In 1860, Edward Oliver, an Englishman and a Mormon convert, moved his wife Sarah and their children to the States and thence westward as far as Buffalo County, Nebraska, before a broken wagon tongue forced them to spend the winter there. When spring came and Edward was ready to move on to Salt Lake City, Sarah declared that she and the children would remain in Nebraska until he had made a place for them. Edward agreed, but he took their young maid Susana with him, and by the time the two had reached their destination, she had become the second Mrs. Oliver. Although there is no official record that Edward's excercising his Mormon option to take another wife had anything to do with the fact that Sarah never did move on to Utah, her descendants say that is the story they have always heard—and that what bothered Sarah most was not that Edward had married again but that he had married her maid.[96]

Frustrated as Sarah Oliver might have been by Mormon approval of polygamy, she likely had no quarrel with that church's disapproval of alcohol. Liquor flowed freely in the gold camps of the West, and reformed drinkers were especially susceptible to the lure of saloons. Hoping to keep her husband away from the "intoxicating bowl," Abby Jenkins wrote Henry about a "heart broken and dejected" neighbor whose hard-drinking husband could no longer "hold his hand still," adding, "When I looked at her I thanked God from my heart that I had been spared from seeing my companion carried along in that awful course." Acknowledging that he could understand her "misgiveings of [his] resisting an old besetment," Henry maintained, "I do not (as formerly) feel any inclination to partake when it is circulating freely all around me."[97]

Apparently many wives shared Abby Jenkins' concerns, for the letters of westering men are filled with assurances that they were not succumbing to the temptation of strong drink. Portraying himself as "the steadiest man in the place," Forty-niner merchant Granberry Rose boasted to his wife, Mary Elizabeth, "I have not drank a glass tumbler of spirits in over eight months." And Alonzo Boardman asked his wife, Nancy, to "tell the Good Templars that I am as good as any of them for I have not tasted a drop of liquor since I have been here and but three times on my way here."[98]

Worried as wives were about the many temptations men faced in the West, the ultimate worry was the danger posed by Indians. Like many other women of her era, Harriet Godfrey feared and hated Indians, although one of her closest friends and neighbors was a woman of Indian ancestry. As her animosity grew in the weeks following the Indian uprising in Minnesota, she talked more and more of "them nasty things" and worried about her husband's safety in Montana Territory, yet Ard himself professed little fear and no disdain for Indians.[99]

Feeling more sympathy than antipathy for the Indians he encountered, Newton Chandler told his wife, Jane, about finding "four Squaws and five young ones" near his camp site. "One Squaw [was] . . . frozen to death and the others nearly froze," he reported, and in his next letter he wrote that the bodies of two of the little boys had later been found in a snowbank. Moved by the plight of the women and children, Chandler blamed the tragedy on the negligence of "the men or Bucks as we call them," who "often stay away [hunting] for weeks leaving their Squaws & young in a bunch of sedg brush to take care of themselves as best the[y] can Such is Indian Life in Utah."[100] If he noted any similarity to life among families of Forty-niners, he did not remark upon it.

John Marsh Smith was eager to correct his wife Lizzie's negative impressions of Indians in the West. Writing from his winter camp in the mountains just above Sacramento, where "the face of white man [had been] unknown" until that previous summer of 1849, he felt "free from harm" and urged Lizzie not to "let horrible tales of California life torment thee. Most are mere fabrications." In 1864, Franklin Friend wrote similar reassurances about Montana Territory to his wife, Martha: "Donte believe anythinge you hear aboute the indians they are friendly." That line was to prove tragically ironic, for a year later Franklin and his brother George were killed in a surprise attack by a party of Blackfeet Indians while logging near Fort Benton, earning extra money as they waited for the arrival of the steamboat that would take them home to Iowa. One of the first men to arrive at the scene of the massacre informed the two widows that all of the loggers had been "shot with guns and arrows, some of them had 7 or 8 arrows in them and some of them had their throats cut from ear to ear and all [were] cut to pieces with tomahawks" and that the Friend brothers themselves had been "shot to pieces very bad and one of them was scalped." In late summer of 1868, Joseph Kenney, en route home to Susan in Iowa, was waylaid on the Yellowstone and burned at the stake by a Sioux war party.[101]

Violent deaths made widows of other waiting wives. Elizabeth Beall of Fond du Lac, Wisconsin, received news that her husband Samuel had been killed in a duel in Helena, Montana. Other women lost husbands to barroom brawls and claim disputes. Still others received word of the death of a spouse from natural causes. Many westering husbands died of diphtheria, cholera, yellow fever, or dysentery, and Lawyer James Hall, who had ultimately gone west himself and made his own wife a "widow" of the sort he had been accused of cheating back in Little Falls, died of a heart attack on his way home from Denver and made her a true widow.[102]

Some wives never even knew they had been widowed. Just as Mary Jane Swilling received no word of her husband's second marriage, she heard nothing whatever about his death in a Yuma jail cell. In August 1854, Granberry Rose wrote informing his wife, Mary Elizabeth, that he was on his way home with "a nice little sum of money" and bidding her "farewell until we meet again." That meeting never took place. Mary Elizabeth continued to hope for her husband's return for many years thereafter, but she and her children eventually concluded that, although it was possible that Granberry had decided to spend his "nice little sum" someplace other than home, it was more likely that he had been robbed and killed by highwaymen, not an uncommon fate for those departing the goldfields.[103]

Accidents claimed hundreds of miners, including John Ewing, who died while working his claim in Montana Territory, leaving his wife, Emily, to support herself as a teacher back in Winona, Minnesota, and fellow Minnesotan Robert Russell, who died in Colorado, leaving his wife, Agnes, to raise their eight children alone. Other accidents maimed without killing. In the summer of 1855, William Jenkins, who had followed his father, Henry, out to California in May of 1852, was "deprived . . . of the sight of both eyes" by the "discharge of powder while blasting." Her son's injury, her husband's long and unsuccessful sojourn in the West, and the emigration of a daughter and granddaughter to the Golden State moved Abby Jenkins to write, "I wish I had never heard of California."[104]

Jane Chandler would no doubt have echoed those words. Having been in the West since 1854, Newton Chandler finally made it home to Massachusetts in the fall of 1860, six months after the death of his little daughter, May, but he was off to California again in the spring, leaving Jane pregnant with another daughter who, like the sister she never met, was destined to grow up without a father in the house. Six years old when his father first left home, Willie Chandler was still writing letters to California well into adulthood. While Jane Chandler chafed at what she viewed as her husband's irresponsible behavior, she did not rue his absence from home, especially after 1869, when widespread rumors of his infidelity led Newton to fear that she might have felt justified in "tak[ing] some other name than [his]."[105]

Constant quarreling with his wife, Mary, coupled with mounting debts, sent Leroy Warner to the Klondike in 1898. Before his departure, Mary had labeled her husband "the meanest man that ever lived," and apparently distance did nothing to alter that opinion. "I've known for 12 or 15 years that you did not care a snap for me if you ever did which I doubt a good deal," Leroy wrote her in the fall of 1905. By the time he finally made it home in 1912, Leroy was badly disfigured and mentally deranged from a logging accident in British Columbia, and although Mary allowed him into her home, she left him largely in the care of fourteen-year-old Don, the baby she had been carrying at the time he set off for Alaska. When Leroy kept straying from home to pan for gold in the treacherous waters of the Black River, Mary had him committed to the insane asylum at Owen, Wisconsin, where the staff allowed him to set up a tent on the banks of a small stream running through the property. There Leroy Warner lived out his days panning for the gold that had so long eluded him.[106]

Other men for whom the lure of gold had once been equally strong came gradually to reassess their decisions to leave wives and children behind and set out for the West. "What is gold to the embraces of an affectionate wife?" Henry Rayner asked, and Henry Jenkins ultimately decided that Calaveras Creek was "a verry poor place for a young man to come to and [that] a married one ha[d] no business to come at all." Conversely, some men felt that the West was not only an ideal place for a married man but also an ideal place for his family. Whether or not they agreed with that assessment, many women did eventually follow their husbands to new homes on the frontier. In some cases, husbands went home in order to accompany their wives and children on the journey west. Cornelius Hedges, who had set out from Iowa for the gold mines of Montana on foot in April 1864, returned to the States in the summer of 1866 to purchase a five-stamp mill for his mining operations in Last Chance Gulch and to bring his wife, Edna, and their two children to Helena, where he practiced law, speculated in mining claims, and held various county and state offices.[107]

Men unwilling or unable to leave profitable claims or sprouting fields made arrangements for their families to make the trip west without them. Riverboat captain William R. Massie reported that many wives and children were on board his Missouri River steamer, *Twilight,* in the summer of 1865 on their way to meet husbands and fathers, many of whom had not seen their families "for years." Some of the men were so eager for the reunion that they traveled down the

Yellowstone by flatboat to intercept the *Twilight* at the river's conflu-
ence with the Missouri. According to Captain Massie, "The scene
that ensued when they got aboard was absolutely indescribable.
Husbands, wives and . . . [children] met. Such a sight I have never
witnessed before or since."[108]

Not all families received such a welcome. After five years of super-
vising her husband William's sawmill in Little Elk, Minnesota, Rosanna Sturgis loaded herself and five of her seven children onto the
steamer *Luella,* which set out from Saint Louis in late spring of 1867.
Arriving in Fort Benton, at the head of Missouri River navigation,
she was met, not by her husband, but by one of his ranch hands. She
and the children promptly lifted their goods into the ox-drawn wagon
William had sent and began the 250-mile trip across plains and
mountains to their new home in the Beaverhead Valley.[109]

Other men sent word that their wives were to come west by sea.
Ann Jenkins Ransom and her daughter, Cordelia, made the long
ocean voyage alone, and Sarah Yesler traveled across the isthmus in
the company of Henry's business friend, G. A. Meigs. Both arrived
safely in San Francisco, but other families were not so fortunate.
Lizzie Smith passed along to her husband, John, "accounts that William Hobsons little son died out at Sea with something like spasms
and that his wife put in at Valperasoe and that William has gone out
there to meet her."[110]

Still other westering men arranged for their families to come to
them by way of the overland trail. When Joseph Avery left his wife
and children in Illinois in 1845, he was so convinced that Oregon
was the place he wanted to settle that he made arrangements with
the wagonmaster who took him west that spring to bring his family
out in another two years. Thus in the spring of 1847, Martha Marsh
Avery and her children joined the wagonmaster's train, traveling in a
wagon drawn by five yoke of oxen and trailed by two cows. Mollie
Kelley, whose firebrand husband had "heid him[self] away to that
Rebel Paradise, Montana," in 1863, followed Robert west to Virginia
City the next summer, driving a "span of mules" that pulled the
wagon carrying her household goods, eight-year-old Kate, and
three-year-old Nannie.[111]

That same summer, Pamelia Fergus showed similar independence
and competence in the face of the exasperating ineptitude of the
man her husband, James, had sent to help her cross the plains.
Although James had earlier proclaimed that his "going away [would

be] of great benefit" to Pamelia by "throwing [her] on [her] own resources and learning [her] to do business for [her]self," he was hardly prepared to resume life with a woman whose new-found independence had so greatly transformed her.[112] After four years of "do[ing] business for [her]self," Pamelia would never again manifest the acquiescent behavior that had characterized the early years of her marriage.

Predictably, there were tensions in the household after the Fergus reunion. Those tensions exploded during a dinner party at the family home some months after Pamelia's arrival in Virginia City. When James criticized her for oversalting the food, Pamelia denied that it was too salty, and in the scene that followed she swore at James, further embarrassing him in front of his guests. In the wake of the confrontation, James, so long accustomed to communicating with his wife by written word, penned a lengthy letter upbraiding Pamelia for her unseemly behavior in public. And he went on to list the many instances—both back east and while crossing the plains—in which she had questioned his judgment, ignored his orders, and acted according to her own wishes. "The great trouble is that you pay no attention to the wishes of your husband," he began. "I gave my wife directions and she did not do them. . . . I wrote you to have it done and that was sufficient [reason to do it]. Mrs. Sturgis Mrs. Ault or any other [wife would] . . . not enquire whether [the orders were] right or wrong."[113]

Gradually the couple readjusted to life in tandem, and James Fergus ultimately came to see the advantages of his wife's independence, noting that she "always kept the purse" after her arrival in Montana and that her managerial skills were largely responsible for the success of the stagecoach station the Ferguses operated on the road between Helena and Fort Benton. In that enterprise the couple "worked together . . . [and] had interests in common," and in later years James maintained that he and Pamelia had never really understood each other "until she had her own way with the . . . Stage Station."[114]

Even though life as a home-front widow brought positive and long-lasting gains to Pamelia Fergus, other women in waiting viewed as burden, rather than privilege, any freedoms attained during the absence of westering husbands. A "sometimes somewhat depressed" Abby Jenkins declared, "I . . . [find] the cares of a large family [for someone] with a mind as week as mine are heavy." Wanting no part "of the fuss that is made about the rights of Woman," Abby maintained that the only right worth claiming was a woman's "right to [her] own husband."[115]

Thus, women in waiting run the gamut—from Pamelia Fergus, who claimed and maintained a position for herself both within the home and in the larger world, to Abby Jenkins, who was eager for the return of her husband so she would have "somebody to look to in all troubles to lift the burden off [her] shoulders and take the lead."[116] Both women managed admirably in the absence of their spouses, yet they would have had considerable difficulty coming to any agreement about exactly what their stints as gold rush widows had meant to them or to their marriages.

As the six chapters that follow will illustrate, no one thesis can possibly encompass the great variety of experience observed in any study of the separated family in the westward movement. There is as much diversity as there is commonality to be found in these stories. Women of varied backgrounds and personalities, married to men whose backgrounds and personalities were equally diverse, were left behind under a wide variety of circumstances to cope with myriad crises until their periods of waiting were ended in any number of ways. Thus it is only through an in-depth study of the experiences of individual families that we can even begin to gain an understanding of this fairly common, though poorly documented, aspect of the history of the settling of the American West.

II

Abiah Warren Hiller

"I Suppose It Is Just in the Edge of the Evening Where You Are"

On a March morning in 1851, sparks from the woodstove in Abiah Hiller's house in McDonough, New York, ignited a loose floorboard, and "the south chamber was all in flames . . . before [they] knew it." Ushering her two young daughters, her mother, and the dozen students in her care out of the smoldering home, Abiah, with the help of neighbors, managed to save "all [her] papers and the greatest part of the furniture," although they were "turned out into the street" in a few short hours. "I have some friends yet," she wrote, a month after the fact, to her husband, William, in the goldfields of Humboldt County, California, "and I shall have another house before long."[1]

Indeed, on June 21, exactly three months after the fire, Abiah Hiller was posting public notice to inform the citizens of McDonough that she would commence school in her new house on the first Monday of September. At the same time, she was writing William that she had used three hundred dollars in the building of the new home. The kitchen, one bedroom, and the schoolroom were finished, but the rest of the house he would have to finish upon his return. "I hope what you have done to your house you have done well so that it will be worth finising when I get home," he replied. "I suppose the roof is too steep to suit you," she responded, "but it suits me."[2]

Abiah Stanley Warren, first child of Oliver and Abiah Stanley Warren, was born May 11, 1805, in Jaffrey, New Hampshire. Growing up in the shadow of Mount Monadnock, little Abiah spent her early years enjoying the pastimes of an only child, wandering in the woods and fields surrounding the old homestead and having the undivided attention of her parents and her paternal grandmother, Martha Warren. She learned needlework, weaving, and other domestic arts from her mother and grandmother and gave early evidence of considerable talent in drawing. As she grew, she excelled in every subject taught in the village school. Blessed with an insatiable curiosity and the encouragement of her parents, she tried everything that caught her fancy, from math to music, and she seemed capable of succeeding in any field she chose to enter. Indeed, by the time she was twelve, she had done so well in all areas that not even the arrival of a long-awaited baby brother lessened the pride her parents took in their firstborn.[3]

Born June 5, 1817, Andrew Oliver Warren became the delight of his older sister, who eventually shared with him all the secrets of the wooded hillsides and spent hours teaching him the letters and numbers he was still too young to be offered in school. Abiah's own studies continued to flourish. Realizing their daughter's need for a more challenging educational environment, the Warrens decided to allow her to board with her uncle Simon Warren and his family in order to attend Chesterfield Academy, an outstanding school located in the village of Chesterfield, some twenty-five miles west of Jaffrey. In her late teens Abiah accepted her first teaching job in a "common district school" close by her home in Jaffrey. Years of teaching in small schools in the area followed, during which time she continued her training in art and in music, attending singing school in nearby Fitzwilliam and taking lessons on the bass viol, which she played for services at the local Universalist church.[4]

Teaching heightened Abiah's interest in furthering her own education, and she intermittently attended classes in Latin, Greek, and other subjects at Chester Seminary in Chester, Vermont, boarding with her cousins, Sarah and Sophia Whitmore. Returning to teaching, Abiah made the world her classroom, leaving textbooks behind in order to take her scholars up "a hill. . . . [to look] through a spy glass." Throughout her early twenties, she continued her studies when she was not teaching. She continued as well her dedication to the domestic arts, producing "exquisite lace needlework" and woven bedspreads. She also developed an interest in astronomy, studying the subject on her own and attending lectures as often as possible. Fascinated by the movement of the heavens and the possibility of life beyond our own planet, she wrote a formal essay on the history of astronomy, signing the piece, "An Astronomer, A. S. Warren."[5]

Her situation varied during her last years in New Hampshire. Although she sometimes lived at home and taught in neighborhood schools, she frequently boarded in the homes of her students while teaching in other districts. Whatever her place of residence or her primary occupation, she "was always busy at some thing." She spun yarn and wove cloth, "dipt candles," made soap, and went to singing school at Fitzwilliam; she scoured knives, sewed frocks and cloaks, and made hats from the "washed and whitened leaves of split palms." She "wrote off" tunes in her handmade music books, and in these same books recorded recipes not only for cakes and cookies but also for the cures of a wide variety of ailments: cancer, corns, stiff joints, and "inflamation of the heart." She harvested cranberries, gathered chestnuts, "seated" chairs, bound flax and rye, and raked and loaded hay. She was, as her brother was later to say of her, "a constant worker."[6]

During the first few years of the 1830s, Abiah kept company with Franklin Wheelock, a young bachelor who shared her interests in music and the arts, but she took no romantic interest in him. Even at twenty-eight, a teaching career and the pursuit of the arts remained her dominant concerns—along with religion. Once or twice a month she made her way to services in her own town or outlying villages, often in the company of friends.[7] Toward the end of the decade, her curiosity concerning religion drew her beyond the Universalist congregation in which she had been brought up and into Baptist, Methodist, Episcopal, Orthodox, and Presbyterian services throughout the area. She sometimes heard two and three sermons on any one Sunday. Sampling so many sermons from so many sects served to increase her doubts instead of her faith. On a visit to Rochester, New York, she gave in to her skepticism: "In the evening there were several bells ringing at the same time to call the different denominations to meeting, they were toned differently, and sounded rather discordant to a musical ear, not more so, however, than the sentiments proclaimed at their respective houses."[8]

While Abiah was pushing beyond the limits of the Universalist faith, her brother Andrew was embracing that faith to the fullest. After completion of his studies at Melville Academy in Jaffrey, he took up theological studies at Westmoreland, New Hampshire. Abiah herself was drawn once more to the seminary in Chester, where, now in her early thirties, she was an "assistant," as well as a student. It was there at Chester in the spring and summer of 1836 that she "learnt to paint portraits." Portraiture proved to be a source of income for her over the next few years, and she regularly traveled through the countryside, moving from Fitzwilliam to Keene to Marlboro and other villages, painting portraits of children and adults— both living and dead—and boarding with the families of her subjects. During this period of painting, she also "t[oo]k a little music as a medicine occassionally." For that medicine, the singing school at Fitzwilliam remained her primary apothecary. She expanded her musical endeavors as well by learning to play an organ that had recently come into the family.[9]

Abiah's love of nature continued to draw her out-of-doors, and the coming of spring often lured her "into the woods." As winter snows melted in the higher elevations, she always managed to find time for a hike "to the top of Mt Monadnock," from which she could, with the aid of her spyglass, look down upon the house her grandfather Warren had built on the road south of Priest Corners. That home and the farmland surrounding it were sold when Abiah was in her early thirties, and her parents moved to McDonough, a bustling village of about fifteen hundred in Chenango County, upstate New York, where her father invested in two hundred acres of good land with solid water rights and proceeded to erect a dam and sawmill.[10]

Her parents' move meant Abiah the younger had to make a choice. Leaving Jaffrey was not an attractive prospect, for she loved the wooded hillsides on which she roamed, and though McDonough's gently rolling landscape reminded her in many ways of southern New Hampshire, there were no mountains to climb. In any event, the decision could wait, as she had a teaching contract to fulfill in Jaffrey that winter of 1838–39. Her class that session was large and included several older scholars, notably William Hiller, a twenty-year-old who was, quite coincidentally, from McDonough but was spending the year working in the Jaffrey area. Having attended school sessions in McDonough only sporadically during his early years, Hiller had been earning his living as a laborer until he traveled up to Jaffrey to learn carpentry from John Towne, a master carpenter of some repute. Inspired to return to the schoolroom by reports of an excellent teacher who welcomed scholars of all ages, Hiller was not

Abiah Warren, self-portrait, at about thirty-five, around 1840,
shortly before her marriage to William Hiller. *(Photo by Peter Ashlock,
courtesy Virginia Ashlock)*

disappointed. Here was a woman who was not only a fine teacher
but was also a tireless learner, ready to listen to and learn from
those she taught.[11]

Though her teaching went well enough to more than satisfy her
oldest student, Abiah was in the process of deciding to seek her

fortune elsewhere. Ever open to new experiences, she had decided to move to New York City, where she knew she would find ample opportunities to continue her own education and artistic pursuits, even while supporting herself through her teaching.[12]

In looking to this new adventure, Abiah was turning down the prospects of a marriage that held little hope of happiness in any event. Her father's partner in the land purchased in McDonough was one Lawrence Brooks, a widower with several children who saw in thirty-four-year-old Abiah the answer to the burdens of childcare. He was also intrigued at the prospect of forming a matrimonial alliance with a level-headed young woman possessed of a sharp mind, an independent income, and noteworthy domestic skills. A man accustomed to getting what he wanted, Lawrence Brooks virtually announced to the village of McDonough his plans to marry Abiah Hiller—at about the same time he got around to writing his intended a letter that sang her praises and set forth the benefits of the proposed union.[13]

Far from being elated at this opportunity to marry off his daughter to a man of some means, Oliver Warren was wary of his partner's motives in seeking Abiah's hand. His wife was equally wary and warned that Brooks was so generally disagreeable that no one would work for him. His offspring were "the worst children you ever saw and Mr b ha[s] not any government [over them]." The situation in the Brooks home was so dismal that the elder Abiah warned her daughter, "If you list with him your happiness is all blasted forever."[14]

Despite her mother's dire warnings and despite the fact that her father, disgusted with his partner's personal and financial dealings, was about to sever their business relationship, Abiah did not immediately refuse Lawrence Brooks's proposal.[15] Instead, she bided her time, turning her attention to her move to New York City. If Mr. Brooks was serious about wanting to marry her, he would wait for her answer.

Once established in her teaching position in the city, she received a letter from Sophia Underwood, a Jaffrey friend, who reported that William Hiller had "been doing nothing ever since you left," implying that Abiah's former student had more than a passing interest in the departure of his teacher. Whether or not she took note of Sophia's comments concerning William Hiller, Abiah had other things on her mind. Her school had grown but slowly, and her city scholars were much harder to manage than she had expected.[16]

Unsettled in the city and weighing the possibility of moving to McDonough to be with her parents, Abiah took a step to facilitate that possibility by finally responding in the negative to Lawrence Brooks's proposal of marriage. Finishing out her year's contract in New York City in the late winter of 1840, she moved to McDonough, where, with her father's help, she converted a sitting room in her parents' home into a classroom and opened a private school. Abiah never had reason to rue her move, for by early March 1840 her new school had proven so successful that her students awarded her a certificate of merit: "We the undersigned tender our unfeigned thanks to you, for the uniform kindness, and attention with which you have treated us, and would also say that we are well satisfied with your school, and believe you have spared no exertions on your part for the promotion of our education." Nine students signed the certificate. The last name on the list was that of William Hiller, who had left Jaffrey and returned to McDonough soon after his favorite teacher had set out for New York City.[17]

Born July 26, 1818, in Rhode Island, William was the last of Wing and Mary Elsbree Hillers' ten children. Growing up as the tag-a-along to three older brothers—Prince, John, and Ira—and three older sisters—Phebe, Susan, and Mary—William had spent his childhood as a typical farmboy, attending school when he was not needed at home. In 1829, when William was eleven, Wing Hiller had moved his family to Chenango County, where he established a homestead near McDonough. There William had joined his siblings in tilling the land and harvesting the sugar from its abundant maple trees. Until his serendipitous decision to pursue carpentry under the tutelage of a master craftsman in Jaffrey, schooling had held but few allures for him. Apparently his months in Abiah Warren's New Hampshire classroom had convinced him of the worth of scholarly pursuits, but if his eagerness to sign up for Abiah's new school in McDonough went beyond that of a devoted student for an admired teacher, he kept his counsel that spring of 1840.[18]

Meantime, Abiah Warren herself focused not on any romance of her own but on that of her brother. On May 6, 1840, Andrew O. Warren married Sophia Underwood of Jaffrey. The young seminarian's first assignment was a Universalist church in Chenango County, and shortly after the wedding the couple moved to the McDonough area. With her family newly reunited and her school succeeding beyond her expectations, Abiah Hiller enjoyed her life in McDonough

William Hiller at about twenty-two, around 1840, shortly before his marriage to Abiah Warren. *(Courtesy Eastern Washington State Historical Society)*

to the fullest. And though romance had never been a priority item on her agenda, she found herself increasingly drawn to student William Hiller. A youthful and energetic thirty-five-year-old, she enjoyed the company of her twenty-two-year-old admirer, and she was certainly not one to let public opinion sway her judgment in such a personal matter as the choice of a companion. William shared her interest in astronomy, botany, and the arts, and she admired his determination to continue his education at an age when most young men were content to turn their energies entirely to the earning of a dollar.[19]

In January 1842, having served the required number of years in preparation, Andrew Oliver Warren was ordained as a Universalist minister. His wife, Sophia, and nine-month-old daughter, Ella, were on hand for the reception that followed, as were his mother, father, and sister. Oliver Warren was grateful to have seen this long-awaited event, for his health had been failing steadily. He had already asked Andrew to add the running of the Warren mills to his pastoral duties, realizing the necessity of keeping the mill in operation even though he could no longer run it himself. His health failed so rapidly thereafter that although he lived to welcome a second grandaughter, Jane, he was dead by April 1842.[20]

His family mourned the passing of a man who had offered his support to each of them in turn, and though they had known him only briefly, the people of McDonough mourned the loss of a good neighbor and respected craftsman. Warren had worked hard all of his life, but he left relatively few earthly goods behind. After creditors were paid, the $959 estate was reduced to less than $500, to be divided among his widow and two children.[21]

If her father had not died that spring of 1842, Abiah Warren's longstanding friendship with William Hiller might have remained only that. But death signaled the end of one generation and served as a reminder of how little time she had left to make her own mark. There was plenty of room in the Warren house to raise a family as well as run a school, and she welcomed the idea of having a helpmate to call upon as she undertook the task of caring for her widowed mother and the farmland attached to the estate. Thus on May 18, 1842, thirty-seven-year-old Abiah Stanley Warren married twenty-three-year-old William Hiller and moved him into the house on East Street. Now a member of the family, Hiller relieved Andrew of the operation of the sawmill and gristmill and saw generally to all of the family business ventures.[22]

Ten months later, Abiah Hiller gave birth to her first child, a daughter, Phebe Amna, born March 20, 1843. With the arrival of a second daughter, Josephine, less than two years later, on January 2, 1845, Abiah considered her household complete. Immediately after her second lying-in period, she returned to her teaching, leaving the little ones in the care of Grandma Warren. William's sisters, Phebe and Mary Jane, were frequent visitors in the home, as was his recently widowed mother, Mary Elsbree Hiller, who had moved in with Mary Jane and her husband, Singleton Kenyon. Andrew and Sophia Warren and their little girls, Ella and Jane, came often, too, and after the fall of 1846 they brought along baby Charles, the first Warren grandson.[23]

The following spring, knowing that his work as a minister left him no reason to maintain his share in the farmland and mills, Andrew Warren sold his portion of the land inherited from his father to his brother-in-law, William Hiller. But only a few months later, having worked faithfully to rebuild the dam and improve water-power potential for the Warren mills, William decided the venture was not profitable enough to justify the continued expenditures of capital and labor, and he and Abiah sold the mills and most of the surrounding land.[24]

Determined to discover exactly what his own occupation should be and not at all sure that his fortune lay in New York, William Hiller spent the next few weeks setting his accounts in order and preparing himself for a trip to the Midwest. All across Chenango County the talk was of better opportunities to the west, and William was determined to check out the possibilities. Sometime during the third week of October 1847, handing Abiah a list of items he had lent to neighbors that she might expect to retrieve in case she had need of them before his return, he bade wife and daughters farewell and set out on his quest.[25]

William was bound for Illinois, where several New York emigrants, including relatives of his brother-in-law, Singleton Kenyon, had found steady work at good wages. As her husband made his slow wagon journey west, Abiah looked after business at home, teaching, tending to the needs of four-year-old Phebe and two-year-old Josephine, driving the team to the mill for grain and flour, and attending to the sundry other duties formerly handled by her husband.[26] Sometime in November, a month after William's departure, she finally heard from him. He had been impressed by the number of wagons making their way across the prairies. Traveling west from Chicago, he had met 439 teams within nineteen miles of the city. "That same road 13 years ago was not plane enough so that a footman could follow it," he declared, "and now . . . it will hold a good comparison with Broadway in New York." He was earning fair wages in Sycamore, a small town some fifty-five miles northwest of Chicago.[27]

Even as she waited for his sporadic letters, Abiah took what time she could to write him of her activities on the home front. She conveyed messages from several Chenango County friends who had relatives in northern Illinois. She also queried him about whether she could hope to make money with her weaving if she followed him west. On Christmas morning, while little Phebe and Josephine were opening their gifts in the presence of their mother and grandmother, their father was making his way across central Illinois in the company of a man named Breed, traveling in a small wagon pulled by a single horse. Remarking on the "broken romantic country" and "large praries," he declared that he liked the country very well indeed. The winter was mild, though they had had a white Christmas, and his health had been good—he "never was rugeder in [his] life."[28]

William had not yet managed to make very much money, but he was confident enough of his prospects to vow, "I would not go home at all if my matters [there] were all settled." As things stood, he was returning to his job in Sycamore and was ambivalent about homecoming plans. All would depend on "how things [went] along." If wages did not improve, he might well need money for his trip home, in which case he would tell her how to send it. Meantime he wanted her to ask their McDonough friend Martin Daniels to write him the particulars about the prospects Martin was checking out in Richmond, Virginia, so that he could compare them with his own findings in Illinois. Since the tone of his letters suggested that Abiah would soon be loading her wagons and joining the emigration west, she began advising her friends back in Jaffrey that they might soon be hearing from her in Illinois.[29]

Yet when William Hiller arrived home in mid-April 1848 after six months of knocking about in Illinois, he brought with him plans of a different sort. Throughout his months in Illinois, he had continued to be intrigued by Martin Daniels's accounts of business opportunities in Richmond, and though Daniels himself had returned to McDonough and was still undecided about a move to Virginia, Hiller was convinced that prospects there warranted his immediate attention. Thus, on June 15, 1848, barely two months after his return to McDonough, William Hiller once again said goodbye to wife and daughters, this time heading south.[30]

The journey to Richmond was slow and indirect, for he traveled by stage, riverboat, and rail, arriving at his destination more than a month after his departure from McDonough. He was not prepared for the cultural differences that awaited him, exclaiming, "Here I am in the City of Negroedom where the darkes are as thick as black berries but for all this it is quite a place and room for it to be mad[e] much more so."[31]

Indeed, he was every bit as sold on moving to Richmond as he had been on moving to Illinois. True to his promise to Abiah, he made inquiries into the schools in the area and learned that there were "a number of Select school[s] in the city" that supposedly paid "verry well." Though he had not "larned much about the kind of books in use" there, he concluded that Abiah could "order a bill of books from New York cheaper than to stop to buy them" now. Although she might have "a chance to use [her] loom," he thought she would hardly earn enough to offset the cost of renting "a room to put it in," and while he saw no problem with keeping a cow, as long as they got "a location in the out part of the city," he thought it best not to do so during their first fall and winter in Virginia.[32]

Boarding with a Mrs. Daws at three dollars per week was an expensive proposition, and William pressed Abiah to come "as soon as convenient." He was paying "25 cts per week for washing," another great expense, but at least clothing was as cheap "as any body can wish." Although money was scarce and that made it "hard doing business," William remained firm in his resolve to settle his family in Virginia. He asked Abiah to write "how you get along and who you have settled [affairs] with."[33]

At home in McDonough, Abiah began settling up outstanding accounts and preparing herself for the move to Richmond. Rather than sell their home, which housed the schoolroom that was her hedge against failure in Richmond, she rented it out. She then secured from the local superintendent of common schools a letter of recommendation indicating that her teaching had "ever been popular and satisfactory to her patrons" and commending her as a role model for other teachers, noting, "most of our female and some of our male teachers have fitted themselves for teaching under her tuition." She collected all the outstanding notes she could from those who owed

William and herself and began sorting out what she should take south.[34]

In the meantime, William located a house for the family in a good, quiet neighborhood, though he feared the house was "too small to be convinent," having only "three good rooms," with one being a basement and the other two "stacked one on top of the other." At least there was a well in the backyard, and the water was reported to be good. The rent was reasonable, and he figured that for the time being it was as good as he could do. An able carpenter, he began to think about partitioning the upper room into two bedrooms and converting the basement into a kitchen. Obviously, Abiah could not hope to conduct her school in such a small house, but there was a "nice church" nearby that William thought "could be got cheap for a school room."[35]

Since space in the house would be at a premium, he advised Abiah to bring as few things as she could get along with. Those things she had to leave behind might be stored at his brother Ira's, "for they [had] plenty of room and . . . [would] take good care of things left with them." She need not bring his turning lathe with her, since he planned to buy a larger one in Richmond. She should give their trunk to his brother John, but in all other matters on the home front, she could "suit [her]self."[36]

Time was of the essence, and William advised Abiah to turn any outstanding notes over to lawyer Lewis Burdick to be collected, instead of remaining in McDonough any longer trying to collect them. Ephraim Frost and Lyman Isbell owed William a considerable sum, but rather than have them pay it at once, he suggested that Abiah should have the two men hold off "untill after navigaton closes" and then deposit the money in a New York bank and send him a certificate of deposit. This would give him money to fall back on in case business in Richmond did not go well in the fall.[37]

The way William Hiller planned it, Abiah would not likely have to travel alone, since he expected Martin Daniels, his partner in the proposed Richmond planing mill, to be ready to travel south by the time she completed her own preparations. Even so, he sent her detailed instructions for the trip. Because baggage was slow, she should send all their goods south ten days in advance of her own departure date. That date would be determined primarily by the steamer schedule out of Baltimore. He urged her to hire a private coach rather than take the stage from McDonough to New York City, where she should anticipate a layover, since Martin Daniels would have business to attend to. He sent further instructions covering her trip from New York to Philadelphia and thence to Baltimore to catch the steamer for Norfolk. Arriving in Richmond, she was to hire a cab and go directly to Mrs. Daws's, where he would be awaiting them.[38]

As thorough as William's instructions were, Abiah altered them to take into account the health of her mother and children. "Mother . . . has the dropsy, which I fear she will not get over, I do not know how it will affect her to ride," she wrote her husband. Furthermore, Phebe had the mumps, and Josephine would likely contract the disease in turn. As a result, she now planned to depart McDonough on Sunday, September 10, assuming Grandma Warren and Phebe were well enough to travel. And despite the fact that it would add two days to her journey, she opted to save money and travel by public stage rather than in the hired coach William had suggested. Martin Daniels would, indeed, be accompanying them, and she anticipated no problems, provided her mother and children were well enough to enjoy the trip.[39]

As she had planned, Abiah Hiller departed McDonough, New York, at 8:45 A.M. on a September Sunday. She came quickly to rue her decision to travel by stage, for her journey was made in fits and starts controlled by the whims of her drivers and the delays of connecting stages. After several days of bouncing over rutted roads with a recuperating five-year-old, a three-year-old coming down with mumps, and a stoical mother, she was glad to arrive in Catskill on the Hudson and transfer to a steamer for the trip downriver to New York City. There Abiah, Grandma Warren, and the girls whiled away a day, waiting for Daniels to conduct his business, before boarding the train for Philadelphia and on to Baltimore. The cruise down Chesapeake Bay and upriver to Richmond was uneventful, and the weary travelers reached Mrs. Daws's boardinghouse about noon on Sunday, September 17, 1848, a week after having departed McDonough.[40]

For two weeks the Hiller family lived at Mrs. Daws's before they were able to move into the home William had secured for them. Adjustment to life in Richmond was not easy for Abiah. For the first time in her adult life she was without an independent income. With her loom, her cow, and her scholars left behind in McDonough, she was obliged to ask her husband for the money she needed to set up housekeeping. Her requests were small—from thirteen cents to three dollars at any one time—but asking for such niggling amounts went against the nature of a woman who had for so long tended to her own business affairs. While she did her best to adjust to the changes necessitated by limited funds, she also managed to take advantage of educational and cultural activities in Richmond. And though she did not yet have a formal schoolroom or enough scholars to begin a school of her own, she began lessons with Phebe.[41]

By early December, William Hiller's planing mill was beginning to bring in some money, and he had become a nominal partner in a concern known as Daniels, Crenshaw, & Co. There was promise of modest success in Richmond, but modest success was hardly enough for a man with sizeable dreams. At about the same time Abiah and the children had arrived in Richmond, so had an issue of the *Philadelphia North American* that featured a first-hand account of the California gold rush. The writer, a Rev. Walter Colton of Monterey, noted that the "farmers have thrown aside their plows, the lawyers their briefs, the doctors their pills, the priests their prayer books, and all are now digging gold." Reverend Colton opined that ten thousand miners in ten years could not exhaust the gold in California's hills. Upon reading such reports, William Hiller's talk about opportunities in the West took a new twist. He searched the papers for reports on the mines and pored over the pages of guidebooks such as *The Emigrant's Guide to the Gold Mines . . . Together with . . . Full Instructions upon the Best Method of Getting There, Living, Expenses, etc., etc, and a Complete Description of the Country.*[42]

Whatever Abiah thought of her husband's gold fever, she was as helpless to ward off its ultimate effects as she had been to prevent Josephine from catching Phebe's mumps. For though William Hiller was with them in the flesh, his head and heart were already bound for California. On all sides he heard talk of the emigration companies that were forming up. These cooperative associations aimed to transport their members to California, where they might engage in mining and other activities beneficial to the group as a whole. While some companies saw mining as their main enterprise, most sought to assemble a diverse membership that included carpenters, millwrights, merchants, doctors, and lawyers, all of whom could expect to ply their trades profitably in the boom towns of the West. For a fixed share, or membership fee, an individual could buy into such a group and be assured of passage west, often on a ship purchased or leased with the money collected through the sale of shares.[43]

Every encounter with persons bound for the West moved William closer to actions he felt his current financial situation more than justified. Ever since calculating his earnings for February and March 1849 and finding he had earned only forty-eight dollars for all his work, he had been haunted by President Polk's message to Congress that reported the earnings of men who made that much in a single day in the diggings out west. The best claims would all be gone if he waited any longer. The time had come. On the morning of March 13 he sold his share of the mill for three hundred dollars, and that afternoon he spent exactly that amount on a share in the "Pacifick Mining and Trading Co," a group of about twenty men who had joined together for the express purpose of getting themselves to California in time to get their share of the riches awaiting them there. Having purchased and outfitted the *Mariana*, an aging, square-sailed barque, the Pacific Mining and Trading Company planned to sail her all the way around Cape Horn and on to San Francisco. A distance of some seventeen thousand miles, the voyage would take about five months, though storms and doldrums might well lengthen the trip.[44]

William Hiller had little enough time to equip himself for the voyage. Over the few days he had left in Richmond, he bought a small blank book, a box of pen points, and three books—a Bible, a millwright's guide, and *Year of the Heavens*, a guide to the night skies of both hemispheres. They were small and insignificant purchases to be sure, but indicative of the special needs of a seafaring man who intended to stay in touch with his family and record with care the adventures that befell him.[45]

On March 16, 1849, William Hiller tucked twenty-five dollars into his pocket and handed his account book over to Abiah, assuring her that he had already paid the next month's rent and had ordered a small supply of wood to carry her over until the warmer spring days. For her other expenses she would have to depend on money Martin Daniels still owed him and would pay as she needed it. Considering his business and family affairs attended to, William hired a coach to carry himself, his family, and his baggage to the dock on the James River, where the *Mariana* lay at anchor. After a last round of goodbyes, he boarded the ship, and Abiah, Phebe, and little Josephine waved as the vessel moved out onto the James, headed for Chesapeake Bay and eventually California. Returning to the wagon that would take her back to the city she hardly knew and the bare walls of her rented house, Abiah Hiller became one of thousands of wives to be left behind that season by gold-seeking husbands who might or might not find their fortunes and might or might not remember the way back home.[46]

Having been given an enthusiastic sendoff by friends and relatives, the gold seekers aboard the *Mariana* sailed down the James in high spirits. But the unwieldy craft, "full as a tick," by William's account, ran aground some twenty-five miles below Richmond. "Yes, by g[oll]y stuck in the mud," he wrote Abiah two days after his departure from home, "[and] I think ther[e] is a right smart chance to stay here . . . but we have a tow (steam) boat ahold of us to start when the tide rises." He and a fellow passenger were appointed "stewarts" of the ship for the first week, and that meant galley duties. In addition to cooking and serving meals, the two were also responsible for cleanup chores, and William boasted to those at home that he was as capable a dishwasher as his little Phebe.[47]

It was two weeks after having left the dock at Richmond before the *Mariana* actually sailed out of the harbor at Hampton Roads and into the rough waters of the Atlantic. As the ship and her company began their long journey south, Abiah contemplated her own journey north. Impatient as she was to leave Richmond, she needed time to weigh her options. William had assumed she would return to McDonough and reestablish her school in the old Warren house, but there was less reason to think of settling there again, now that her brother Andrew and his wife Sophia had just been assigned to a new pastorate in Montrose, Pennsylvania, a village some fifty miles south of McDonough. In fact, just before William's departure, Andrew had written urging her to consider setting up a school in Montrose so that the family could once again be together. The prospect was attractive, especially since she could depend upon Andrew's support during William's absence. And she had no idea how long that absence might be, for her husband had declared that he did not intend to come back until he had "seen the Elephant," however long that might be. Although William had advised her against taking a chance on starting a new school in a strange town, she fully intended to visit Montrose and decide on its merits for herself.[48]

As Martin Daniels and his laborers packed up Abiah's household goods, she addressed each trunk and barrel to herself, in the care of Rev. Andrew Warren, Montrose, Pennsylvania. If Montrose was not to her liking, it would be easy enough to have them shipped on to

McDonough. Having dispatched her bundles northward, Abiah packed valises and bandboxes for herself, her mother, and the two little girls, and in early April they set out for Montrose, this time taking the packet *Greenway* all the way to New York City. Taking advantage of the new railway that had just opened between New York and Elmira, the family rode the train as far as Binghamton, where Andrew met them in his wagon. All five of the Warren grandchildren had grown, of course, in the six months since the Hillers had left McDonough, and there was much news to catch up on. There were also discussions of the pros and cons of Abiah's opening a school in Montrose. In the end, though she and her mother hated to part with Andrew, Sophie, and the three little Warrens, Abiah decided that resuming her well-established school in McDonough was a far safer venture than opening a new one in a strange town. Toward the end of April she once again made out shipping labels for her household goods, addressing them to Abiah S. Hiller, McDonough, New York, for this time she was really going home.[49]

Arriving in McDonough the first week in May 1849, Abiah set about at once to reclaim her home and restore the schoolroom. Retrieving her loom and the other items she had left in Ira Hiller's care, she reestablished her family in the familiar rooms of the house on East Street. She also procured a cow and some chickens, knowing that she would need the income as well as the milk and eggs. The girls could help tend the hens and gather the eggs, and they could churn butter, which was selling at a good price that summer. By late May, with the house in order and the schoolroom restored, Abiah S. Hiller began to advertise for scholars for the coming term.[50]

While his wife had been in a flurry of activity during the month of May, William Hiller had been sailing slowly, but steadily, toward Rio de Janeiro. On Monday morning, May 21, the *Marianna* was just off the Brazilian coast, waiting only "for a wind to run into port." The company was somewhat behind schedule, having met with a fierce storm that had blown them off course and cost them several days' travel. Since then they had had relatively smooth sailing. Life at sea was not particularly to William's liking, mostly because of the slow passage of time. He had not been seasick "but a few days," as was the case with most of their company, and it had not been as hot "under the troppick[s] as [he] had expected to find it." There was "no prevailing disease" on board the ship, and his own health was "first rate, except for "a lameness in [his] back" and swollen feet and "ancles," all of which he attributed to "want of exersize and land to be on." He was therefore looking forward to a layover in Rio.[51]

Because the *Mariana* was in need of minor repairs, that layover stretched into a week's duration, allowing William time enough to enjoy the sights and sounds of the city. Finding the festive Brazilian capital "clean and nice," with "very narrow" streets, he was impressed by its architecture and layout. Built mostly on a level plain "elevated but a few feet above the bay," Rio featured "many building[s] on the sides of the mountains." He walked up some of the steepest streets and gained "a most comma[n]ding view of the city" that afforded him a study of rooftops "covered with a sort of Stone . . . made in half circles and covered first with the hollow sides up then another set put over the joints with the rounding sides up." He sketched a section of the roofing he described and sent the sketch home to McDonough to be exclaimed over by his friends.[52]

It did not escape Hiller's notice that the labor in Rio was done by slaves. Slaves built the fine homes and churches, and slaves waded out to load heavy bundles onto the scows that took freight out to ships waiting in the harbor. Unlike the slavery Hiller had seen in Virginia, here there was "but little distincion in color," yet the line was clearly "drawn between bond and free." While he found all the people of Rio "very polite and hospitable," Hiller was at times ashamed of his fellow travelers. "Some of our company drink ashore and act like fools," he wrote home, "and it is the case with most other companies." Brazil was in "the first days of winter," but the days were "as warm as our August at the north and the trees and herbs [were] of a most beautiful green." While observing the region's flora, Hiller also observed the night skies of the southern hemisphere: "As to the heavens and the stars therein I can say they are very beautifull and I shall take a map of the Southern hemisphere before we git out of it." In walks along the beach, he picked up shells he planned to take home to Abiah and the girls—if he was not "so loaded with Gould" that he could not carry them.[53]

While Hiller's own optimism remained high, some of the men in his company had already "got enough of sea life" and were turning back at Rio. The others planned to disband the company as soon as their contracts were up, having decided they would do as well or better to strike out on their own once they were in California. By the end of his week's layover, William was eager to be away from Rio and en route to San Francisco. Even as he thought ahead to California, he was also thinking of the people at home. He could only surmise that Abiah and the children had arrived safely in McDonough. He was well aware that both his mother and his mother-in-law were aging, and he wondered whether he would see either of them again "on the shores of time." Removed as he felt from them all, he could only hope that his wife and friends were receiving his letters and that both his family and his business concerns were faring well in his absence.[54]

Sometime during the first week of June, with repairs completed and the hold loaded, the *Mariana* raised sails to begin the treacherous journey around Cape Horn. Once they passed the Falkland Islands, they could expect to spend at least thirty to forty days in the frigid waters surrounding the cape. With no heat on board and temperatures ranging from zero to freezing, they expected to be cold, damp, and uncomfortable and braced themselves against the ordeal.[55]

At home in McDonough, Abiah read such news with anxiety, knowing it would be weeks or months before she learned the outcome of her husband's journey. She sought news from all sources. In addition to the letters William sent directly to her, she knew she could depend on Martin Daniels to write her any news William might have addressed to friends in Richmond. Daniels was also keeping her apprised of her husband's business concerns in Virginia. He had managed to sell "the Old Inn" and pay all debts associated with that enterprise, had made "most all the collections," and had sold much of the lumber, some of which had belonged to Hiller. Having made a full accounting to Abiah, Daniels wrote William that Hiller's business dealings in Richmond had now been completed. Daniels himself expected to "earn one thousand dollars more" than he had the year before. His mill was running well, yet his success in no way lessened his interest in activities in the goldfields. He and his business associates had "learned all the news" from the "many letters" they had received from Virginians aboard the *Mariana*. Having read in local papers that California was already holding meetings "for the purpose of forming a government and asking admission as a state," Daniels advised Hiller, "Tell them they will miss it if they recognize slavery."[56]

At home in McDonough, Abiah had already "commenced weaving and teaching," and she and the girls were thriving. William's sister, Susan Barrows, came to visit them with her baby boy, and Phebe and Josephine were delighted to play with their brand new cousin. They also enjoyed visits from their favorite aunt, Mary Kenyon, who was anxious about their father, her brother William, and awed by the distance that stretched between them. "I scarcely know how to address you at so great a distance from us," she confessed, for it seemed to her "to be among the impossibilities for a letter written in McDonough Chenango Co. ever to arive safe in San Francisco." Still, she wrote William the news. A severe drought had struck Chenango County, and "crops of oats buckwheat and corn" were all "injured." The pastures were "vary short" and fruit was scarce. Mother Hiller was doing well, though she was worried about William and hoping he would soon "git as much gold as [he] want[ed] and return home and be content to stay."[57]

Abiah was kept very busy that fall with caring for her children, her mother, her house, and her school, all the while juggling her absent husband's concerns. She went to attorney Lewis Burdick with her worries about a lawsuit filed in regard to William's hay, and she turned over to him several overdue notes she had been unable to collect, though Burdick warned her that it would be "very difficult to effect any thing with them in [William's] absence." She found it increasingly frustrating to deal with her husband's affairs, little as she had been involved in them before his departure. For example, she had no way of responding to Lyman Isbell's inquiry about exactly which section of fence William had repaired on the land Isbell had bought from them, and she had no idea what to charge the man for an iron bar Hiller had left behind. All she could do was hold up her own end of things and dash off letters relaying the news and the queries.[58]

Abiah's letters were also filled with comments on the health of her daughters and her mother. Six-year-old Phebe had been bothered by a persistent cough, and her mother, Abiah Warren, had "failed very much" on her return to McDonough. Despite her chronic cough, Phebe was moving quickly through her first course of arithmetic and begging "to study Colburn," a more advanced text. For her own sake as well as to satisfy the curiosity of her children and her scholars, Abiah constantly pressed William for news of his progress, asking how he "got around the Horn," what the "face of the country" was like, and whether he'd gotten "a sight of the Andes."[59]

Even while focusing on the needs of her students, Abiah continued to indulge in many other projects. After school hours she turned to such chores as weaving diaper cloth, doing the family's laundry, and, in the late evenings, writing to her husband. "It is now ½ past ten o'clock and all the rest are asleep and I must go to bed too," she wrote him one night that fall, adding, "I suppose it is just in the edge of the evening where you are," though she really had no way of knowing exactly where William was.[60]

He was, in fact, already in San Francisco. Rounding the Horn had been less hazardous and more comfortable than anticipated, but the company had been glad enough to sail back into the heat of the tropics after the "squals of hail and snow" that had been their weather during their southernmost passage. Unfortunately, "the chance for stargazing around Cape Horn" had not been good, for it had been "cloudy most of the time." However, during a stretch of clear nights off the coast of Chile he had sketched "several maps of the southern cross." One of these he sent off to Abiah, labeling his work the "apperance of the southern cross as seen Aug 17, 1849, in Lat 14 3 S, Long 96.24 W."[61]

But that was all behind him now as the *Mariana* sailed triumphantly through the Golden Gate on Sunday, September 30, 1849, six and one-half months after having left Richmond. Finally in safe harbor, William Hiller joined his fellows in selling off the "company property and closing up the concern as fast as possible," then went ashore to establish himself in the city. He immediately found a carpentry job paying six dollars a day, but carpentry was not what he had come to California to do. Declaring himself "bound to see the whole of it," he spent but a week in San Francisco before writing Abiah that he was "fixing to go to the mines," admitting, "Yes i am going to see the Elephant."[62]

Over the next few months, William made good his promise, wandering here and there in various mining towns and staying just ahead of the mails so that by early February 1850, nearly eleven months after his departure from Richmond, he still had not heard a single word from home. Even so, he dashed off notes whenever he could. In early spring he wrote Abiah from Texas Tent, some twenty miles outside Stockton, describing the country as "containing all kinds of a face." There were "mountain ranges with scattering timber shrubs etc and large extincive planes of good land." In the fall, plains and hills were "dry and barron as the desarts of Arabia," yet "when the rain commences every ravine gulch and slough is full of water." The hills and valleys were green and beautiful during the rainy season, so even though "the higher mountains were covered with snow," he had picked flowers down in the valley below. The snows that drove the deer and other game down out of the mountains to "seek a warmer location" led many of them to "a warm one" sure enough— "in the miner['s frying] pan."[63]

He admitted to his wife that he had not made "much of a pile" in the towns around Stockton. He had a few gold dollars to send Phebe and Josephine and some gold for his mother-in-law to make into beads—all of which he would send in good time. Other than that, he had nothing yet to show for his trip to California. Still looking for a windfall, he had decided to go "on a wild goose chase up the coast to Trinidad Bay," some 250 miles to the north, hoping to find a good townsite and plenty of gold. Downplaying her concerns for his health, he noted, "I shall live till I die and that is as well as the best of men do."[64]

Hiller was far from ready to start home again, but he was already making plans for life in McDonough, writing Abiah, "I want to buy a snug farm and there I will stay the balance of my life." Nostalgic for land that would provide security, he urged his wife to "buy some good farm . . . and pay in what [she could] spare," taking out a note they would pay off later, "say part next fall and the rest one year from next fall." He sent not a penny toward his suggested purchase, and he urged Abiah to keep this plan "a secret from the world" until they were ready to act on it.[65]

Soon thereafter William left Texas Tent for Trinidad Bay, first going back downriver to San Francisco to catch a boat up the northern California coastline. In San Francisco, on the last day of February 1850, almost a year after his departure from Richmond, William Hiller received his first word from home, a letter from Abiah dated December 20, 1849. Juggling all his work and her own, she was tired and discouraged and finding it hard to get into the holiday mood. She was also deeply pained by attacks on her husband's reputation, especially those launched by William Stanley, her uncle and neighbor, who had threatened a lawsuit over an uncollected debt. William sent no money and offered no advice—except to suggest that she not pay the debt unless she absolutely had to and that she "tell Mr Stanley that I am not an absconded debtor onely gone to Cal and that is nothing in these days."[66]

With money scarce, William no longer pressed Abiah to buy a farm in his absence, asking her instead "onely [to] keep a good look out for a chance" to buy. Still, he held fast to his plan of settling down to stay, once he returned, vowing, "I have romed till I am satisfied. . . . I shall know how to appreciate the comforts of home and friends if I ever live to get to them." Although carpenter's wages were high—up to twelve dollars per day—work was scarce and the economy sluggish. While laborers in the San Francisco area were expecting to make more "as soon as the weather becomes settled and the gold begins to come down from the mountains," William Hiller did not feel inclined to wait. He could make much more by going north. "I hear a thousand stories about those new diggins and very conflicting," he wrote Abiah on the eve of his departure, "but I am bound to go and see for myself." The trip would be a major investment, but he was optimistic about recouping his expenses in the mines, plus earning enough to pay for his return trip home, which he now planned for "next winter," reasoning, "if I am a going to make any thing at all I ought to do it this summer."[67]

After delaying his departure some two weeks in order to book passage on the schooner *Paragon*, the best of the ships available for the risky trip north, William sailed from San Francisco in mid-March. The journey began well enough, with unusually smooth seas and easy sailing, but while the ship was anchored in the harbor of present-day Crescent City, a gale came up and both anchors pulled free, letting the vessel run aground. The ship foundered, but William and his stock of goods survived the wreck, and he eventually made his way down to Union Town on Humboldt Bay.[68]

Realizing that his wife had no way of knowing where he was, since the coastline he had just traveled had been "but little known before this spring," William drew her a map "on a small scale," adding a detailed, but somewhat inaccurate, description of the rivers that led back into gold country: "Smiths river is large and is formed by the Trinities Chaster and Clamith rivers and has a midling harbor Port Trinadad is a crook in the Cost and makes a safe anchorage for northerly winds . . . Humbolt Bay has a good entry and is from 1 to 10 miles wide and 20 to 25 long it has 3 or 4 small strams runing in to it but no large ones."[69]

Even though Hiller had come north to pan for gold, carpentry work remained the key to his good fortune. Union Town had "commenced about May 1," but construction had not gotten fully underway until several weeks thereafter, and Hiller had arrived in plenty of time to land good contracts. By mid-June he had hired out at fourteen dollars a day, and until mid-August he worked steadily, laboring some fifty-nine days and earning over six hundred dollars plus occasional payments "in dust" on debts his fellow workers owed him. For the first two months of the fall, he took still another carpentry contract, earning close to five hundred dollars.[70]

As autumn of 1850 came on, although Abiah had no way of knowing the extent of her husband's earnings, she was relieved to hear that he was "doing something." She also knew that he had, as yet, received only one of the many letters she had sent him, and she was frustrated, noting that it was of little use "to write a long letter for uncle Sam's clerks to read." Still faithful to her husband's dream of settling down on a "good snug farm," she was determined that farm should be close by McDonough, for she did not "intend to go where [she] must give up teaching school." Lawrence Brooks's farm was close enough to her home and school to allow her to continue her profession, and she felt there was no farm "better situated than that." But prompt action was required, since Brooks himself planned to build on the land if he could not sell in good season, and she was frustrated by William's inability to see her point of view. As astute and frugal as she was in all matters, Abiah knew a good buy when she saw one. "I do not care if he does ask a large prise for it," she wrote William, "if I owned it, I would not take what he asked for it." Land was rising in value, and she and William would surely be able to sell the farm at a profit later if they could secure it now. "If you will send me $1000 I will buy it before next spring," she wrote her husband that fall, yet she knew that unless mail service to California improved, chances of William's getting her letter in time to send the money were slim indeed.[71]

In general, farming in the state went well that season, even though late summer and early fall were unusually warm and wet so that by early October Abiah still had not dug any of her potatoes and fully expected to find that most of them had rotted. Despite such disappointment, she had done very well in the one sphere over which she had complete control of her own fortunes. That fall she had already enrolled twenty scholars, noting, "more are coming, so I have business enough for the present." Her teaching provided the cash she needed for everyday affairs, and she was grateful that she did not have to rely on shipments of gold from William in California to sustain the family. Nonetheless, she was delighted to receive that fall some evidence of her husband's success in the mines—a nugget, worth about $1.50, from Union Town. The packet also contained a comparable nugget for her mother, along with the long-promised gold dollars for Josephine and Phebe.[72]

Although he was earning enough money to afford to send along a little gold, Hiller had relatively little cash on hand, since he was working on credit and most of his contracts would not be paid until spring. By mid-October he stood to collect about $1,150, and he was confident his employers would come through with what they owed him. The evidence of his handiwork and that of his fellow laborers was mounting. Since early summer, Union Town had grown from a few shanties to a town of sixty wooden buildings and ten "iron" ones. The town's twenty stores and its three hotels catered to the miners who passed through on their way to or from diggings up the Klamath and Trinity rivers. Few women were among their number, and only ten to fifteen families had settled in Union Town, though a school had been erected. As of mid-October, there was still no post office, and William advised Abiah to continue to direct her mail to him via San Francisco, but to keep a sharp lookout for newspaper accounts of the opening of a post office in his area. Without knowing exactly what the papers were reporting of Indian encounters in the West, William assured his family that the Indians were "some troublesome," but they had done nothing to bother him personally.[73]

An epidemic of dysentery had hit the area, and although William was in constant contact with those who suffered from it, he himself escaped. Even after nursing one of his fellow carpenters while the disease ran its course, he reported that he felt "first rate," having practiced "some prudunce" in his habits in order to maintain his health. As the winter came on, he began to fashion plans for the future. He was earning good wages in construction work, but he had not satisfied his curiosity as to what he could make in the mines and was reluctant to go home without trying his luck there. "Reports . . . [had] been quite flatry" concerning the "Trinity and Klamith and there tributaries," and he determined that if he could "find good mines" in the spring, he would stay on and work them through the summer. If not, he would return home come spring.[74]

William still had but one of his wife's letters on hand, but he knew her well enough to anticipate her questions concerning the countryside. He described for her—and for those with whom she shared his letters—the abundant wildlife in Union Town: "Elk & Grisley Bear are quite plenty and wild geese and brants are comeing down from the north in multitudes—also ducks." The grasslands were dry and sparse in the summer, but the forests were magnificent. There was little hardwood along the coast, but redwood, spruce, and red and white fir abounded. He was fascinated by the size of the redwoods, some trees being "about 300 feet high and many . . . 20 to 30 feet through."[75]

Knowing it would now be at least another half year before he saw them, William directed "One word to the children," beginning with his elder daughter. "Phebe I hope you are a good girl and are a learning you[r] books and other useful thing[s]." Mindful of how peevish the child could be, he added, "You must be good to your little sister and not plage or hurt her you must be good to your Grand Mother and wate on her and be a good girl untill I see you again." He then admonished Josephine, "You must be a good girl too and I will bring you both Something when I come home."[76]

Abiah read these notes to seven-year old Phebe and five-year-old Josephine some two months later, in early December 1850, as she prepared the house and family for a second holiday season without William. Reviewing her situation, she found it secure enough, even though yet another school had been established in the village. She had earned twenty-five dollars in tuition that fall, and although she did not expect as many pupils in the winter term, she had other sources of income. Myron Wooster was rooming and boarding with her and helping out with chores, and a young woman named Rowena Beebe was rooming at the house, though boarding in town. Over the winter Abiah expected to take in one or two more renters and would be happy to have the added income. She had also made a personal investment with an eye to profit. "I have bought me a Daguerian apparatus," she wrote William, "but have not got it quite paid for. I have not done any business with it yet, but I thought I would have it."[77]

She still held to the possibility of buying the Brooks farm, if only William would agree and send her a down payment. "Brooks' farm is just the thing to cut into village lots, and if you want land in this vicinity, that is the place to buy," she wrote him. "They talk of building a plank road from Green to Grant's and from Oxford to Norwich, if they build one through this place it will raise the price of land in the hollow very much." While keeping her eye on real estate, Abiah was busy with other projects as well. That fall she had got the wall "laid over half way," between her property and that of Ephraim Frost; the rest was Frost's to build in the spring. She had had to replace the cellar drain, for when neighbors had put in a new dam and filled their pond, the rising water table had caused Abiah's cellar to fill to a depth of eighteen inches. She had also finished a quilt and set out a dozen apple trees. She and the girls had turned her cow's milk into 136 pounds of butter over the autumn months, and they had sold fifty-four dozen eggs at ten cents a dozen. Her corn crop that season yielded seven or eight bushels, and she was fattening a hog on rotten potatoes and corncob meal, hoping to get him to two hundred pounds before Christmas.[78]

Thanksgiving Day fell on December 12 in 1850, and as she celebrated the day with her family and boarders, Abiah felt she had much to be thankful for. She had her health and enough projects to keep her happy, and her children were thriving. The "best scholar of her age" Abiah had ever seen, Phebe was already well into *Adams' Arithmetic,* and both she and Josephine could name and identify "the bodies of water, capes, etc. around all the countries except Africa." Though Phebe did not read quite as well as Josephine, she was well ahead of her sister in all other subjects. As much pride as she took in her elder daughter's academic achievements, Abiah was less happy about Phebe's temperament: "She is too selfish, and jealous, she is afraid I will give Josephene, more, and better things than I do her," Abiah wrote William. Josephine, on the other hand, was "the reverse of that, she alwa[y]s wants Phebe to have some of every thing she has."[79]

It would be many weeks before William read those words, long after he'd passed a lonely Christmas. Fortunately, he was able to stay busy. By late January he had earned another six hundred dollars. One of his employers, Benjamin Kelsey, was impressed enough by his finish work to hire him to refurbish Kelsey's own house, a large dwelling just west of the public square in Union Town. Transactions with Kelsey and others were duly noted in a daybook Hiller began in December 1850 with a front-page entry that clearly tied his fortunes to those of his family back in New York:

> Wm Hiller
> Union Town 1850
> I belong in McDonough
> Chenango Co., New York
> So if I should
> Misstep and die
> please collect my funds

and send them by
the first good chance
you meet with
To my wife
Mrs Abiah S. Hiller
McDonough
Chenango Co NY[80]

As her husband worked in the West, Abiah began a new school term in McDonough with a dozen scholars. But even as she called her classroom to order every morning, she was mulling over other possibilities. She thought she might like to go to California to teach, once "they get a rail road across, which congress begins to talk about." Teaching in Montrose, Pennsylvania, near her brother Andrew remained an attractive possibility, since she could probably make more money there than in New York. However, living expenses would be higher and Grandma Warren did not want to leave McDonough, even to move closer to her son. Neighbor Hiram King had tried to rent her place, but Abiah had refused, since she had no serious intention of moving. "I do not want to go any farther from a village than I am now," she wrote William early in the new year, "for I mean to teach school as long as I can see, & I think that will be some years yet."[81]

Not having received from William the money she needed to invest in Lawrence Brooks's farm, Abiah used what capital she had in other ways, lending $150 to Abel Breed, $25 to William Burdick, and $218 to John Nichols and collecting good interest. Not every local lender fared so well. The town was shocked by the behavior of Luther Blivin, who had borrowed large sums, "gambled away some 2 or $3000 . . . of other peoples property," and was now "gone, no one knows where." Lyman Isbell had lost $300 to Blivin, and William Burdick had lost $100. Having been prudent enough herself not to have lent anything to the scoundrel, Abiah reported, "our money matters are all safe." Although "Uncle Bill" Stanley continued to dun her for the money William owed him, she stood her ground and refused to cover a debt she had no part of.[82]

Abiah's spirits that winter were raised not only by her solid financial position but also by the fact that she was now hearing regularly from her husband. William's letters not only provided a tenuous connection to him but also provided her with classroom lessons. She asked him to "press some leaves and flowers" for her and to specify their names. She also sent news of his mother and of the Kenyons and the Barrowses, his sisters' families. She noted that snowfall had been abundant that winter, with drifts "three feet deep in the woods." She reported that her hog—fattened on rotten potatoes dug through the fall—had reached 213 pounds before she slaughtered him in early January and that with all else she was handling, she had not yet had a chance to use the "Daguerreotype apparatus."[83]

Apparently she never did, for on April 10, 1851, she wrote, "I have bad news to tell you. Our house was burnt on the morning of the 26 of March." The fire had been discovered about 9:30, before most of her scholars had arrived, and no one had been hurt, though the house had "burnt down in a very short time." The cause of the fire remained a mystery, but the wind that morning had been unusually "strong in the southwest," and she believed the fire had "caught by a sparks blowing down between the [stove] pipe and the iron that it goes through and blowing on the loose boards near the pipe." Her own carelessness had not been a factor, for she had taken "the pipe down and burnt it out, the last of Feb. in both rooms." Whatever the cause, "the south chamber was all in flames on the upper side of the ceiling before [they] knew it," and only with the help of her neighbors had she managed to save "the greatest part of the furniture."[84]

It was an overwhelming loss—"in a few short hours we were turned into the street"—yet she had no intention of giving up. "I have some friends yet," she wrote, "and they have got up subscription papers, and I shall have another house before long." Not that she wished to become a charity case. "I do not expect to have a whole house given me, but the people will help me all they can." Already she had begun her plans: "I think I shall build 24 by 30, and 1½ stories high and finish the kitchen one bedroom and a schoolroom, and leave the rest for you to finish. I have got a plan that I think I shall like; the rooms are not quite so large as I should like, but they will do. They are going to begin next week to dig the cellar."[85]

In the meantime, Phebe was living at the Beebes', where she would stay through the summer, and Abiah, Grandma Warren, and Josephine were at Dr. Frost's house, though they would be moving in with the Stanleys "as soon as it [was] warm enough to be comfortable." Determined to "get along some way," she urged William, "Do not give yourself any trouble on our account." She had saved their "provisions" and would have enough to eat, and she had $541 loaned out at interest that she could call in as she began to build the new house. Martin Daniels also had some of their money out on interest, but she had no idea how much it was and would not know until Daniels got home from Virginia that summer. She expected to use "$200 or $300 in building," but she promised to be "as economical as I can and have it answer the purpose." Money for other needs would be short, of course, so she pressed William one last time for the gold she needed "to buy Brooks farm, for it will bring the money and I want it." Having posted the letter that told William of her loss and of her plans for regrouping, she got on with her life. No one had been injured in the fire, she had managed to save all her papers, and as soon as the house was restored, she expected to resume her classes.[86]

Unaware of the loss at home, William continued to ply his trade as a carpenter, putting up the stores that served Union Town's burgeoning population, finishing homes, and giving many of his off-hours to building coffins for those who succumbed to the illnesses of the gold camp. Although he was doing well enough, he still had outstanding debts to collect from his sojourn a year earlier in the Stockton area, and he continued to press his debtors, sending notes with friends who passed between the gold camps of northern and central California.[87]

While the rapid growth of the settlement on Humboldt Bay worked to William's advantage, the natives of the area chafed under the rush of the Anglos to their lands. Just before William's arrival in Union Town in May 1850, local Indians had plundered the *Eclipse*, the vessel that had brought the first miners into the bay. The incident had set off a series of confrontations between whites and Indians. Despite the weight of opinion in Union Town, Hiller was sympathetic to the plight of the Indians, calling his fellow whites "brutes." In July 1851, heightened conflict over fishing rights led to a series of public meetings in which the citizens of Union Town decided the natives could hunt and fish wherever they wanted to in the outlying areas, but not in town.[88]

As William Hiller debated the issue of Indian rights, Abiah was fully engaged in rebuilding her home, driving her team to Greene and Smithville, where she chose bricks, shingles, and other supplies that she loaded into her wagon and hauled home to McDonough. Out on the building site, she supervised the carpenters and masons, painted all the sash, set all the glass, and attended to countless other rebuilding chores. In late June of 1851, thinking ahead to the fall session, she had handbills printed announcing the opening of a "Select School." Throughout the village she posted broadsides proclaiming, "Mrs. A. S. Hiller Respectfully informs the citizens of McDonough that she will commence School in her new house, near McDonough Village, . . . where she will teach the branches usually taught in similar schools." She gave her terms as $1.50 to $3.00 for a twelve-week quarter for the traditional subjects, though students could opt to enroll in "EXTRA STUDIES," including "Drawing and Painting with water colors, Theorem Painting, Map Drawing, Card Drawing, Wax work," all "taught on reasonable terms." The notice also declared that "Board can be obtained in the family of the teacher on reasonable terms."[89]

After going public with her plans to reopen, Abiah reported to William her progress on the house. "It is a very long time since I heard from you," she wrote him in August 1851, some five months after the fire and some eight months after having last heard from him, "and many have been the trials I have been called to pass through; but I am alive . . . and hope I shall see happy days yet." Against the very good chance that her letter containing news of the fire had never reached him, she repeated the details, adding, "since then we have been scattered, like sheep without a shelter." Explaining once more that she was building a new house and expected to move into it and begin her school in about four weeks, she advised her husband, "I finish [it] for present necessity and the rest I leave for you to finish," though if "I had some of your gold, I would finish it now." Impatient as she was to receive the long overdue gold, Abiah had long since given up on using any of it to purchase Lawrence Brooks's farm. In fact, Brooks had by now sold out—for eighteen hundred dollars—and she once again predicted that the land would soon be resold for "building spots, [for] we shall have a village here soon."[90]

William's brother John had not been heard from in some time, Mother Hiller was "not very well," and Grandma Warren's health was "very poor." "People die and are born here as usual," Abiah reported, "only some"—like little Phebe and Josephine—"do not have any father [at home] to own them; there are 30 such in the county." Still lodged at her uncle's home, she had been weaving diaper cloth on his loom, tending to her own small orchard—a dozen apple trees, all growing "first rate"—and overseeing the construction of her house and school. Letter writing was relegated to late hours when she had a quiet moment to herself.[91]

Out in Union Town, William at last received word of the fire that had occured in McDonough three months before. Although he was slow in responding, he was concerned. "I was sorry to hear of your bad luck," he wrote a month after receiving the letter that first told him of the fire, "for I well know that it has made you a good deal of hard work and trouble besides the loss of property." As to her plan to design the new house herself, finishing out only what she needed for living and teaching quarters and leaving "the rest for [him] to finish," he was somewhat peevish: "I hope what you have done to your house you have done well so that it will be worth finising when I get home." Impressed by Abiah's plan to enlist the help of her neighbors, he offered to repay anyone who helped her rebuild the home, an offer met with some skepticism by those in McDonough who believed that William himself ought to be at home taking care of his family.[92]

In truth, despite his generous offer, William was little better off than he had been a year earlier when he first arrived in Union Town. As Abiah had predicted, working for deferred wages had proved to be risky business, and he had "done but little" all summer except try to collect "something" for what he had done in winter and spring. Having "made but little progress" toward that goal, he found himself with considerably less money than he had been promised, though he hoped to "gett some more." Whether out of disregard for his hard-won lesson or because he had no choice in the matter, he took on a job that would require two months of work and bring him four hundred dollars. Upon completion of that project, he planned to get his "outher matter[s] settled" and "set out for home," though he warned his wife, "You must not look for me until you see me befor you."[93]

Tired as he was of "living away from my family and friends and the comforts of life," he was reluctant to leave California. In the event that he decided not to come home that season after all, he promised to send Abiah what money he could, but it would not be "enough to buy a good farm with." As to the Brooks property, he was blunt: "I do not fancy it [since] it is cut off to[o] much with the creek to suit me and too frosty I want a farm on a hill if any." He had little interest in hearing any more about her real estate plans but was very curious to know more about Martin Daniels' business in Virginia.[94]

Back in the South after spending five summer weeks in McDonough, Daniels was equally curious about Hiller's situation in California. He was skeptical about the truth of rumors concerning large shipments of California gold coming into Richmond. By his own observation, some of the returning miners had made "a little," some had come out "about even," and some had returned "poor creatures indeed." Daniels was uncertain which category his friend would fall into, but he was fairly confident that William could have done better there in Richmond, where the two of them "might [have] made about 500 per year to lay up" had they "continued together." Now Daniels planned to leave Richmond and move on to Florida, although he confessed, "I wish I had a good steam mill in your country to cut up those large redwood trees." Having received no reply to two letters he had sent to Hiller in San Francisco, Daniels could only hope his latest letter would eventually reach his friend and elicit a response.[95]

Abiah held similar hopes. She was quite concerned about William that fall of 1851, for the last letter she had received from him had been postmarked December 1850. When she finally heard from him again, late in November, she noted, "I was glad to hear that you are alive; I had almost given you up for lost." With nothing in this letter to indicate that others had been written before it, worry turned to annoyance as she noted, "I believe I have got all your letters," thereby blaming her husband's long silence on his own negligence rather than on the vagaries of U.S. mails. She overcame her annoyance sufficiently to acknowledge that "the children were much pleased" with the small nuggets of gold their father had sent them.[96]

And she was much pleased to report that on September 15 she had not only moved into her rebuilt home but had also welcomed seventeen scholars for the opening day of fall term. On some days she had as many as thirty in attendance, leading her to lament an unforseen problem with her house plan: "I laid out the plan myself, [and] I find only one fault with it, it is too small for my business." Apparently she had reason to believe that William might find her design flawed on another count: "I suppose the roof is too steep to suit you but it suits me."[97]

As much as she liked her new house, she was not particularly enamored of the heavy snows that had influenced her decision to design a roof with a one-third pitch. "I do not like this climate," she wrote to William, "it is too cold and stormy to suit me. I think I should like the climate of Cal." Clearly, there was money to be made in warmer locales, for a Mr. Calendar of nearby Smithville had paid three thousand dollars for a farm nine miles outside of Astoria, Oregon, and was confident of raising and selling enough vegetables to pay for it in a single year.[98]

By Christmas her view of life in McDonough had softened, and she seemed less inclined to dwell on money-making opportunities afar. "I have a first rate school room in my house," she wrote William, "and I earned $45 last quarter. I see now what I could have done if I had had a good place for a school in times past." Still one of her best scholars, Phebe was "quite good in Arithmetic, she has ciphered 180 pages, and understands it quite well." Abiah and the girls were in good health, her mother's health was improving, and William's mother and the rest of the Hillers were all doing well, but she was worried about William himself. "I have been dreaming that you are sick," she wrote. "Is it so? If it is, write . . . and let me know."[99]

Into the personal news she dropped a rare comment concerning events on the national scene: "I have just heard that the Capitol is burned at Washington, but I suppose you will hear of it before this will get to you." That comment aside, her concern was with household affairs, which were in good order, though winter had come early and had been unusually harsh. Potatos were scarce, but she would have had plenty to feed her own family had she not had so many workers and students boarding with her during the fall. Since running low on potatoes, she had been substituting apples and turnips in their menus. The weather in McDonough was very cold, and there was plenty of good sleighing, but Abiah longed to be in "the good climate you spoke of."[100]

Over that Christmas season of 1851, William continued to while away his hours at odd jobs in carpentry in the Humboldt Bay area. He passed the holiday itself in relative solitude. There was "but little mirth" in Union Town, and he chose to write in his daybook rather than join those who "spent the day in drinking." By late January, Union Town had a post office, even though mail steamers still stopped only at Trinidad, leaving the Union Town mail to be delivered by overland stage. William declared that Abiah's letters still seemed to be coming by way of "Jam[ai]ca or the Holy land," judging by the time it took them to reach him.[101]

Although McDonough was in the grip of winter, Humboldt Bay

weather was "very fine." The grass was green and flowers were in bloom, "summer birds" were singing, and all things were "cheerful as May." A few days before Christmas, William had managed to gather some flowers and seeds in the valley and had sent them home to McDonough. He continued to describe astronomical events for Abiah as well, including an eclipse of the moon on the night of January 6, 1852: "The air was clear and the nigh[t] was beautifull and everything seemed to be clothed in gloom and darkness but after it had remained so for some hour and a half the shadow passed off and the moon shone again in its usual splendor and seemed to guide the traveler [on] his way, as if nothing had happened to her fair face."[102]

If flowers in late December and the beauty of a lunar eclipse made northern California seem an idyllic place, an Indian uprising soon shattered William's illusions. "The great toppick of excitement is the troubles with the Indians," he wrote Abiah that winter of 1852, "and trouble it will be I fear if some of the whites continue the course that they have begun." When two miners were killed some thirty miles up the Eel River, the murders were quickly blamed on Indians. Nevertheless, William suspected the crime could as easily have been committed by miners. In retaliation, a group of whites made an early morning raid on an Indian village, killing twenty or more "regardlys of there guilt or innocence." Fearing a counterattack, Union Town had posted nighttime guards, and William stood his turn. Within a few days he reported that people were "coming to the[ir] sences on[c]e more," yet he predicted more trouble, since "the least insult from the Indians set[s] them (the whites I mean the Demonical portion of them) all in a rage again." Although he was interested enough in the conflict to keep a journal account of daily events, he reassured Abiah, "Don['t] think that the Indians will get my skelp for I let them a lone and they have me so far."[103]

Despite the unrest and the unpredictable economy, more and more men were sending for their families, and single men eagerly sought the hands of the few available women in town, since "them that cant get maried have to do with out." William took pains to describe the town's weddings to Abiah, counting on her interest in ceremonies so different from the rituals with which she was familiar. One of those weddings had taken place "after a long and tedious courtship of some 10 days in which they both bore with Christian resignation untill the last minute when nature gave way and they were made one." During the solemnities, some townsmen "had there round with tin boxes &c fireing cannons but some one put a stop to there shoting by spik[ing] the old thing. . . . The surenade party went in to the house where the wedding was held and they all being to[o] hevy for the floor it gave way," the wedding party and guests falling through to the hollow underneath the house. The resultant "pile was made up of the od[d]s and ends of all things in the shape of humanity."104

Intending to "amuse [her] a little," William continued to keep Abiah posted on the follies of life in Union Town. He wrote most frequently of "how the old bachelors get along way out [here]"—he included himself in the number—noting that "they eat something two three and sometimes four times a day and it takes them ther rest of the time to digest it." As to "there houses and furniture," the men usually built "a hut called a log cabin perhaps something like old Tip's," but he predicted that should any of them "ever be candid[ates] for the presadency . . . there cabins would not be drawn about the streets as a momento of there wortheness for the sufferage of the people." For utensils, the bachelors had "a pot or kettle fry pan" that they scraped off "when it gets so durty they cannot tell what they eat on it last," plus "a tin cup to drink there coffee out of." Their clothes "they wash now and then."105

In stark contrast to the life William so lightly described in his letters of early March was the life Abiah was living in McDonough. A year had passed since she had been burnt out of her home and livelihood, and she was comfortable once again. Because she had taken up classes the same day she had moved back into her house, the finishing work had gone slowly, being squeezed in between teaching duties. She had finished out "more than I should have done" in order to have "a decent place" to put her scholars; even so, there was still plenty of work left to do, and she wrote William, "I left the parlor, back room, and one chamber for you to finish, if you ever get home."106

Her finances had been tight since the fire. She had taken out a loan to complete her building project and now owed some $150. Although she already had $218 set aside with which to pay that debt, she was biding her time, since the note did not fall due until December. She had been pinched primarily because community support for her building fund had waned and she had not had "so much given" as she had expected. "The excuse of some was that you was getting rich," she explained to him, "and would come home better off than any of them. Others reported that you had already sent me several hundred dollars. Some signed [the subscription list] but have never paid." In any event, she had no intention of asking for the money now, though she knew "who did give, and how much."[107]

Her income was supplemented by the money she received from the students and others who either boarded or roomed with her. Ten scholars had continued to attend her classes through the sparse winter session; with spring coming on, she expected enrollment to increase. The winter had been not only harsh but long, and by late March Abiah was ready for spring. She was somewhat lonely as well, for eight-year-old Phebe had moved out to the old Hiller place to help her Uncle Ira look after Mother Hiller after he lost his house-girl. Both little girls looked daily and fruitlessly for more gold tokens from their father. Abiah had set aside the gold he had sent in the fall in order to make rings for them, thinking it best to "keep it till their fingers get their growth."[108]

Abiah's old suitor, Lawrence Brooks, was preparing to leave town at last, having bought a tavern near Binghamton. She still toyed with the idea of buying "an acre or two, off of the Brooks farm for a pasture, if I can get a pay day so that I can pay for it; they ask $25 an acre but that is cheaper than to hire a cow pastured for 10 years for $5 a year" and then not own the land. There had been a variety of births and deaths, and two separations. "She that was Sally K[enyon] has left her husband and works out in the village," Abiah wrote William, adding that she did not blame the woman, since George Kenyon was "a perfect hog." The Frosts, the couple with whom she and her family had briefly stayed after the fire, had also separated, and Mrs. Frost had gone off with her children. Abiah was sure that Ephraim's drinking "was the first cause."[109]

Noting that twenty more men from Chenango County had "started for Cal.," Abiah added, "I think I should like to go," despite the fact that William had never extended her an invitation to join him in the West nor had she herself ever done more than hint at the idea before. Still looking for money from William, Abiah suggested he consider sending home the gold piecemeal—perhaps five dollars at a time in a letter—since the postage would be only twenty cents. True, the money could be lost in the mail, but William could also "get robbed in crossing the Isthmus."[110]

Meantime, William was giving more and more thought to home if not to homecoming. He looked forward to each of Abiah's letters, though fewer came than had been promised. He himself wrote "about every chance there [was] to send them down to San Francisco." The news his letters carried was not always welcome at home. In one, written after nearly three years of absence, he declared, "I am here yet and I dont know but I shall be for some time if I do not go away and some body don't carry me a way but I am well so I may as well stay here as to go somewhere else." In another, he playfully compared Abiah's situation with his own. In health, he decided, they were both well, so that she had "none the start" on him there. In income, she had made forty-five dollars that fall, while he had made two hundred dollars, so he had "some the start ther[e]" on her. "You eat turnips and apples I eat taters and turnips," he wrote, "so we are about even there I sle[e]p alone and I suppose you do so we are about even there I cook my own grub and so do you so thats even." But by all other measures, he was by far the more unfortunate: "I am here ten thousand miles from home and a darned ways from any place and cant get the knews onece in a dogs age and then its not new." Then, as if to punctuate his claim to the better income, he enclosed three dollars in gold dust for Abiah's mother.[111]

Hardly impressed by the small amounts of gold she received from her husband, Abiah was still relieved that he was not involved in Martin Daniels's financial misfortunes in Virginia. Daniels had lingered on in Richmond just long enough to lose nearly eight hundred dollars in the bankruptcy of the man to whom he had sold their planing mill. Currently looking for new opportunities in Canada, Daniels had not given up thoughts of relocation in Florida. Abiah herself was still toying with thoughts of going west. "I believe we had better go to Oregon some time," she wrote William, noting that yet another company of Chenango County residents was forming up for the purpose of following the Oregon Trail. Worn out by the long, cold winter, she added, "I would like to be one of that Co. [myself] if my children were large enough to take care of themselves."[112]

When spring finally did come to McDonough, Abiah turned to all the chores the new season entailed, "drawing stone in a wheel barrow to wharf up the back side of the house," preparing the garden, and sowing some of the flower seeds William had sent from California. She was productive as ever, but she was "very unwell" that spring of 1852 and decided against offering a summer session.[113]

While his wife tended her garden back in McDonough, William

built a house for a family newly arrived in Union Town from Brooklyn. Upon finishing the structure, he accepted a commission to
make many of their household items—a washboard, a knife box, a
mush stick, a rolling pin, a ladle, and a child's high chair. With more
and more families moving into the area, the Brooklynites were "not
alone in their wants," and newly arrived mothers looked to William
to build cradles "to jog there babies in" and little wagons "to draw
them in."[114]

Union Town was booming, despite the "many vessals that have
been lost at this Bay." The Indian troubles were apparently at an
end, as the natives now came and went "at there plasure." Despite
these improvements and despite the fact that he had plenty of carpentry work to do, William was now seriously considering the best
time and route for going home. He wrote Abiah in late August that,
all things considered, he should be able to close out his business in
Union Town sometime in September and "be home in Nov or Dec
next." He dismissed her plan to go to Oregon Territory, for if he
moved west "for life" it would be in the vicinity of Humboldt Bay. In
mildness of climate and fertility of soil that region exceled anything
he had seen before; certainly it promised a much better life than did
Oregon Territory, and his goal now was to provide an easy life for his
wife. Abiah's health, he feared, had suffered that spring because of
overwork. He advised her to refrain from stressful activities, since "it
is of no use for who will thank you for it when you have worked your
self to death."[115]

Although his advice was no doubt well meant, it was hardly practical, in view of his continued absence from home, and it was hardly
in keeping with the personality of the woman to whom he wrote,
one who had always been "busy about something" and whose hard
work had never been motivated by thoughts of the thanks she might
receive for her efforts. Having heard from William more than once
that he intended to come home whenever he "finished out" his business in California, Abiah now knew better than to look for him before she saw him "comeing down the hill."[116]

This time, however, William was serious about starting home. On
October 23, 1852, he began a trip diary with the first entry, "Bound to
McDonough Chenango Co. NY." In a small pocketbook he carefully
noted obligations he had taken on in behalf of friends in California;
he was to carry "B. F. Wymans respects to his father" and to go up to
Poughkeepsie to see D. H. Snyder's brother, financing his passage

with the eight dollars Snyder had given him. He was also to go to North Oxford, Massachusetts, to carry to "Miss Clarrasa H. Barton" a message from William E. Phillips, a blacksmith in Union Town. Once very much involved with Miss Barton, Phillips wanted Hiller to ascertain her current feelings toward him. For William's efforts on his behalf and to cover expenses entailed in the trip to Massachusetts, Phillips gave him fifty dollars.[117]

Hiller's travel diary also contained a careful listing of the various bags of gold hidden among his gear, since getting his money home safely was a primary concern. Bags 1 and 2 contained one hundred ounces of gold apiece and were each worth $1,600, while bag 3 contained but seventeen ounces ($282) and bag 4 held only thirteen ounces ($219). In addition, he carried a small pouch of dust worth approximately forty-six dollars, specimens worth forty-seven dollars and twenty-five dollars, respectively, and forty-six dollars in gold coin, for a total of $3,865, a far greater sum than Abiah could have expected and likely more than William could have earned in the states over a three-year period.[118]

With all his preparations complete, William Hiller left Union Town and secured passage aboard a schooner for San Francisco on October 25. After a two-week sojourn in that city, he boarded the steamer *Golden Gate* and started south, by way of San Diego and Acapulco, arriving in Panama on November 28. Hiring two natives to pack his belongings up the Chagres River, he reached Cruces on November 30 and the next day boarded the *SS Illinois*, arriving in Boston the morning of December 15.[119]

Mindful of the obligations he had taken on in Union Town, he at once "took the cars" for Worcester, bent on locating Miss Barton. Upon his arrival in North Oxford on the next morning, he learned that she was now teaching in Bordentown, New Jersey. Exhausted as he was, Hiller was not inclined to give up the search for his friend's intended. Returning to Boston, he took a steamboat down to New York City, riding out a fierce winter storm. Despite the onset of "an augue chill," he left the city, bound for Bordentown, on December 18 and succeeded in locating Clara Barton. This sensitive, lively young woman at once impressed William Hiller, perhaps because she, like his wife, was a woman fully dedicated to her teaching career. Convinced that the city's poor would send their children to school if no fees were charged, thirty-one-year-old Barton had persuaded the officials of Bordentown to allow her to teach for three months without a salary. Enjoying the success of her educational experiment, she was not at all interested in marrying "Friend E," though she talked long and earnestly with William Hiller as to how to break that news to Phillips.[120]

On December 22, William Hiller, still ill with chills and fever, bade farewell to Clara Barton—who would, some thirty years later, establish the American Red Cross—and set out for New York City and thence to Poughkeepsie to deliver D. H. Snyder's message to his family. Finally having fulfilled his obligations to his California friends, Hiller departed Poughkeepsie on the morning of December 23, traveling by train to New York City and on to Binghamton. The next day, Christmas Eve, he took a stage to Greene, arriving at noon, too sick to travel any farther. After spending the night with friends, he paid $2.50 and thus "procured conveyence home," arriving, "very sick," in McDonough at 11 o'clock on Christmas morning, 1852.[121]

While his return after almost four years' absence greatly heightened his family's holiday spirits, William himself was far too ill to fully enjoy the reunion. Adding ten days of train, steamship, and coach travel around the Northeast to an already exhausting journey home from California had broken the good health he had enjoyed during his years away. Abiah and her mother took him under their care at once, and nine-year-old Phebe and seven-year-old Josephine were obliged to play quietly while the bearded stranger who was their father rested from his travels.

Although William first blamed his illness on exhaustion, he grew worse, not better, after reaching home and found himself in the first stages of what was to be, in his own words, "a hard run of sickness." Ill with "the shakes," most likely malaria or some other fever picked up during his crossing of the isthmus, Hiller stayed close to home during the early months of 1853, writing letters to friends in California and catching up on the business affairs Abiah had handled in his absence.[122]

Old Union Town friends who had returned to the East continued to write him of their plans to go west again, some of them by way of the overland trail out of Saint Joseph, Missouri. However, if Hiller himself had earlier entertained any thoughts of returning to California, his illness and his apparent satisfaction with life in McDonough kept him close to home. He sent apple seeds to friends in Union Town and read with interest news of the settlement's continued growth. Friends who had been miners and laborers were now fencing their land, buying animals, and planting crops. Union Town was "fast filling with a permanent population."[123]

Whatever the progress of Union Town, William Hiller was happily settled in McDonough, his wanderlust apparently well satisfied and his activities at home profitable. He spent most of 1853 in small carpentry jobs—building a shop for himself, repairing tables and chairs, making cupboards and bookcases. But as 1853 drew to a close and his strength returned, he established a new trade, one backed by the gold brought home from California. In the month of December alone he bought up $1,175 in mortgages. Soon he had lent out over $3,030 in mortgages for land and homes as far distant as Cortland and Oxford, and from this point onward, most of his income was derived from real estate dealings. He also engaged in some farming, largely on land owned by his brother-in-law, Singleton Kenyon, with whom he planted and harvested crops, sawed logs, chopped and hauled wood, and gathered sap from the maples owned by both families.[124]

All the while, Abiah continued to run her school, much as she had run it in William's absence. In the summer of 1855, she had a surprise letter from a former student in Jaffrey. Olive Towne Burpee wrote of the "great changes" since Abiah left, noting that "the buildings . . . [are] all gone at your former home." Only the Stanley well house remained, and Olive looked upon that small structure as "a momento of the past." Abiah's ensuing correspondence with Olive Burpee allowed her to indulge her new interest in spiritualism, a movement that now surfaced in McDonough and Jaffrey as well as other towns throughout the nation. The possibility of communion with the dead was an intriguing theory that sent Abiah to scientific and religious journals as well as to seances held by McDonough residents.[125]

While Abiah and William explored their joint and separate interests, their daughters were developing their own individual talents. In 1857, fourteen-year-old Phebe was granted a temporary teaching certificate by the county school commissioners, one of whom was her own father, William Hiller, and the following year she was given a more advanced certificate. Over the years, Abiah continued to conduct her highly praised school, even as she expanded her butter business, having finally invested in pastureland and several cows. In her dairying she was assisted by Grandma Warren, who remained in fair health, though William's mother, Mary Elsbree Hiller, died in the spring of 1859. As innovative in the dairy business as she had been in her other activities, Abiah joined William in an experiment with an "air pressure churn" in December 1859, and their butter account sheets give evidence of a thriving business.[126]

In April 1861, the same month fifteen-year-old Josephine took her place beside her mother and sister as a schoolteacher in Chenango County, Confederate forces fired on Fort Sumter and sent the country into civil war. Over the next few years, McDonough sent many volunteers into the Union army, and the patriotic spirit of the settlement was encouraged in the classrooms presided over by the Hiller women.[127]

In the fall of 1863, Abiah came down with diphtheria. For a month, the usually robust and energetic woman required constant care. In the course of nursing her mother, Josephine, then eighteen, also contracted the disease. While Josephine began almost at once to recover, Abiah grew worse. By mid-November, her diphtheria seemed to have "resolved itself into a dropsical consumption." William now called in a Mrs. Hodgkiss to help care for his wife.[128]

Whatever the exact nature of the complications that set in, William wrote in his journal that Abiah's illness "run her down rapidly to the grave." As her husband and daughters watched, she grew weaker and weaker, and on November 15, William Hiller faced the inevitable. Sitting at his wife's bedside, he entered her words in his journal: "My wife's requests in case she dies," he began, then jotted the following entry: "My wife wishes that Phebe have $100 that she has on hand and that Josaphine has the Melodian and $50 that She has also on hand;—That she has a bill vs Widow Meeker of $20 and a bill vs Miss Gault—and she wishes to be bured by the side of her father." The next morning, on November 16, 1863, William made yet another entry: "She died this morning at about a quarter to 5 Oclk droping away very easy." At fifty-eight Abiah Warren Hiller was dead. William turned at once to practical matters. He telegraphed his brother-in-law Andrew in Montrose, Pennsylvania, and prepared for the funeral by purchasing a shroud for Abiah and a new hat and suspenders for himself.[129]

The funeral was attended by family members and by many friends and former students, but not by Abiah's brother, Andrew. "I received your dispatch last night about 1½ o'clock," he wrote to William. "I regret that it was not possible for me to be present." He sent his sympathies: "You have lost a beloved wife, the mother of your children, the sharer of your joys and trials," and he advised William to accept Abiah's passing as the act "of an all wise being that is to[o] good to do a wrong."[130]

On the back of his letter to William, Andrew wrote a note to Phebe and Josephine, reminding them that "in the midst of life we are in death." Acknowledging that they had "lost a good mother, a faithful teacher whose place no other can fill," he also reminded them that their mother was now with God and "in the full enjoyment of her precious faith." To his own mother, Andrew wrote yet another note, expressing especially his regret that he had not made it up to McDonough in time to have seen his sister, mistakenly thinking "she would have a few weeks longer."[131]

Within three months of Abiah's death, her eighty-five-year-old mother was also dead. Phebe and Josephine, who had now lost the two most influential women in their lives, continued their teaching, and their father continued his real estate dealings and farm work. Then, on April 27, 1867, some three and a half years after Abiah's death, William married Abigail Roe. Though hardly the independent businesswoman Abiah Hiller had been and in no way her intellectual equal, Abigail Roe Hiller was a faithful companion to William. She was also a good stepmother to his daughters, now young adults though still living in the family home.[132]

In 1873, the tenth anniversary of Abiah Warren Hiller's death, her brother, Andrew, was summoned back to Jaffrey, New Hampshire, to present an address at the centennial celebration of the town in which he had been born and raised. Andrew used the occasion to deliver a belated eulogy to one of Jaffrey's most accomplished citizens—his sister, Abiah Warren Hiller. He praised her as a worthy wife and mother and as "a kind neighbor ever ready to assist in time of need." Noting her many accompishments in music, art, and teaching, he asserted that "few women more fully filled the proper sphere of woman than she." Abiah, he said, "possesed a truely independent spirit that caused her ever to go forward in what she considered her duty without stopping to consider what others might think of it Her first thought was ought it to be done, if so, she did it next. Would there were more such women in the world. She has left a bright example for her daughters & all young ladies to follow. May they be able to walk in her foot steps."[133]

Abiah's daughters did indeed follow in her footsteps. Phebe established herself as an excellent teacher and astute businesswoman, helping her father in his real estate ventures. Four years after her mother's death, Josephine married Charles B. Dunning, who had come to McDonough as a school principal, and in due time she made William a grandfather four times over.[134] When the Dunnings moved to Spokane, Washington Territory, in 1880, William Hiller periodically made plans to visit the West again, but that trip was never made.

In early August 1884, sixty-six-year-old William Hiller grew seriously ill. On the twentieth of that month he suffered a "hemorage of the bowels." That day Phebe Hiller made an entry in her father's Journal & Cash Account Book: "Wm Hiller died this morning at 2 oclck after 11 days sickness. Died easy." The man who had wandered out to Illinois, down to Virginia, and on to California, all the while insisting, "I belong in McDonogh, Chenango Co., NY," was at last laid to rest beside the woman whose "truely independent spirit" had served her well in all his absences.[135]

III

Almira Fay Stearns

"The Thought of Another Six or Eight Months Absence Makes Me Sad"

In 1911, Daniel Stearns, then eighty-nine years old, wrote out a detailed description of his adventures as a Forty-niner. Calling his first journey from Boston to San Francisco "the roughest . . . I experienced in making three trips . . . [across] the Isthmus," he described that 1849 crossing in great detail, gave less attention to his second passage, and dismissed the third in a few sentences: "In the latter part of September [1853] my wife and son and baby and I started back to California. . . . . We made this trip via the Nicaragua route."[1]

Had his wife, Almira, recorded her memories of that 1853 passage, they would surely have taken more than the few lines Daniel devoted to the experience. Just a little over a year earlier she had been so near death that her in-laws had called Daniel home to her bedside. Predictably, barely nine months after her husband's return to New Hampshire, she had given birth to their second son, and that baby was four months old when the Stearns family steamed out of Boston Harbor, en route to a new life in the West.

In the course of that month-long journey, Almira endured long days and nights confined to the ship's cramped quarters before beginning the arduous overland portion of the isthmus crossing, during which she made her way through tropical forests on muleback, her infant in her arms. Upon reaching the Pacific, she boarded a steamer bound for California—only to find the ship was carrying yellow fever. The Stearns family survived the journey, but it was hardly the uneventful trip implied by Daniel's memoirs.[2]

⚜

Almira Fay Stearns was born in Monson, Massachusetts, on May 26, 1825, one of eight children of farmer Simeon Fay and his wife Desire. By the time Almira was twelve, the Fay family had moved some fifteen miles north to Belchertown, a mill town close to the rapidly expanding industry of the Springfield area in western Massachusetts.[3]

Sometime in her late teens, prompted perhaps by her mother's death and her father's remarriage, Almira followed the course of many other young women of her day and station and moved into Cabotville in order to find work in one of the new cotton mills springing up on the banks of the Chicopee River. While it is conceivable that Almira's move was made in order to contribute to family finances, it is far more likely that she was escaping an unhappy home situation, for estrangement from her father's household is evident from this period on.[4]

At the time eighteen-year-old Almira arrived there, Cabotville was a heavily industrialized village of about four thousand people, boasting seven mills and block after block of tenements. Almira took up the mill girl's life, not in one of those tenements, but in a family home operated as a boardinghouse for the mill company. A factory whistle summoned her from sleep at 5:00 six mornings a week, and whistles punctuated every segment of the twelve hours she spent in front of her power loom. Half of her weekly wages of $2.50 was passed on to her boarding-master. Such wages were relatively good for a young woman of the mid-nineteenth century, but working conditions were abysmal. Each workroom was filled with clattering looms, and the cacophony of sound heightened the tension imposed by the constant pressure of production schedules.[5]

Nonetheless, to Almira Fay, life in Cabotville was better than life in Belchertown. She had escaped an uncomfortable situation at home, had established her independence, and was being courted by a man who wrote to her of parties they would attend and holidays they would share.[6]

Almira's suitor was Daniel W. Stearns, an ambitious young merchant some three and a half years older than she and a resident of Ware, a village thirty miles northeast of Cabotville. In his early twenties, Daniel Stearns was a "sedate, thoughtful, easy going" man of solid Yankee stock. Born at Chesterfield, New Hampshire, on December 31, 1821, into a family that could trace its American roots through four generations, Daniel, like Almira, was one of eight children. The oldest son of Arba and Harriet Whitcomb Stearns, he attended the village school and lived and worked on the farm his father acquired near Swanzey, just east of Chesterfield. A serious student throughout his childhood, at twenty Daniel tried his hand at teaching, spending two years as an instructor in the local school before deciding to explore the larger world. In 1844 he left Swanzey for Boston to clerk in a cousin's store, but he soon moved on to a similar job in Thorndike, a town some ten miles south of Almira Fay's family home in Belchertown. At about the same time that Almira left Belchertown for the factory in Cabotville, David left his work in Thorndike to take up a sales position in Ware. By August 1845, a year or so after their respective moves, he was well established there and well enough acquainted with a certain young mill girl to be writing frequent letters to his "Respected Friend Almira."[7]

Daniel seized every opportunity to visit Cabotville, and between visits he wrote to assure Almira that "there has not been any days nor but few hours that you have been absent from my mind." Over the 1846 New Year's holiday, Daniel Stearns took Almira Fay home to Swanzey to meet his family; thereafter he filled his letters to her with hints at an impending marriage. When he bought tinware from his brother-in-law, Nathaniel Pomeroy, he wrote Almira that his having chosen "a good family assortment" had led "a good many people" to think he planned to be married soon. When he was told that his sister Emily Pomeroy had received a note from "sister Almira," he teased Almira about the use of the term, remarking that he could only assume that his family must be "very willing to acknowledge some things that are but anticipated."[8]

Even as he teased Almira, he was solicitous of her health, and with good cause. Long hours in the mill had taken an emotional, as well as a physical, toll. After a visit to Cabotville, Daniel was especially concerned: "I must say that I was very sorry to find you in no better hopes and with so much doubt and fear as to make you less happy than what I wish always to see you." As the year wore on and the couple began to discuss wedding plans, Daniel encouraged Almira to remember "that this winter will be your last in the mill."[9]

In fact, Almira did not even finish out that season, for she gave her notice in November, and on January 3, 1847, twenty-one-year-old

Almira Fay and twenty-five-year-old Daniel Stearns were married at Belchertown. They were well settled in Ware by late October, when a son, George Jones, was born to them, but sometime during the next year they moved east to Boston, where Daniel again took up clerking in his cousin's grocery.[10]

Late in 1848, Daniel began to browse the exciting reports that appeared with increasing frequency in the Boston papers. On the other side of the continent, gold had been discovered, and Daniel Stearns "got a touch of the California fever." He was hardly alone; to contemporary observers, the entire country seemed in the grip of "a prodigious mass hysteria, with normal pursuits all but forgotten."[11] Daniel's decision "to set out for the Golden West" was apparently impromptu and unilateral. From Almira's point of view there were far more compelling reasons for her husband to stay home than to chase after riches in California. Their child was barely a year old, they were relatively secure financially, and everything Almira could have wanted for the family was to be found right there in Boston. But like thousands of other shopkeepers, schoolteachers, farmers, and physicians that year, Daniel Stearns wanted a part of the wealth and adventure promised by the stories coming from California.

In February 1849 he and twenty-four other men invested three hundred dollars each in an entity called the Massasoit Company. The company's first act was to charter a schooner, the *Harriet Neal,* for the voyage to Panama, the first leg of their journey west. Another member of the Massasoit Company was Loyal Brown, a young man whose roots were also in New Hampshire. It was an auspicious meeting for Daniel Stearns, for, in one way or another, his fortunes were to be intertwined with those of Loyal Brown and his brothers for the rest of his life.[12]

After taking Almira and little George home to his family in New Hampshire, Daniel returned to Boston to board the newly refitted schooner, expecting to be in San Francisco within six weeks. On March 10, 1849, the *Harriet Neal* sailed out of Boston Harbor, the men of the Massasoit Company aboard. A month later, after weathering a storm Stearns later described as "the grandest and most fascinating [he had] ever seen," the 128-ton schooner arrived in Chagras, the port city of Panama. There the ship's company rented six bungos— long, narrow canoes hollowed out of a single log—and two whaleboats, loaded their belongings onto the small crafts, and started up the Chagres River. Three days later they arrived at Gorgona, at the headwaters of the Chagres, where Daniel and his partners loaded their goods onto the backs of bulls and natives for the one-day overland trek to Panama City.[13]

Caught now in the crush of travelers seeking passage to the goldfields, Daniel and his companions languished in Panama City for weeks. In the course of this long delay the Massasoit Company was dissolved, although Daniel and six or eight of his original companions, including Loyal Brown, remained together. This group, and thirty or so other stranded travelers, were eventually able to engage the services of a twenty-nine-ton sailing vessel for the trip to San Francisco—a move they soon regretted. With more than forty people—and all their baggage—on board, the little craft was so overcrowded that there was no room for anyone to lie down. Twice the ship ran out of drinking water, and the passengers were reduced to catching rainwater in a large rubber sheet. After forty-nine days essentially adrift in the Pacific, the hapless boat docked at San Blas, Mexico. There the vessel was condemned by maritime authorities, and Daniel Stearns and his fellow passengers were compelled to find other means of getting to California. Over two weeks passed before they were able to secure passage on a steamer, arriving safely in San Francisco on the third of July, almost four months after having left home.[14]

Daniel Stearns went to California as a merchant, not as a miner, and though the goldfields did not always yield the sought-for rewards for the prospector, they proved to be a packer's paradise. Even so, the rewards did not come easily. Arriving in California with no capital at all, Stearns spent the first summer haying in the Sacramento Valley in order to earn enough to launch himself in the merchandizing business. Soon he and fellow traveler Loyal Brown were able to buy four horses and a wagon, which they put to use over the next two years, packing supplies in season between San Francisco and Sacramento and mining camps to the north—Yuba City, Shasta City, and Trinity Center. Over the winters they operated outlets for miners' supplies, first in Trinity Center and, during the second winter, in Sonora, in the heart of the Sierra Nevada camps.[15]

Then in the spring of 1851, having dissolved his partnership with Brown, Daniel Stearns decided to pack into the Salmon River mines of nothern California, where he made a substantial profit. He spent the winter of 1851–52 running a pack train between San Francisco and Yreka, a gold camp near California's northern border. By this time, Loyal Brown had moved some 140 miles north of Yreka to Scottsburg, a booming new port city in Oregon Territory. There he invested his own money and some of Daniel's in a store in partnership with his twenty-year-old brother, Henry G. Brown, newly arrived from New Hampshire. This investment in Brown, Drum & Company would eventually tie the destiny of Almira and Daniel Stearns to Oregon Territory.[16]

Through these three years, Almira Stearns and little George were in New Hampshire, living with Daniel's parents and several of his siblings: two of them young adults (Priscilla, a teacher, and John, a farmer) and three of them teenagers (Ellen, Miriam, and Martha).[17] When, in the winter of 1852, Almira suffered a sudden and serious illness, Harriet Stearns wrote Daniel that if he "ever wanted to see [his wife] alive again" he should return home at once. Upon receiving his mother's letter, Daniel immediately closed out his business in Yreka and set out for home, arriving in New York City in late July, then hurrying on to New Hampshire. There he apparently found Almira all but fully recovered, for on May 2, 1853, almost exactly nine months after their reunion, she gave birth to a second son, whom Daniel named Loyal Brown after his friend and business partner.[18]

In late September of that year, Daniel Stearns again left New Hampshire for California, this time accompanied by his wife and sons—six-year-old George and four-month-old Loyal—and his two younger siblings, Priscilla, twenty-nine, who intended to teach school in the west, and John, twenty-five, who planned to go into business with Daniel. Although Daniel's first journey had been via Panama, now with his family along he chose the Nicaragua route, which was ostensibly healthier and less dangerous than the more southerly isthmus route.[19]

The entourage boarded a steamer in Boston, putting in briefly at New York and then continuing on down the coast and across the Caribbean to Nicaragua. From the Caribbean side of the isthmus, they took a stern-wheeler out of the port city of San Juan del Norte, going upriver to Lake Nicaragua. After a full day's passage across the lake, they engaged native guides and mules to travel the twelve miles of jungle that lay between them and the Pacific Coast. Arriving in the port city of San Juan del Sur, they immediately boarded the steamer that was to take them on to San Francisco. Just out of port a case of yellow fever broke out on board, and over the duration of the voyage, five young women died while Almira watched helplessly and prayed that none of her family would contract the disease.[20]

The Stearns family arrived safely in San Francisco in the latter part of October 1853, a month after having left Boston harbor. In the city, Daniel quickly rented a house for $50 a month and invested $250 in furnishing it. He also rented a small frame building close by for an additional $50 a month and opened a store. But this proved to be a temporary measure. Business in San Francisco was in a slump, and Daniel was influenced by reports of the success Loyal and Henry Brown were enjoying in Scottsburg. By early 1854, within months of his arrival in San Francisco, Daniel Stearns had decided to become an active partner in Brown, Drum & Co. Pulling up stakes, the entire Stearns household boarded a steamer that took them along the Pacific Coast and up the Umpqua River to Scottsburg.[21]

While Daniel and John went to work at Brown, Drum & Co., Almira and Priscilla settled the children into a small house the family purchased in Lower Scottsburg, a dwelling built right on the river bank. But Daniel's affiliation with Brown, Drum & Co. was even more short-lived than his tenure in San Francisco. Quickly dissatisfied with the arrangement, he convinced his partners to split up the business. Then, leaving Almira and the boys in Scottsburg with Priscilla, Daniel and his brother, John, took the Stearns share of the merchandise by pack train some ninety miles south to Jacksonville, where Daniel had earlier been packing goods for Brown, Drum. There in August 1854 he established his own store, which he left in John's care while he moved back and forth between Scottsburg and Jacksonville, constantly restocking supplies.[22]

On October 24, 1854, scarcely a year after her arrival in the West and only months after having settled in Scottsburg, Almira Stearns gave birth to her third son, Arba Fay. Before the baby was a year old, the Jacksonville store became a casualty of the Rogue River War, the result of several years of increasing tension between the Rogue River Indians of southern Oregon Territory and the fur traders, farmers, trappers, and miners who had invaded their lands. On October 9, 1855, twenty-two Jacksonville settlers were killed in an Indian raid in which Daniel Stearns's store was burned to the ground. Having lost the store and stock, valued at over $4,100, Daniel Stearns was, by his own account, "practically broke." But he was resourceful. He contracted with the federal government to carry merchandise and military supplies from the Willamette Valley in the north down into southern Oregon Territory, thereby turning to his own profit the war that had destroyed his business.[23]

Although the Stearns family's location in Scottsburg made them relatively secure from Indian raids, Almira suffered a loss of another kind. In September 1856, her sister-in-law Priscilla, whose company had sustained Almira over the years, married Henry Brown, Daniel's former partner. The newly married couple moved to Elkton, some twenty miles to the east, to establish a homestead on the fertile farmland there. With Priscilla no longer in the household and Daniel frequently away on government packing trips, life in Scottsburg was lonely for Almira, who found it increasingly difficult to care for three young boys alone, now that she was expecting a fourth child. Under these circumstances, Daniel decided to look for another and more permanent means of livelihood. In 1857 when the government offered him livestock in lieu of the money they owed him for his months of packing, he decided to leave the mercantile world behind him. Taking the cattle offered, he purchased a section of land bordering Priscilla and Henry Brown's farm near Elkton.[24]

Two weeks after she made the move to the new homestead, Almira gave birth to her fourth son, John Warren. The ensuing years at Elkton were trying, for the vagaries of ranching soon proved to be as real as those of merchandizing. If Daniel's profits were not increasing, his family obligations certainly were, for on April 14, 1859, Almira bore her fifth—and last—child, another son, Ralph L., quickly dubbed "Rallie" by his brothers. That same year, Daniel stood for election as treasurer of Umpqua County, soon to be renamed Douglas County.[25]

By the time he was well into his term as county treasurer, Daniel Stearns was seriously considering a proposal made to him by yet another of the Brown brothers. John Brown, who had come to Oregon Territory at almost the same time as had the Stearns family, had a chance to buy the American Hotel in Roseburg, a settlement located thirty-five miles southeast of Elkton. But he needed a partner in the enterprise, and, in what was becoming a Brown family tradition of sorts, he approached Daniel Stearns. The proposition was attractive to Daniel, who had found times hard for farming and ranching, and to Almira, who had found farm life too isolated and looked forward to moving into town. In the eight years since its establishment, Roseburg had enjoyed rapid growth as a mercantile center, and though it was a smaller community than those in which Almira had lived and worked back east, it promised far more amenities than did the farm at Elkton. White frame cottages lined neatly laid out streets, and its eight hundred residents were served by two doctors, two dentists, several taverns and stores, a school, and two hotels.[26]

Agreeing to John Brown's plan, the Stearnses invested three thousand dollars in the American Hotel, a sum that covered half interest in the building and its accoutrements—furniture, dishes, bedding, and fixtures. By the end of September 1859, Daniel had rented the Elkton ranch to the mother and stepfather of the Brown clan, Caroline and Alexander Brown, who had just arrived from the East. Soon thereafter Daniel and Almira Stearns and their five sons, ranging in age from twelve years to five months, plus Daniel's youngest sister, Martha, now twenty-one and also newly arrived from New Hampshire, moved into the American Hotel in Roseburg. Martha was a particularly welcome addition to the Roseburg community, for the school was badly in need of a teacher. The Stearns family adjusted quickly to life in town, and the American Hotel venture seemed destined to be a success. In addition to housing a steady flow of travelers, the hotel was home to a number of more-or-less permanent residents, including several farm workers, a blacksmith, and the area's first minister, an Irish emigrant under whose leadership the town was building its first church.[27]

But Daniel's partnership with John Brown was not a stable one, and exactly a year after their initial agreement, the Stearnses bought out the Brown interest in the American for twenty-five hundred dollars. Shortly thereafter, John Brown took over the proprietorship of Roseburg's other hotel, the Eagle, which stood a block away. Still optimistic concerning his chances of success, Daniel added a livery and a stage barn to his establishment, improvements that may have been a wise enough investment but which threatened his financial stability. Although he was renting out the Elkton property, he had not been able to sell it, and, by his own reckoning, his debts of four thousand dollars nearly equaled his assets. He was able to maintain his precarious situation only because his creditors gave him great latitude—as well they might, since they were charging 20 percent interest on the borrowed money.[28]

Uneasy as he was to find himself in such a position, Daniel Stearns began to listen in earnest to the tales of instant riches coming out of newly discovered lodes in the Salmon River country to the east in what was, at that time, still Washington Territory. Recalling his profitable days a decade before in the Sierra Nevada camps, Daniel felt sure his fortune could be recouped once again by supplying the needs of the two thousand miners who had swarmed into the Nez Percé country six hundred miles northeast of Roseburg. Almira had coped well enough in his absence before; she could do so again. He recognized the burden of caring for the boys, but he was reassured by the close presence of his bachelor brother John, who had bought a saloon in Roseburg. Various Brown brothers and their families were also close by, should Almira need help: John and Clara, their former partners in the American, were just down the street at the Eagle Hotel; Loyal and Sarah were living only a few miles to the north; and Alonzo and Ada, who had come out with Alexander and Caroline the year before, were now farming just outside Roseburg.[29]

If Daniel could count on the Brown families to keep his wife company in his absence, he could no longer count on his sister Martha. That June she married Thomas Hyland, the twenty-six-year-old Episcopal minister who had been boarding at the American ever since his arrival in town. The newlyweds stayed on at the hotel after their wedding, but Father Hyland was expecting word of a new pastoral assignment, and Martha had little hope of remaining in Roseburg.[30]

Less than a month after his sister's wedding, Daniel Stearns set his plans in motion. Having leased the American Hotel, with an option to buy, to Silas Crane, a twenty-seven-year-old goldsmith from Ohio with a wife and small child, he rented a home for Almira and his sons, set his brother, John, in charge of his business affairs, and, on July 20, 1861, left Roseburg for "the North"—specifically for Walla Walla, the entry port to the newly discovered goldfields.[31] His timing was most auspicious, although he could not have known it. Within a month of his departure, the biggest gold stampede in Idaho history would be triggered by a rich strike at Florence, south of Walla Walla in the Salmon River country.

Word of the new strikes in the North spread quickly, and the news was convincing. Three months after Daniel's departure for the mines, the *Oregonian* promised prospective miners that "the rumored riches of the Salmon River Gold Mines are to be fully realized." The paper forecast "tremendous stampedes from California to the mines,—a flood of overland emigration,—a vastly increased business on the Columbia river." Such articles, of course, never mentioned the incipient Indian dangers to be anticipated as prospectors swarmed over the favorite hunting grounds of the Nez Percé.[32]

Daniel was on the road months in advance of the stampede. Traveling by stage to Portland, he boarded a steamer going up the Columbia to The Dalles, where he caught a stage to Walla Walla. On the streets of that bustling town, he met a Dr. Baker, who offered to stake him to an inventory of goods if Daniel supplied the outlet. Taking that as a generous offer, Daniel bought his teams of mules and their rigging, loaded the goods, and began the trek to Elk City, the hub of all gold country activity, some two hundred miles to the east. When he arrived there in August 1861, the town was barely a month old, yet it was already home to a thousand miners, eight stores, and six saloons.[33]

From the beginning, Daniel's store was a profitable operation, and by early fall, with his inventory running low, he hired a man to tend shop for him while he returned to Walla Walla for new stock. On his way back to his store, early snows forced him to forsake all thought of reaching Elk City and turned him southwest, toward Florence, "an excited mining camp of about 1000 people." Within ten days, he had sold six packloads of goods at a profit of five hundred dollars. Still unable to reach Elk City, he returned to Walla Walla to winter over.[34]

In the meantime, Almira had settled herself and the boys into a life without Daniel. She was living in a house rented at ten dollars a month from John and Emma Floed, a prominent Roseburg couple. As comfortable as she found that home, Almira did not find life itself particularly comfortable in Daniel's absence. Even though Daniel had left his business affairs in the care of his brother, John, Almira was necessarily involved in all matters that touched on family finances, an area with which she had not before concerned herself. Now in her letters to Daniel she constantly posed questions about family and business matters. From the beginning, the situation at the American Hotel forced itself on her attention. A heavy drinker, Silas Crane was a woefully negligent manager. "The house looks dirty and the Roaches are getting thick again," Almira wrote Daniel in her very first letter after his departure. She suspected that Crane himself would have preferred to strike out for Walla Walla and noted, "I do not think he would stay in the Hotel if he could sell his things."[35]

The Cranes stayed on, but the Hylands did not. Two months after Daniel's departure, the couple left Roseburg for their new parish in California. "I felt verry bad to part with them," Almira wrote Daniel. "It seems but a short time since Martha came to us and now to have her leave. . . . It sometimes seems hard to be seperated from those we love best." With Martha's departure, not only had Almira lost a friend, but Roseburg had also lost its teacher. Citizens held a meeting to resolve their problem, but no teacher was hired, and Almira was faced with the prospect of finding the money needed to send her three oldest sons—George (nearly fourteen), Loyal (eight), and Arba (not quite seven)—to school under a tutor who would charge her five dollars a quarter for each boy. Money was scarce that fall, for Alexander Brown had fallen behind on his rent on the Elkton farm and Silas Crane's mismanagement meant that there was little income from the hotel.[36]

Over the course of the winter, Almira's worst fears about the situation at the American were finally realized: Silas Crane gave her his notice. He was leaving, not for the North, but to take occupancy of the Eagle Hotel, which he had purchased from John Brown. Faced with the closure of the American, Almira hoped for a while to receive an offer on the property from Nancy Kent, who ran a boardinghouse in town and whose son Benton had already approached John Stearns about assuming the lease on the hotel. An astute judge of most situations, Almira noted that "people are so changeable in this town that you cannot tell whether they mean what they say or not," and her reservations proved well founded when Nancy Kent made no offer. Unwilling to run the place herself, Almira had the American boarded up that spring, thereby losing her primary source of income.[37]

If she felt powerless in the business world, Almira was more than competent in meeting the needs of her neighbors. In the fall of 1861, Alonzo and Ada Brown had lost their year-old son, Edgar, and she shared the grief of the stricken parents. She also befriended Helen Dearborn, a frightened nineteen-year-old, who, far from her home in Connecticut, gave birth to a stillborn child after a difficult labor. And she sympathized with neighbors who lost property when the Umpqua River flooded its banks early in 1862, inundating two blocks of downtown Roseburg and destroying a great many barns and houses outside town. Although the Stearnses lost no Roseburg property to the swollen waters, their livestock on the Elkton ranch were threatened by the bitter cold and snow that followed the flood and held the area in its grip until March.[38]

If the winter of 1861–62 was a hard one in the Umpqua Valley, it was legendary in the mines of the Salmon River country, where record snows and frigid temperatures brought almost all activity to a standstill. Daniel Stearns was esssentially confined to Walla Walla, where he had trouble finding feed for his mules and had to pay thirty dollars a cord for wood. In February, as the weather began to moderate, he managed to pack twelve hundred pounds of flour from Walla Walla to Lewiston, a town eighty miles to the northeast that was then barely six months old. There he sold the flour at three times the price he had paid for it. Encouraged by his success, but concerned with the condition of his store in Elk City, he left his snowbound pack train in Lewiston and started eastward alone, covering the 125 miles on snowshoes.[39]

Arriving in Elk City seventeen days later, Stearns discovered that the people of that mining center had not had word from the outside world for months, and he was a very welcome man. He also discovered that the man he had left in charge of the store had sold his entire stock—some eleven hundred dollars' worth of goods—but had lost three hundred dollars of that sum gambling away the long winter days. Deciding that the boom in the spring would center to the south, Daniel collected his money from the contrite gambler, closed down his Elk City store, and returned to Walla Walla to buy provisions for a new store in Florence.[40]

Out of touch though he was with the outside world, Daniel Stearns had assessed the situation accurately. Adventurers who had heard the exciting reports out of the Idaho mines in the fall of 1861 were only waiting for the arrival of spring to begin the trek to the goldfields. Among them were many men from Roseburg. Three of the Brown brothers were on the move. Daniel's old traveling companion, Loyal, had decided to "go north," but he planned to take his family with him. As restless as ever, John Brown wanted to go with his brother but did not know "what to do with his wife," a question that apparently did not bother his brother Alonzo, who was "going north soon," leaving his pregnant wife, Ada, and six-year-old daughter, Minnie, in a rented house in Roseburg.[41]

Hearing such plans only increased Almira's loneliness. By March 1862, Daniel had been gone from home for more than seven months, having left the summer before with the promise of returning in the spring. Though there were clearly signs of spring now in Roseburg, Almira had not yet heard from him. "I am quite low spirited and homesick and have been thinking for the last few days if you are not coming to live with us I should like to come and live with you," she wrote him. Loyal and Sarah would leave for Walla Walla the first of May, and Almira had plenty of time to prepare herself and the boys to make that trip with the Browns, if Daniel "had any place" for them.[42]

Her despair about her situation in Roseburg was aggravated by the stark contrast between the rundown and empty American Hotel and the newly refurbished Eagle. Silas Crane had sobered up enough to make major improvements in the rival structure. "He has torn down the Chimney in the New part and made one large room of the two," Almira reported to Daniel. Having "papered and lined the house all over [and] finished off the dancing Hall," Crane was planning to open his hotel "with a grand Ball." John Stearns continued to encourage Almira about prospects for leasing out the American again, but she knew that John himself had plans to leave his saloon behind and go north. It might be in John's best interest to keep her believing in a rosy future that would not depend on his continued presence in Roseburg, but she knew the situation as well as he. Even if she could manage to find someone to clean up and reopen the American, the remodeled Eagle would be stiff competition for the relatively few boarders in town.[43]

Her situation was dismal. "We cannot live without money," she wrote Daniel: "Every thing is verry dear . . . and very scarce at that I have not had any . . . vegetables since New Years and upon the whole we have lived verry poor this winter I do not think our expenses have been more than fifty dollars a month since you went away but the Children have not had any clothes except boots and shoes. I have had two Callico dreses and that is all but we shall all have to rig up some this spring or we cannot go to church or sabbath school." Obviously, her dire straits could be laid to Daniel's long absence, and there were some who pointed out that fact to her. Loyal Brown himself believed that if Daniel had remained in Roseburg, things would have gone differently with the hotel. When he said as much to Almira, she hastened to pass the opinion on to Daniel. "But still I dont know," she added. She and Daniel almost seemed fated "not to prosper hard as wee have worked and ecenomical as wee have lived." She hesitated to "complain at the dispensation of God for I have many things to be thankful for blessed with health and my children and Husband spared to me."[44]

Though spared to her, that husband was far distant and long overdue; indeed, a mid-March visit from a Mr. Park brought Almira the unwelcome news that Daniel would not be coming home until fall. Casting about for some way through the disappointment, she could only "hope it [was] all for the best." "I have been verry contented all winter thinking it would soon pass away," she wrote to Daniel, "but now the thought of another six or eight months absence makes me sad." And she repeated an earlier question: "Could I come up there and live some where near you so that I could see you once in a while?"[45]

The responsibilities of five sons and the defunct business were almost beyond her. There had been no school all year, and she had little hope that sessions would be held in Roseburg that summer. The boys were bored; George, especially, was in need of something to occupy his time. He had worked briefly for Silas Crane in readying his new hotel, earning seven dollars for his chores, and there was a possibility that Addison Flint, who kept a bookstore, could use him, but in the meantime, George was restless and was pressing his mother to let him go north with Loyal and Sarah Brown. In fact, all of the boys wanted to make the trip to the mines. "They tease me all the time to go for they want to see papa," Almira wrote her husband, trying to rouse some response in him. "I tell them that prehaps you dont want us there but I cant make them believe it. I should like to come verry much but you know better than I do and you must decide."[46]

By late March, Almira at least had company in her misery when Alonzo Brown bade goodbye to Ada, who was six months pregnant, and left for Portland, where the rush for the mines was so much in evidence that he had trouble fitting his buggy onto a steamboat for the trip to The Dalles. From The Dalles eastward, he found the road lined with prospectors, most of them on foot, all the way to the mines. In Lewiston he sold his buggy, bought another pack horse and merchandise, and proceeded to Florence with bacon, flour, and syrup. Although it was by now late April, the vestiges of that record-setting winter still held the country in sway; horses and men carrying packs struggled through deep drifts of snow and were stymied by swollen, ice-packed rivers. Sixteen miles short of Florence, the trail became impassable to horses and mules, and Brown was forced to divide his provisions and pay willing prospectors to pack the goods in on their backs.[47]

Once in town, Brown soon found Daniel Stearns, who had himself just arrived with merchandise from Walla Walla. Although Alonzo had never kept shop with Daniel, three of his brothers had, and yet another partnership was formed. By nightfall the two men had paid twenty-five hundred dollars for an unfinished log building and had opened up shop as Stearns & Brown. For the rest of that season, Alonzo Brown managed the store in Florence while Daniel Stearns ran the pack train back and forth from Lewiston to provide the merchandise for the shelves. At the peak of the summer season, there were ten thousand miners in Florence, and Daniel and Alonzo sold flour at seventy-five dollars a sack and bacon at three dollars a pound to miners who were willing to pay any price for provisions.[48]

The new inhabitants were a rough breed: "The town was filled with the worst element of the Pacific Coast and thieves and gamblers from the East," Alonzo recalled later. "The saloons and gambling houses were wide open night and day and a man was killed nearly every night." That description matched the one that Daniel himself finally relayed to Almira, when, in April 1862, nine months after his departure, she finally received his first letter. She was, of course, "truly glad" to hear from him, for she had heard "bad reports from the North" about "much suffering for the want of food [through the winter]." Although she was still uncertain of the full extent of winter's toll at home, Alexander and Caroline Brown had reported that all their stock in Elkton had been lost. Almira feared she had lost her milk cows in Roseburg as well, since George had not been able to find them when she had sent him out to reconnoiter the town and its outskirts.[49]

There were larger losses to be counted, and she felt helpless to remedy them. Her fellow citizens had done nothing to restore the bridge taken out by the winter's flood, and as a result, no stage ran north to Portland. With no through traffic, there was even less business in Roseburg and less hope than ever of reopening the American Hotel. The town's lack of civic responsibility not only increased Almira's financial worries but it also compounded her concern for the welfare of her children. Nothing had been done to organize a school for the coming year, and there were no longer regular church services. Contemptuous of the town's attitude, she noted that "Roseburg is asleep and I am afraid that it will never wake up every one is discouraged and want[s] to get away as soon as they can."[50]

Everything was "scarce." The Stearns family had had no potatoes from January to April, when the Floeds, the couple from whom she was renting, had shared some newly acquired produce. With money even more scarce than potatoes, Almira saved all the cash she could. But she disparaged her own efforts, writing Daniel that she wished she "could do something to help support us." Her only good news was the fact that John and Emma Floed had decided against leaving Roseburg to summer in Portland, a loss for which she had been bracing herself.[51]

In addition to enjoying the company of her friends in Roseburg, Almira enjoyed the letters of friends and relatives from afar. When Daniel's siblings wrote, she invariably passed their news along to him. In addition to letters from relatives in New Hampshire, she received infrequent notes from the Hylands, who reported in mid-April that Martha had had a fine, healthy boy. At about the same time, Almira received some unexpected news from her sister Polly Blodgett, who wrote that their father had died the previous August from "disease of the heart."[52]

As alienated as she was from her family back east, the news of her father's death was probably less traumatic than news that her husband had decided to stay on in the North, but she and the boys were not to join him there. Disappointed once more, Almira began to realize that if she wanted to improve her lot, she would have to act on her own. Having noted that if she were in Daniel's place she "would give up the Farm for the Mortgage and find a new home in some place where wee could send our boys to school," she went even further, vowing that if her husband could not come home, then she herself would "go to some other place where there is good schools." Declaring herself "willing to make any sacrafice for the sake of the boys," she expressed particular concern over fifteen-year-old George, who was certainly "not learning much" in his present environment.[53]

Despite her threats, Almira was in Roseburg to stay. Even as she resigned herself to that fact, her brother-in-law, John Stearns, closed his saloon and left for Lewiston and the gold mines. He knew he had only "faltering" prospects in the mines, but his prospects were even poorer in Roseburg. Almira did not begrudge John the leaving, for it was "useless to think of making anything here nearly all the men are going North." As had been earlier predicted, gold seekers from California were now streaming through town, headed north. "The road is lined with people . . . some on foot some horseback and in wagons," she wrote. And she did not fail to observe, nor hesitate to report to Daniel, that "a good many take along their families."[54]

Perhaps because of that remark, perhaps simply because Stearns & Brown experienced a new prosperity that spring, Daniel's largesse increased at this point. Almira received several sacks of gold dust in early summer of 1862—and with it the promise that Daniel would soon be coming home. With that news to sustain her, life brightened, and Almira felt magnanimous enough to insist that he "must not come on [her] account." They were all well and she had "never had such health in [her] life."[55]

With the money Daniel sent her—a little over two hundred dollars— Almira paid her rent to the Floeds and still had forty dollars left. On that forty, plus fifty dollars that Henry Brown owed her, she expected to be able to "get along for sometime." Relying heavily on Daniel's promise to be home sometime that summer, she advised him not to send any more dust. It cost too much to convert it to currency, and besides, her credit was good in town.[56]

And her spirits were high, for Bishop Scott, the Episcopalian chancellor, had visited Roseburg; for Almira it was "a blessed privalage to have Divine Service once more in our own Church." Other blessings sustained her. On May 27, Ada Brown gave birth to an eleven-pound boy, whom she named Frederick, joyous news that Almira asked Daniel to pass along to Alonzo. Less joyous was news of another Brown pregnancy. Daniel's sister Priscilla was expecting again in Elkton, and Almira was ambivalent about what would no doubt be expected of her: "I am not shure what they will do when she is confined," she wrote to Daniel; "I do not feel it is my duty to go. I pity her but it is all I am able to do to take care of my [own] family and often more than I can do."[57]

Depressed by the prospect of even a brief visit to Elkton, she made it clear that she hoped never to have to live there again herself. At least in Roseburg she had companionship, and the promise of schooling for her boys, both courtesy of Emma Slocum, the teacher hired to conduct sessions that summer of 1862. Miss Slocum not only provided classes each day for the Stearns boys but also provided company each evening for Almira, with whom she boarded.[58]

School came too late for George, who opted to skip the summer session in favor of staying on at Mr. Flint's bookstore. Although he did well at his job and acted "quite dignified," Almira still thought that the boy should be in school. Indeed, during Bishop Scott's recent visit she had asked him about the Episcopal school in Portland and had learned that George could be enrolled there for the fall term. But it would cost sixty dollars for his room, board, and tuition. It was a decision Almira did not want to make on her own, and she begged Daniel to let her know how he felt about the matter.[59]

Meantime, the younger boys were doing well enough under Emma Slocum. Nine-year-old Loyal was an excellent student, but Almira found that she had constantly to prod seven-year-old Arba in his schoolwork. His mother's most willing helper with the chores at home, Arba had absolutely no interest in learning to read and write and was outshone even by five-year-old Johnny, who had his first taste of schooling that year. As the summer set in, Almira became concerned about Loyal. He had been hoarse all spring, and when he grew noticeably pale weeks after the onset of the hoarseness, Almira feared he might have consumption. She took her fears, and the young patient, to Dr. Eugene Fisk, who prescribed some "linement" to be rubbed on Loyal's neck. If that treatment didn't work, the doctor advised "blistering." Almira had no confidence in such a remedy.[60] Fortunately, though, the salve worked and Loyal improved, but by the time he was fully recovered, the school term had ended and Miss Slocum had departed, leaving Almira without her companionship and raising once more the nagging question of whether there would be any schooling available in Roseburg.

When Mr. Flint let George go from the bookstore, all five of Almira's boys were footloose once again, and she lamented, "I often wish I lived where there was a good school all the time." She pressed her husband to consider a new plan. "What do you think of my moving to Salem where the boys could have a chance to go to school?" They could live more cheaply in Salem than in Roseburg, and moving expenses would be minimal, since there was constant traffic between Salem and Roseburg and any of the merchants' teams could carry them in the coming fall. If Daniel were not home by summer's end, she would prefer to move on, but she deferred to his judgment: "It is for you to decide. It is not on my own acount that I wish to go but for the boys."[61]

Almira had other concerns that summer. She continued to look in on Ada Brown and to send word of her progress and the baby's to Florence. She also sent periodic reports of her own deteriorating financial status. She had received fifty dollars from the sale of one of the horses that had survived the winter, but she still had not received the fifty dollars that Mr. Crane owed her. She was about out of money and wrote Daniel that if he did not intend to come home any time soon, he had better send her "the coin."[62]

That letter was posted in mid-July, and two months passed before Almira received an answer. Written in early September, Daniel's response arrived within two weeks of his having posted it. Delighted "to get a letter so quick after it was written," Almira urged him to "send them all by Express." While the letter contained the money she had requested, it also contained Daniel's veto of her plan to leave Roseburg. Disappointed as she was to learn she would not be moving the boys to Salem, Almira took some comfort in Daniel's assurance that at least he did not intend to move them back to the ranch at Elkton when he got home from the mines.[63]

Anticipating his arrival sometime before Christmas, Almira had dried a bushel of corn and was making lots of plum sauce, putting up fresh peaches and pears, and trying to get all of her sewing done so that she could just sit and "look at [him] a long time with pleasure" when he arrived. To her surprise, Daniel appeared on her doorstep in late September—only to leave again some two weeks later. His unexpected business trip home was so sudden and so brief that she later had trouble believing he had come at all. And this leavetaking left her lonelier than ever. George had gone with his father as far as Portland and was well settled in Bishop Scott Academy by the time Daniel was back in Florence. In addition, her closest friend, Ada Brown, had joined Daniel on his trip back to the mines. There was little hope of Almira's following her there, for, although Alonzo Brown eagerly welcomed Ada, seven-year-old Minnie, and baby Freddy to their new home—"a pole house, chinked and daubed with mud"—Daniel Stearns remained convinced that Florence was not the place for Almira and his sons.[64]

Disappointed that Daniel had not, after all, come home to stay and that she and the boys were not destined to join him in Florence, Almira was at least glad to have George in school in Portland. And in the wake of Ada Brown's departure, she changed her mind about the wisdom of traveling to Elkton to help Priscilla Brown and her family. There was little to hold her in town, since there was no chance of school for the term, and whatever her own feelings about life on the ranch, the boys thrived there. Thus when Henry came to town with the news that they had a fine new baby girl, Almira loaded boys and bundles into his farm wagon and made the trip to Elkton, where she found Priscilla and her baby—and the other two Brown children—doing well. Upon her arrival, she busied herself in doing what she could to help her sister-in-law catch up on her sewing and baking.[65]

Despite her resolution to make the most of her visit, Almira was uneasy in Elkton. When Henry drove her by the ranch where she had spent over two years of her life, it seemed to her that she had never lived there, and she was "sure [she did] not wish to again." The farm was deserted and in disrepair, for the elder Browns had abandoned it to move onto Loyal's place when he and his wife set out for the mines in late spring. And though Henry had managed to work the Stearns fields through harvest, it was not likely he would be able to manage both ranches through another season. Ironically, a neighbor's ranch, not nearly as good a property as theirs, had sold that fall, and Henry agreed with Almira that the buyer would probably have preferred the Stearns ranch if Daniel had been home to present the terms. But that was spilled milk, and, for lack of a better plan, she accepted Henry's offer to hire a man to oversee the place for her.[66]

While Almira passed her days in Elkton, Daniel and a companion were beset by three highwaymen during a trip to Lewiston for supplies. The packers succeeded in outrunning the gunmen, "at a pretty rapid gait for five or six miles," and the robbers were later apprehended near Lewiston and "disposed of," vigilante fashion. Daniel wrote of the escapade to Almira, likely without realizing how unsettling the news would be to a woman who had already "heard [far too] much about Indians and Robbers." Thankful that he had survived this misadventure, she pressed him to "be cautious in the future."[67]

With winter coming on, she was preoccupied with problems of her own. Without asking Daniel's advice, she authorized the building of a new woodshed, ordered enough wood for the season, and had the boys stack it.[68] After purchasing her flour and vegetables, she felt quite well fixed. The winter of 1862–63 turned out to be a mild one, bringing "quite cold weather with heavy frosts but little rain," a marked contrast to the floods and snows of 1861–62.

Although Almira had the company of Daniel's brother John, who had returned from the mines to winter over with her and the boys, she had little help from him in the matter of the vacant American Hotel. Indeed, John Stearns gave but scant attention even to his own real estate interests. He had still not sold his saloon, though it was "offered . . . for 15 hundred." Almira had no idea what he intended to do with himself and was convinced that neither did he.[69]

Pleased as she was that Roseburg would offer a school term that winter, she was dismayed to see the community politicize educational concerns. The new schoolmaster, "a Mr Gale of Eugene," arrived in early December, bringing as his assistant Winifred Lane, neice of Joseph Lane, the first territorial governor of Oregon and most lately its senator. Soon thereafter a group of citizens who were still rankled by memories of the bitterly contested election of 1860 called for her dismissal. Almira Stearns promptly obtained her landlord John Floed's permission to offer the ousted assistant the use of space in her rented house, and there Miss Lane opened school for twenty-seven youngsters, with Loyal, Arba, and Johnny Stearns among them.[70]

His mother's idea of the perfect student, nine-year-old Loyal could already read and spell as well as George, who was six years older. While Almira credited Loyal with "good ideas" and predicted that "with opportunity" he would "make a good scholar," she was worried about her reluctant scholar, seven-year-old Arba. Yet it was Arba who offered her the most help at home, rising early every morning to build the fire, grind the coffee, and put on the teakettle. Johnny was "learning some," in the way of an almost-five-year-old, and everything he learned at school he shared with little Rallie, who frequently tried to talk him into staying home to play. Lonesome through the school day, the three-year-old followed his mother from room to room, "driv[ing] away the blues" with his many questions. "Darling boy," she wrote Daniel, "I should indeed be lonesome without him." Her thoughts were often with George, who wrote her frequent, satisfying letters that told of his progress at Bishop Scott's school, where he was "happy and contented."[71]

Although neither George nor his father made it home over the holidays, the Stearns family enjoyed a festive Christmas, complete with firecrackers. Silas Crane gave a Christmas ball at the newly refurbished Eagle Hotel and invited "quite a number of Citzens." Almira herself "did not wish to go," but she got a full report of the event from John Stearns, who had escorted a fifteen-year-old redhead, news Almira relayed to Daniel, who spent New Year's Eve, his forty-first birthday, in Florence at Alonzo and Ada Brown's pole house.[72]

With the coming of the new year, Alonzo's brother, John Brown, was home from the mines, but Almira did not know "whether he brought home any money or not." Dr. Fisk was gone from Roseburg, having received "an appointment from Washington as Surgeon in the Army." The war news concerned Almira, for things looked "worse than ever."

She expected that McClellan would be removed as commander of the Union forces, since some blame should fall on him for the losses at Fredericksburg. War news came from closer to home, too, as she reported to Daniel that "The Pirate [ship] Alabama stop[ped] the California Steamer coming this way and got eight hundred thousand dollars in Greenbacks" to fund the Confederate war effort.[73]

Having had no letters from Daniel since early December, Almira noted, "Five weeks is a long time not to hear from the dearest friend on earth." She was also lonely for Ada Brown, from whom she had not heard at all since Ada's arrival in Florence, and she was eager to hear her friend's opinion on life in the mines and to share the Roseburg news with her. Longing for a chance "to gossip a little" with Ada and to spend time with Minnie, who had been like a daughter to her, and with little Freddy, whom she imagined as "fat and good natured and very sweet," Almira closed each of her letters to Daniel with an injunction to "kiss the children" for her.[74]

Up in Florence, Ada and her family had also found the winter of 1862–63 relatively mild. It had snowed there "for one hundred and thirteen days, more or less," so that Minnie Brown was able to ski over the roof of their house, but the deep drifts kept the house warm and snug. Come spring, Stearns & Brown anticipated record sales. They had bought a large stock of goods late in the fall of 1862, figuring that "if business remained as good as it bid fair to," they "would clean up a good stake" the following summer. But the merchants had not given sufficient thought to the mercurial nature of the gold camps. The discovery of gold in Placerville and Bannock (soon to become Idaho City) in the Boise Basin of southern Idaho some three hundred miles to the south sent reports of fabulous new riches circulating throughout Florence. Even those miners holding good claims made plans to move on with the coming of spring. Stearns & Brown, as owners of the second largest stock of merchandise in Florence, made plans to move with them. But not as far as southern Idaho. Warren, or Warren's Diggins, just forty miles to the southeast, had been the site of a promising strike in the summer of 1862, and Daniel Stearns predicted correctly that it would be the busiest mining camp of the north in the coming season. He was already planning his first pack trip from Florence over the mountain, eager to take advantage of the new market.[75]

The economy at home in Oregon was promising, too. Henry Brown was able to find a man to live and work on the Stearns ranch at

Elkton, and John Stearns had rented out his saloon for twenty-five dollars a month. John still had no plans, and though Almira enjoyed his company well enough, she found his lack of direction and his complaints about Roseburg irksome, and she fully expected him to leave for the mines again soon. It was, in fact, the time of year when the people of Roseburg began to talk again of who was going and who was staying. Andrew Sawyer had come home in the dead of winter with "lots of presents" for his children, but whether or not he brought money was a question that was debated about town. Dr. Leander London, the dentist, left for the North, taking his family with him. And Loyal Brown and his family, after wintering at the Elkton farm, had returned to the Salmon River country with ambitious plans. While maintaining his store in Elk City, Loyal intended to undertake an enterprise some forty miles to the west—the expansion of the crude way station at Mount Idaho, the western terminus of the Milner Trail, a rudimentary forty-five-mile road scratched out the season before from Camas Prairie south to Florence.[76]

Everyone else seemed bound for somewhere, but Almira was stuck in Roseburg. As the winter wore on, her spirits sagged. Money was once again a scarce commodity. With only seventy dollars in cash and the rent not yet paid, she considered her prospects. Henry Brown owed her fifty dollars, but she doubted that that sum would be forthcoming before late spring. John Stearns owed her money as well, but she knew he was saving what he could for his trip north, and she was reluctant to ask him for it.[77] She would have to bide her time and hope for money from Daniel.

George wrote of homesickness, and Miss Lane closed her school late in February in order to prepare for her impending marriage to merchant Horace Barton. Although she did not want the boys to lose such a good teacher, Almira was happy for Winnie Lane, since she considered being "married . . . of more importance than Teaching." Even as one friend left, others were still on hand and in need of Almira's company. She and Emma Floed spent several days taking care of Winifred Mosher in her confinement, and she and Mrs. Heineberg gave one day in late winter to calling on the Flints, the Roses, and the Sawyers, all of whom asked for news of Ada Brown.[78]

Miss Lane's resignation meant the boys were once more out of school, and Almira kept them occupied with lessons in the art of housekeeping—not so much because she needed the help but because "they had better do it than to run [around] all the time." In

early April, her fears about her sons' use of leisure time were compounded when George, whose homesickness had interfered with
his studies in Portland, returned to Roseburg, having "grown a good
deal and . . . improved in his appearance." Delighted as she was to
see him, Almira was soon contemplating sending him up to Elkton
to work on the ranch with Henry Brown, since it was "bad enough
for Loyal and Arba to be runing the streets" without having George
on the loose as well. To her, no schooling meant no intellectual
growth, and she concluded, "It seems to me that boys raised in
Oregon are of no account." Fortunately, other parents shared her
concern, and in the spring of 1863, Roseburg finally took "the first
step towards Civilization" by holding a citizens' meeting to discuss
the issue of a "free school." Opening a school meant the imposition
of new taxes, but Almira was a staunch supporter of the group who
favored the project. When the question came to a vote, John Floed
"took the lead and of course the rest followed," and Roseburg gained
its first public school with only two dissenting votes."[79]

Students once again, the Stearns boys suffered the customary
colds of springtime, and Almira doctored them even as she endured
her worst ever attack of "Neuralgia." Her medical skills were tested
to the limit when little Rallie experienced a series of vomiting and
fainting spells. Diagnosing the ailment as a case of worms, she
treated him accordingly and was relieved the next day when "there
was a very long tape worm came from him." Poor communication
with those in the high country meant she had no way of knowing
that while she dealt with colds and worms, Ada Brown dealt with
despair and scarlet fever. Both Minnie and Freddy had contracted
the disease, and though both had recovered, Ada and Alonzo had
decided that she must take the children back to Oregon as soon as
the trail to Lewiston opened up.[80]

Unaware of her friend's dilemma, Almira was caught up in visits
to Roseburg's new babies. Jane Chadwick, wife of the local attorney,
had had a fine nine-pounder. Libby Flint Morgan, fourteen-year-old
daughter of bookseller Addison Flint, seemed to be taking to moth-
erhood well enough, although Almira had earlier rued her engage-
ment to Eby Morgan, a farmer in his late thirties—"She seems so
young and innocent and him so old and has a wife living." Helen
Dearborn, whose first child had been stillborn, now had a healthy
infant. Richard Dearborn, the new father, had already gone north to
work as a purser on a steamboat. Having seen so many new babies,

Rallie asked his mother to "write to papa to bring us a little sister." And though she had more than once lamented the fact that she had no daughter, Almira hastened to assure Daniel, "I think we can get along very well without one so you need not fetch one."[81]

Even as the arrival of new babies swelled the town's population, the predictable spring and summer exodus of male citizens reduced it once again. Growing "tired of this town," Benjamin Heineberg had left too, promising his wife he would send for her when he found a place to suit him. And John Stearns finally carried out his plan to return to the Salmon River country, but he, like his brother Daniel, sent only sporadic word to Almira from the mines. Back in Roseburg, John's real estate woes continued, as his saloon was boarded up again.[82]

The American Hotel also stood vacant. Nancy Kent and "one or two others" still talked of taking it over, but no one had, and Almira suspected Silas Crane of frightening off all prospects in order to limit competition with the Eagle. Something had to be done. While her own hotel stood empty, she was paying rent to the Floeds. Although both she and the boys would prefer to remain where they were, if the American did not rent soon, Almira planned to move in. The property would be far more attractive to prospective buyers if it were occupied instead of vacant, and she could use what she saved in rent to make improvements on the building. She had no fears for their safety, for sixteen-year-old George had gotten to be a good-sized boy. Unless Daniel sent some word of disapproval, she would move herself and the children into the American in October, if it was not rented by then.[83]

She was short on cash, even though John Stearns had paid what he owed her before heading off to the mines and Henry Brown had paid twenty-five of the fifty dollars he owed her and promised to send the balance. That was all the money she had. Everything was "dear" that summer, and it took "more cloth to make the boys pants this year for they have grown tall and they eat more." She had once hoped to make her cash last until Daniel's as yet unscheduled homecoming, but she now wondered if she could stretch so few dollars so far.[84]

Because of such concerns, she had allowed George to close out his schooling at the end of the term and take up a position in a store, though she questioned whether he had "sufficient learning." Loyal wrote his father that the new teacher, a Mr. Hall, was strict with his sixty scholars—they could not "use any profane words," and if they missed "more than one word in spelling" they had to stay in after school—but he was well liked. All the boys thoroughly enjoyed the Fourth of July holiday, when residents of Douglas County gathered for a festival at Wilbur, just seven miles north of Roseburg. "About a thousand people" attended the celebration, but Almira was not among them, since she did "not enjoy such things much any time" and enjoyed them even less when she could not have Daniel's company. In her husband's absence her socializing was limited to "calling," traveling in the company of women friends who dropped in on other friends for an afternoon's visit. And she happily received company into her home. The summer of 1863 was particularly filled with visitors. Priscilla and Henry Brown spent eight days with her in June, a visit Almira enjoyed, although she commented later to Daniel that "they have got some wild children."[85]

In early June 1863, Almira welcomed her dear friend Ada Brown back to Roseburg, noting that she "could hardly believe it was her" when the stage stopped. Having left Florence as soon as the roads were clear, Ada arrived home little the worse for her travels. Minnie, too, had survived the trip well, but year-old Freddy had been feverish and restless throughout the long journey.[86]

As his family settled in with Almira in Roseburg, Alonzo sold the pole house for one hundred dollars and moved back into the unfinished frame building that bulged with Stearns & Brown merchandise that had lost its market with the spring stampede to Warren and other new gold camps further south. Seeking to cover their potential losses, Daniel Stearns rented a building in Warren to use as an outlet for the surplus stock on hand at the warehouse in Florence. While Stearns sold goods in Warren for "a fair profit," Brown sold them at Florence "at a loss, sometimes for half of the cost and the freight." It would not be a good season for Stearns & Brown.[87]

In Roseburg the arrival of Ada, Minnie, and Freddy Brown had changed Almira's thoughts about the hotel. Even though Daniel had not yet written his opinion of her plans to reclaim the place, she was no longer willing to delay until autumn. Why not clean and refurbish the long-empty rooms at once so the two families could take joint occupancy there as soon as possible? Excited by the prospects of solving the problem of the vacant hotel in such a pleasant way, she paid the place a visit to survey the possibilities. She was devastated at the extent of the vandalism. Someone had broken in through a door, removed the locks, and stolen mattress tickings, leaving the straw contents on the floor. Nine feet of pipe had been cut from the plumbing system and carried off, and repairs on the pump would amount to seven dollars.[88] Almira was discouraged but determined, and she and Ada set out together to clean the place up.

At least her financial position was not so desperate anymore. Henry Brown had finally paid the last half of his debt, and Horace Barton, the merchant newly married to former teacher Winnie Lane, had promised her rent on the hotel barn. When she opened the American Hotel again, she could count on two boarders: Ada Brown and children, who would pay whatever rent Daniel thought just, and a Mr. Lathrop, a sometime resident of the hotel who had periodically slept "in the parlor" even as the building deteriorated around him.[89]

The prospect of a steady income again was all the more appreciated after Almira received word from Daniel of the losses Stearns & Brown faced in the Salmon River country. That same letter dashed whatever hopes Almira had of seeing Daniel that fall. Resigned, she responded that since he did "not think[it] best to come [home]," she would "try to make the best of it," relying on "an all wise providence in all things" and trusting that if they were not to be reunited in this world, they might at least be "an unbroken family in heaven."[90]

Although it was carried out without Daniel's knowledge or approval, work on the hotel was tonic against discouragement, and it progressed rapidly through the weeks of late July and early August. Moving day itself was hectic but happy, for Almira had finally taken her biggest problem in hand. This may not have been the best solution—certainly she would have preferred to have stayed closer to her friends and neighbors in the Floed house—but at least she was doing something about a deplorable situation. And she was doing it in company with Ada Brown.[91]

Within a few days of having made the move to the American, Almira carried through with a promise she had made to the boys, and to herself, and set out for Elkton to spend a week's vacation with Priscilla and Henry. It was a good break after weeks of heavy work cleaning the hotel and moving a household, and Almira was happier than she had thought she could be at Elkton, spending her days visiting with Priscilla and discussing farm management possibilities with Henry, who thought he could find someone to work the Stearns place again if she would take payment in bushels of wheat. George worked the fields with Henry, who reported that the boy "works like a man," and the younger boys fished and generally "[ran] wild."[92]

Though she enjoyed Priscilla's and Henry's company and though the cousins all "got along first rate," Almira soon grew homesick at Elkton. Ambivalent as her feelings about the ranch were, just being there made her all the more lonely for Daniel, since there were "so many things to remind" her of him. She was concerned about some unfinished business at home in Roseburg; Mr. Lathrop had not paid his rent for "the several months" he had lived in the parlor of the hotel, and Almira wanted to go home to address that question. She was also having second thoughts about the radical move she had just made without Daniel's approval. "I have felt very anxious and uneasy about the change which I have made and do not know but you will think I am crazy," she wrote him from Elkton. She wanted to "get home and get settled" so that she could think things through in her proper place.[93]

As fate would have it, Almira had no sooner taken definitive action on the hotel than another possibility presented itself. Soon after she returned to Roseburg, Mr. Putnam, who had just sold his hotel at Wilbur, approached her about renting the American. His plan gave her pause. "As buisness is dull," Mr. Putnam wanted her to stay on and board at the hotel for a while. Although she would much prefer to do her own "housekeeping," she felt "willing to make that sacrifice hoping . . . it may be the means of selling [the hotel]." Besides, she "was [already] there and had all [her] things there." She would pay forty dollars a month for two rooms—one for herself and one for the boys—and she would do her own washing and "wait upon herself." She and Mr. Putnam came to agreement on the sum he would owe her for the month of September, but she reserved the right to consult with Daniel before setting a final figure for his leasing the American in subsequent months. While she would have liked to collect more to offset the forty dollars she would be paying Putnam for room and board for herself and the boys, she doubted he could afford "to give any more," since there was not enough business in town to support two hotels. Less than satisfied with the new arrangement, she added yet another condition to her agreement with Mr. Putnam: at the end of one month, if he did not like the situation or if she herself was not satisfied, Almira and the boys were free to leave the hotel.[94]

The bargain was struck, and Almira and the boys became guests at the American Hotel, along with Ada Brown, who contracted with the Putnams under much the same conditions. As she settled in for the duration, Almira assessed the arrangements for Daniel. She liked what the Putnams were doing. "They take good care of things . . . the kitchen wants repairing . . . the stove was useless . . . so they set it out in the yard and bought a new one, they have three girls bourding here . . . and expect more when school begins they have had some Travelers everyday to dinner." With this new arrangement, and with the hotel barn being leased by Mr. Barton for the care of the stage horses, she did not project a need for any money from Daniel until spring, by which time, in any event, she hoped to have him home. The Stearns family did well in their new environment, and Mr. Put-nam did a good business in the hotel that fall, even though he was "sickly" and most of the work fell to Mrs. Putnam. The number of regular boarders increased to eight, not counting the Stearnses and the Browns, and there were a "good many transients."[95]

That fall an outbreak of scarlet fever "rag[ed] all over Oregon," even-tually touching Almira's own household. Loyal was sick for three days before his mother recognized the illness for what it was. She had doc-tored him herself at first "with homepathy medicine," but she would not have done so had she known what she was dealing with. She "felt very anxious" about her second son for a couple of weeks thereafter and was relieved when none of his brothers came down with the dis-ease. While none of Roseburg's children died of scarlet fever that year, several children in surrounding communities did die, and Almira con-tinued to write to Daniel of the epidemic for months thereafter.[96]

Her letters also contained other Roseburg news. Mr. Flint and Mr. Crane had "brought on a stock of dry goods and Groceries," and all the merchants had shipped in large stocks of goods in anticipation of an active winter market. A Mrs. Gaddis was "crazy by spells," Mrs. John Drum had a "nice fat boy," Mrs. Abraham had a little daughter, and Antonio Fink, the baker, had left Roseburg "for good." There was also "a large distillery going up in town down by the brewery," but Almira had not yet discovered exactly who was building it.[97]

Ada and Almira moved about Roseburg, delighting in each other's company and once in a while enjoying an outing with other families. Despite such diversions, each woman was preoccupied with con-cerns about her husband's welfare, for correspondence was not forthcoming from the gold camps that summer and fall of 1863. From late July through mid-November, Almira heard nothing at all from Daniel other than second-hand greetings delivered early that month by two men from the North who dropped by and gave the youngest Stearns boys "four bits apiece to buy candy with." Finally, on November 16 she received from Daniel himself a packet containing not only a letter but also some poetry and a "handsome" ring. Wishing she "had something to [send in] return," she could only offer "lots of love." The boys were obviously as proud of their mother's gold ring as she was, and she asked Daniel to be sure to "bring each one some little thing they will prise it so much comeing from you for they all think papa is more than common."[98]

The arrival of the packet indicated to Almira that Daniel was probably not planning a trip home anytime soon. She shared her fears with Ada, and the two women took a joint stand against further disappointment: "When you and Mr Brown find out where you are going," Almira wrote Daniel, "[we] hope you will keep [it] to yourselves for we do not want to know." In response to Daniel's comment that Alonzo had been "complaining that he does not get letters from his wife," Almira replied that Ada had written often, as had she, but perhaps their letters were not getting through.[99]

Life in the hotel offered Almira a spectacle of activity that she had not known within the quiet confines of the house she had rented from the Floeds. Her fellow boarders were an interesting lot—especially a Mrs. Whitmore, whose quarters were next to hers and who seemed to be given to entertaining men in her room during her husband's frequent absences. The unfortunate woman was surprised in the act one night when someone, perhaps Mr. Whitmore himself, "threw two large stones" in her window, breaking "two lights of glass." The disturbance alarmed Almira sufficiently to cause her to support Mr. Putnam in his decision to ask the woman to leave the hotel. Despite the eviction notice, Mrs. Whitmore managed to stall for time, so that even as Almira described the episode to Daniel, she could hear Mrs. Whitmore and Fred Johnson, her "most ardent admirer," in the next room, "talking low."[100]

There was more gossip to be shared. The wife of Mr. Pierce who owned the sawmill up Deer Creek had run off with "a man by the name of Priest a young man," while Mrs. Pierce herself was "about fifty." Having come into the American Hotel for dinner saying they were "going to the canyon on a visit" by stage, the lovers had actually headed for Sacramento, taking with them some six hundred dollars of Mr. Pierce's money. "Mr. Pierce says he is sorry to lose the money," Almira reported, "but don't care for the woman."[101]

The American was becoming the social center of Roseburg, and when Mr. and Mrs. Putnam held a grand-opening ball, Almira Stearns broke her rule about attending social affairs without Daniel and made it a point to be on hand. Although Ada Brown, a youthful twenty-seven-year-old, joined in the dancing, Almira, a sedate woman of forty-two who considered herself beyond the coquetry of youth, chose to enjoy the festivities as spectator rather than participant.[102]

Sixteen-year-old George also danced at the Putnam ball, something that his mother was not prepared for, though she admitted that he danced "first rate." But that was only the beginning. The ball having seemingly "set him crazy," he had subsequently gone to "a kitchen Party," where he danced a good deal. "It seems strange to have him going around," Almira remarked to Daniel, "but I suppose he must have some Amusements and he had better dance than to visit Saloons." Grateful that her son did "not seem to have any inclination for drink or smoke," she was also "very glad he always [went] to Church when [they had services] although he dislike[d] the Methodists as much as [his father did]." While Almira herself attended the Methodist service whenever it was available, she welcomed the irregular visits of the Episcopal Bishop Scott, whose preaching was always "fuel to [the] soul."[103]

The school term began again in late fall, and the Stearns boys, including George, were once again under the tutelage of Mr. Hall. Arba, now nine and as helpful around the house as ever, still had problems with reading and writing, though Almira helped him far more with his studies than she did the others, who were all apt scholars who "[did] not need much urging." Even Rallie, not yet five, was "learning very fast" according to his brother Loyal, who was the most faithful of the boys in writing their father. George got along well enough in his studies, but he was lazy and cross at home, and Almira had begun to doubt whether school was the best place for him. It was a situation that once again made her wish that his father were home to see to things—or that he would take George to the mines to work with him there. George was not a bad boy, but it was time he began to earn his way. Indeed, she had thought for some time that he was old enough to work for his board.[104]

It was a natural enough thought, for Almira was once again feeling the weight of financial problems as the winter of 1863–64 came on. Although entirely out of cash, she felt she could not raise the rent on the hotel, partly because she figured the Putnams were paying all they could afford to pay, since "it costs so much to keep up fires and lights" and business was not likely to be nearly as good through the winter as it had been that fall. Besides, she liked the couple; they were hard workers who had "made something" of the place.[105]

Almira fretted over Mr. Putnam's ill health and lamented the extra load Mrs. Putnam was forced to shoulder. Indeed, she and Ada were so sad "to see that old lady always at work" that they did all "the chamber work" for her, as well as washing dishes and taking on other chores around the hotel. "Always pleasant" and ready with "a kind word for every one," Mrs. Putnam was grateful for their help. Almira was called on to help another friend that fall when the Moshers lost the newborn that Almira had helped care for in the spring. Lafayette Mosher, an attorney, was away when the infant died, and they "had to bury it before [he came home]." Almira spent several days with the distraught mother, offering what comfort she could, taking care of the two older children, and sewing a tiny shroud for the infant.[106]

That fall of 1863, although their families down in Douglas County could not know of it, Daniel Stearns and Alonzo Brown were busy trying to cut their losses in the Salmon River country by centering their energies on the new mining towns in the Boise Basin. Closing up the store in Florence, Alonzo spent two months packing goods from Lewiston to Warren, where the mining, and hence the merchandizing, was still good. As the heavy snows began, Daniel left the store in Warren in charge of a friend and joined Alonzo in his winter camp in the Blue Mountains between Lewiston and Walla Walla.[107]

At home in Roseburg, with no recent word from their husbands, Almira and Ada prepared for the holidays. Almira complained in each letter to Daniel that it was hard to continue to write when her letters drew no response, but she admitted that Roseburg was "very gay" that winter of 1863–64. The Putnams had a New Year's ball at the American, which drew about thirty couples—"all the Married people that dance"—and everyone had a "very pleasant time." Holiday festivities did not ease her worries about George, who was "very anxious to go north" with his father. Anticipating Daniel's contentions that life in the mines was too rough for a boy of George's age, Almira noted, "I am sure he could not get into a worse place than this drinking and Gambling are the chief amusements night and day sundays and all."[108]

Others were equally disillusioned with life in Roseburg. Times were hard for most of the townsfolk, and early in 1864 there was much talk of relocating. The Heinebergs headed down to California, the Dearborns left Roseburg "for good," and John Floed again went north to check prospects in Portland and Walla Walla. Unable to consider a move herself, Almira was once again hard pressed for cash. After loaning Ada Brown twenty-five dollars, she had only enough left to pay her February room and board and the impending school taxes. She tried to sort through her expenses, noting, "It seems to me that I spend a great deal, but five boys wears out a good many Clothes and boots and shoes." Her world brightened considerably when she received from Daniel two early February letters carrying not only news to ease her loneliness but also money to ease her financial worries.[109]

In answering Daniel's letters, Almira shared news from her long-silent brother-in-law, John Stearns. He had moved south into the new gold country and wanted her to advise Daniel to join him in booming Bannock. Although Almira dutifully passed the word along, she would have preferred to advise Daniel to come back home instead of heading off to new goldfields.[110]

Inspired by his brother's invitation, Daniel set out for Bannock in early spring, sending Almira no word of his whereabouts and thereby jeopardizing yet another opportunity to end their indebtedness. In April, while Daniel was off in southern Idaho, Silas Crane, owner of the highly successful Eagle Hotel, approached Almira with an offer to buy the American. She immediately took the matter up with Stephen Chadwick, a local attorney, asking him to draft whatever legal release would be necessary in order for her to complete the transaction on her own. But all the while she feared Crane would reconsider and withdraw the offer before either she or Chadwick could get a response from Daniel.[111]

As she had predicted, by the time Daniel wrote to Almira saying he was back in the Salmon River country, Silas Crane had, indeed, "got off the notion" of buying the American and had invested seventeen hundred dollars in the house and store the Dearborns had newly vacated. That was no small loss, but Almira blamed the fates, not her husband, for their misfortune: "It seems to me that you and I were born under an unlucky planet for if other people buy property they can sell it but not so with us. . . . I fear we shall always have a farm and Hotel."[112]

At least she would have a bit of cash on hand as well, for upon his return to Florence, Daniel sent home enough greenbacks to allow Almira to pay most of the debts that had accumulated over the long winter. The money was "all gone so quick" that more bills remained, and in mid-May of 1864, for the first time in her husband's three-year absence, Almira asked Daniel to send a specific amount—$150— feeling that sum should allow her to pay bills and "get along for some time."[113]

Financial pressures had begun to ease somewhat now that George was earning his keep by clerking for John Fitzhugh, "a very stern man of good habits" who had taken over the Heineberg store when that couple left for San Francisco in the spring. The new job kept the young man well occupied, since he not only worked in the store, but also slept there and took his board with Mr. and Mrs. Fitzhugh. Happy in his work, George seemed "just fitted to the store" and was looking "more manly than he did when he went to school."[114]

With George no longer in residence at the hotel and Ada Brown and her children off visiting Priscilla and Henry in Elkton, the early summer of 1864 was relatively quiet for Almira. There was some political activity, including "a great deal of stump speaking." Governor A. C. Gibbs, who had managed the American Hotel before the Stearnses bought it in 1859, came back to Roseburg to speak. Mrs. Gibbs had sent Almira "a nice Book by the Gov so it seems with all her prosperity and station she has not forgotten her old friend." While Almira had agreed with what the governor had to say, she feared that the "secesh," who had "mustered quite a force in and around Roseburg," might beat some of the Union candidates.[115]

The town was abuzz with other news. Mr. Rinehardt "got tired of living and took 12 grains of sthrychine," dying three days thereafter. Mr. and Mrs. Kearny, a young couple wed only that spring, had been "both very much surprised with [an early summer] baby." Though Mr. Kearny had denied he could possibly be the father and had left bride and baby behind, Almira was convinced the infant was indeed his. Along with Thomas Hyland's other former parishoners, Almira was saddened to hear that the Hylands had lost their little boy to dysentery. Having heard but little from Martha and Tom since their move to California, she felt awkward about responding to such tragic news herself and sent their letter on to Daniel, urging him to write condolences to his sister and brother-in-law.[116]

She had happier news to share when her friend Ada Brown finally returned to Roseburg from her long visit at Elkton. In early June, Daniel had sent her $750, far more than she had asked for and far more than she thought she could use. Because no letter had accompanied the money, Almira remained mystified about what Daniel intended her to do with it. After using $150 to pay off all her remaining debts, she sequestered the remaining $600 against her husband's instructions, which she felt must surely be forthcoming. Puzzled as to why Almira received far more than she had requested and Ada received none of what she asked, the two women were also left wondering what plans their husbands were making for the new season in the mines.[117]

That season was to be far easier than the previous one for the partners. Without the store in Florence to concern them any longer, they concentrated on the new store in Warren and on packing supplies between Warren and their supply base in Lewiston. In their absence, their families in Roseburg faced new crises. In mid-July Freddy Brown, now just over two years old, was seized by a fit. Undecided about its cause, the doctor prescribed a dose of "gallop and Rheubarb." With the boy deathly ill for an entire week, "better one day and worse the next," Almira remembered as clearly as Ada the fall of 1861, when the Browns had lost year-old Edgar, and she advised Daniel that "Mrs Brown is nearly crazy for fear [Freddy] will die you can tell Mr Brown what you think best."[118]

At about the same time Almira was helping Ada through Freddy's illness, the Putnams gave their notice. Managing the American had been a year-long struggle for them, and at the end of their lease, they returned the hotel to Almira, worn out by the effort. With no hope of finding another manager, or a buyer, Almira once again took over the hotel herself. Discouraged, she wrote to ask Daniel if he intended for his family to stay in Roseburg through yet another winter. "It seems ages since I have seen you," she wrote him. "I dream of you often but something is always wrong." What was wrong, of course, was the seemingly endless separation. She longed for the time when the family could be together and live without struggle. Still mindful of Ada Brown's recent crisis, she hastened to add, "I think it would be very wrong for me to complain with all the comforts of life and good health [and] my children."[119]

Even so, she longed for Daniel's company and support and was both amazed and delighted when, just before Christmas 1864, both he and Alonzo Brown suddenly appeared in Roseburg, set on wintering over with their families. Predictably, the partners set out for the mountains again in the spring of 1865, and this time eleven-year-old Loyal Stearns went with them. Ever since his bout with scarlet fever, the boy had been given to bronchial infections, and there was reason to believe that a season in the mountains might restore his health. Almira would miss her son, but she knew he would be in good hands, for Loyal Brown had invited his young namesake to spend the summer at his family's hotel at Mount Idaho. Even if mountain air did not cure her son's ailments, at least his journey north would give him what Almira had always wanted to give George—the opportunity to escape the monotony of life in Roseburg.[120]

After dropping his son off with the Browns at Mount Idaho, Daniel continued on up into the mountains to open up shop for another season. Yet even as he made his way toward Warren, Daniel Stearns was revising his plans. Although he and Alonzo had already decided to move their operations to the busier mining camps in southern Idaho, Daniel could muster no enthusiasm for the move. At forty-four, he had finally had enough wandering; he was ready to return home and settle in with his family. While he had not made a fortune in the mines, he had made more than enough to pay off his debts in Roseburg, and with the savings he had sent Almira the spring before, plus what he could get now by cashing in his assets, he should be able to buy cattle and equipment needed to reestablish his family on the farm in Elkton.

With this plan in mind, he sold off the remaining stock in Warren, closed down the store, and set out for Walla Walla, where he found Alonzo ready to depart for Boise with a string of loaded pack animals. When Daniel told his partner of his decision to sell out and go home, Alonzo was readily amenable. He himself had entertained similar thoughts. The two men divided the pack train in half—right there in the street—then proceeded to Baker & Boyer, where they took their gold from the vault and divided it in half. As simply and as quickly as that, the partners who had known "three years of ups and downs" without ever "a discordant word" passing between them dissolved the business.[121]

Converting his share of the gold dust to greenbacks, Daniel Stearns sent the money home to Almira and then made one last trip to Florence to sell his share of the stock and the train left there. Then, having disposed of all his goods and equipment, Daniel Stearns started home. After stopping off at Mount Idaho to pick up a hearty and robust Loyal, he continued on to Lewiston, thence to Walla Walla, and eventually to Portland. From there he took the stage to the state fair down in Salem, where he invested some of his packing profits in the family's farming future. Thus it was that on an Indian summer day father and son arrived in Roseburg in a farm wagon pulled by two mules and followed by a mare and her colt, two horses, and several head of cattle.[122]

Whether Almira had had the pleasure of anticipating her husband's homecoming or whether Daniel and Loyal simply appeared at the American Hotel that mid-September day in 1865, one look at the entourage accompanying them must have told her what she had no desire to know—that the farm in Elkton was to be their home. Daniel had his reasons for ignoring his wife's oft-repeated statements about never wanting to live in that "lonesome place" again. After all, Almira herself had complained often enough about the problems of raising children in Roseburg, and "not knowing what [else] to do with [the boys]," he had "decided to return to the farm at Elkton for their benefit." The American Hotel was again put on the market, and the Stearns family packed their household goods and moved to the ranch.[123]

Although the farm had fared well enough under Alexander and Henry Brown, the later years under less careful tenants had taken their toll. In essence, Daniel and Almira started over in Elkton, but they reentered farming at a fortituous time. Partly because of the activity in the mines to the east and partly because of the natural fertility of the surrounding country, Douglas County prospered from 1865 into the 1870s, and Daniel prospered with it. Having brought home sufficient capital for expansion, he added more acreage to the 640-acre farm. He added livestock as well. When sheep raising, primarily for wool, became an important industry, he invested in sheep. When hogs became a good source of income, Daniel raised hogs. For his own pleasure, he raised and traded horses, and "for a number of years he had the fastest trotting horses in the county."[124]

Despite all the signs of prosperity, Almira's second sojourn at Elkton was no more to her liking than had been her first. Having lived in the midst of Roseburg's bustle for more than six years, she was suddenly confined to the relative isolation of the farm. Ada Brown, her dearest friend, was now some twenty-five miles away, living on 320 acres Alonzo had bought in Oakland.[125] At least with Priscilla and Henry Brown living less than a mile away there were shared Sunday suppers to look forward to, but those visits were virtually Almira's only contact with society. And she no longer had the children for company. George was clerking at a store in Oakland, and his brothers were intermittently away at boarding school.[126]

Whether because of Elkton's unbearable isolation or because of the exhaustion that set in after so many years of coping alone during Daniel's time in the mines, Almira's health began to suffer soon after the family's move back to the farm. Having handled all things in Daniel's absence, she was unable to handle even her own accustomed duties for some years after his return. As depression and the "change of life" took her in their grip, Dr. James Cole became a frequent visitor at the farmhouse. He advised Daniel to get someone in to help Almira with the chores and to "get her out more." As a result of Dr. Cole's advice, Marietta Ransom, a thirteen-year-old girl from Scottsburg, came to live with the Stearns family in the winter of 1867, taking on the responsibilities of the household whenever Almira was confined to her bed, a frequent event throughout the Elkton winters. Arba's age at the time of her arrival, Marietta became the daughter Almira never had, becoming as much apart of the "schooling done around the dining room table in the evening" as were the Stearns boys themselves. Even so, when the boys were gone, the house seemed empty, and over the winter of 1868–69, with both Loyal and Arba away from home at Umpqua Academy, Almira rarely got out of bed.[127]

Her spirits lifted with the coming of spring and the promise of good company. In response to an invitation from his brother Loyal to run a store he had just bought in Elk City, Alonzo Brown sold off his livestock, rented out his Oakland farm, and moved Ada, Minnie, Freddy, and baby William onto a farm near those owned by Henry and Priscilla Brown and Daniel and Almira Stearns. The reunion that ensued was to prove as important to Ada as to Almira, for while Alonzo was away in the mines, fourteen-year-old Minnie died of typhoid fever.[128]

Soon thereafter, Daniel began to take seriously Dr. Cole's prescription of more "outlets" for Almira. With the boys now of an age to look after things at home, the couple traveled more, visiting with Martha and Thomas Hyland up in Astoria and taking in the state fairs at Salem. In the early 1870s, Daniel decided to seek public office once again. Fourteen years earlier he had served as treasurer of

The Stearns family, about 1885.
Almira and Daniel, seated, with
their five sons: *(left to right)*
Arba, John, Loyal, Ralph, and
George. *(Courtesy the Stearns
Family and the Douglas County
Historical Society)*

what was then Umpqua County, and in 1872 he ran an active, though unsuccessful, campaign for a seat as state representative of Douglas County. In 1874, when "the people quietly nominated" him on a reform ticket, he did virtually no politicking and yet "was elected by a good large majority" of the citizens of Douglas County.[129]

Shortly thereafter, he and Almira bought a second home in Oakland, where George, now married, had settled. They stayed there more and more frequently, leaving ranching responsibilities to their younger sons. The move into town not only acknowledged the coming of age of the boys but also brought Almira back into the company of Ada Brown, who had returned to Oakland after Minnie's death brought Alonzo home from the mines.[130]

Since Almira's loneliness at the ranch had been all the more acute during Daniel's trips to the legislature in Salem, the move to Oakland came just in time. Over the course of the decade, Daniel Stearns became increasingly involved in politics, and in 1878 he was joined in the Oregon House of Representatives by his son Loyal, who had read law with former Governor Gibbs. In 1880, Daniel ran for, and was elected to, the state senate. At about that same time, he began to invest in land outside Oakland, putting together eleven hundred acres a mile and a half west of town. This time, Almira welcomed a move to the country, for her new home was not only conveniently close to town, but also next door to George and his wife, Nettie, who owned the neighboring acreage. With two grandchildren at her doorstep, Almira found that her needs had finally coincided with those of her husband.[131]

Over the next decade, with the help of his son Ralph, Daniel Stearns developed the ranch outside Oakland into one of the county's most prosperous, and George did equally well on the adjoining acreage. Never one to let progress pass him by, Daniel, at well over seventy years of age, planted thirty acres of hops and twenty acres of prune trees, opening up two lucrative and relatively new agricultural ventures at a time when most men of his age were enjoying retirement. On Sunday afternoon, January 3, 1897, in the company of children and grandchildren, Daniel and Almira Stearns celebrated their golden wedding anniversary at their home in Oakland.[132]

In the fourteen years left to them, the couple continued to travel frequently, enjoying visits with Loyal and his family in Portland and with Martha and Tom Hyland in Astoria. At home in Oakland, they had a vigorous social life, highlighted by frequent dinner parties.

Almira Fay Stearns at eighty-two, 1907. *(Print Collection, A6354, Special Collections, University of Oregon Library)*

During their visit to the World's Fair in Portland—the Lewis and Clark Centennial Exposition of 1905—their only concession to age was to "hire chairs" to take them out to the midway.[133]

Soon thereafter, advancing age began to curtail their activities, as Almira, now well into her eighties, grew increasingly frail. Death took their closest friends—first Ada Brown and John Stearns, then Priscilla and Henry Brown and Thomas Hyland—and on Sunday, February 6, 1911, at the age of eighty-six, Almira herself, "one of the oldest and most highly esteemed pioneer women of Douglas County," died of pneumonia at her home in Oakland, with her husband and her five sons at her bedside.[134]

Daniel spent the next few months composing a history of his life for his sons and grandchildren, ending his memoirs with a telling sentence: "I have lived in this country fifty-four years and have never had a fight or a quarrel with my neighbors or anybody else, which I think is a pretty good record, considering the strenuous times we passed through in the early days." On October 27, just eight months after Almira's death, Daniel Stearns died at age eighty-nine. His property was divided among his five sons, with his youngest, Ralph, who had stayed on to farm the Elkton place with his father, inheriting that acreage and carrying on the farming and ranching operation that his father and mother had begun.[135]

IV

Sarah Burgert Yesler

"I Will Endeavour to
Look upon the Bright Side"

When, in the fall of 1857, Henry Yesler finally wrote to his wife, Sarah, in Massillon, Ohio, to ask that she and their son, George, make plans to join him in Seattle, she was torn. She had by then been separated from her husband for six long years while he was exploring the Pacific Northwest in search of the best location for a sawmill that would supply the lumber needed in California's boom towns. Once before she had made elaborate preparations to join him, only to be told at the last minute that he had changed his mind and preferred that she wait until he was better established. Faced now with a second invitation, Sarah wavered. She hesitated to subject a twelve-year-old boy to the perilous ocean voyage and to expose him to the frontier conditions in the rough little settlement that was rising on Puget Sound—especially since Henry envisioned their move west as temporary.

Thus Sarah made up her mind. She herself would join Henry, but she would leave George behind in Ohio to board with her brother in Cleveland. His schooling would not be disrupted, and he could wait for them in a familiar, stable environment. Although her decision went against Henry's wishes, in the end he acquiesced. In June 1858, Sarah said goodbye to her son, assuring him that they would all be together again in a very short time, and left for New York, where she had booked passage on a steamer with the five-hundred-dollar draft Henry had sent to cover her expenses. She could not have known it at the time, but that fateful passage marked the end of her life in

Ohio, for, despite her husband's predictions to the contrary, she would spend the rest of her years in Seattle.[1]

❧❧❧

A child of the frontier, Sarah Burgert Yesler was the daughter of Ohio pioneers. Her father, David Burgert, had come as a young boy to Stark County with his family in 1814. Six years later, David married Elenor Huet and settled in the newly formed township of Paris. Late that same year, their first daughter, Elizabeth, was born, and, on June 18, 1822, their second, Sarah, arrived. Over the course of the next few years, three more children—Adam (1824), Catherine (1826), and Mary Ann (1828)—were born to David and Elenor.[2]

By the time little Sarah was six, the family had moved some forty miles southwest of Paris to New Bedford, in the corner of Coshocton County. There life went on much as before, punctuated by the arrival of Sarah's five youngest siblings: George (1830), James (1832), Lucinda (1834), Amanda (1835), and Amos (1836). Then in 1837, either during childbirth or shortly thereafter, Elenor Burgert died, leaving her husband with ten children, ages sixteen to one. Care of the children fell briefly into the hands of the two older girls, Elizabeth and Sarah, though David Burgert eventually remarried.[3]

During the years immediately following their mother's death, David Burgert's children made lengthy visits to their Grandmother Burgert's and to the households of various Burgert aunts, uncles, and cousins back in Stark County, catching what lessons they could in whatever schools were in session and drawing upon experience for the rest of their education. By 1838, the year Sarah turned sixteen, she was spending as much time with relatives in and around Paris as with her father and his new wife down in New Bedford, and she had begun keeping company with an ambitious young Massillon carpenter, whom she met through mutual friends in Paris. Twenty-eight-year-old Henry Leiter Yesler had been settled in Massillon for about a year at the time and was feeling quite at home in a community almost as German in its heritage as his hometown of Leitersburg, Maryland.[4]

Born on December 4, 1810, in a brick-faced log house on Antietam Creek, Washington County, Maryland, Henry Yesler was the son of Catherine Leiter, grandaughter of the German immigrant for whom the town had been named. His father, Henry Yesler, reportedly married his mother just before or shortly after she gave birth. The marriage, if indeed there was one, lasted only long enough to give young Henry a paternal surname. The divorce, if indeed one was necessary, freed both parties, and Catherine Leiter soon married D. L. Lowman, with whom she had three sons and two daughters. Growing up in the home of his stepfather, Henry had almost no contact with—and very little use for—the father he felt had deserted him. Toward his stepfather Lowman he felt gratitude, if not love, and he was quite fond of his half-siblings.[5]

Henry barely tolerated school, preferring fishing and swimming with a group of boyhood friends, among them Louis Ziegler, Tim Roath, Christian Welty, and Josiah Harris. At seventeen, Henry became a carpenter's apprentice, thus beginning the trade that was to be his support for the next decade. After three years of apprenticeship, working for his board and twenty-five dollars a year, he advanced to journeyman.[6]

This promotion seems to have prompted an urge to wander, and in 1832, at twenty-one, Henry Yesler set out to visit the German-American settlement of Massillon, a favorite destination in those years for many of the emigrants who poured over the National Road that passed through Maryland near his boyhood home. Founded some six years earlier, in 1826, Massillon was an important part of the Ohio canal system. A bustling village of about one thousand people, it offered ready work to the young carpenter.[7]

Despite his apparent success in Massillon, Henry remained restless, and in 1835 he moved to Cleveland. Soon thereafter, he joined a boyhood friend, Christian Welty, in an exploration of the Ohio and Mississippi rivers, a trek that took them as far south as Natchez and New Orleans before discouragement and low wages sent them north again to New York, Philadelphia, Baltimore, and Washington, D.C., then back to Leitersburg in 1836. Upon his return home, Henry began calling on Barbara Ziegler, the sister of his friend Louis. But in late fall Henry left Barbara and Leitersburg behind and headed for Natchez once more, trying to entice another boyhood friend, Josiah Harris, now a physician, to join him there. Harris was tempted, but ultimately decided against the move, since "the sickly season" was over and there would not likely be enough business to warrant making the trip.[8]

Finding the economy in Natchez little improved, Henry traveled back to Massillon, where he quickly established himself in the community. Almost as quickly, he met and began to court a petite young woman with bright blue eyes and a ready smile. Sixteen-year-old Sarah Burgert was not at all intimidated by the fact that Henry Yesler was twelve years her senior, nor did she mind that having the affection of the ambitious young carpenter meant having that of his boyhood friends as well, for they had, one by one, established themselves in Ohio. Tim Roath, who had opened a print shop in Gnadenhutten, not far from Massillon, shared Sarah's love of books and exchanged some favorite novels with her. Josiah Harris included messages to her in notes written to Henry from Coshocton County, where he had taken up practice near Sarah's family. Both Tim and Josiah were present on New Year's Eve 1839, when Henry Yesler and Sarah Burgert were married in the Baptist Church in Massillon.[9]

Even though their closest ties were to Henry's friends and Sarah's siblings, the newlyweds participated in the larger world of Massillon. An agricultural and industrial center, the city had nearly doubled in population in the few years since Henry's arrival there, and such growth provided plenty of work for carpenters. Among his other projects in the early 1840s, Henry built two water-powered sawmills and the Charity School of Kendall, "a substantial brick structure."[10]

In the course of this work, Henry met John E. McLain, a kindred spirit whose entrepreneurial endeavors had made him a wealthy man. In January 1839, during the early months of Henry's courtship of Sarah Burgert, John McLain had married Eliza Austin, and the friendship of the two wives grew quite naturally out of the amiable business relationship enjoyed by their husbands.[11]

Although Sarah's friendship with Eliza meant she was often a part of the nursery scene in the McLain household, which welcomed a daughter and two sons over the next few years, Sarah herself continued to read novels, entertain friends, and visit relatives, unencumbered by the arrival of children. Then, sometime around 1844, Sarah gave birth to a daughter, who died before her first birthday. By 1845, Sarah was pregnant once more, and late in that year or early in the next she bore a son, Henry George. The baby's arrival gave Henry reason to rethink the future. Taking stock of the opportunities afforded by Massillon's building boom, he sought to increase his profits by acquiring a water-powered sawmill on the Tuscarawas River, an operation that produced the lumber for many of Massillon's new structures.[12]

But over the next few years, the boom slowed in Massillon, and as

Henry Yesler approached his fortieth birthday, he had little to show for years of hard work. Once again he fell prey to the old wanderlust that had set him on the road in his younger days. Burdened by a good many debts, he still had enough money to take him west and enough faith in the booming economy set off by the rush for California gold to believe there would be work aplenty for him there. Others from Massillon had already made the trip and were reporting favorable opportunities in every line of endeavor. He would go west, leaving Sarah in the company of good friends and caring relatives. Once there, he would consider the possibilities, establish himself in some sort of work, and send for her—or else come home with enough money to give them a financial boost there in Ohio.

When Sarah agreed to the plan, Henry began to prepare in earnest for his journey. By the end of September 1850 he had sold his sawmill, dam, and all adjacent property for five thousand dollars. Throughout the fall he continued to liquidate his assets and pay off his most pressing debts, though he was hampered by his inability to sell several town lots he and Sarah owned.[13]

On April 1, 1851, having done all he could to close out his real estate dealings, Henry transferred power of attorney to his friend John McLain, whom he also entreated to act on Sarah's behalf in all personal matters. Several of Sarah's relatives agreed to check in on her, and her bachelor cousin Levi Burgert, who was clerking in Massillon, arranged to take his meals at the Yesler house on Muskingum and Charles. Sometime during the first week in April, confident that his wife and son were in good hands and having settled his business matters as best he could, Henry Yesler said his goodbyes and set out for New York, where he took a steamer bound for the Isthmus of Panama, some five thousand miles south and west.[14]

Even though there had been nearly two years of heavy traffic along the water route Henry Yesler took to San Francisco, the difficulties of travel had lessened little since the first group of easterners pushed off in search of gold. Passengers were still subject to the whims of weather during the nine-day voyage from New York to Chagres, Panama, and once disembarked at Chagres, Henry faced a three-day trip in a dugout canoe poled by a native bungoman up the Chagres River to Gorgona, then a day's journey by muleback along narrow, muddy trails through a countryside rife with tropical diseases.[15]

Having survived the discomforts of the isthmus crossing, Yesler arrived in Panama City and, within a day or so, boarded one of the newer Pacific Mail steamers bound for California. Traveling second class, he enjoyed the relative comfort of one of several bunks in a cabin on the main deck as the ship plied its way toward San Francisco, some three weeks to the north.[16]

Arriving in California in good health and high spirits, Yesler quickly surveyed job opportunities and determined that his best chance lay in Oregon Territory, since most of the lumber coming into San Francisco was being shipped from Portland. Booking passage on still another steamer, he arrived in that city sometime in May 1851. As he had anticipated, the lumber business there was booming, and his skills were sorely needed. He at once secured work as a carpenter and millright, earning eight dollars a day. By mid-June he had surveyed the situation and made a decision. There were already two mills operating in Portland, but neither could saw long, square timber. By building a mill that could cut timbers in great demand and short supply, he could set his own terms with contractors in San Francisco.[17]

Convinced that the opportunity warranted the risks it would entail, Yesler wrote John McLain, outlining his plans and asking his friend to research the availability and cost of the mill he envisioned —a portable unit powered by a twelve-horsepower steam engine. McLain estimated that such a mill would cost at least two thousand dollars and wrote Henry that he would "Scratch around and get the cash." It would take time to find the right manufacturer and raise the money, but McLain thought he could have the mill delivered to Portland on or before the first day of April 1852, "without I Should kick the bucket."[18]

In return, McLain asked Yesler to garner information on whether he might not be able to "make a fortune" by sending out plow irons, along with a man to "wood them." Ever the entrepreneur, he was ready to take advantage of any opportunity Henry thought might turn a profit. He was even ready to go out himself, should Henry think it wise. And should he make that trip, he might have company, for Sarah was discussing the plan with him, trying to figure out "what kind of trip it would be for her . . . wheather it would be good for her health or not and wheather she could cook for her board when she got out their."[19]

From the day Henry left Massillon, Sarah focused on the means and the timing of her trip west. Yet her days in the first year of Henry's absence were filled with many of the same activities as they had been in his presence: visiting with cousin Levi as he came in for meals; with her twenty-three-year-old sister Mary Ann, who visited frequently in Massillon; and with Eliza McLain. She also stayed in close touch with John McLain, who was hearing from the West more often than she. Sarah was well aware of the interest those around her took in her husband's welfare. Frequently people stopped her on the street to ask after him. Some wrote directly to Henry, asking for his opinion as to the opportunities, climate, culture, and economy of the West Coast in general and Portland in particular. In February 1852, Sarah learned that at least two couples, the Buckinses of Cleveland and the Canes of Massillon, had made firm plans for a trip to California, and she began to favor making the trip with them rather than waiting on John McLain, who seemed so unsure as to when and whether he would go west.[20]

McLain was not alone in his ambivalence. No matter how Sarah pressed Henry on the topic, he remained, for the most part, unresponsive to her proposals to go west. Not getting answers to "letters that ought to have been answered long ago" caused Sarah "a great deal of anxiety," since without his advice she could not "tell how to calculate or know what to do." Then, soon after deciding to set up his own mill in Portland, Henry sent the long-awaited letter, advising her to sell all her furniture and prepare herself and George for the trip. Eager for the promised reunion, she quickly rented out her house to Mr. and Mrs. Harper Partridge and began pricing her goods for the sale—only to receive a follow-up letter from Henry stating that "for various reasons" he could not advise her to come. Having already signed the rental agreement with the Partridges, Sarah was now faced with the dilemma of whether or not to carry on with the sale of her household goods. Since the only reason Henry had given for the suggested delay was that "she might not like it there," she reasoned that if he could "stand it," she could, and she carried on with her sale and her plans for a trip to Portland sooner or later.[21]

Unable to discern exactly where her husband was, and uncertain as to what would happen if she and George reached Portland and found he had moved on, she reluctantly gave up her plans to sail with the Buckinses and Canes. With half of Ohio bound for the West Coast, she chafed at being left behind. "Mr. and Mrs. Cane take the cars at 11 oclock tomorrow on there way to Cleveland," she wrote Henry. She regretted the loss of such "a golden opportunity" and doubted she would ever have "a nother such a chance."[22]

She was disappointed not only in not making the trip but also in not making what she had hoped from the sale of her goods. She had taken in less than two hundred dollars, a sum she felt would have been considerably higher had any one of her friends or relatives "interested them selves for me." She was particularly distressed over the behavior of her cousin Levi, with whom she had been quarreling over the increase she had asked in his board: she needed at least $1.75 a week, a fair enough rate, since others had been asking $2.00. Levi justified haggling for a lower rate because he "brought [her] home a little marketing occasionly" from the store in which he clerked, but since he had been known to charge her for some items she requested but never got and to charge her twice for some of the things he did manage to bring home, she hardly felt obligated to give him special consideration. Ever since their falling out, Levi had, in effect, ceased to care "how [her] affares" got settled. During the sale she had "had to depend on strangers altogether," and the experience had been a sobering one that left her uncharacteristically despondent—"feel[ing] at times as though [she] had not a friend in the world."[23]

Now that the Partridges were leasing her home, Sarah had become a renter herself—in her own home—an arrangement she liked "better than housekeeping" and thought might be cheaper in the long run. Pleased with their new quarters in the Yesler home, the Partridges seemed to enjoy having Sarah and George live with them and saw no reason for her to make any other arrangements before her move to Oregon. Having her near was a comfort to the couple, especially since Mrs. Partridge was pregnant and had been "threatened with an abortion."[24]

McLain had first promised Henry that he would have his mill equipment by April 1, but unforeseen delays in its shipment raised the possibility of Sarah's going west that summer on board the same ship that would carry the machinery. After due consideration, she decided that since it would be "very sickly to go in June," she would wait until the following spring. Less patient than his mother, six year-old George entertained himself with fantasy trips to the frontier and sent his father imaginary tickets home.[25]

Both George and Sarah were strong and well, though she was frequently bothered by problems arising from Henry's unsettled business affairs. A coffee merchant had presented her with a bill for one hundred dollars, claiming her husband had taken coffee beans west with him. Should she pay it or insist that he write Henry? She wanted to stop the *Star* and the *Massillon and Canton Democrat*. What papers did Henry see in Portland? Would he like the *Star* sent to him? She had been thinking that vegetables must be very dear in a sparsely settled place. Might they not profit from raising produce for sale? Would Henry consider starting a garden so that it would be well seasoned by the time she and George arrived? After more than a year's separation, she was eager for reunion, and she assumed Henry would send for them as soon as he had his machinery.[26]

She was to be disappointed. Eager as he was to pick up his mill, and assuming it had, indeed, been shipped on April 1, Henry left Portland for San Francisco without waiting for word as to which ship would be carrying the crucial cargo. His abrupt departure was triggered by another factor. He had decided that Portland was not the place for a mill of the kind he'd envisioned. The Columbia River bar presented major problems for heavy cargos, as the recent wreck of the *General Warren* had graphically demonstrated. Furthermore, he now saw that getting timber out of the forests and down to his mill would not be the easy task he had once supposed. Resolved to find a better situation, he set out for California to learn what he could from mill operators there while keeping an eye out for freight shipments from New York.[27]

Henry's unexpected departure from Portland left Sarah and John McLain at a loss. Further delays meant that the mill did not actually leave New York City until May 27 of 1852, though Henry was already making inquiries at the wharf in San Francisco as early as mid-April of that year. Frustrated after weeks of waiting for equipment that never arrived, Henry decided that there was little future in hanging around the San Francisco wharf and hired a man to wait in his stead, ordering him to inquire after all freight shipments coming in from New York City and to notify him as soon as the mill arrived. Now free to explore opportunities elsewhere in California, Henry set out to learn what he could about commerce in the area. Over the course of the next few weeks, he packed salmon in Sacramento—for the cash and the experience—and mined gold along the Bear River, where provisions and lodging were so high and wages were so low that he quit after realizing that he had, in effect, lost thirty-three dollars in three days' labor. Moving on to Marysville, north of Sacramento, he found work as a carpenter that paid eleven dollars a day. By mid-May, Henry had decided to stay there until his mill came in, and he wrote Sarah to that effect.[28]

She, too, was on the move, making the most of George's summer holiday by joining Eliza McLain and her children on a leisurely trip to see friends and relatives in northern Ohio and Illinois. Sarah looked forward to the visiting—and to the chance to be away from the house at Muskingum and Charles for a while. With the coming of hot summer days, life there had begun to wear on all parties, and the very pregnant Mrs. Partridge had found George "to[o] stir[r]ing and noisy."[29]

The trip began under conditions that were hardly more pleasant than the situation she left at home. On the first night out on the packet that carried them up the canal to Cuyahoga Falls, seven-year-old George "had quite a hard chill," then a high "feaver all night and vomited freely." After transferring in the middle of the night to "the cars," Sarah, the desperately ill George, Eliza McLain, and her four children arrived in Cleveland in mid-morning. With all due haste Sarah proceeded to the home of friends, where she practiced a bit of hydropathy, putting George "in a whet Sheet which brook up the feaver," and from that moment "he commenced getting better."[30]

So much better, in fact, that by the following evening Sarah, Eliza, and all the children boarded a Lake Erie steamer bound for Toledo. There the two friends parted company. Sarah and George spent nearly a month stopping over with friends from earlier years. Visit after visit filled Sarah's days in that month, and no new enterprise missed her astute business eye. She could see that Toledo itself was "a great buissness place." However, she did not think that she would like to live there, for it was "a very durty looking place" and "so scattered that it is a long walk to any place." Even so, she predicted "in 4 or 5 years [it would] look very different when they get all the swamps and hollows filled up." One of the families she stayed with had about twenty-five acres of land under cultivation just outside Toledo and were "raising vegetables for the market," an activity she had earlier suggested to Henry might be a profitable enterprise in Oregon.[31]

Bidding goodbyes to friends in Toledo, the two women loaded children and trunks onto the steamer and retraced their route across Lake Erie to Cleveland, where Sarah and George set out on another round of calls to various and sundry acquaintances. Among them was an old friend, Dr. Sam Underhill, who had become a medium and was "buisy with the spirits." Cleveland was preparing for a spriritualism convention over the Fourth of July holiday, and Sarah predicted there would be "an awful shaking of Dry bones." She was familiar enough with such goings on, since she and Henry had known several spiritualists in Massillon, where the movement was quite popular. Skeptical as she was about the validity of table rappings and other such activities, Sarah nonetheless found her curiosity aroused by those who professed to cross known borders and commune with the dead.[32]

Leaving Cleveland behind them, the Yeslers and the McLains spent the week of the Fourth in Akron with Sarah's brother Adam before finally taking the packet south again to Massillon. When Sarah and George at last arrived home in mid-July, they found they needed to be quieter than ever in the house, for Mrs. Partridge had been delivered of a son in their absence. Sarah wondered once more at the wisdom of having gone through with the sale of her household goods, thereby committing herself to a peripatetic life. The prospect of a long wait without the comfort of a home of her own looked less and less attractive, now that her departure date for the West seem more and more distant.[33]

Henry had good reason to be reluctant to send for Sarah and George. His summer in California had made him even more doubtful about where to place his mill. How could he ask his wife and son to join him when he had no clear idea of where he would be by the time they got there? At one point he had been as enthusiastic about settling in Marysville as he had been earlier about settling in Portland. In fact, he had almost signed a contract for a partnership with a "mill man from Maine" who proposed to share in the expenses of setting up a mill and then "go halves" in the profits with loggers who would cut timbers all winter and float them down the Feather and Yuba rivers during spring runoff. But, at the last possible moment, Henry had reneged, pronouncing the plan too risky because the streams were "too precarious." The more he thought about it, the more convinced he was that the best prospects were to be found in the Northwest. Henry's opinion in this regard was strongly influenced by reports he heard from an enterprising ship's captain who saw vast lumbering possibilities along the thickly forested shoreline of Puget Sound. The area was also reported to have the excellent agricultural land that would be needed to sustain a settlement. Impressed, Henry Yesler determined to check out the captain's story.[34]

Returning to Portland, he picked up his mail and settled various business matters before taking a boat up the Columbia and Cowlitz

rivers. Traveling overland to Olympia, he transferred to a dugout canoe in which he made his way through the islands along Puget Sound, past the tiny settlement of Tacoma, and on to New York, a village on Alki Point. Although the area boasted fine forests and there were already several families living there, Yesler dismissed Alki as a mill site because it was not a suitable location for loading ships with heavy cargo. Leaving Alki behind him, he poled his dugout along the Elliott Bay shoreline to the mouth of the Duwamish River, where he staked his claim to land he thought might be suitable for a mill site. But he was unwilling to settle there until he had checked out the fledgling village of Seattle; pushing off again, he continued up the coastline, arriving at his destination—a mere clearing in a towering forest—on October 20, 1852.[35]

Settled in the spring of 1852, Seattle, like Alki Point's New York, was engaged primarily in cutting timber and piles for shipment to San Francisco. Rustic and rough as it was, the place seemed promising to a man looking for the ideal site for a steam-powered mill, and its citizens welcomed the idea of a mill that would build up the trade essential to their economic survival. However, because all waterfront property had already been claimed, Yesler realized he could not possibly operate in Seattle and resigned himself to returning to the claim he had staked at the mouth of the Duwamish. Unwilling to lose the prospect of a mill, two Seattle men, Carson D. Boren and David S. Maynard, who had staked their own claims in the spring, offered to adjust their boundaries to give Yesler the frontage he needed on Elliott Bay, plus a connecting strip of land that would link the frontage property to the rest of his holdings. That strip was the key to his future in Seattle, since access to open water was essential to his plans for shipping his products down to San Francisco. Such boundary adjustments were simple enough, since the claims had not yet been officially filed at the land office in Oregon City. In fact, Maynard himself had received a similar favor upon his arrival and was ready enough to do what he could to entice Yesler to stay on in Seattle.[36]

The Oregon Donation Land Law enabled Yesler to claim 160 acres for himself and 160 for Sarah. The claim was most irregular in shape, for the deal he had struck with Boren and Maynard meant that, in addition to the main portion of his land, Yesler owned a long panhandle about 500 feet wide and a mile and a quarter long stretching down to the bay. The bulk of Henry's claim, plus Sarah's, was a

rectangular block on the eastern end of the panhandle, with the "pan" falling on the north side of Henry's corridor to the sound. The bulk of their acreage extended well beyond the boundaries of the village to within half a mile of Lake Washington.[37]

The village itself was primarily confined to a small, bulbous peninsula around a quarter of a mile long and not more than thirteen hundred feet wide. Stretching out south of Yesler's panhandle, the peninsula was connected to the mainland by a marshy neck of land so low that during high tides Seattle became virtually an island. On the east the peninsula was bordered by an all-but-impassable slough that separated it from the hills beyond. The mainland along Yesler's narrow corridor consisted of heavily timbered hills crossed by a few Indian trails.[38]

All through the late summer and early fall of 1852, while Henry was drifting around California and contemplating possibilities in the Puget Sound area, Sarah and George were caught up in another round of visiting. Both of them were in good health, and George was growing so "tall and sli[ght]" his father would not know him. The boy's growth was remarked on by all the Burgert relatives they visited in Canton, Paris, New Bedford, Nashville, and Navarre. After "put[ting] in the summer pretty well," Sarah and George returned to Massillon, once more as boarders in their own home.[39]

Having adjusted somewhat to her state, Sarah was nonetheless discouraged at the prospect of still another year in Ohio without her husband. "It looks far ahead to wait another year," she wrote him. "As long as I was preparing to go to Oregon the time seemed to fly. I never knew the weeks to be so short, but since that, time lags." She could manage anything for a while, but she warned, "2 years is as long as I can think of staying alone, if you intend staying longer I think I must come out. Life is but short at most, and I think it is well to spend as much of it together as we can, and then I think it will be better for George."[40]

Adrift as she was and almost totally reliant upon the kindness and hospitality of relatives and friends, she expressed a deeper concern: "If fortune is propitious and you live to return all will be right, but there are so many chances against you, it is this which causes me so much anxiety could I be assured of your safe return I should be quite content, but should anything so unfortunate happen which I pray God it may not I should be much more contented to be housekeeping or at least to have the means to go to housekeeping. . . . I should

not feel so dependent." Despite these fears, she added, "As you say it is no use to cry for spilled milk what is done can not be undone [and] I will endeavour to look upon the bright side."[41]

That became increasingly hard to do as fall came on and she received no definite word as to her husband's whereabouts. By late October, while Henry was filing the papers that would link his destiny to Seattle, Sarah and his friend John McLain were growing more and more uneasy about what might be happening to the mill McLain had shipped to San Francisco. Their latest letter from Henry, sent in late August or early September, had told them of his plans to explore the Puget Sound area and advised them to address all correspondence to him at Seattle. This news precipitated a crisis, for Henry himself had to be at San Francisco when the mill arrived or risk having it "sold for transportation," about five hundred dollars.[42]

With the fate of the mill resting on Henry's appearing at the dock, shipping papers in hand, in time to prevent the agent from selling off the cargo to cover freight charges, Sarah was unwilling to trust to the new Seattle address alone. Ever since receiving the first letter that told them Henry was no longer in Portland, McLain and Sarah had both written multiple copies of all letters concerning the mill, sending them to every address they thought might be valid: Portland, Sacramento, Marysville, San Francisco. Now that Puget Sound had been added to the list, McLain had washed his hands of the matter, saying he was "tired [of] writing so often and about the same thing." Leaving this final round to Sarah, he had entrusted to her the one remaining copy of the shipping papers. He had sent his other two copies in previous letters, and Sarah advised Henry that he could expect to find them "at one or the other" of the places to which McLain had mailed letters. She now directed the final copy of the shipping papers to San Francisco, assuming that the mill and papers would at least be in the same city at the same time. Weary with copying letters over so many times, she wrote the bulk of her news in the letter she sent to San Francisco, keeping the November notes sent to the other locations to a minimum: "The mill was shiped on the 27 of May on a shipe called the Wm H. Harbeck concined to yourself at sanfrancisco. Mr Mclain has sent you 2 lots of shipping bills and i now send you in your letter to sanfrancisco the third and last lot if these get lost Mclain says he can do no more for you." Frustrated by her inability to contact her husband, Sarah noted, "Mr. Mclain thinks it passing strange that you do not get his letters and none of mine."[43]

Communication on the home front was proving to be almost as frustrating to her as communication with Henry. In December, Sarah's twenty-three-year-old brother George decided on impulse to take a steamer to California. Traveling down to Massillon to say goodbye to Sarah and her son, he found they were away in Paris, attending the funeral of Grandmother Catherine Burgert. Although Levi Burgert told him that the two were "both in the Enjoyment of good health" and would likely want to accompany him west, George was due back in Akron the next day and could not afford to wait for them.[44] Thus Sarah returned from the funeral to find she had missed still another chance for reunion with Henry.

Not that she would necessarily have been as eager to pack up and go as her cousin Levi had supposed. Henry's letters had been so sporadic that she had no way of knowing what progress he was making in Seattle—or whether or not he was even still there. Indeed, he was not, but was instead en route to San Francisco to meet the vessel bringing the engine and saws shipped months earlier. During his absence, workers began construction on a shed to house the mill, and in early 1853 the mill and other machinery finally arrived in Seattle and were rafted ashore.[45]

Within a few weeks, Yesler had established a pattern of operation that was to serve him well for years to come. Loggers felled trees and cleared land in the hills above the mill, then sent timbers sliding down a skid road etched into the panhandle of the Yesler property. After splashing into the bay just north of the mill, the logs floated within the confines of Yesler's boom until they were needed, at which time they were taken from the water and deposited in a sluice extending from shore to millshed. Within that shed, Yesler turned out the rough-hewn lumber that helped raise the city of Seattle. By late summer of 1853, twenty frame buildings dotted the shoreline. While sawing lumber for early Seattle dwellings was an important service to that tiny community, milling profits obviously lay elsewhere, and most of the lumber was rafted out to ships bound for San Francisco and other California boom towns.[46]

As more and more California orders were received, Yesler's mill began operating around the clock to keep up with the demand, turning out fourteen thousand to fifteen thousand board feet of rough lumber during two twelve-hour shifts. The largest—and for a while, the only—industry in Seattle, the mill employed most of the able-bodied laborers in the area. When no white workers were available, Yesler hired Indians, establishing a new precedent. An anomaly among Seattle's white settlers, Henry not only treated his native employees fairly, but also found no fault with his white employees who lived with "their squaws."[47]

Back in Massillon, Sarah received relatively little news of such matters. Indeed, she continued to know virtually nothing about her husband's life in Seattle—not even where he lived, though that dwelling would eventually become legendary. Some months before he had set up the mill, Henry had used hewn logs to build the twenty-five-foot-square cookhouse that would serve as his home and office for the next six years. But the cookhouse on the shore of Elliott Bay became far more than a roof over Henry's head and a place for hired hands to take their meals. Just as his mill became the center of industry, so his cookhouse became the center of civic activity. As the only lodging available for visitors along a hundred miles or more of shoreline, the cookhouse served Seattle, with its population of fewer than fifty, as courthouse, post office, church, jail, town hall, military headquarters, storehouse, tavern, hotel, and meetinghouse.[48]

The Yesler mill was off to a good start. During 1854, Yesler shipped out a dozen loads of lumber, most bound for San Francisco, but one to Honolulu and one to Australia. Frustrated by the difficulty of rafting lumber out to the deep water where the ships were moored, he constructed a makeshift pier out of slabs, the beginnings of what was eventually to be a sturdy wharf one thousand feet long. Optimistic citizens believed that Seattle would become the San Francisco of the North and talked of the coming of the transcontinental railroad that would one day make the city as easily accessible by land as it now was by sea.[49]

If high hopes and fine profits tempted Henry Yesler to send for his wife and son, he soon had reason enough to be glad he had not done so. In 1855, lumber prices dropped sharply in California, and Yesler's market collapsed. Competition had been growing steadily, and there were now some twenty-four sawmills on Puget Sound. Yesler was competing with mills controlled by wealthy San Francisco businessmen, who often owned the ships on which lumber from the Sound was transported.[50] He did what he could to find markets beyond California, but he soon had no need to run the mill day and night. As he was forced to lay off more and more of his millhands, settlers began to worry about a recession.

In addition, they worried about growing Indian unrest. Governor

Isaac Stevens had signed treaties with the tribes on both sides of the village, but those documents did nothing to end recurring disputes. The Yakimas beyond the Cascades were furious when miners crossed their hunting grounds en route to gold strikes beyond, and white settlers feared the Yakimas would influence the more peaceful tribes around Puget Sound. Tension between whites and natives heightened when an Indian agent ordered the removal of Seattle's "canoe Indians" to the west shore of the sound. Yesler had denounced this decree as certain to cause more racial troubles. Persuading the Indians to camp close to his mill, he continued to allow them to work when he had lumber to cut, a move that prompted critics to dismiss as self-interest his plea on their behalf. As tension mounted, a blockhouse was built in the middle of the village, a company of volunteers was raised, a U.S. naval ship was sent to patrol Elliott Bay, and nearly one hundred settlers from the surrounding area left their homes and sought the security of Seattle.[51]

In early January, with the Indian seige and winter weather keeping him confined to quarters, Henry found time to pen a letter home. It was this New Year's letter that gave Sarah her most detailed look at the realities of her husband's life in Seattle. "I inhabit a portion of a castle situated in the center of the city at the waters edge," Henry wrote, "in fact the castle is on pillows [pillars] one half over the sea and the other half at times on dry land." The main dining hall boasted a gigantic fireplace, and a modest woodstove stoked by an Indian boy warmed his own room. He sat in one of two chairs that faced the stove, his gun by his side. In the far corner were the stretcher and blankets that served as his bed. Although his "castle" served as cookhouse for millhands, Henry himself generally took his meals at a boardinghouse and, occasionally, at a private home.[52]

Henry had company in his residence. "On the next floor there lives a large number of people of different shapes [and] forms . . . and they speak all sorts of languages." He shared his home with a variety of animals as well: "On the floor and in the hall and other rooms near me there is a great variety of inhabitants such as dogs a tame deer hens cats etc etc etc Directly under my room there is a space that the sea does not wash into and that is the favorite resort of Hogs of all sises."[53]

It was to this "castle" that the Duwamish Indians brought word one day in late January 1856 that warriors from across the Cascades were preparing to attack Seattle. Acting on this tip, Marines called ashore from the naval ship in the harbor fired a howitzer toward the woods where, according to Yesler's informants, hostile natives were lurking. When the shot roused the Indians hiding in the brush, what was to become known as "the Indian attack on Seattle" began. In the brief siege that followed, two townspeople were killed. The Indians themselves sustained no casualties, but they were quickly routed. Having successfully withstood the assault, Seattle residents used lumber from Yesler's mill to erect a double-walled stockade around the village on three sides. When they added a second blockhouse, the small settlement took on the appearance of a fortress.[54]

Appointed acting Indian agent for the area in the wake of the attack, Henry Yesler persuaded 150 Indians to move from Seattle to a site on Bainbridge Island. By late 1856, no more than fifty natives remained in Seattle proper, most of them living in shacks built from scrap lumber donated by Yesler's mill. Believing that trouble with the Indians could be traced to "worthless white [men]," Yesler did what he could to establish peaceful relations between the two races, work for which he received the praise of the *Olympia Pioneer and Democrat.*[55]

Yesler's efforts at peacemaking notwithstanding, the conflict of 1856 took its toll on the population of Seattle. With outlying homes destroyed, food supplies low, farmers bankrupt, roads impassable, and business stagnant, the *Olympia Pioneer and Democrat* reported that the area was "literally used up and rubbed out, so far as population, property, or the necessaries of life are concerned." With the mill operating at far beneath its capacity, unemployment was high, and many loggers and millhands moved to Port Gamble or other settlements on Puget Sound where larger mills offered more job security.[56]

Ignoring the exodus, Henry Yesler stayed on. Seattle held too much promise for him to give up now. Those who hung on after the Indian attack talked once more of the need to establish a new economic lifeline, perhaps a railroad linking the city with the coal mines of eastern and southern Washington. As the Indian conflict had shown, there was great need for an overland route into the town, perhaps even a road stretching from the Mississippi to the Pacific by way of Snoqualmie Pass.[57]

While the railroad and highway were no more than wishful thinking, such thoughts helped keep Henry Yesler in Seattle—even when his wife was writing to urge him to cut his losses and come home.

Certainly, by spring of 1857, Sarah Yesler had had her fill of waiting. Having vowed she would stay behind no longer than two years, she had, in fact, already spent six waiting for her wandering husband to come home or send for her. Not quite five when his father set out for the west, George was now almost eleven and hard put to remember the man whose sporadic letters were filled with talk of a sawmill on Puget Sound. In Sarah's view, further waiting was not to be tolerated. For over two years she had heard nothing but bad news from her husband. Clearly, it was time for him to sell out and come home. Although Massillon, like the country as a whole, was suffering economically in 1857, at least she and Henry could weather difficult times together.[58]

Henry was equally eager for a family reunion, but he had no intention of leaving Seattle. In late August 1857 he admitted to having "fooled nearly two years away," yet insisted, "I think it will pay to stop here awhile longer. . . . To leave now at a sacrifice, at a time, too, when I can make something, looks like bad management." He would prefer "to come home . . . if it were possible, and stay there," he assured Sarah, but he had had no decent offers for his mill and could hardly afford to sell at a substantial loss. Things would surely pick up again soon, and when that happened, he would be in a position to make sufficient profits to ensure their future. On the other hand, with business at a standstill, his days and nights were long and lonely; if Sarah and George would come out for a visit, they would be able to share whatever time remained to him there and to see Seattle for themselves.[59]

Coming after them himself was out of the question, since he could hardly afford to be that far from Seattle when the lumber market might shift for the better at any moment. Rather, if it suited her, Sarah and George could travel west in the company of a Mr. Meigs, a Bainbridge Island mill owner who had returned to the East for supplies and would be leaving New York sometime early in 1858. Not knowing whether Sarah would be comfortable traveling in the company of a stranger, he suggested that, should she decide to come, "Perhaps there might be some one of your female friends or acquaintances who might like to come with you. If so bring one along perhaps some girl might be willing to cook for the mill for which she would get 40 or 50 $ per month." Now that the mill was running only daytimes, her cooking load would not be heavy, since "our family consists of about 5 white men and about as many Indians." In any event, the decision was entirely up to Sarah. He would send her the money needed for the trip, and "if it suit[s] you to come when Mr. Meigs [does] it would be all right, and if it [does] not suit you, . . . you could come at another time," he wrote her.[60]

Faced with the alternatives outlined in Henry's letter, Sarah debated her course of action. While willing enough to make the journey herself, she was uncertain about what to do about George. A well-traveled lad who had seen all there was to see of the country that lay between the many friends and relatives they had visited during the years of separation from Henry, the boy had long been promised the greatest journey of all—the voyage to Seattle that would reunite him with his father. Yet how could she justify exposing him to the dangers of ocean travel and the diseases of the tropics, especially since he would be facing those same risks all over again on the return trip to Massillon? And why interrupt his studies and take him to a frontier town where his schooling was sure to be inadequate? Why not leave him for a year or so with her brother Adam and his wife, Lizzie, who were now living in Cleveland? George knew his aunt and uncle well and would feel perfectly at home with them. Why take chances, when he would be safer and perhaps even happier in a familiar environment?

Even though George would be disappointed at first to be left behind, Sarah concluded that making the trip alone was the wiser choice. On November 14, 1857, her mind made up, she sat down to write her husband that after nearly seven years of separation, she was on her way to Seattle to be with him. That letter was filled with questions about what to bring, what to do about matters at home, and what to expect upon her arrival, but when Henry received it in early January, one section caught and held his attention—the paragraph explaining Sarah's decision to leave George back in the States.[61]

He sat down at once to pen a reply: "I do not like the idea of George not coming out." His forthright objection was followed by lines implying far greater emotional ties to his son than he had ever expressed before: "I want to see him very much. I have bin deprived of him so long that I am nearly crazy to see him as well as you." As to her argument concerning the importance of having George continue his schooling back east, he noted, "His being out here two years would not deprive him of a good Education," for education did not take place in classrooms alone. The very experience of spending "a couple years in this country would be equal to several years in an old place," he claimed. If

Sarah insisted on formal schooling, there was "a first rate school taught in Olympia" and the boy could be sent there to board.[62]

As much as he disagreed with his wife's decision, Henry realized that his years of absentee fathering left him little room to argue with her. A fair man, he noted, "I will not urge the matter too strongly, as you have had all the care of him for several years and I have not. It is perhaps no more than right that you should do as you think best." Having begun his letter on a negative note, Henry went on to answer Sarah's questions as best he could. As to her "effects" at home, he had no words of wisdom but advised her to discuss the matter with Mr. McLain and "do what you think best." His own books and papers could be left in McLain's care.[63]

In the years since his own journey west, there had been so many changes that he could not answer any of her questions concerning what to expect on board ship. Aware that she might be too frugal to take proper regard for her own safety, he added, "This I will say take passage on a first class boat and come comfortable . . . unless there were several of you togather and all concluded to go second cabbin, and even then it would not be so pleasent for a lady." She was not to worry about the cost of the trip. He was forwarding five hundred dollars to her through a Mr. Blinn in San Francisco. He himself planned to meet her in San Francisco, but if anything happened to detain him, she could count on Blinn to meet her and entertain her until his own arrival from Seattle, provided she wrote the man to inform him of the name of her ship and her anticipated time of arrival.[64]

As he drew to a close, Henry came back, once more, to the topic with which he had opened: "The more I think about George not coming the less reconciled I am. I want to have him about me not-withstanding he will be well provided and cared for, still he will. . . ." Scratching through those last three words, Henry let the matter stand, adding "The steamer is coming & I must close."[65]

In less than two weeks, Henry received yet another letter from Sarah, one in which she noted that she planned to sail in January, meaning that he had little hope that any reply he sent now would reach her before she left Massillon. Nonetheless, he dashed off a few lines to warn her that the five-hundred-dollar draft he had sent her through Blinn had been drawn on a company that had subsequently "suspended" business. The draft might not be honored; if that was the case, she must let him know at once, so that he could make arrangements to have another one sent.[66]

Other things were on Henry's mind. In discussing with friends and relatives the advisability of taking George west, Sarah had obviously shared her husband's plans to return to the East within the next two years. He now cautioned her against "saying too much about your returning in two years as it will show that I am determined to sell out and those who intend to buy may take advantage of it and not give me as good a bargain as I otherwise might get. It is always best not to let every one know all your plans & calculations." And he added a note of resignation: "As regards George I have concluded to be satisfied with what ever you think best."[67]

He might as well have been satisfied, for Sarah remained resolute in her plans to go to Seattle alone—even though her departure was delayed when she was, as Henry had feared, unable to cash the draft Mr. Blinn had sent her. She wrote at once to inform her husband of her plight, but letters from Massillon were usually several weeks in transit. Under the best of circumstances, it would be early March before he received her letter, perhaps mid-March before he could make arrangements to have Mr. Blinn send her a second draft out of San Francisco, and sometime in April before she would receive the new draft. When Mr. Meigs insisted that he was not at all inconvenienced by postponing his departure on her account, Sarah settled down to await the arrival of the new draft. The long delay would not make saying goodbye to George in May or June any easier than it would have been in January or February, but it would at least give them a few more months to enjoy each other's company.[68]

Out in Seattle, Henry was also making the most of those months. Satisfied that Sarah would soon be arriving and certain that she would not be pleased with life in the "castle," he set out to build her a house. With plenty of time and lumber at his disposal, he planned and constructed a six-room frame house not far from his mill site. An ample front porch ran the width of the dwelling, and a six-foot facade rose above the porch roof, giving Sarah's new home the storefront look common to California gold-rush towns. Whatever its limitations, the house represented a considerable improvement over the old cookhouse Sarah had assumed would be home.[69]

Unaware of the surprise that awaited her, Sarah continued her preparations for the journey west, leaving Henry's books and papers in the care of Mr. Mclain and outfitting George with clothes she hoped would be sufficient to get him through at least the first year of her absence. Around the end of May, she completed the last of her packing, made a farewell visit to her father and stepmother down in New Bedford, said her goodbyes to the McLains and other Massillon friends, and made her way to Cleveland to establish George in the home of Adam and Lizzie Burgert. By early June 1858, she was kissing her son goodbye, bound for New York, from whence she embarked for Panama, traveling first class, as Henry had advised, in the company of the patient Mr. Meigs.

The ship stopped only once on its way to the isthmus—in Kingston, Jamaica. Soon underway again, the passengers arrived in the Caribbean port city of Aspinwall a scant eight days after their departure from New York. In stark contrast to Henry's trip across the isthmus six years earlier, Sarah's was made in relative ease by train, which carried her to Panama City in approximately four hours so that she was able to board her ship on the Pacific Coast that evening. Stopping only at Acapulco for fuel and supplies, Sarah's steamer made the voyage to San Francisco in fourteen days, arriving in early July, her entire trip having been accomplished in three weeks.[70]

When the steamer docked, thirty-six-year-old Sarah Burgert Yesler made her way onto Central Wharf, where she was not surprised to be met by Mr. Blinn instead of Mr. Yesler. To compensate for his absence, Henry had arranged for her to meet and be entertained by several of his acquaintances in the city, captains of the ships that transported Yesler lumber from Puget Sound to San Francisco. Quite accustomed to being on her own among relative strangers, Sarah quickly warmed to the people who surrounded her while she waited for the steamer that would take her up to Seattle. She particularly enjoyed the company of Louisa Goodwin, a young woman who shared her interest in the theatre, and of Captain Pinkham, who escorted the two women to various social events.[71] So enjoyable did Sarah find the company and the culture in San Francisco that she was even somewhat reluctant to leave the city and embark on the last leg of her journey toward reunion with Henry. Nevertheless, a week after her arrival, she sailed north out of San Francisco toward Puget Sound.

Nothing she had read in Henry's letters could have prepared her for the sight that met her eyes as her ship eased its way toward Yesler's Wharf. Seattle was little more than a rude gouge in an otherwise unbroken expanse of trees. Smoke from her husband's mill hung in the air above the rough-hewn shanties that were home to the sparse populace, and behind the mill stretched the long, deep scar of the skid road that carried logs from the hills above to the boom below. The waters no longer lapped at the pilings of Henry's "castle," for sawdust from the mill had so completely filled in the upper reaches of the marsh that the cookhouse now sat on something resembling solid ground. And beyond the scatter of houses and shops were acres and acres of stumps, testament to the extent of the logging and clearing operations of early settlers.

Even as Sarah peered out at the ragged skyline of the village, its residents were observing the approach of the steamer. By the time the ship nudged against the pier, a small welcoming committee was on hand, led by a short, stout, bewhiskered man dressed in a proper, if disheveled suit. The acknowledged leader of those in his wake, forty-eight-year-old Henry Leiter Yesler stepped forward to embrace his wife and introduce her to Seattle and its inhabitants. Her arrival was cause for rejoicing, for "well-reared white women" were in scarce supply on Puget Sound, where males outnumbered females nine to one.[72] There was less cause for rejoicing on Sarah's part. Making her way down the wharf and onto the muddy trails that served as streets, she had reason to question the wisdom of her decision to see for herself the wonders of the West.

Even as she traversed the sea of mud and building debris that surrounded her new home, she saw at once what had to be done. Henry must have his men clean and level the lot and lay out a large garden in which she could plant the seeds she had been given by her sister Elizabeth Wilson back in Ohio. Since there was only one other building on the block, there would be plenty of room for an orchard as well. A line of saplings set out along the length of the house and small evergreens planted in the front yard would add warmth, and she countered Henry's protest that wandering deer would soon strip the bark from young trees with a plan for the construction of triangular corrals to protect the transplants through their first few growing seasons.[73]

Having satisfied herself that her new home would soon be quite livable, Sarah toured the mill site with Henry. The skid road so vital to his industry now had a log-lined bed that was greased periodically to hasten the speed with which timbers could be sent down into the sound. There was great demand for lots along the road—later to be known as Mill Road and ultimately as Yesler Way—and buyers were setting up a variety of businesses to meet the needs and satisfy the urges of the laborers. Backed by monies from Adams, Blinn, & Co. of

San Francisco, and in partnership with Captain August Rand, Henry had extended the wharf some two hundred feet into Elliott Bay, opened a general store, and set up a small gristmill. The sawmill, busier that season than it had been in a while, now employed about twenty men, including two engineers, four sawyers, three loggers, and two millwrights. Recently elected county commissioner, Henry Yesler was in a financial and political position to make a difference in Seattle.[74]

And so was his wife, Sarah, although her first business at hand after her whirlwind tour of Henry's empire was to sit down and write to the loved ones she had left back east—brothers, sisters, father, friends, and, of course, young George—and she began that task in the middle of July, within a few days of her arrival in Seattle. Hungry for any scrap of news she could obtain concerning George's adjustment to her absence, she asked about him in letter after letter, entreating those to whom she wrote to see him as often as they could and let her know how he fared. To all her correspondents she also wrote the expected news—details of what had turned out to be a very pleasant voyage to San Francisco, a description of her new home in Seattle, and discreet comments on Henry's business success.[75]

Having caught up with correspondence to relatives and friends in the East, she began a series of bread-and-butter notes to those who had befriended her on her trip west and during her week's stay in San Francisco. High on her list was Louisa Goodwin, whose company she had especially enjoyed in the city. Eager to have her friend see the contrasting sights of Seattle, she urged her to catch a mail steamer up to Puget Sound. But until Louisa arrived, Sarah had to content herself with entertaining local callers, most of whom were male. On the day after her arrival she had received two dozen calls from young men, and traffic had hardly slowed since.[76] In between visitors, she gave her attention to the many tasks attendant upon getting settled in for her first winter on Elliott Bay. Never too busy to walk down to meet the mail steamer, she continued to be disappointed at lack of mail from home until late October when she was handed an envelope in her father's ample, sprawling hand.

Not having been up to Cleveland since Sarah's departure, David Burgert had not seen George himself, but he reported that "Levi [Burgert] & wife were here in August and told me that he was doing very well." At any rate, he was confident that George "could not be plased in better hands." Sarah's youngest sister, twenty-three-year-old Amanda, had also spent the summer with Adam and Lizzie, studying music at Cleveland Conservatory, and she too wrote Sarah of George's happiness there: "George appears to be in very good spirits all the time and very well contented and enjoys himself very well. He says I shall tell you he wants you to write him a long letter. He wrote you last mail." All of them had thoroughly enjoyed Sarah's most recent letter, which carried a photo of Henry, and George had been pleased to see what his father now looked like. His Aunt Amanda insisted that Henry had "grown a good deal better looking" since leaving home.[77]

With letters from home renewing her confidence in her decision to leave her son behind, Sarah threw herself into the myriad chores that faced her in her new home and resolved to make the most of her relatively unencumbered days. Though she still looked forward with great anticipation to the long-planned visit of Louisa Goodwin, in the interim she enjoyed the company of Seattle's men and its few women. By the time of her arrival, Henry had already established an open-door policy that meant his wife might expect frequent company. Holiday entertaining, while necessarily considerably less elaborate than it had been in their old home in Massillon, could not have been any more appreciated, for settlers were starved for reminders of the life they had left behind. Caught up in her new rhythms, Sarah celebrated her first Christmas with Henry in six long years—and her first Christmas without George and without holiday visits from her siblings.

Homesick for friends and family, she wrote frequent and lengthy letters to Ohio. From one of George's former teachers, M. A. De-Votre, she learned that the Partridges had sold out in preparation for moving west. Massillon was "extremely dull . . . [with] nothing going on of consequence & property down to the lowest terms." The list of business failures was long and included solid citizens; the litany of the dead was equally long and included one of George's former classmates, young George Benskin, who had "died very suddenly with lung fever & pleurasy."[78]

The death of George Benskin made Sarah all the more eager for news from her own George—and all the more aware of how suddenly death could come, even to those who were in good health. She was stunned to receive word of the death of her brother-in-law Aaron Wilson, a robust man who had put off his own dreams of going west partly on account of the poor health of his son, Horace. The boy tended to be taken with "fits," and the shock of losing his father had precipitated a long round of seizures, leaving Sarah's sister Elizabeth bearing a double burden. While friends and neighbors had come readily to her aid, Elizabeth had been left in a precarious financial situation. Dependent largely on the money Aaron Wilson had been owed by his customers, she soon found that his debtors felt under no obligation to make reparation to a man who now lay in his grave. Seeing no recourse but to sue for payment, she had engaged a lawyer but was not looking forward to the legal battles she faced.[79]

Sarah's brother George was another frequent correspondent. Having decided that Nebraska offered more opportunities for him than California, George was settled now in Nebraska City, where he was a partner with his brother-in-law Jacob Hockstetter in the merchandising business, serving the thousands of emigrants who yearly passed through that settlement on their way across the plains. George sent news of his own situation in Nebraska, but he could not tell her much about his young namesake in Cleveland, since the boy had not written him "Since the Cows came home."[80]

As George Burgert wrote those words on June 1, 1859, he had no way of knowing that neither he nor anyone else would ever again receive a letter in his nephew's childish scrawl, for before month's end, Henry George Yesler was dead. Stricken quite suddenly with some virulent disease, George had grown steadily worse, despite all that the physician and his aunt and uncle could do for him. Just hours before his death, Lizzie Burgert had been forced to leave his bedside when she went into labor. The joy Adam and Lizzie felt at the birth of their first child, little Emma Amanda, was stifled by the sorrow—and the overwhelming sense of responsibility—they felt at the loss of their nephew. He had been entrusted to their care, and now he was dead. How could they write such news to his parents? Incapable of finding the words himself, Adam wrote to his father instead. A man of faith, David Burgert would be able to set the boy's death in perspective.[81]

Completely unaware of the tragedy back home, Sarah and Henry Yesler carried on with life in Seattle. San Francisco lumber orders were back up, and the mill was once again running steadily. Most of the trees Henry had set out around the house had taken, and Sarah was busy directing the planting of the promised orchard. Nothing they heard concerning business affairs back home made them eager to give up what they had begun there in Seattle. If things continued to go well, perhaps they should consider staying on. Sarah could go back for George, or someone could bring him out. Amanda, her youngest sister, still unmarried and intrigued by Sarah's stories of all the single men in Puget Sound, might be persuaded to bring the boy west.[82] And there was always his Uncle George. If trade in Nebraska City continued to dwindle, they could no doubt convince him of the advantages of a free trip west—in the company of his favorite nephew.

Oblivious to the tragic news that was making its way down the Atlantic, across the isthmus, up to San Francisco, and thence to Seattle, Henry and Sarah planned for their future and that of their son. When they met the mail steamer that midsummer day, there was no reason for them to register anything but delight at the sight of an envelope bearing an Ohio postmark. Yet when they had read the contents of that envelope, there was no reason for them to think of ever going back to Ohio again. To turn back now was to betray the dream that had taken them so far from their child. If they had no further hope of raising a son, they could at least do their part in raising a city.

Well aware that madness lay in dwelling on what they could not hope to change, the couple staved off the grief that threatened to consume them by directing all their energies toward the tasks at hand. Henry investigated new markets and shored up relations with old ones. If there was to be no selling out, then he would do what he could to make a success of the venture he had begun. For Sarah, diversions were harder to find, for the letters from home that had so long sustained her had taken on a peculiar and bothersome tone. No one, it seemed, could bear to mention the death of her son. Aside from the one letter that brought her the news, George's name was never mentioned. Week after week, month after month passed, and though she received about the same number of letters from home as before, she was at a loss as to how to answer them. Should she be stoical and follow the lead of her eastern correspondents, prattling on about personal and business affairs as if George Yesler had never existed? Or should she break their silence by admitting the grief that had overwhelmed her and the depression that threatened to engulf her? Choosing the middle ground, she wrote of life in Seattle, while carefully and openly responding to any news of death or suffering on the part of those to whom she wrote. Perhaps her response to even their smallest losses would inspire them to offer an honest, caring response to her larger one.

But if friends and relatives at home could not be depended upon for solace, those near at hand most certainly could. As she had earlier become close friends with Eliza McLain, wife of her husband's business friend, so now she drew close to several other women whose husbands had business connections with Henry, and to those women she talked freely of her loss. Since many of them were wives of the various ship's captains who boarded at the Yesler house during their layovers in Seattle, Sarah was soon entertaining friends from up and down Puget Sound, as well as from San Francisco. She and Henry particularly enjoyed the company of thirty-two-year-old Captain William Bushnell and his twenty-one-year-old wife, Rosa, residents of Olympia. Rosa Bushnell frequently accompanied the captain to Seattle, sometimes staying with the Yeslers while he continued on his journey through the sound. The Yeslers also visited the Bushnells in Olympia, where Sarah quickly made the acquaintance of Rosa Bushnell's closest friend, Eliza Ann Hurd, a twenty-six-year-old widow. To support herself and her infant daughter, Ella, Eliza had for a time run a small dressmaking shop in Olympia, though by 1860 she had rented it and her house out and had taken a room in the same boardinghouse as the Bushnells.[83]

Despite all the diversions offered by her new friends, Sarah's heart remained heavy, and early in 1860 her health began to fail. When her Olympia friends urged her to avail herself of "the water cure," she joined Eliza Hurd's mother, Salome Woodard, for several weeks at the baths in San Francisco.[84] Rejuvenated as Sarah was by her time at the baths, her return to the harried atmosphere of her home in Seattle almost instantly drained her energies, and she began to plan frequent trips away from home, counting particularly on visits with Eliza Hurd and Rosa Bushnell to sustain her. The frantic pace of the Yesler house, as well as the ache of George's loss, were left behind whenever she sailed to Olympia.

As important as her friendships were, Sarah still longed for the company of family members in the East. Although she had written her widowed sister Elizabeth, inviting her to come out to Seattle with her son Horace in the spring, it was early May before she finally received the long-awaited letter from West Bedford. It brought disappointment. "I can not go to Oregon this spring," Elizabeth wrote her, "for I can not get in my money." She had been successful in several suits against her husband's debtors, but Elizabeth had found that "it takes almost half the principal to fee the lawers." She did not hold out much hope of ever recovering her financial security, concluding, "Every person seemes to think that a widow can live on nothing."[85]

According to Elizabeth, Adam and Lizzie Burgert had left Cleveland for Toledo, where they now lived with their baby, Emma Amanda, who was nine months old and thriving. But this news had barely reached Sarah when it was countered by news from her brother George, still living in Nebraska City. Adam and Lizzie had lost their beloved little Emma in early April. "It sets hard on them," George warned her, "The[y] worshiped her to[o] much . . . . But why talk. They have given you the particulars long e're this."[86]

Adam and Lizzie had not, in fact, yet written Sarah the "particulars" of their loss, most likely because they had not yet found the courage to write her the "particulars" of young George's death. It was not until two months after his own baby's death that Adam finally penned the letter to Sarah and Henry in which he at long last acknowledged the death of their son. "All is lonely and desolate now Since we lost our dear Sweet little angel," he began. Thirty-five by the time of the birth of his long-awaited first child, Adam had seen in that little girl "our future hope prospects and happiness," and her "Sad loss" had thrown him into deepest despair. "Oh how I wish you could have seen her," he wrote Sarah. "She was a perfect Beauty and Smart and loved by Every Body that saw her."[87]

Having spoken of his own great loss, Adam at last confessed, "When I wrote you before I Never mentioned the death of Your Sweet darling Son George Yes darling I must call him for I thought quite as much of him as I could have if he had been my own son." He had never said as much to Sarah and Henry in the past because

When I wrote you I dared not mention his name knowing your grief was alrady quite as much as you could bare. I Recolect what you told me before you left that I could never appreciate the feelings a parent had for a child until I had one of my own. God knows I can Simpathise with you now for if Ever a child was loved by Mortal Man My dear little Emma was loved by me. . . . My only Consellation is now that the dear little Angle Babe is with her Father in heaven and much happier then I could have made her in this Sinful World. . . . You have the same conselation with your dear Boy he is reaping the benefits for his good and Kind Conduct and actions in this world. Oh how I wish I knew that George and My Baby would know One another in heaven I know that George would be so happy with my sweet little Emma Amanda.[88]

While her brother seemed reconciled to the idea that reunion with those who had departed this earth could be anticipated in heaven, Sarah herself had reason to hope for a more immediate reunion. Since George's death, spiritualism had taken on new meaning for the Yeslers. In Ohio they had dabbled with the movement; now they took it up more seriously. Almost from their first meeting with Eliza Hurd, they had been told of sessions in which mediums had enabled her to communicate with her deceased husband, James. Confessing that she would be totally crushed by the loss of her husband's physical presence were it not for the hope of reunion in a brighter world beyond, Eliza explained to Sarah how, through "the aid of Fancy," she was often "almost there."[89] Perhaps through mediums the Yeslers themselves could learn to commune with their beloved son.

As their friendship grew, Eliza Hurd's passionate attachment to her dead husband was transferred, in part, to a passionate attachment to Sarah, whom she declared to be "a darling & a great deal more that I cannot express," exclaiming, "If I only had hold of you I would squeeze you for half an hour." The women's friendship developed over frequent visits to each others' homes, during which time their affection frequently found physical expression. "Oh Sarah I wish to say so much and I cannot say anything—I want to sleep with you again! hey!" Eliza wrote her "darling sister Sarah" after a visit in Seattle. "I would like to step into your bathing room tonight and take an ablution, and you might shower me too, and I think I wouldnt squeal so bad." Apparently, the passionate nature of Eliza's attachment to Sarah caused Henry Yesler no great concern. Taking delight in the company of charming Eliza Hurd, he not only welcomed her into his household when he was away on business but also took no exception to Sarah's preferring to have Eliza share her bed on visits when both husband and friend were in the house.[90]

Eliza enjoyed an equally intimate relationship with Rosa Bushnell. Writing Sarah from "Rosa's cozy little home," Eliza reported that their mutual friend was ill and she was "putting her through a course of wetsheets, and she endures it like a hero." Disconcerted at Rosa's failure to take better care of herself, Eliza wrote, "Yes, I scold, and at the same time pet her, and rub her, etc., but I think all the time she needs a good spanking." Dependent as she was on Rosa's friendship, Eliza naturally fretted a good deal over the Bushnells' move from the boardinghouse they shared with her into a home of their own and over their subsequent plan to move to California. As the move to San Francisco loomed, she pressed Sarah to come down to Olympia, for if she did not come soon, she would miss what might be "the last time we three can be together."[91]

The pace of life at the Yesler household kept Sarah from making that trip to Olympia, and Rosa's disappointment matched Eliza's. "I have a powerful affinity for you . . . [and Eliza] is in love with you too," Rosa wrote Sarah on the eve of her move to San Francisco. With Rosa caught up in her move, Eliza concentrated on the sewing that supported her and four-year-old Ella, though she was eager to be done with it so she could be off to Seattle, since she was "just aching to get down there with [Sarah]." Planning to arrive within two weeks, she urged her busy friend to "work now" in order to enjoy "pleasure by and by on a more extensive scale, hey?"[92]

Even as Sarah looked forward to Eliza's next visit to Seattle, she was kept busy managing her household, which at that time counted, in addition to herself and her husband, eleven men, all between the ages of twenty-five and thirty-five, and all in the employ of the Yesler mill. Yet, having become a horsewoman since her move to Seattle, she reserved some time each morning for exercising herself and her horse, Jim, "a noble fellow." And she maintained business and social ties with acquaintances throughout Puget Sound. She kept her friend Eliza Hurd apprised of her travels, and after receiving a description of a trip to Fort Madison on Bainbridge Island, where Sarah had visited with her old traveling companion, Mr. Meigs, Eliza congratulated her on her "daring boldness" in "walk[ing] right into the affections" of a man, adding, "You are the most bewitching little Muggins I know of."[93]

While Sarah was enjoying such correspondence with her female friends, Henry Yesler was enjoying with several Seattle men a camaraderie that mirrored the male friendships of his more youthful years. In addition to his closeness to the sea captains who were often house guests in the years before Sarah joined him in the West, he had developed social ties with a select group of area businessmen. He and his cronies made it their business to socialize freely with members of the opposite sex, frequently playing elaborate pranks on prominent women of the city, a practice that Sarah apparently found quite acceptable, despite the obvious element of flirtation.[94]

Their increasing social ties in Seattle notwithstanding, Sarah and Henry remained closely connected to family and friends in Ohio, with Sarah writing frequent letters back east and relishing the letters that brought her news from home. Her sister Mary Ann, now thirty-two and still unmarried, wrote of the problems of remaining in her father's house, a dour environment at best. She had just finished a course in "pedagogical skills," and though she disliked teaching, she saw it as the best way to self-sufficiency and freedom from her domineering stepmother. With the dawn of 1861, her brother Adam wrote of political as well as personal matters, noting, "Our Cunt[r]y is in trouble and business of all kinds is dull and there is no telling when it will turn for the better." South Carolina's secession from the Union had triggered the withdrawal of four other states, and Louisiana and Texas were sure to follow. With rumors of war rampant, Adam was "looking forward to the glorious 4th of March when the Man old Abe will fill the place . . . and . . . their will be a change in the affairs of things."[95]

Sarah's widowed sister, Elizabeth Wilson, was, by her own admission, a terrible correspondent, but when Lucinda Hockstetter began to talk of a trip home from Nebraska City with her three little boys that summer, Elizabeth begged Sarah to make Lucinda's visit a real reunion and plan a trip home at the same time. They could "all meet at Fathers," since they could no longer gather at Sarah's home in Massillon. Elizabeth needed to see for herself that her two younger sisters were doing well, for she had long thought of Sarah and Lucinda as living in the midst of "Savage nations." Now she conceded that Sarah, at least, seemed to have "every thing convenient and nice about [her]," and she gave Henry "praise for always being a good man about having every thing nice and handy about a house," adding, "The[re] are but few that have the taste he has got about a house." While she was quite impressed by Sarah's report of Seattle's Fourth of July ball and pleased to know that her sister had so many "enjoyments" at her disposal, Elizabeth was sorry to hear that Sarah's failing health made life in Seattle less than ideal. "I hope you will attend to that in time," she wrote. "See some good doctor and get cured [for] health is more precious than wealth."[96]

Long before her sister's letter made its way into her hands, Sarah Yesler was already following the advice it carried. Persuaded by her friends in Seattle and Olympia, she had entrusted herself to the care of Dr. G. M. Bourne of San Francisco, a specialist in the water cure that had helped her in her months of depression following George's death nearly two years earlier. With the Bushnells now settled in San Francisco, Sarah did not lack for company in the city, including that of the well-traveled Eliza Hurd and daughter, Ella.[97]

Strengthened by her sojourn in San Francisco, Sarah was greeted by cruel rumors upon her return to Seattle. There were those who felt she had stayed away an inordinately long time—and for less than good reasons, since her illness had not been obvious to many of her Seattle acquaintances, who had thought her in excellent health. And while there were few, if any, who chastised Henry for having left his wife in Ohio for more than six years, there were a number who took umbrage with Sarah for having left her husband in Seattle for more than six weeks. Henry's reputation was now threatened by gossips who suggested that Sarah preferred the company of her women friends to that of her husband. Thus, however improved her health might have been by her treatment in San Francisco, Sarah fell back into the depths of depression shortly after her homecoming.[98]

Eliza Hurd did what she could to raise her friend's spirits: "Do let it all go a[s] idle chaff, which is not worth sifting," she counseled: "You who merit no such base slander—for slander it is when undeserved and I know from my associations with you Sarah—I think I know something of the innermost feelings of your heart—know them pure, enobling and true—and there are others, perhaps that know you equally as well, and knowing can not—will not—doubt your motive in coming to California."[99]

Writing from her sister's home in Santa Cruz, California, Eliza noted that little Ella was thriving in the fresh country air and that she, too, was empowered by the beauties of nature that surrounded her. Unfortunately, her sister's skepticism had limited Eliza's ability to commune with her late husband, and she longed for a "harmonious circle" in which she could "yield [her]self entirely . . . [to] "the Clairvoyent Sleep." Toward that end, she made plans for a summer visit with Henry and Sarah, when "We will indeed try to be harmonious and happy, [and] thereby be enabled to communicate with the unseen world."[100]

At about this same time, another Eliza sat down to write a letter to her dear friend Sarah Yesler, opening with a play on current events. "I begin to think that you have seceded entirely, if not from the United States from your friends who have been waiting very anxiously to hear from you," wrote Eliza McLain. Sarah's last letter, written to John McLain almost a year earlier, in August 1860, had informed him that she and Henry wanted to give the McLains the clothing, furniture, and household goods she had left stored in her old house, now occupied by the Hatmakers. Although they had done as she directed, Eliza had written to suggest that Sarah might want to consider keeping a few of her old things, and she had, to date, had no reply on the matter. "Are you tired of your old Friends?" she asked, adding, "I assure you that they are not tired of you."[101]

The Hatmakers were remodeling the old Yesler home, Eliza McLain reported, turning a closet into a bedroom, changing the kitchen chimney, and painting all the rooms. Lovina Hatmaker herself wrote Sarah, sending more news of Massillon and telling her "dear friend" how often her mind wandered back "to the happy days we spent together sitting hear together in this room how often I wish you were hear now."[102]

Despite the cheerful, caring tone of letters from her friends, Sarah's depression continued. The smoke that rose from Henry Yesler's mill and mingled with the mist that so often shrouded the little settlement lent an air of gloom that not even increased lumbering profits and interesting civic projects could dispel. All that spring of 1861, Sarah remained indisposed, and several letters from Dr. Bourne urged her to return to San Francisco, while warning her against putting too much faith in traditional medicine. He reminded her of the advantages of the water cure, especially in cases like hers. "Start with a determination to make everything secondary to the regaining of your health," he told her. "I am fully satisfied you never will recover unless you do take such a resolution."[103]

Friends from San Francisco wrote of the cures they had enjoyed at the baths, and Rosa Bushnell was especially eager to have her come down. The Bushnells had recently moved from the temporary quarters where Sarah had visited them in the winter to a new suite of rooms in a building on Montgomery Street, just off Market. Captain Bushnell added his own note, urging Henry to tell Sarah that "we enjoyed her visit very much and hope she will come again soon" and promising that if Sarah came down for a visit, Rosa might go up to Seattle and stay for a while.[104]

Rosa's invitation was tempting, but Sarah's experience with Seattle gossip kept her at Henry's side through the summer months. They were long and lonely months, for Eliza Hurd, who had been so eager to join Sarah in Seattle so that they could communicate "with the unseen world," had found sufficient diversions to keep her happily ensconced in Santa Cruz.[105] Both she and Rosa, who had never been as faithful a correspondent, wrote less and less often now, though Sarah kept up a flow of mail to California.

The buzz of activity on Elliott Bay helped Sarah to cope with her depression and get through the summer of 1861. Henry was completing Yesler Hall, a two-story frame building that housed not only the company store but also a theatre and meeting hall. Serving as hostess for events in the new hall, making her appearance at the annual Fourth of July ball, and taking care of her garden and orchard filled Sarah's days. But with the coming of fall, "the blues" once again got the upper hand, and she returned to California to take another course of water-cure treatment in Dr. Bourne's clinic.[106]

Completing that treatment, she took up life again in Seattle with new resolve, throwing herself into civic activities and assuming, at long last, the "first lady" status she had so long resisted. Focused as she was on her work in Seattle, she gave only passing thought to her friend Eliza Hurd's new fascination with Dr. Charles Henry DeWolf, a phrenologist, minister, and proponent of free love, newly arrived in Washington Territory from Philadelphia. From their first meeting, DeWolf had charmed Eliza with his talk of things beyond the ken of most mortals.[107] Her attentions were now directed more and more toward DeWolf and less and less toward Sarah. Accustomed to fluctuations in fortune and affections, Sarah carried on in style.

Then, in May 1862, some six months after Dr. DeWolf had arrived in Olympia, Puget Sound papers printed news that rekindled gossip concerning Sarah's association with a certain Eliza Hurd. In a free-love wedding ceremony performed without benefit of clergy or any other official personage, Eliza became the bride of Dr. DeWolf. The news rocked the region. DeWolf was described as a "peacock, whose little heart is one beating pulse of vanity," and many who had professed friendship with Eliza now renounced all ties to her.[108] In Seattle, Sarah Yesler was more understanding. In Charles Henry DeWolf, Eliza had at last met a man whose spiritualist leanings were equal to her own. No one any less liberal could have made her friend happy, and Sarah was quick to express her support of the couple.

From her new home in Victoria, British Columbia, Eliza responded at once: "Yes! dear Sarah, it made my heart glad . . . to still be able to count you as a _true_ friend." Praising her for "stand[ing] up bold and independant against the rushing tide of public or popular opinion" and for refusing to be swayed by "newspaper and gossip which is activated by nothing but prejudice and malice," Eliza urged, "Come! Yes! Self and husband come and see and hear for yourselves, then, of course you can better decide upon the merits or <u>demerits</u>, of the case." The good doctor, too, invited the Yeslers to come up and see them in Victoria, where they were doing a brisk business in phrenology, astrology, and seances, although they had been open for only two weeks. Despite the ardor of the invitation, the Yeslers never visited the newlyweds in Victoria nor entertained them in Seattle, and Eliza Hurd eventually faded from Sarah Yesler's life.[109]

Left on her own in Seattle and resolved to put behind her once and for all any gossip concerning her lack of devotion to her husband and the city he was determined to build, Sarah spent the next decade helping Henry Yesler achieve his dream. Sometimes her activities were those of businesswoman, notably during the mid-1860s, when she negotiated with George Plummer of San Francisco, who was principal stockholder for an unhappy while in the Yesler holdings in Seattle. Making frequent buying trips down to the city, she sympathized with Plummer's complaints about Henry's running his store on credit, all the while working to persuade Plummer that he must be more judicious in choosing the wholesalers he used to fill her orders and more prompt in shipping those orders to Seattle. Back home, true to her word, she worked to move Henry toward a "cash-and-carry" basis of operation, though Plummer's continued delays in stocking her shelves meant the store was never to be solvent.[110]

Social concerns also received Sarah's attention. In 1863 she joined Asa S. Mercer, the first president of the territorial university, in planning and executing what became known as "The Mercer Expeditions," trips organized to bring out from the East "a few hundred good women"—many of them Civil War widows—in hopes of improving the culture of the area and providing prospective brides to its many bachelors.[111]

During this same decade, Yesler Hall began to flourish as a theatre, and by April 1864 Seattle had seen its first traveling minstrel show. In 1865, Henry bargained with supporters of the annual Fourth of July ball for two hundred dollars as their contribution to Yesler Pavilion, a permanent replacement for the makeshift pavilions that had been erected and dismantled in years past. Larger than Yesler

Sarah Burgert Yesler at forty-six, 1868. *(Courtesy Special Collections Division, University of Washington Libraries, neg. no. UW2439)*

Hall, the new pavilion soon replaced the older structure as the city's cultural center, and a new stage was built. "Ventriloquists, magicians, minstrel shows, and elocutionary lectures" trod the boards of that stage, and it was there that Seattle's first grand opera and first Shakespearean drama were performed. Although such events gave Sarah Yesler a taste of the culture she had left behind in the East, Shakespeare at Yesler Pavilion was not unlike Shakespeare at the Globe, for latter-day groundlings who indulged in chewing tobacco made the floor "the receptacle of numerous large pools of tobacco stained saliva, through which the ladies had to wade upon retiring from the hall."[112]

With business booming, Yesler borrowed money enough in 1869 to erect a new mill, one large enough to enable him to compete more successfully with his rivals up and down the sound. Since he could now plane lumber as well as cut big timbers, he was in an even better position than before to be an integral part of the building boom that Seattle was enjoying. That summer of 1869, he tore down the old sawmill and put up new frame structures in its place so that a post office, tinsmith's shop, drug store, and several markets stretched out in what became known as Commercial Row. The 1875 *Weekly Intelligencer* cited Yesler as having "contributed more largely to the building of business structures in this city than any other property-holder." Expanding into real estate in outlying areas, Henry began to sell portions of the northern, or "pan," segment of his panhandle, offering "Suburban homes and retreats upon the delightful shores of Lake Washington," and the demand for lumber from Yesler's mill increased as new homes were erected in the subdivisions carved from his and Sarah's holdings.[113]

Yesler's interest in utilities also continued to grow. In 1865 he had expanded his primitive water supply system and established the Seattle Water Company, an enterprise that brought water down to the city by means of a pipeline of eight- to twelve-foot logs bored to four-inch diameters and joined together along a trestle. Primitive as it was, it met the needs of the townspeople and enabled Yesler to hold onto his water monopoly for a few more years. In 1869 he tried, unsuccessfully, to start a gaslight business so that the new homes on Elliott Bay could enjoy the latest in lighting. Though he failed in his first attempt, by 1873 he was a partner in a successful enterprise that lit up the homes of Seattle. Gaslights also lit up Yesler Pavilion, where district court meetings and public forums on the coming of the railroad were regularly held. Seattle was booming, and at the center of the boom was a bearded, burly little man who was hardly ever seen without a few sticks of whittling wood poking out of the pockets of his rumpled suit.[114]

While Henry Yesler hustled and bustled his way through Seattle society, Sarah found new outlets for her lifelong interest in women and their affairs. By the early 1870s, suffrage had become the cause of the day, and Sarah Burgert Yesler was at the forefront of the movement. A founding member of the Female Suffrage Society in Seattle, she was one of four delegates chosen to attend the convention in Olympia. On November 6, 1871, she was elected temporary president of that convention. She hosted Susan B. Anthony's visit that month to Seattle, and over the next few years, as Elizabeth Cady Stanton, Abigail Scott Duniway, and other leaders of the suffrage movement came to the city to speak from the stage of Yesler Pavilion, Sarah Yesler was always on hand to offer hospitality and support.[115]

Sarah also used her status to further other causes. In 1860, Henry had been one of the founding members of a short-lived Seattle Library Association, and by 1868, Sarah was one of twenty Seattle residents who formed the second such association. The library was housed in Yesler Hall, and for a time Sarah served as librarian. Throughout the early 1870s, both Yeslers were active in the Library Association, and in 1873, Henry built a new library on First Street.[116]

While their support of the library and other civic projects earned the Yeslers the status of good, upstanding citizens, there were those who condemned the couple for their failure to join a church. Indeed, Henry twice offered free land to churches seeking building sites, and both times his offers were summarily rejected; perhaps building a church on land donated by so liberal a thinker was considered suspect by conservative ministers and their flocks. Plymouth Congregational Church did accept his offer of rent-free use of Yesler Pavilion for their services, and the ladies of that congregation took part in a comical, but effective, fund-raising scheme Henry devised in which he and several of his cronies walked around the pavilion whittling, then were fined by the ladies for the "muss" they had made on the floor. Not deeming such actions sufficient evidence of Henry's salvation, the Reverend Daniel Bagley, pastor of the "Brown Church" on Second Avenue, openly prayed for the "God-forsaken couple" in Sunday services.[117]

In truth, although Sarah and Henry refused to join a church in

Henry Yesler at about sixty, around 1870. *(Courtesy Special Collections Division, University of Washington Libraries, neg. no. UW3997)*

Seattle, they were by no means out of touch with spiritual matters, and all during the early 1870s they maintained their interest in spiritualism, frequently hosting sessions presided over by W. E. Cheney, a well-known spritualist-astrologer and an open proponent of free love. Henry Yesler's political affiliations were almost as loose as his religious ties. Having switched from Democrat to Republican in the years following the Civil War, he was nominated as mayor in 1870 and touted as "the Best Friend that Seattle has ever had." Losing that election, he was nominated again in 1873 and again lost. Finally engineering a successful campaign, he served as mayor in 1874–75, but he was hardly able to concentrate on running the city that year, for his business had begun to collapse on every front. No one mourned the end of his tenure in office, since he had been little more than a figurehead, and his name had more often appeared in the newspapers because of business catastrophes than because of civic activities.[118]

If the 1860s had been years of success for the Yeslers, the 1870s were years of disaster. By 1872, with the lumber boom subsiding, Henry had rented out his new mill and was doing his best to shore up his other properties. By mid-decade, only his real estate holdings kept his assets above his liabilities. He owed over $76,000—most of it to John McLain of Massillon—and though he was conscientious in meeting the interest payments, the principal remained unpaid. Realizing that many of his and the city's financial difficulties stemmed from the fact that Seattle still had no overland access route, Yesler devised a desperate scheme to finance a long-discussed wagon road over the Cascades. He proposed a state-run lottery, first prize for which would be the Yesler Mill. Valued at $100,000, the mill was considered a desirable property, even though Henry had had no luck in selling it at that price. Setting the drawing for July 4, 1876, the country's centennial, Yesler had tickets printed up and began to sell them, planning to pocket 90 percent of the proceeds and give 10 percent to the legislature for the proposed wagon road. Declared illegal in late April, the lottery was halted, and Yesler moved even closer to bankruptcy. McLain, unable to trust his friend's good intentions any longer and now holding over $91,000 in Yesler notes, finally brought suit in 1878. A temporary truce reached the following year saved the Yesler enterprises and the Yesler-McLain friendship.[119]

The newspapers had been fairly kind to Henry Yesler through his financial troubles, but the editor of the *Weekly Intelligencer* turned on him in 1877, noting that the buildings he had continued to erect along the wharf and in the industrial area now constituted a fire hazard that could only spell disaster. Charging that Henry was getting such high rents for mere shanties that he could not be bothered to replace them with brick structures, the editor suggested that Seattle should have "fire limits" like those in other major cities. Hoping to assuage public outcry, Yesler made haste to add twenty-five fire plugs to his already overtaxed water system and attempted, in vain, to use the improvement as a means of continuing his monopoly of the water rights in the city.[120] Seeing Yesler's vulnerability, old creditors brought suits against the entrepreneur, and he responded with countersuits that led to a series of courtroom battles that kept the Yeslers—and the city of Seattle—unsettled and uneasy into the next decade.

With attacks coming from every quarter, it is little wonder that Sarah Yesler's old ailment, depression, returned, sending her down to San Francisco for a month's water-cure treatment in 1877. Returning to the chaos in Seattle, she managed to weather the legal battles that marred the end of the 1870s and emerged, with Henry, early in 1880, in fairly stable shape, both emotionally and financially. Success bred success. In 1882, Yesler joined John Leary in constructing the most elaborate business building in the city, a five-sided, three-story structure on the corner of Mill and Front. By 1883 real estate was booming, and both Sarah and Henry Yesler bought and sold properties at a rapid pace.[121]

With renewed prosperity, Seattle suffered serious growing pains. Long known as the most wicked city on the coast, the settlement had courted that dubious honor as far back as 1861, when the first brothel was established near Yesler's sawmill. Indeed, the bars, gambling houses, and brothels along the mill's skid road were so legendary as to lend the English language a new term for a city's roughest section. By the early 1880s, when upstanding citizens began to call for change, the Law & Order League, which sought to regulate liquor and improve the morals of the town, was ranged against the Business Men's Ticket, a group opposed to regulation on the grounds that it might hurt prosperity. While the Law & Order League spoke out against Seattle's "two distilleries, eleven drinking establishments, one bawdy house . . . and gambling," businessmen reminded citizens that vice brought in business. Not surprisingly, Henry Yesler was touted as the businessman's candidate, and though he owed the city for numerous assessments he had refused to pay for street improvements and other refinements, he won the election of 1885 and again became mayor of Seattle.[122]

At seventy-five he hardly seemed up to the task, especially since he took office at a time when the city faced a serious problem. The Chinese workers who had been so instrumental in laying the railroads and working the mines of the West were now being condemned by persons who felt that the cheap labor they provided was detrimental to the economy. Anti-Chinese disturbances broke out across the region, and when unrest became evident in Seattle, Yesler called a civic meeting in which he insisted that only lawful means be used to remove Chinese from the city, if removal was, indeed, the will of the people.[123]

In early February 1886, matters came to a head, and groups of workers began invading Chinese homes across the city, rounding up their inhabitants and marching them onto a boat waiting at the dock. When Sarah Yesler's Chinese cook sought sanctuary in her home, she refused to turn him over to a group of men who demanded that she do so: "I must stand by the law," she insisted, "This is my house and I will protect it." She remained firm in that stand, even after fake bombs were placed on her lawn and two cows and a horse were poisoned in the field beside her house.[124]

In the mid-1880s, Sarah Yesler became a founding member of the Seattle Ladies Relief Society, one of the first organized benevolence groups in what was, at that time, a city of twelve thousand people. By February 1885 that group had founded the Seattle Children's Home. Even as she watched the orphanage take shape, Sarah Yesler was also observing the construction of another home, a magnificient edifice at the corner of Third and James. In 1883, in celebration of his return to prosperity, Henry had begun making plans for his new house. Sarah's exact role in this enterprise is not clear, though she must certainly have had mixed emotions, since her orchard was sacrificed to make room for the imposing structure. Furthermore, her thrifty nature no doubt balked at the idea of borrowing still more money in order to build a house they could well do without. Three stories high, the 112- by 80-foot home rested on a stone foundation. Crafted in a "modified Queen Anne style," with "numerous bay windows and verandas," the house had forty rooms—finished out in ash, oak, cedar, and redwood. When the elaborate structure was finally finished, Sarah lingered on in her old home, and rumors flew that she was reluctant to leave its cozy, familiar rooms for the laby-rinthine hallways of what had become known as the Yesler man-sion. Whatever her feelings, in June 1886 she and Henry finally left the old home behind and moved into the new one that awaited them.[125]

Within months of that move, Henry Yesler realized what Sarah had known all along: the house was far too large for just the two of them. To fill the emptiness, he rented out rooms as business and professional suites, so that even in her new home Sarah was not removed from the concerns of the Yesler enterprises. Whatever her feelings about life at Third and James, her days in that house were numbered. She had not been particularly robust since her arrival in Seattle, and her health deteriorated rapidly after her move into the new house. In early August 1887 she was stricken with "gastric fever," and on Sunday morning, August 28, after several weeks of severe illness, sixty-five-year-old Sarah Burgert Yesler died.[126]

As the news swept across Seattle, flags in the city and its harbor were lowered to half-mast as citizens mourned the woman who had given so much to them. Stores and businesses closed their doors out of respect for "the aged lady," and hundreds poured through the doors of the Yesler mansion and into its north parlor, where her body lay. The *Post-Intelligencer* noted that "no person within [the city's] borders was better known or more generally respected than she" and reported that the Yesler home, large as it was, "would not hold half of those who came to pay last respects." Praised for the western hospitality she had shown to visitors on the sound and for her "unwavering faith in the growth of the city," she was mourned by all of Seattle.[127]

Chief among her mourners was her seventy-six-year-old hus-band, who, according to newspaper accounts, was "bowed with grief at loss of his life partner who has always been a loving and devoted wife and from whose loss he will never recover." Yet recov-ery for Henry began almost immediately with the appointment of his nephew, James D. Lowman, as the executor of his wife's estate. Sarah Yesler, who died intestate, was survived not only by her hus-band, but also by nine of her siblings. When those siblings brought suit against the estate, Henry was thrown into five years of legal battles. A veteran of court actions, he was hardly perturbed by the threat of impending lawsuits, and in September 1887, barely a month after Sarah's funeral, he and his nephew set out for the East. Apparently invigorated by the trip, Henry maintained a pace that so tired his nephew that Lowman eventually returned to Seattle without him. After visiting Sarah's relatives in Ohio and his own boyhood home in Maryland, Henry returned to Washington Territory by way of San Francisco, where he negotiated with backers to clear himself of bothersome debts. Back in Seattle, he rented out still more rooms in his mansion and set himself to the task of planning a four-story building that would honor the pioneers of the city.[128]

Before he could get the building underway, an oft-predicted disaster struck the city. On June 6, 1889, fire raced through the heart of the business district, razing almost all structures there, including a good many owned by Henry Yesler. The mansion at Third and James was spared, but it was surrounded by the ashes of the commercial section of the city. A man who thrived on crisis, Henry Yesler threw himself into rebuilding the city he loved, and by September 1890, he had not only restored most of the properties he had lost in the fire but had also completed the Pioneer Building.[129]

He was rebuilding his life in other ways as well. In 1888, a year after he had visited them in the East, Henry's second cousin, Minnie Gagle, her parents, and her younger sisters followed him to Seattle and moved into the Yesler mansion. An attractive, grey-eyed woman of twenty-two, Minnie was soon seen on the arm of her septuagenarian cousin, a spectacle that set Seattle tongues wagging. Gossip intensified when, on September 29, 1890, in a civil ceremony in Philadelphia, Henry, three months shy of his eightieth birthday, married Minnie, then twenty-four. The newlyweds returned to Seattle to live in the mansion at Third and James.[130]

Henry Yesler's remaining years were spent in relative seclusion. Minnie did not approve of most of his cronies, and he saw less and less of the old crowd. Even though he continued to take an interest in his business affairs, his nephew handled most of his dealings while he contented himself with wandering about the wharf area and puttering around in the Yesler mansion. Early in 1892, he was touched to hear that a group of women who had established a home "for the benefit of respectable women and girls who were dependent upon their own work for a livelihood" had named their new building "The Sarah B. Yesler Dwelling." He immediately wrote them a letter, offering to furnish the building, an offer that was promptly accepted.[131]

In early December 1892, a newspaper reported that Henry Yesler was suffering from "a dropsical trouble" with attendant stomach disorders. Although he protested that he was "good for some time yet," on the morning of December 16, Henry Leiter Yesler "simply ceased to breathe." Among those at his bedside were his wife, Minnie, and his nephew, James D. Lowman.[132]

Over three thousand people flocked to the mansion to attend his funeral services, among them the members of the Women's Home Society he had so recently aided. His funeral oration, printed in its entirety by the *Post-Intelligencer,* was filled with accolades to one who had believed enough in Seattle to link his fortunes with those of the city. After the bombast and ceremony, a long line of carriages followed the hearse up the hill down which Henry Yesler's logs had once been skidded and into the tree-lined lanes of Lake View Cemetery, where Sarah Burgert Yesler's body had been laid to rest some five years earlier. Today, visitors to that plot observe a large stone marker and three plain white tablets, one engraved with the name of Sarah Yesler, the second with the name of Henry Yesler, and the third still blank, reserved—in vain—for Minnie Gagle Yesler, who slipped from public view after several years of bitter litigation over her husband's estate.[133]

Harriet Burr Godfrey

"Gold or No Gold, Come Home, We Cannot Spare You Longer"

When Ard Godfrey, a Minnesota lumberman, joined the Fisk Expedition of 1862 and set out for the goldfields of the Salmon River country of what was then Washington Territory, he left his wife Harriet behind with sixty dollars in her pocket and seven children in her care. As she said her last goodbyes, her major concern was Ard's safety on the long journey through Dakota Territory, for his wagon train would be crossing through prime hunting grounds of the Plains Indians.

Ironically, Ard's passage was made without incident, while his family at home soon found themselves in the midst of what would become known as the Dakota Conflict of 1862. "Everything is looking dark," Harriet wrote Ard that September. "We are in trouble . . . the Sioux have been fighting the men, and killing the women and children." Nineteen-year-old Abner Godfrey added sentiments of his own: "The sutheners are on the south and the indians are on the north and I guess that we will have plenty to do."[1]

Surrounded by children aged four to twenty-three, all living at home, Harriet struggled to make the best of a life fraught with uncertainties. "It seems sometimes that I cannot endure the suspense," she wrote to Ard during the worst days of the Indian uprising, "but when I look on our little ones who are depending on me I try, and pray for strength that I may be spared to them."[2]

Born in Brewer, Maine, a small settlement across the Penobscot River from Bangor, on February 5, 1816, Harriet Burr was the tenth child, and youngest daughter, of Joseph and Sally Proctor Burr. Joseph Burr, a farmer, was a fifth-generation American and a member of the committee that carved the town of Brewer from Orrington in 1812. He was also a member of the first school board elected in Brewer that same year, and his interest in education was not lost on his children, particularly his youngest daughter, who was a quiet, bookish girl.[3]

Harriet remained a member of the Burr household until she reached young adulthood. Sometime over the course of her years at home in Brewer, she met a young man from Orono, a community some five miles to the north, who, like herself, came from a large and prominent family. Ard Godfrey, Jr., born on January 18, 1813, was the son of Catherine and Ard Godfrey. As the seventh of thirteen children, and the oldest son, Ard came into responsibility early, being trained as a young boy in his father's trade, that of millwright. By the time Ard, Jr., was eighteen years of age he was given full charge of the construction of a sawmill, a position that placed one hundred men under his supervision. The tall, muscular youth had soon earned a reputation as a craftsman that extended beyond the boundaries of Maine.[4] Over the next few years, he contracted for the construction of mills along the eastern seaboard. In addition, from the time he was twenty-one years of age, he dealt frequently in real estate in the area around Bangor, buying and selling lots in Bradley, Brewer, Orono, and Old Town.[5]

On January 31, 1838, the twenty-five-year-old millwright married Harriet Burr, who was then just a week shy of her twenty-second birthday. The ceremony, which took place in the bride's family home at Brewer, was a quiet affair, for Harriet's father, Joseph Burr, had died only nine months before. Immediately after the wedding, the young couple set out on a week-long sleigh trip to Saint John, New Brunswick, where Ard was in charge of the construction of a large sawmill. There they remained for the greater part of a year, but with the completion of the mill, they returned to Maine, where they built a small house near the old Godfrey homestead in Orono.[6]

The house was no sooner finished than Harriet delivered her first child, Helen. Although the baby's birth delighted Ard, within months of that event he had signed a contract to build a mill in Savannah, Georgia. Unwilling to pass up an opportunity to earn twelve hundred dollars, plus living expenses and passage, for a year's work, he left Harriet and the baby at home in Orono and sailed for Savannah. Already a bustling city of upwards of ten thousand people, Savannah was a far more exciting place than the village of Orono, and it offered Ard a contentment he had not known in his native state. Happy where he could "get a little money once in a whyle," he was undecided as to whether he would ever return to Maine. "It is my sole object to get a situation of my own that we can get a living withou[t] slaving all the days of ou[r] lives," he wrote Harriet. "I know very well that it would be quite pleasent to be situated among our friends But all this dose not afford us an indenpendant living."[7]

At home in Orono, among her friends and Ard's family, Harriet was far less disposed to think in terms of a permanent move to Georgia. She was managing admirably in Ard's absence, though she was lonely enough that she would have rented out her home and boarded with a family had she been able to make satisfactory arrangements for her cow. Ard, too, was lonely, and when it became obvious that he would have to stay south for the winter, he begged Harriet to join him in Georgia. The invitation was readily accepted, and late in 1839, Harriet and nine-month-old Helen sailed for Savannah. Although their ship was caught in a violent storm off Cape Hatteras, they eventually reached safe harbor, and Ard rejoiced to be reunited with his wife and baby. Still thinking in terms of staying on in the South, he wanted Harriet to see the city and to give her "opinon [of the place] in regard to [her] own comfort."[8]

Whatever Savannah's charms, the city was, in Harriet's opinion, too far from Maine. On May 30, 1840, Ard's contract was "cancelled by mutual consent of the parties," and the Godfreys returned to Orono. There, in mid-September of 1840, settled once again on the Godfrey homestead, Harriet gave birth to their second child, a son they named John Reid after a brother of Ard's who had died in infancy.[9]

Over the next few years, the young couple experienced a series of setbacks and tragedies. In February 1841, Ard entered into a subcontract with Samuel Valentine to replace six saws in the mill operated by the city of Bangor. At $540, it was a good contract. The work proceeded well through the spring, and in May, Ard received his final payment for the job. But claims of faulty workmanship surfaced soon after the newly repaired mill went into operation. By the end of the year, the claims had reached the courts, and the sheriff attached all of Ard's and Harriet's real estate and personal property.[10]

Even as their financial difficulties mounted, the couple faced personal tragedy. Early in October 1841, just before his first birthday, John Reid Godfrey died. Although Harriet was soon pregnant again, their third child, Laura, survived her birth by barely a month. In less than a year, Harriet and Ard Godfrey had buried two children. Helen, their only surviving child, was a now healthy three-year-old, but there were few other bright spots in their lives.[11]

On March 1, 1843, with the Valentine case on appeal, Ard Godfrey, Jr., filed for bankruptcy in the Penobscot County Courthouse in Bangor. Still, his losses continued. In June, three months after that filing and less than nine months after the death of his infant daughter, Ard lost his father, a man with whom he had worked closely since adolescence. Two months later, the Supreme Court of Maine ruled in the *Valentine* vs. *Godfrey* case: Ard Godfrey, Jr., millwright of Orono, was assessed $1,093.35 in damages and $11.70 in legal costs. To cover the judgment, Ard surrendered the property that had been attached by the court order issued a year earlier.[12]

There seemed to be little left to Ard, other than his family. In addition to little Helen, he and Harriet had a healthy infant son, Abner Crossman, born on August 2, 1843, the day the supreme court handed down its decision. He had, as well, his mother, his brother Alfred, and his seven sisters and their husbands, whose support he had never lost. And, miraculously, he still had his reputation. He must have had credit as well, for he was soon buying land again in the Bangor-Orono area. In 1846, Ard secured a parcel of land in Bradley, across the Penobscot River from Orono, and in May 1847 he moved Harriet, Helen, and little "Crossy" from the homestead in Orono to the new home he had built on their Bradley lot. It was there, a month later, that the couple's fifth child, Sarah Catherine, was born.[13]

When that infant was only a few weeks old, Ard Godfrey was offered another lucrative contract that would take him far from home. Franklin Steele, a native of Pennsylvania, had migrated to the northwestern frontier in 1837, eventually becoming the sutler, or shopkeeper, at Fort Snelling, an outpost that played a major role in the development of Minnesota Territory. From his post at Fort Snelling, Steele spent some time studying the local area for potential development and eventually decided that the Falls of Saint Anthony, just upriver from the fort and some ten miles northwest of the newly established port city of Saint Paul, offered unrivaled promise as a source of water power for future settlement on the banks of the Mississippi.[14]

In 1847, as the federal government reached an agreement with the Dakota and the Chippewa that opened up the land on the east bank of the Mississippi to white settlers, Steele staked a claim on 160 acres at the falls. Now rich in property, he began a search for partners who would provide the funds to build a dam and sawmill in exchange for a share in his claim. In July 1847 he reached a provisional agreement with two Massachussets financiers, Caleb Cushing and Robert Rantoul, Jr., prominent lawyers and politicians who had already invested liberally in the development of the western frontier. Despite the fact that the government had not yet passed title to Steele's claim to land on the eastern bank of the Mississippi, the investors pledged twelve thousand dollars for a nine-tenths interest in the property. On the strength of their agreement, Steele wasted no time in sending out crews to build a mess hall, carpentry and blacksmith shops, stables, and a bunkhouse. Then, on a tip from a lumberman from Maine, he contacted Ard Godfrey, offering him fifteen hundred dollars plus living facilities and an option to buy a one-twentieth interest in the property in return for overseeing the construction of a dam and a millpond at the Falls of Saint Anthony.[15]

Thirty-four years old and again looking for new opportunities, Ard accepted the offer quickly and departed Bradley in July 1847, once again leaving Harriet behind, this time with three children—eight-year-old Helen, three-year-old Crossy, and infant Sarah Catherine—to care for. When Ard arrived in Saint Anthony in October 1847, he found a crude village of some three hundred people, among them only one woman. Steele's crews had finished the preliminary buildings—the mess hall, bunkhouse, and carpentry shop—and there were a few log houses around the site. Across the river, on the west bank of the Mississippi, were the vast lands of the military reservation at Fort Snelling, where government mills were already making use of the water power from the falls.[16]

Construction work on the dam began with Ard Godfrey's arrival. As superintendent, he worked side by side with laborers who stood waist-deep in the river, fighting its currents to put in the foundations. By month's end, the men had partially completed a "temporary dam," but they suffered a setback a few weeks later when the boom upriver broke, freeing the logs it had held for the dam's construction. Although Steele at first feared that the loss of raw mate-

rials would delay the work for a year or more, the dam was completed in late spring of 1848, almost on schedule.[17]

While Ard worked on the frontier in what was soon to become
Minnesota Territory, Harriet was managing on her own in Bradley.
House-bound with three small children, she was as lonely as she
had been during Ard's earlier absence. All through the summer, fall,
and an especially hard winter, she counted the days until February,
the date of her husband's promised return. Her disappointment over
news of the broken boom that would delay his homecoming turned
to near-panic when a tumor was discovered in her six-month-old
infant. She had "pretty good courage," she wrote Ard, though she
sometimes lost heart and was more than grateful when her mother
came up from Brewer to help her through the crisis.[18]

In mid-March, with winter letting up and her baby "about well of
her tumor," she received an optimistic letter from Ard. The work had
gone much better than he had first supposed; the dam was "most
don," and they had already begun construction of the piers for the
boom. He was now considering leaving for home around the first of
May. In the meantime, he had written a Mr. Little, telling him to give
Harriet "what money" she wanted.[19]

The money from Mr. Little was indeed welcome, since Harriet had
not been able to collect "one cent" for hay she had sold to a Mr.
Dudley nor any of the money a Mr. Chiley owed her for rent on the
use of her wagon. Hard-pressed as she was for cash, she cast about
for a means of steady income. She was intrigued by her brother
Joseph's suggestion that she open a tavern, and she was also considering turning her home into a boardinghouse.[20]

Harriet mulled these plans with no knowledge of the one that was
simultaneously developing in Saint Anthony. Buoyed by the offer of
a new contract with Franklin Steele, Ard was now convinced that
the family's future lay not in the East but on the frontier. The new
contract reflected the fact that the financial support Steele had been
promised by the Boston capitalists had not materialized, and he did
not have the fifteen hundred dollars Ard had originally been promised for his work on the dam. In lieu of full wages, Steele now offered him a partnership in the Saint Anthony Mill Company, the firm
he had formed for the express purpose of developing the town of
Saint Anthony. In addition, Steele would also provide "a dwelling
house" for Godfrey and his family. In return, Ard was to superintend
construction projects and engage "in such other employment as

may be deemed to be the best interests of the owners of the property."[21]

Satisfied with Steele's offer, Ard Godfrey signed the contract and prepared to return to Maine to bring his family west. Before his departure, he saw to the cutting of the timbers to be used in the construction of the "dwelling house" and set its foundation with the help of two other laborers. The building was to be a very special one. Not only would it be the first frame house in the village, it would also be a replica of Harriet Godfrey's childhood home in Brewer, Maine. Even in a primitive mill town far from home, she would be living in a house designed to evoke memories of happy times with loved ones.[22]

In early May, leaving directions for the completion of the house and collecting $975—the cash portion of Steele's payment for his work to date—Ard started for Maine. He arrived in Bradley in late summer to find his family in crisis: fourteen-month-old Sarah Catherine was once again critically ill. Within weeks of her father's homecoming, the baby died.[23]

Suppressing their grief, her parents threw themselves into preparations for a new life in the West. But the delay caused by the baby's illness and death became a significant factor in the family's plans. Working against time now, Harriet readied the household goods for the move while Ard disposed of holdings in Maine that would no longer benefit them. Choosing what to bring and what to leave behind was difficult for Harriet. Difficult as well were her farewells to family members who had always been close at hand. She was especially reluctant to leave her seventy-four-year-old mother, whom she would likely never see again, and her sister Ann Eliza, who, though ten years older, had been her close companion all her life.[24] Even so, the frontier's promise of a fresh start was as strong a magnet to Harriet as to her husband, and nine-year-old Helen and five-year-old Crossy were filled with excitement over the trip.

On an autumn day in 1848 the Godfrey family left Bangor harbor, bound for Boston by boat, where they visited briefly with Ard's sister, Harriet Emery. The visit was a trying one, for Harriet Emery openly questioned her brother's decision to take his family west "to a country where there were only wild Indians and where his children would have to grow up without education or advantages of any kind."[25]

Leaving Boston, the family took the train to Buffalo, the western terminus of the railroad, where they boarded a steamer to cross the

Great Lakes. In Milwaukee misfortune again delayed them, as little Crossy was taken seriously ill. Giving up all hope now of reaching Saint Anthony before winter set in, Harriet and Ard instead did what they could to find medical assistance for their sick child in a strange city, all the while wishing they could at least have reached Beloit, some eighty miles to the southwest, where Ard's oldest sister, Cynthia, and her husband, Alexander Gordon, anxiously awaited them.[26]

As soon as Crossy improved, the family pressed on as far as Beloit. There the parents made a decision: Harriet and the children would have to wait until spring to see Saint Anthony. A harsh and early winter had set in, making the trip difficult for even the heartiest wayfarer and all the more imposing for a thirty-two-year-old woman who was traveling with two children while in the early weeks of yet another pregnancy. Although the Saint Anthony sawmill had been completed in early September in Ard's absence and was now producing finished lumber for construction, his commitment to his other obligations to Steele led Ard to push on through on horseback, leaving Harriet, Helen, and Crossy to winter over with the Gordons.[27]

The season passed slowly, both in Beloit and in Saint Anthony, and even before the coming of spring, Harriet and the children were eager to be on with their journey. In February, Ard wrote that their house would be ready by mid-April and Harriet should plan to be in Galena, Illinois, no later than the fifth of April in order to be aboard the first boat bound upriver for Saint Paul.[28]

Because Ard himself would not be able to come to Beloit to accompany his wife and children on the remaining leg of their journey, his brother-in-law, Alexander Gordon, offered Harriet his services as escort. Eight months pregnant and in sole charge of two lively youngsters, she gratefully accepted Gordon's offer. She soon had reason to be glad she had, for when the stage left Beloit in early April, she was the only woman on board and Helen and Crossy were the only children. The roads were so rough and so deep in mud that the travelers frequently alighted—either to help disengage wheels mired in the muck of spring thaw or simply to walk beside the stage rather than endure more of the endless jostling.[29]

In Galena, Harriet barely had time to shop for a few pieces of furniture—a tall poster bed for herself and Ard, beds for the children, and a full set of dinner dishes—and to pick up materials being held for the Saint Anthony Mill Company. Embarking on the first vessel to steam north that spring, Harriet, the two children, and Alexander

Gordon arrived in Saint Paul on a rainy Saturday night. Ard Godfrey was there to greet them, as were most of the town's citizens, since their steamer was the first to dock in over five months and brought fresh food supplies and long-awaited news of the world back east.[30]

After an overnight stay in Saint Paul, Harriet, Helen, Crossy, and Ard bade early-morning goodbyes to Alexander Gordon and boarded the stage to Saint Anthony, ten miles to the northwest. Appropriately dubbed the "mud coach," the stage took almost five hours to cover those ten miles of thawing roads, and it was early afternoon on that sunny April Sunday of 1849 before Harriet Godfrey saw the village that was to be her home for the next fifty years. Despite his best efforts, Ard did not yet have the family's home ready for occupancy, and so for the first few nights after their arrival in Saint Anthony the Godfreys were quartered in the mess house, in lodgings shared with construction workers and millhands. But Harriet was soon unpacking their possessions and arranging their furniture in her own home, dodging as she did so the men who were still plastering and painting its walls.[31]

The first night under their own roof was a special one for the Godfrey family, marked by a sparse but festive meal of Harriet's homemade biscuits, served with strawberry jam delicately scooped from a jar that had broken during the long trip from Bradley. The evening was highlighted by Ard's rendition of "Home, Sweet Home," the song he was to make a part of all special family occasions thereafter. The table at which the family dined that night was fashioned from the chest that had carried Harriet's good dishes—and the rag doll ten-year-old Helen had smuggled west against her mother's wishes.[32]

Ecstatic to be in Saint Anthony, Harriet was unfazed by its primitive aspect, for the house Ard had built carried her back thirty years to her mother's home. Because Minnesota pine did not match the natural golden color of Maine pine, Ard had had the home's exterior painted yellow to more nearly approximate the hue of his wife's childhood home. With the coming of another spring, Harriet would plant the dandelion roots her mother sent her, and in subsequent seasons, as she made coffee from dandelion roots or salad from the leaves or wine from the blossoms, she was transported back to her mother's kitchen in the house on the Penobscot. Years later, Harriet would still claim that her happiest days were the ones spent in that little home, no matter the hardships and deprivations.[33]

Even as she familiarized herself with her surroundings, Harriet found herself hosting a good many of the new settlers who arrived with each docking of a boat from downriver. Because there were still no "public houses" in town, the Godfrey home at the river's edge, overlooking the magnificent falls, became a temporary residence for many of Saint Anthony's newly arrived citizens. Harriet accommodated as many as fifty overnight guests at a time by spreading straw mattresses on the floors.[34]

And she did all of this in the last six weeks of a pregnancy that ended on May 30, 1849, with the birth of her namesake, Harriet Razada, who was from the first called Hattie. Mother and infant were tended during the delivery by Dr. Zachariah Jodon, a physician carpentering for the Saint Anthony Mill Company. Dr. Jodon delivered the baby in sawdust-covered overalls, but it is evident that he soon had sufficient business to enable him to forsake carpentry in favor of medicine, since some forty babies were born in the months following the arrival of the Godfrey infant.[35]

Saint Anthony's growth was phenomenal, and the Godfreys became major figures in the life of the bustling village. Their house not only gave temporary shelter to newly arrived settlers but also served as hospital to eastern immigrants who arrived in Saint Anthony suffering from various stages of typhoid fever, cholera, and other illnesses contracted during or exacerbated by the rigors of travel. While Harriet ran household affairs and took care of the new baby and her two other children, Ard carried on with the business of the Saint Anthony Mill Company, working out of offices in a shop built directly across the street from the Godfrey house.[36]

Early in the summer of 1849, Elizabeth Backus, a resident of the Godfrey house who had originally come to Minnesota Territory as a missionary teacher to serve the Chippewas and Dakotas, opened a school in Saint Anthony, and Helen and Crossy Godfrey were two of the fourteen children enrolled. Ministers of several denominations —Baptist, Congregationalist, Episcopalian, and Catholic—stopped over with the Godfreys on weekends, providing the small community with regular religious services even before the town had any churches. In the fall of 1849 the settlement's first post office was installed in the shop across the street from the Godfrey house, Ard Godfrey was appointed the postmaster, and weekly mail service to and from Saint Paul was inaugurated.[37]

The family's first Christmas in their new home was a quiet, thankful affair. Two Christmases before, while far from his family and home, Ard had written Crossy, then four years old, that sleds "grew on trees" in Saint Anthony, and for Christmas 1849, Ard presented the boy with his first sled, crafted from strips of Minnesota pine.[38]

As her first year in Saint Anthony drew to a close, Harriet Godfrey's day-to-day activities had become almost routine. By the late spring of 1850, with the Saint Anthony Mill Company producing sufficient lumber for the completion of homes and the town's first hotel, the Saint Charles, she and her family gained some privacy in their living quarters. Wall-to-wall straw mats gave way to new furniture. The chest that had served as dining table was replaced by an elegant six-footed black walnut table bought from a family quickly discouraged by life in Saint Anthony and eager to sell whatever they could before returning to the comforts of the East. From that same family Harriet also purchased a black walnut cradle for baby Hattie.[39]

No longer providing lodging for Saint Anthony's latest immigrants, Harriet and Ard Godfrey still remained integrally involved in community affairs. Early in the summer of 1850, townswomen began gathering in Harriet's parlor, planning the flag that was to be flown in the town's Fourth of July celebration. Having sent to Fort Snelling to get the design for the flag—how the thirty stars should be arranged, how the stripes should be alternated—the women now raided wardrobes and piece bags to get the materials for its construction. The celebration, the community's first full-fledged civic event, was a marvelous affair. The flag drew everyone's admiration, Ard Godfrey was the parade marshal, and the Honorable John W. North, town attorney, read the Declaration of Independence.[40]

As the summer of 1850 came to a close, the census taker found only Ard, Harriet, Helen, Crossy, and Hattie living in the house that had been listed as the residence, if only temporarily, of fifty-three people little more than a year before. Secure in their privacy and eager to add the final touch to their household furnishings, Harriet and Ard ordered a Chickering piano from the Boston factory through Hiram Emery, Ard's brother-in-law. Emery chose a top-of-the-line model with a six-octave keyboard, justifying the three-hundred-dollar price by citing the rigors of shipping that the instrument would have to withstand. With the piano due to arrive in the spring of 1851, Helen began to take lessons from Ann North, an accomplished pianist who lived across the millpond from the Godfreys on Nicollet Island. For lack of ferry service or even a bridge, the eleven-year-old crossed the pond on logs—or on ice—to get to her weekly lessons.[41]

A month or so before the piano's scheduled arrival, the first Masonic lodge meeting in Minnesota Territory was held in the parlor of the Godfrey home, and Ard Godfrey was elected treasurer of the Cataract Masonic Lodge. By late spring, Helen was playing her piano, which had been shipped from Boston to Saint Louis and thence to Saint Paul by river boat—"at great trouble to stage drivers and boatmen." That summer she and Crossy did well in the town's new academy under the instruction of a Professor E. W. Merrill and his wife, their father continued to prosper in his work with the Saint Anthony Mill Company, and their mother prepared for the birth of another child.[42]

Even as Harriet nursed the new baby—Martha Annie, born on July 29, 1851—change was underway for the Godfrey family. In April 1851, Arnold Taylor, a Massachusetts businessman who now held half interest in the Saint Anthony Mill Company, had sued his partners, Franklin Steele and Ard Godfrey, claiming they owed him for the use of the sawmill and for his share in real estate that Steele and Godfrey had rented or sold. The courts ruled in favor of Steele and Godfrey, but Taylor continued to be vexatious, and Steele eventually agreed to buy out the man's interest for twenty-five thousand dollars. Despite the buyout agreement, litigation was to tie up the company for the next few years.[43]

Although Franklin Steele retained Ard Godfrey's respect throughout their association, Ard was increasingly uneasy with the power struggle and the politics that were now tied to the conduct of the mill company. In 1852, when the federal government opened up part of the Fort Snelling reservation across the river to settlement, Ard seized his chance to leave Saint Anthony. Selling his interest in the company, he took a claim on a 160-acre section of land lying between Minnehaha Creek and the Mississippi River, drawn to that site by his instincts for dam and mill building. Quickly erecting a claim shanty, he began work on the family house, located on the highest point of land above the Mississippi, close by Minnehaha Falls. While the house was under construction, Godfrey dammed Minnehaha Creek just below its falls—called Little Falls in contrast to the mighty Falls of Saint Anthony. There, at the junction of the creek and the Mississippi River, at what was to be called Godfrey's Point, he built a small sawmill and a wharf. To underwrite his venture, Ard formed a partnership with Charles Borup, a well-known early fur trader and banker, in a new firm called Borup & Godfrey. From his sawmill at the mouth of Minnehaha Creek, Ard rafted lumber to Saint Paul, where Borup & Godfrey now maintained an office.[44]

That summer 1853, as she prepared her family for the move across the river, Harriet had mixed feelings. She was moving into a larger, finer home, but she was leaving a house connected to childhood memories. In addition, in Saint Anthony she had been at the center of things. From the beginning, her home had been the hub of the village. Across the river she would be more isolated. Evenings of whist and afternoon sewing circles with friends would be harder to arrange. Minnehaha was a half day's outing from Saint Anthony and another half day's drive on to Saint Paul. Even the village of Minneapolis, just a few miles north, was an hour's drive by horse and buggy.[45] But if friends could not easily drop by her new home for a visit, her husband's business could expand, the family could enjoy the benefits of their own farm, and her children could have growing room. Besides, the move across river seemed minor compared to the move across country she had accomplished just five years earlier.

In the fall of 1853, Harriet and Ard sent fourteen-year-old Helen back to Maine for a year's schooling. The following spring, while her oldest daughter was away, and just eight months after she had settled into her new home, Harriet gave birth to another daughter, whom she named Sarah Catherine, for the daughter who had been born and buried in Bradley some six years earlier. As little Kittie slept in the black walnut cradle, Harriet's older children romped in the fields and forests that surrounded their Minnehaha home, sometimes taking the path down to the sawmill, sometimes collecting herbs along the creek bank for the kitchen and the medicine chest, sometimes visiting the Kernons, an Irish family who lived in the claim shanty by the falls. During sessions, Crossy went to school in Minneapolis; in season, he helped his father in the fields or with the livestock, which now included not only Old Suke, the milk cow the Godfreys had owned since first arriving in Minnesota, but horses, cattle, pigs, and sheep as well.[46]

Even as Ard oversaw the farm and the mill, Harriet spent her days in activities characteristic of any other woman of her era and her situation. She made all her own bread—indeed, she made everything the family "ate, wore, and used," including three or four barrels of soap each year. Although she was not a regular churchgoer during these years at Saint Anthony and Minnehaha, she was a deeply religious person, of "old Puritan stock," who faithfully refrained from any work on the Sabbath, spending all day Saturday readying everything needed for the family's Sunday meals.[47]

Harriet's closest neighbors in those years were the Kernons and the Robinsons. Both men worked at the Godfrey mill, and their wives and children were considered a part of the Godfrey family. Delia Pettijohn, the daughter of a Dakota Sioux, was another friend and neighbor during Harriet's early years at Minnehaha. Although these friendships sustained her, Harriet's closest ties were still to her family in the East, and she looked forward to the letters that kept her in touch with happenings in Brewer, Orono, and Bangor. Her sister Ann Eliza continually entreated her to come home for a visit, since their mother's health was failing, but as much as she wanted to, Harriet could not consider such a trip. The children kept her close to home, as did her husband's activities, which were ever-expanding. A year after he built the sawmill at Minnehaha Creek, Ard put up a gristmill on the same site. He also bought land at the mouth of the Elk River, some twenty miles north of Saint Paul, where he built another sawmill and gristmill.[48]

Although business operations, farming, and childcare made it impossible for the Godfreys to consider a trip east, family members occasionally found their way to Minnesota. Alexander and Cynthia Godfrey Gordon came periodically from Beloit, and Margaret Godfrey Fuller and her son came out from Bangor. Ard's younger brother, Alfred, a minister who later served as a chaplain in the Union Army, brought his wife, Martha, for a visit to Minnehaha Creek. Harriet and Hiram Emery, who had so feared to have Ard and his family go west, finally came to see the land for themselves. Nancy and John Jameson, Ard's younger sister and her husband, came west to stay in the middle of the decade, taking up a farm at Stillwater some ten miles east of Saint Paul.[49]

In April 1856, Ann Eliza Chamberlain wrote Harriet of the death of their eighty-one-year-old mother, Sally Proctor Burr. Some eighteen months later, on November 1, 1857, Harriet Godfrey, forty-one years of age, gave birth to the last of her seven children—identical twins who weighed eight pounds each and were named Mary and Minnie. In addition to nursing her twins, tending her other children, and managing her usual household affairs that winter of 1857–58, Harriet also boarded her husband's millhands. Besides her oldest daugh-

ter, Helen, Harriet had the help of two "housegirls" as well as that of
Martha Godfrey, a cousin visiting from the East. While eighteen-
year-old Helen stayed home to help her mother, Hattie, age seven,
and Mattie, age five, began their schooling in a little clapboard
building not far down the road from the Godfrey house. Abner, now
thirteen and no longer called Crossy except at home, was away at
boarding school in Saint Paul, although he got home on most weekends, walking the ten-mile distance when he could not get a ride.[50]

Home was a special place to the Godfrey offspring, as it was to the
woman who was its center. And while Ard was a quiet, self-effacing
man who rarely spoke at social events, especially at the large dinner
parties the Godfreys frequently hosted, within the family circle he
was a man of easy laughter who frequently joined the children in
their games, often exasperating Harriet by roughhousing with the
little ones at bedtime. Conversely, he could just as quickly bring a
peaceful mood over the house by playing his rosewood violin, which
always lay at the ready on the Chickering piano.[51]

But Ard was restless that winter of 1857–58. The fact that he kept
the Minnehaha mill open that season despite the poor market was
indicative of the family's financial pressures. He began to spend less
time playing with his children in the evening and more time sitting
at his desk, "calculating his expenses." Having known nothing but
financial success since his arrival in Minnesota, he suddenly found
himself prey to forces beyond his control.[52] The nation was in the
grip of an economic slump, and nowhere were the effects felt more
directly than on the frontier. Still, Ard kept the mills going, hoping
with each passing month that the trend would turn.

His assets were solid—real estate valued at twenty thousand dollars and personal property valued at five hundred dollars—but cash
flow was at a standstill, and his responsibilities were heavy. In residence in the home, besides the nine family members, were four
millhands, even though Borup & Godfrey received ever fewer contracts. Hard-pressed as she was to feed thirteen people on a tight
budget, Harriet continued to convey nothing but optimism in her
letters to the family in the East. "Times have been hard in Minnesota
for the past three years," she admitted to her sister Ann Eliza early in
1861, "but all feel in hopes the coming year will bring a change."[53]

The year 1861 did, in fact, bring change—but in the form of a civil
war, which neither helped the economy of the frontier nor reversed
the Godfrey fortunes. Indeed, in the first call to arms for Minnesota

men, Ard lost so many of his millhands that he could not keep the Minnehaha mills running. And the year also brought severe spring floods that swept away the dam at Elk River. In order to rebuild it, Ard mortgaged the homestead at Minnehaha Falls.[54]

With a mortgage on the farm and a lien on the mills, Ard Godfrey now took a seemingly desperate course of action. In the summer of 1858 the discovery of gold in the Rocky Mountains had kindled the imagination and roused the hopes of many who had ignored the California rush a decade earlier. Minnesotans were especially heedful of the promise of the "new El Dorado," since the frontier economy had suffered so drastically in the recession of the late 1850s. Ard Godfrey was no exception. Discouraged by the continued decline of his fortunes and attentive to the prospects in the mining camps of the Salmon River Country of the northern Rockies, in what was then Washington Territory, he began to fashion a plan to pull himself out of debt. When he confided that plan to Harriet, she responded as he knew she would, arguing that at forty-nine, he was too old to undertake the rigors of the trip across the plains, let alone the rigors of life in the mountains. More than that, she feared for his safety in the land of hostile Indians. Despite her arguments, Ard saw the goldfields as the only means by which he would be able "to get anough to pay [his] debts."[55] As the plan grew more definitive, it became the focus of dinner conversations, and the Godfrey children, especially the older ones, were caught between a natural excitement over their father's proposed journey and an empathy for their mother's anxieties.

As Ard worked the fields that spring of 1862, the family was keenly aware that Abner would be the one harvesting them in the fall. Intending to leave Old Doll and John for his son to use on the farm, Ard bought himself a new team of horses and equipped a covered wagon with provisions to last a year—enough for the four-month trip across the plains and for all the months when he would be prey to extractive prices in the mining camps. Then, on Wednesday morning, June 18, 1862, his preparations complete, Ard said his goodbyes to Harriet and the twins, who stood waving on the front porch of the house as the wagon pulled away. The older girls rode with their father as far as the schoolhouse two miles distant, where they climbed down from the wagon to begin the walk home, while Abner continued on horseback as far as Minneapolis. Cautioning his son to be strong in his absence, Ard bid Abner goodbye and headed his wagon north and west toward Fort Abercrombie, where he was to join up with the main party of the Fisk Expedition, commissioned by the federal government early in 1862 to escort citizens through the Indian territory that stretched between Minnesota and the untapped treasures of the northern Rockies.[56]

At forty-six, Harriet Godfrey was once again left to manage family affairs at home. As had been the case before, she had limited financial resources to call on as she began her task. But this time her children were old enough to provide economic as well as emotional support. Realizing the importance of being at home with her mother and siblings, twenty-three-year-old Helen had decided against teaching another school term and had instead purchased a sewing machine, intending to supplement family income as a seamstress.[57] The principal farming and livestock chores would fall to eighteen-year-old Abner, who also planned to hire out for odd jobs when he wasn't working his family's fields. The rest of the brood—Hattie, thirteen; Mattie, eleven; Kittie, nine; and the twins, four—were hardly aware on that spring day of all the ramifications of their father's absence. Nor did they sense their mother's trepidation as the separation began.

Ard himself had sensed his wife's fears and now did what he could to allay them. Immediately upon discovering that he was "not the only old man in the company" assembled at Fort Abercrombie, he hastened to write his wife that some of his fellow argonauts on the Fisk Expedition were even older than he. And as far as her fears of an Indian ambush as they crossed the northern plains, she should be reassured to know that the expedition's leader, Captain James Fisk, had decided to take a "small canon" from Fort Abercrombie with them as a hedge against attack.[58]

Ard's news of the maturity of his traveling companions and the security of the cannon did little to ease Harriet's mind, but she pushed her fears aside and made the necessary adjustments to her husband's absence, soon establishing a comfortable family routine that allowed life at Minnehaha to continue much as it had before Ard left. The summer of 1862 was filled with pleasant weather, good crops, a Fourth of July family celebration, and frequent visitors. The younger girls, including the twins, spent weekdays learning their lessons in the little clapboard schoolhouse, while Helen and Abner helped their mother around the house and the farm. Abner also made frequent trips to Elk River to take grain to the mill, to bring back flour, and to carry messages to a Mr. Welles, who was managing the business there for the Godfreys.[59]

The idyllic scene at Minnehaha was suddenly shattered in the late summer by the violence of an Indian uprising. From their reservations along the upper Minnesota River, the Dakota Sioux—frustrated by the continued encroachment of white settlers and traders, by the effects of a poor harvest the preceding fall, and by delay in payments for land they had newly ceded to the federal government—rose up against the settlers in south central Minnesota. Before the uprising could be brought under control by troops siphoned off from the Union forces, at least 450 settlers and soldiers had been killed and a considerable amount of property destroyed.[60]

Though neither the members of the Godfrey family nor the homestead on Minnehaha Creek suffered directly during the crisis, Harriet's agitation could not be contained: "We are in trouble. . . . everything is looking dark," she wrote her husband. "You know how nervous I ever have been about Indians. . . . I hope I may be strengthened from day to day, but we cannot promise ourselves any thing, we know not what to-morrow may be." Despite her concern for his safety, Abner continued his trips between Minnehaha and Elk River, even though it meant traveling through unsettled country. Ironically, he was actually in greater danger than his father, since the expedition crossing the plains that summer encountered very few Indians, and those few were "so closely watched" by the company that "they did not get only what was given them."[61]

Of more interest to Ard were his encounters with miners passing the expedition on their way back home. With some of them reporting earnings of "20 to 95 dollars per day," Ard was eager to have his journey behind him and to be settled in the West. Since he did not yet know exactly where in the West that would be, he asked his family to write to "diforant points" so that he would be assured of getting at least some word from them.[62]

As the months passed at home, Harriet's major worry moved from fear of Indian attack to concern over financial matters. Upon Ard's departure, she had urged him not to send money home. She was sure he would need cash more than the family, for she planned to get by as "economically" as she could. Yet, by summer's end, after only three months on her own, she was already uneasy about her situation. Thinking ahead to the payment she would soon owe against the mortgage held on her home, she approached Mr. Welles in Elk

River about repayment of a one-hundred-dollar note she held from him. By mid-October, when she finally received the money from Welles, she had decided to put the major portion of it to another use, giving Abner seventy-five dollars to purchase a good, strong horse to match with Old Doll so that he could bid on government contracts to haul goods from Saint Paul to Saint Cloud. Although she was still worried about meeting the mortgage payment, she was convinced that at this point it was best to use the money to make more money.[63]

With his new horse and a new double harness, Abner began to haul supplies for the government. But after his first trip he was discouraged enough to reconsider the prospects; he was neither paid in a timely fashion nor given the full amount for which he had contracted. On the other hand, it was income, and hauling for the government could prove to be steady work, since federal troops, mostly cavalry, were still being sent west to guard against further trouble with the Indians, and government supplies inevitably followed those troops.[64]

Troops in the East and South also caught the family's attention. Louis Meeker, a former boarder and millhand, was serving with McClellan, who was dug in on the Potomac, and the "Southern war seem[ed] more dismal than ever before." In about the only encouraging news out of Washington, the president had announced his plan for freeing the slaves. To keep her husband abreast of such events, Harriet periodically sent Ard packets of newspapers that carried reports of the progress of the war—and news of a good harvest at home. The younger children had helped Abner to dig potatoes for the family larder and to pull turnips to feed the cattle, since despite the otherwise good harvest, hay would be in short supply for the winter.[65]

Such news from home was shared with Ard each Sunday afternoon as Harriet sat at the desk in the parlor to write him. Sunday afternoons were also given over to visits with neighbors. Most often, Mrs. Chapin, the new tenant now living in the claim shanty by the mill, dropped in, and the two women knitted and talked for hours. "There is quite a chattering between Mother and Mrs Chapin," Helen wrote her father. "[Mother] is quite a different person since Mrs Chapin moved here. She [Mrs Chapin] is real pleasant . . . and is always lively and has something interesting to tell everytime."[66]

After months with no word, the family at home finally heard from Ard, receiving in late October a letter he had written the first week of

September at the end of his crossing. Although the news was almost two months old, it was welcome. He was at Fort Benton, in what would eventually become Montana Territory. In the course of the crossing he had decided not to push on to the Salmon River country, but to try his luck at a new strike on the Beaverhead, some 250 miles southwest of Fort Benton. News of her husband's safe arrival in the West prompted high spirits in Harriet: "It gave us all much joy to hear of your good health. We could hardly contain ourselves we were so happy," she replied to Ard. In her expansive mood, almost all her worries dropped away: "The Indian war they think is about played out. . . . It does not worry me at all. . . . All that troubles me is anxiety for you, and fearing Abner may be drafted [though] the drafting is put off until the 10th of November."[67]

She was in the midst of negotiations with a D. L. B. Johnston over the sale of the millstones at the now-abandoned mill on Minnehaha Creek. The man was very interested in acquiring them, but to make the sale, Harriet would have to carry a contract, with twenty-five dollars down and payments over the next three months. She hesitated to accept the offer without the advice of someone with experience in such affairs. She received little help when she approached Mr. Welles, since the man simply told her to do whatever she thought best. Deciding to trust her own instincts, she accepted Johnston's offer.[68]

At about the time Harriet was negotiating the sale of the millstones, Ard was settling himself at Bannack, in the Beaverhead Mining District. The camp was temporary home to about four hundred people, most of them working for wages of three or four dollars a day, mining for those fortunate few who had staked out the earliest claims. This situation hardly squared with the optimistic accounts Ard had heard on the trail, but he was not discouraged. He had found an Indian who promised to guide him into the mountains to a "rich gold mine . . . whar [the gold was] in lumps." Confident of his own success, his greatest concern was lack of news from home. He had "some very anxus fealings" about his family, for in the four months since he had left Minnesota, he had not received a single letter. Nor could he know for sure that any of his letters had reached home.[69]

Eventually deciding not to go into the mountains with the Indian guide, Ard invested instead in the construction of a "Saw Mill with 5 orther men in companey." With Bannack's rapidly increasing popu-

lation in need of lumber for homes and stores, prospects for investment in a mill were promising. Still, Ard Godfrey considered his
investment a temporary one. "You [should] not think because I am
building a mill that I intend [to] stop here any longer then I first
intended," he wrote Harriet. "If I do not sell out befire it is finished [I]
shel soon after. . . . you may depend apon me comeing home next
summer."[70]

Harriet was pleased to hear that Ard was involved in a business in
which he had experience and skill. Surely the construction of a mill
would prove more rewarding than panning for the elusive gold, since
her husband was, after all, first and foremost a millwright—and a
good one. If he was now building a sawmill, then he should soon be
able to earn enough money to meet his needs back home. Still prey
to fears and prejudices heightened by the Indian uprising, she saw
the sawmill plan as far superior to his idea of going off with the
native guide, who was, in her opinion, likely to be as "treacherous
and ugly" as others of his kind.[71]

Indeed, Ard had, by how, had problems of his own with Indians,
having lost both of his horses to a band of Snakes. One of the horses
was "good for nothing," but the other was the little mustang that had
been Abner's favorite. Still, he saw his troubles as nothing when, in
mid-December—four months after the fact—he finally received
newspapers that told him of the "Indians troubles in minnasota."
From that time on, he felt "so anxus" about his family that "sometimes [he could] hardley contain [him] Slf."[72]

While Ard was filled with belated worries over his family's troubles with the Dakotas, Harriet and the children were enjoying the
holiday season, which brought "plenty of company" and helped time
to pass more quickly. Nancy and John Jameson, Ard's sister and
brother-in-law, had come down from Stillwater, as they did periodically, "on purpose to hear [Ard's] letters." On their return home
they left their oldest son, eighteen-year-old Henry, behind at Minnehaha so that he could spend the winter going to school with his
cousin Abner.[73]

The holiday season brought more than visitors. Whooping cough,
which had reached epidemic proportions in central Minnesota,
found its way into the home on Minnehaha Creek. By Christmas all
five of the younger girls had symptoms of the disease, and by New
Year's they had contracted the measles as well. Hattie and Mary
were especially sick. Complications followed. Upon her recovery

from measles, Kittie was "afflicted with biles." The eight-year-old had a dozen boils on her face and scalp, and Harriet applied "mustard" and hoped "soon to subdue them."[74] For over six weeks the house was under siege from whooping cough and its aftermath.

As the winter wore on and the children recovered, Harriet found a new confidence born of experience. Throughout the long illnesses, she had "got along without a physician," relying on her own good sense and her herbal medicines. Despite her great fear of Indians, she had comported herself well during the crisis of the fall, when she had never "had so good courage in [her] life." She had collected on notes and had negotiated the sale of the millstones. She felt secure—and thankful that she had a "house to live in and plenty to eat and drink and wood plenty to burn." She also had all the money she needed, having received partial payment on the millstones from Mr. Johnston. And Mr. Welles had assured her that they stood to receive one thousand dollars or more in the final disposition of a case involving a suit Ard had brought against the Borup estate. Even the discovery that there were delinquent taxes on the Minnehaha property did not discourage her. She simply sent Abner to the courthouse in Saint Paul to find out the amount owing and the years unpaid. "I wish you could see how well we do without the Maine Spoke," she bragged to Ard, and then cushioned the statement, "that is for a little while, [but] I do not think we can get along much longer without Father."[75]

Her feelings of security did, indeed, fade every time she thought of Ard. On January 18 he had celebrated his fiftieth birthday in a gold camp in the Rockies, and she had been able to do nothing to make the day special for him. Fearing that he lacked the "comforts and necessaries" and was suffering needlessly "in that far off country," she did not want him even to think of staying away another winter. "You must have a hard time I . . . feel it night and day. I miss you so much. . . . Rich or poor come home so we can fare alike," she wrote him. His letters—her only connection to him—were sporadic at best. By late January she had received only five letters from Ard since his departure seven months before.[76] Few as they were, each letter from Bannack was treasured, and each was shared with relatives, friends, and acquaintances, some of whom also had loved ones in the West.

Despite being a major emotional and financial support for his mother, Abner was increasingly eager to go west to be with his father. His sisters mentioned his restlessness several times to Ard, concluding that the only thing that kept Abner at home was the fact that he could not leave his horses. Well aware of her son's dream of going west, Harriet would have preferred that he do so rather than be drafted. Still, she hoped that his position as the only male in the household meant that choice would never have to be made. Even as Abner himself dreamed of a trip west, he pushed for his father's return home. The economy was improving in Minnesota; wheat, corn, and oats were all selling better than they had the year before; and young Godfrey advised his father not to stay too long in the West trying to "make any thing . . . for their is a living for you at home and a good one."[77]

On the first day that his little sisters were well enough to leave the house, Abner drove the family a few miles down the road to Fort Snelling to look at the seventeen hundred Dakota men, women, and children who had been interned there since September "in a little pen fenced round 2 acres of ground." The Indians, Harriet noted, were "dying off pretty fast with the measles and other diseases." The antipathy stirred by the uprising was still strong, and she showed no remorse at the abominable conditions she saw at the fort, writing, "I think it a pitty they do not all die off."[78]

With her younger children now fully recovered, Harriet concentrated again on business matters. It had been agreed on Ard's departure that if she got a reasonable offer—five hundred dollars was the base figure mentioned—she was to sell the Elk River property. As the winter of 1862–63 moved on, she became more and more anxious about the condition of that property. It was rumored that the railroad was soon to run as far north as Saint Cloud, and thus the value of the property would be greatly enhanced, but she did not want to gamble on that possibility. Already in poor shape, the dam would likely go out with the spring floods, and since she lacked the money to replace it, it was imperative that she sell before the river broke up. L. C. B. Nash of Saint Paul had expressed serious interest in the property, but the sale price had not yet been agreed upon nor had the papers been drawn up. A Mr. Martin was brokering the deal for Harriet, and she was hopeful that the men would come to a settlement quickly. In the course of the negotiations, Abner made several trips to Elk River with Mr. Nash to show him the place and to answer his questions concerning the operation.[79]

When—and if—the sale of the Elk River property went through,

Harriet was determined to put the five hundred dollars gained from it against the mortgage on her home. They had been under heavy debts for several years, and she wanted to get out from under the load. Time weighed heavily as winter turned to spring. Harriet had endured nine months of Ard's absence, months given to prolonged and confusing financial negotiations, to whooping cough and measles, to the loss of neighbors and friends to war and illness, and to the terror of the Indian uprising. "Hellen and Abner keep up good courage, and will not allow me to get discouraged or fear," she observed to her husband. But even with their unflagging support, the worries and the responsibilities had been mainly hers. She was tired. She had not had a letter from Ard in six weeks, and since he had written that letter in early December, anything could have happened to him in the intervening months. "I feel very lonely," she wrote, "if it were not for the children I feel that I could not stay here much longer alone."[80]

By mid-April, Harriet still had had no more recent word from Ard than the lines he had penned on December 3—five months earlier. She was consumed with worry: "_Gold_ or _no_ Gold, come home," she begged in early March, "we cannot spare you longer." She could only hope that the opening of navigation with the spring breakup would hasten the arrival of mail from the West. Desperate for news from her husband, she had Abner drive her into Minneapolis to call on two women whose husbands were also in the Beaverhead Mining District to see if they had received any word from the West. Both women had had recent letters saying that all the "Minneapolis folks" were well, and though neither miner had mentioned Ard by name, Harriet felt some reassurance.[81]

With that worry somewhat relieved, Harriet turned her attention to financial matters. Nash had not yet come to terms on the Elk River property, and Johnston had asked for an extension on his final payment on the millstones. The Borup suit, though decided, would not generate payment until "the Legislature rose." If she had heard nothing more of the settlement by that time, she intended to "go to Saint Paul . . . and see about it" herself, but how glad she would be "to have Father at home again to see to things." She had had advice from others in these matters, but she could not be sure what Ard would have done. "We need your advice so much," she wrote. "If only we . . . could hear often."[82]

As Harriet fretted over her husband's silence, Ard himself was reading the first letters he had received since leaving Minnesota. On March 21, he responded immediately to three letters received all at once from his "dear & loveing famaly," admitting that, not having heard from them in eight months, he had "had so much anxiety . . . it was hard . . . to content my slf to remain [out here]." Still, because he had remained, he had all but finished building the sawmill, a project to which he had given the winter months. Within a month he would be producing lumber, and, as one-sixth owner of the mill, he figured to realize about two hundred dollars out of his first run. Once the mill was in operation, he planned to move back into Bannack, just a few miles west of the mill site, and pick up "some mecaincal work" that would pay good wages. He had made up his mind to start home before the first of September, but before he did so, he intended to work a claim he had staked on Grasshopper Creek above Bannack, to "get a little gold dust to take home . . . for the Benafit of our littl flock."[83]

Harriet clung to the good news from the West as she dealt with rumors that were now circulating throughout Minnesota. It was said that Little Crow, who had escaped capture through the long winter, was putting together a coalition of Dakotas, Winnebagos, and Chippewas; that he had "collected 5000 warriors"; and that he would march "as soon as the grass [was] as high as the hand." Against that eventuality, the federal government assigned more troops to Minnesota forts. While there was hope that such preparations would at least take the advantage of surprise away from the Indians this time, such hopes were little consolation to Harriet.[84]

Worried about Ard's safety as well, she fell back on the faith that had so often sustained her. "We must trust in Him who is able to Save and preserve us from all dangers both seen and unseen," she wrote Ard. "May he bless and keep you and return you safely to your dear family again is my constant prayer." Other matters, such as the cost of goods, were also beyond her control. With prices "very high," she had tried "to be as economical as possible," yet found that "when there is so many it takes some money to get along."[85]

The winter of 1862–63 had been one of the mildest in memory, and spring had come early. In mid-April Harriet set out her strawberry plants, Abner put in the peas and corn, and they both expressed hopes that Ard would be home to enjoy the harvest. In May, when the school term took up again, the newly hired teacher, Viola Shepley, a young woman from Minneapolis, moved in to room with the Godfreys, and Abner's thoughts began to turn more and more often to the young woman who escorted his sisters to school each morning.[86]

While Abner tilled fields and sheared the sheep in Minnesota that spring of 1863, his father was making the final arrangements for his homecoming. He had sold out his interest in the mill at a profit "wich is not much," he warned Harriet, but enough so that they could "clear the Place sow that wee can have a home clear." Whether or not he had significantly improved the family's fortune, Ard Godfrey had, without a doubt, "got anough of the Mountain life." On May 26, 1863, he sat down to write his last letter from the West: "I tak this moment to in form you that I Start for home this Day by the way of Fort Benton and if thare is a Boat I will go down the Missiuri river And per haps I may get home not far behind this."[87]

Thus, eleven months after having left Minnesota, Ard Godfrey set out for home. He left Bannack with a group of men who had organized themselves into a quasi-military company against the dangers of highwaymen and marauding Indians. Arriving safely at Fort Benton, at the head of navigation on the Missouri, they found themselves a good month ahead of the river's opening. Impatient and restless, Ard and two of his fellow travelers spent the next few weeks building a flatboat and were on the river a good two weeks before they met the first steamer coming up from Saint Louis. Hailing Ard and his friends, the riverboat captain insisted that they give up their foolhardy idea of proceeding through Indian country on such a vulnerable craft and return with him to Fort Benton. Ard acceded to the captain's orders only after being offered free passage to Sioux City, Iowa, in exchange for work as a member of the ship's crew. Although the decision to return to Fort Benton cost him another three weeks, he arrived safely in Sioux City in late July. Hiring a horse and sulky, he covered the remaining 250 miles to Minneapolis in ten days, and on Sunday, August 9, 1863, Ard Godfrey arrived home in Minnehaha after an absence of fourteen months.[88]

The household exploded in celebration. The younger children knew immediately the significance of the strange horse and buggy in front of the house when they returned home late that morning from Sunday school. Inside they found their father already comfortably settled, as if he had never been away. The afternoon was filled with visits from friends who, with the family, had long anticipated Ard's homecoming. The next few days were spent in paying calls to others, passing on news and money sent by friends in the mines.[89]

Eventually, some semblance of routine settled over life at Minnehaha, and Ard resumed once more the rhythms of the world he had left so many months before. Spending the balance of the summer and fall in the fields with Abner, he spent his evenings laying plans to reopen the mill. The mortgage on the Minnehaha property had been redeemed, lumber prices were attractive, and all Ard's instincts were those of a millwright.

He prepared for the future by leaving Harriet one more time. He had an appointment to meet an old friend in New Orleans, a man who, like himself, had arrived in Saint Anthony some fifteen years earlier and had got his start in the area through his partnership with Franklin Steele. In the intervening years, John Harrington Stevens had become a leader in territorial affairs and a dabbler in many business ventures. Now he was in the South, speculating in cotton and working in a general store. Whether to join Stevens in speculating or simply to reestablish contacts for future mill operations, on February 1, 1864, less than six months after his return from the West and during the height of the Civil War, Ard Godfrey set out for New Orleans.[90]

Because the Mississippi did not open up until mid-June that year, and because of the war raging up and down the river's banks, Ard likely traveled east to New York, then down the Atlantic Coast to the Gulf of Mexico. Whatever his route and his rationale, the trip south surely brought no comfort to Harriet. Having suffered great anxiety during the time he spent in "Indian country," she now waited at home for another three months while he walked the streets of war-torn New Orleans. Only his safe return in mid-May eased her anxieties. His return also meant the beginning of a new enterprise, for within a week of his homecoming, the old sawmill on Minnehaha Creek was set afire and a new mill began to rise in its place.[91]

Change was the one constant in Harriet Godfrey's life. While her husband worked to reestablish his mill, her son and daughters were moving in and out of the family house, beginning to establish their own lives away from Minnehaha. That summer of 1864, Abner's participation in a military expedition commissioned for the purpose of establishing Fort Sisseton in Dakota Territory gave him at least a taste of the adventure he had yearned for and had been denied during his father's year on the frontier. In Abner's absence, his four oldest sisters—Helen, Hattie, Mattie, and Kittie—moved from the homestead into rented rooms in a house located on the outskirts of

Minneapolis and belonging to a Mrs. Bigelow. There, with Helen serving as "housekeeper," the other three girls, now fifteen, thirteen, and ten, attended classes at the public school that served Minneapolis.[92] With the girls and Abner all gone from home, the household at Minnehaha was reduced in size to husband, wife, and seven-year-old twins.

Other changes were in store. On January 19, 1865, twenty-two-year-old Abner Godfrey married Viola Shepley, the young school-teacher who had boarded with the family in the spring of 1863. After a wedding trip to Monticello, Minnesota, the couple returned to Minnehaha, where they lived in a house not far from the senior Godfreys and Abner resumed work with his father, who was putting up a new gristmill. A year later the couple presented Harriet and Ard, now in their early fifties, with their first grandchild, a boy named for his grandfather.[93]

That spring, on the day after her seventeenth birthday, Hattie Godfrey left home to take a teaching position at Dayton, Minnesota, but she was home in time to be a part of the preparations for her older sister's wedding. On August 26, 1866, in a ceremony at the home of her parents, twenty-seven-year-old Helen Godfrey became the bride of Mark Berry.[94]

With Helen and Mark settled in Minneapolis and Hattie away teaching school, Harriet had only her four youngest at home: Mattie, fifteen; Kittie, twelve; and the twins, nine. But Abner and Viola were not far away, and little Ardie was the delight of his grandparents and aunts—as were the other babies that arrived in succession in Abner and Viola's home: Horace in 1867 and Eugene in 1869. Harriet's visits to Minneapolis increased in frequency when, early in 1869, Helen Berry gave her parents another grandson, a nine-and-one-half-pound boy. Seven months later, little Hiram Berry died, and Harriet and Ard Godfrey felt once more the pain of losing a child, an experience they themselves had shared three times as young parents.[95]

There were other kinds of losses. In October 1870, the original mill at Saint Anthony, the one Ard Godfrey had come to Minnesota twenty-two years previously to build, burned to the ground. An era seemed to be ending. At fifty-seven, Ard was increasingly aware of the passage of time and more and more discouraged over the prospects of ever gaining a fortune from the Minnehaha mills. The falls were of impressive height, but they were narrow, and the volume of water that flowed down Minnehaha Creek varied widely from season to season,

Ard and Harriet Godfrey and five
of their daughters, about 1873:
(left to right, standing) Hattie,
Minnie, Mary, and Mattie; *(seated)*
Ard, Kittie, and Harriet. *(Courtesy
Hennepin History Museum)*

making the falls such an unreliable source of power that there had been times when Ard had been forced to buy finished goods from other mill owners in order to meet his contracts for lumber or flour.[96] It was hardly a lucrative way to run a business, and Ard talked more and more of selling out and moving into Minneapolis.

As much as she loved the house at Minnehaha Falls, Harriet concurred in the decision to sell. Abner and Viola were also talking of moving into town, and she could not conceive of life at Minnehaha Falls without them. Minneapolis held other attractions. Now a city of more than thirteen thousand, it was vibrant, full of the activity from which she had been isolated for the fifteen years she had lived on the homestead. Thus she made no objections when, in 1871, Ard found a buyer who was willing to take only the mills, leaving the Godfreys ownership of the house and the land. With profits from this sale, Ard and Harriet bought a home on Chicago Street in Minneapolis, and in October, though still weak from a summer bout with typhoid fever, Harriet packed up the Minnehaha household for the move into the city.[97]

Harriet Godfrey's life in those Minneapolis years was focused on her children and grandchildren—on weddings, births, and deaths. All of her children, with the exception of Hattie, who devoted h to a teaching career, were eventually married, and from these marriages came sixteen grandchildren, five of whom died in childhood. In August 1882, Harriet and Ard lost another one of their own children, twenty-eight-year-old Kittie, who left a nineteen-month-old son. The child, John Godfrey Osborne, remained with his father, though the Godfreys maintained close ties with him.[98]

Harriet and Ard remained active, enjoying civic as well as family affairs. They made visits to the East Coast, and, after the Berrys moved to Los Angeles in the 1880s, they traveled to the West Coast as well. In the spring of 1888 they sold the Minnehaha homestead to the State of Minnesota, which converted the property into a park that also housed a soldier's home for Civil War veterans.[99]

As the years moved on, Harriet was given more and more to spells of depression. Hers had been a busy life that centered on the care of her many children. Now that they were adults, her ability to guide or assist them was limited, and she felt the loss. "No one thinks much of Mother," she confided to her diary early in 1890. "My day is past. . . . Cannot do any one any good." "Feel sader than usual," she told her diary in the fall of that year, "when will this trouble cease It

Harriet Burr Godfrey at about sixty-five, about 1881. *(Courtesy Hennepin History Museum)*

seems more than I can beare Father is the Same Thank God that it is so. I could not endure it all alone!"[100]

And yet in the end she did have to endure it alone, for on October 15, 1894, at eighty-one years of age, Ard Godfrey died quietly at home. As stipulated by his will, his widow was his sole heir, and

Eugene Godfrey, Abner's son, now a practicing attorney in the city of Minneapolis, was named executor of the estate, which amounted to more than forty thousand dollars.[101]

For most of the nearly two years that she survived her husband, Harriet Godfrey was largely housebound with depression. Hattie and Mattie both lived with her now, and together with Abner, who lived nearby, they tried to ease her loneliness, taking her out on rides and arranging visits with friends and relatives. But she grew increasingly hard to please, even "fractious."[102] Then, on Wednesday afternoon, June 24, 1896, "at twenty minutes after four with a few struggles to swallow & breathe," eighty-four-year-old Harriet Burr Godfrey died, with Hattie and Mattie at her side. Two days later she was buried alongside her husband and her daughter Kittie in the family plot at Lakewood Cemetery. All her surviving children were present, with the exception of Helen, who arrived from Los Angeles too late for the funeral. Abner, her only son, was inconsolable, and Hattie, who had become the heart of the family, observed and recorded it all.

Hattie's records and the reminiscences of her siblings were to prove invaluable some eighty years later when the Minneapolis Women's Club mounted a civic project that restored the yellow pine cabin Ard Godfrey had built for Harriet at Saint Anthony Falls in the winter of 1849. Today that dwelling stands in the middle of a metropolis as a lasting reminder of the lives of a pioneering couple.[103]

VI

Emma Stratton Christie

"If We Only Had a Place of Ourn and You Was with Us"

In late September 1885, having finally chosen a homestead for his family in Montana Territory, David Christie sent the first in a series of letters to his wife Emma, giving her explicit instructions about settling their affairs in Minnesota and preparing herself, the children, and the household goods for the trip west. "Sell the cow to Merrill if he wants her," he wrote, "get the cash for everything you sell if you can for we will need it. . . . Keep your knives forks and spoons you can wrap them up in some of the clothing but the dishes you had best sell they are so heavy and they are just as cheap here take the bell of[f] the cow before you sell her. . . ."[1]

The plans called for Emma to travel from Mankato, Minnesota, to Bozeman, Montana Territory, by train, and he admonished, "You must not come second class because you would be put into the Smokeing carr with a lott of rough men so you must come on first class ticket if it does cost a little more it is the proper way."[2] Having followed her husband's instructions to the best of her ability, Emma traveled to Saint Paul in the company of her sister-in-law Sarah Stevens, and on October 11, 1885, she boarded the train with her five small sons and eleven-week-old Eliza, a product of David's last visit home. Three days later, David met them at the depot in Bozeman, loaded them into his wagon, and took them ten miles up Bridger Canyon, where he introduced Emma to her new home—a one-room cabin with a lean-to kitchen.

❧❧❧

Born into a farming family in Clyman, Wisconsin, on March 15, 1854, Emma Mary Stratton was a daughter of frontier America. Her father, James Stratton, was a native of Vermont; her mother, Martha, a New Yorker. The family had migrated from Ohio to Wisconsin by the time Emma, the seventh of James and Martha's nine children, was born.[3]

Then, sometime between Emma's sixth and eleventh birthdays, the Strattons moved on to Minnesota, settling in Blue Earth County. The family moved en masse, Emma's older married siblings and their families settling on acreage near the senior Strattons. As Emma entered her teen years, she and two brothers, Wilbur and Fred, lived on the family homestead, while two other brothers and a half-brother worked neighboring farms. Emma's older sister, Ellen, her childhood friend and confidante, was now married and living in Amboy, some twelve miles to the southwest.[4]

In the spring of 1868, when Emma was fourteen, family friends from Wisconsin, James and Persis Christie and James's nineteen-year-old son David, settled a few miles north of the Strattons on a quarter-section in the rolling plains between the Blue Earth and Maple rivers. The Christies, like the Strattons, had moved to Minnesota in search of good farmland, the same quest that had caused James Christie to leave the textile mills of his native Scotland some two decades earlier, emigrating to America in the company of his teenaged son, William; his second wife, Eliza; and his three youngest children, Tom, Sarah, and Alexander. David, James's fifth and last child, had been born on September 8, 1848, a year after the family settled in Wisconsin. Some two years later, Eliza Christie died in labor, and James subsequently married Persis Noyes, who raised his four youngest children. Now, with William farming in southeastern Minnesota, Tom and Alexander (Sandy) away in school, and Sarah teaching back in Wisconsin, it was David to whom James looked as he settled into life in Blue Earth County.[5]

And it was David to whom a certain young woman looked as well, for on July 4, 1870, in a ceremony held at the bride's home in Good Thunder, Minnesota, sixteen-year-old Emma Stratton married twenty-year-old David Christie. The groom, a severe asthmatic, was so ill on his wedding day that he "had to lie down . . . before coming down to the parlor to be married," and he collapsed after the rites with what was diagnosed as "pleura pneumonia." What was to have been a

honeymoon soon became a death watch; by dawn friends and relatives feared for David's life. But the young man rallied and within a
week was back at work on his father's farm, where he and his bride
shared a room in the James Christie home, a living arrangement that
was to become uncomfortably common for them in the years ahead.[6]

In November, four months after the wedding, David Christie bought
the eastern half of his father's acreage, and in the center of that land,
about a quarter of a mile from his parents' house, he built a home for
himself and Emma. It was there, on March 7, 1872, that Emma bore
their first child, "a wonderful Large pretty Blue Eyed Boy," who was
named James James, after his two grandfathers. The young parents
doted on their firstborn, and David, a loving, attentive father, shared
news of the baby's growth in frequent letters to his brothers, Tom
and Sandy, and his sister, Sarah. David was a caring brother as well
as a caring father, and shortly after his baby's birth, in order to help
his sister through a financial crisis, he compromised his own position by remortgaging the Christie farm. Even before David assumed
Sarah's debts, his financial situation had been precarious, and for
the next two years, he and Emma struggled to stay afloat.[7]

Then, in the summer of 1874, money matters were forgotten in the
wake of a new crisis. Two-year-old Jamie suddenly developed an
"affection of the brain and spinal chord" and died after a brief illness. Within hours of her son's death, Emma Christie went into
labor, and "While [Jamie's] Body still lay in the house . . . [she] was
delivered of a Boy," promptly named Alexander for his Uncle Sandy,
who was now studying at Harvard. That very afternoon, August 11,
1874, little Jamie Christie was buried beside his grandfather, James
Stratton.[8]

Stoically, Emma carried on, tending to her baby, seeing to her
other tasks about the house and farm, and worrying over family
finances. As 1874 passed and the harvest of 1875 came around, she
and David were optimistic about their crops but despairing of their
financial situation—and with good reason, for Sarah had signed
David's name to a loan on which she had made no payments. Even
the excellent harvest that fall of 1875 did not yield enough money to
cover the new note in addition to the Christies' other debts. Knowing his father's great need to hold on to the farm at all costs, David
bought time by borrowing money at 30 percent interest.[9]

In November 1876, Emma gave birth to "another Little Christie . . .
a fine healthy Stout boy" named Donald. She was on her feet again

within two weeks of the birth, and David reported to Sandy that she was "real Smart sewing on the Machine tonight" and that the baby was "real good sleeps and Eats most of the time." When the mortgage came due soon after little Don's arrival, David was able to save the farm only by writing Tom and Sandy to ask for money.[10]

Any hopes he had of repaying his brothers were dashed when that season's crops were devastated by grasshoppers. Reporting that he had never worked so hard in his life, David described days that began at 4 in the morning and went on "as long as we can see fighting them." He was exhausted and discouraged as he watched "the Best Promiseing Crop [he] Ever had melting away before [him]." Sensing the futility of his struggles, he began to question the wisdom of staying on in Minnesota. He knew a number of young men who were leaving Blue Earth County to claim government land in the Black Hills; from Wisconsin Sarah reported that farmers there were also heading for the Dakotas, many of them leaving wives and children behind.[11] Although David envied those who were leaving, he held on to the farm through yet another dismal season rather than disappoint his father.

Ties to the elder Christies remained as tight as ever—and the work as heavy. During the harvest of 1877, David suffered another serious attack of asthma. Recovered, he toyed with his brother Sandy's proposal that the two of them seek renewed health in the invigorating climes of Colorado. The idea was attractive, but he shook it off, resolving to stay where he was until he got "out of these troubles of Debt." He was resolved as well to stay close by his wife and children. Family life suited him well, and he tried to convey his delight in his little ones to Sandy: "I have just stopped and rocked Sandy and Donald to Sleep Sandy says good night pa good night ma good night Aunt Sarah good night Don . . . and goes to Sleep and then I took Don and sang him to Sleep they are two very nice Boys if I do say it—don is a very Large Strong Built child he has a very large head Brown eyes and light hair Sandy is more slight is growing quite tall is intelligent he knows all his letters is very quick to understand anything."[12]

There were soon two more sons to be rocked: David Bertie Christie II, born August 20, 1878, and George Alfred, born November 4, 1880. With four boys to feed and clothe and little hope of otherwise getting out from under his debts, David thought again of selling the farm and beginning anew. But his father's need to hold on to the land continued to control his fate.[13]

Any hope that 1881 might be a better year faded in the face of yet another major setback. On a bitterly cold January day, while David was at work in the woods and Emma and the four boys were alone at home, the house caught fire. With the help of the hired man, Joe Dodge, Emma carried baby George and his brothers to safety. After piling blankets over the children to ward off the near-zero temperatures, she and Dodge returned to drag what possessions they could from the burning house. Minutes after they had pulled out her sewing machine, the roof collapsed. The house was a total loss, and only a prevailing north wind saved the granary, woodpile, and hay.[14]

In the wake of the fire, Emma, David, and the boys moved once again into the home of James and Persis Christie. Due in part to the added stress he was under, David suffered a major asthma attack. Ill and broke as he was, his thoughts returned to the one hope he had left: the trip west. Thirty-three years old, mired in debt, and responsible for a wife, four children, and elderly parents, he wrote his brother Sandy, "If I can only get out to Colorado next Spring and get so I can breathe why I can get into Some employment that will pay."[15]

The plan became feasible early in 1882 when William Stevens, a well-to-do widower who had married Sarah Christie a few years earlier, agreed to assume the note on David and Emma's house and farm, along with several other Christie debts. With his financial worries now eased, David pondered other aspects of his plan. What would he do with Emma and the boys if he did go west? It seemed best to accept the offer made by Emma's brother, Fred Stratton. If she and the boys moved in with the Strattons, they could have the upstairs of the large house to themselves, Emma could do the milking and light chores for her brother and sister-in-law, and the older boys, Sandy and Don, now seven and five, would be close to school. Having resolved the situation in his own mind, David purchased a ticket to Leadville, Colorado.[16]

Emma's involvement in her husband's decision and preparations was minimal. From the first, Sandy had been his primary confidant, and Emma knew little more than that he might go west and that she must see to things if he did. In the end, she lacked even the comfort of a farewell embrace, for when David left Blue Earth County on the evening of May 15, 1882, he sent her a message from the depot that he was underway sooner than expected and would write as he could en route.[17]

Within two weeks, he was settled in the Arkansas River valley of

Colorado, where he had gained twelve pounds in eleven days, had no sign of asthma, and had taken a job promising wages of sixty dollars a month, plus board, loading coal at the Malta Lake kilns. The mountain air was bracing, the coal dust did not bother him, and he had finally written to Emma, sending what cash he could spare. Yet by late August, having taken sick and lost his job, David wrote his brother Sandy for train fare home. By early October, four and a half months after having left Minnnesota, David was back in his rebuilt farmhouse with Emma and the boys. Although he was still suffering the effects of asthma, the money he had earned in Colorado, plus the money sent by Sandy, had, to some extent, eased the family's financial situation.[18]

Determined to return to the mountain air that had so improved his health and to the booming western economy that had provided more cash than he could ever have accumulated in Blue Earth County, David now laid plans to go to Montana Territory in the spring. Two of his former hired hands, Joe Dodge and Emma's nephew Myron Stratton, were doing well out there, and David hoped to join in some venture with one or the other of them. Granted, he would be leaving Emma and the children behind again, but he justified his plan to Sandy: "I think it would be a very foolish thing for me to take out a wife and family of small children and expose them to hardships, and then come home some night and find them all murdered by a lot of Damned Crow Indians or some other outlaws. . . . Untill we [k]now more about the country and get started then we could make it pay to come back and get the family and take out a small herd of heifers and then the children will have a chance to go to school here now."[19]

Eager to be off, David chose "the most direct rout" on the newly laid Northern Pacific line. Unsure as to how livestock would fare in the harsh Montana winters, he had given up an earlier plan of taking sheep with him, deciding instead to wait and see how well Myron Stratton's sheep fared.[20] Besides, unencumbered by livestock, he would be free to take the best job he could find working for wages. That was by far the fastest way to gather the money he would need to bring his family out, once he found a good place in the West.

In mid-May of 1883, hopeful for David's success and confident that he would be home by early September, Emma put her husband on the train, then took eight-year-old Sandy, six-year-old Donald, four-year-old David, and two-year-old George home to the lonely farmhouse. Their separate adventures were underway, though David's had a less-than-auspicious beginning. Prostrated by yet another attack of asthma by the time he arrived in Miles City, Montana Territory, David had to be carried off the train by his traveling companions. Unwilling to admit defeat so quickly, he insisted on being loaded into the wagon they bought for the trip across the plains and into the mountains surrounding Bozeman, some three hundred miles to the west. That journey was restorative, for by the time David reached his destination, he was in hearty good health again.[21]

Delighted to hear of the healing powers of the mountain air, Emma looked forward to other letters that would bring equally encouraging news of all that her husband found in the land that was to become her home. The news was not what she had hoped for. While good homesteads were still available in the more mountainous areas of the territory, David was in no position to stake his claim. He was earning $1.50 a day, plus room and board, for his work on the Godwin ranch in the Cherry Creek area, about thirty miles west of Bozeman, but he sent little money home to Emma, and she lived in constant fear that notes would be called in and creditors would seize their house and farm before David could return. Hers was not a comfortable situation, but it was a familiar one, since she had lived all of her married life under the shadow of heavy debts. Nonetheless, things were especially dismal that summer of 1883. Because the farmland went unworked, there was no prospect of income from a cash crop. With the help of her brother Fred, Emma tended her garden and livestock. Milking two cows, she even managed to earn some cash from the extra butter she churned, but that meager amount was barely sufficient to keep the boys in shoes and clothes and left her little to apply toward retirement of their debts.[22]

Although she had no way of repaying what they already owed, Emma had no intentions of borrowing anything more. Frugal to the point of sacrifice, she was determined to avoid signing any more of the hated notes, vowing, "As to our running [further] in det we have not nor wod not if we had to do with out grocers."[23] She was not afraid of going hungry, because the garden provided most of the food they needed, and she kept David informed of the state of their crops and those of their neighbors. She wrote detailed news of family and community affairs as well, yet neither her letters nor David's specifically mentioned the fact that she was carrying their fifth child.

In September, Emma wrote for David's advice as she faced a major decision. Mr. Eberhart, a neighbor, wanted to buy their eighty acres.

Prospects of a sale raised David's hopes as well as hers, and he advised her to sell the land at $2,100 with the timber or $1,900 without it. Upon hearing the price, Eberhart lost interest, letting it be known that he would soon enough be able to buy the land at auction for much less than the Christies were asking. His predictions seemed likely to come true, with Christie fields lying fallow and a six-month note to William Stevens falling due. Emma advised David that all he needed to do was to write Stevens for an extension, but either pride or carelessness kept him from doing so. Caught in a bind, Emma approached Sandy, asking him to write Stevens on David's behalf.[24]

Instead, Sandy fired off letters to both Sarah and David, accusing Stevens of taking advantage of Emma in her husband's absence and questioning whether he had been giving Emma credit for the small, but sacrificial, payments she had been making. In the midst of unsettled accounts and flying accusations, Emma carried on her household duties and struggled to maintain good relations with Sarah and William Stevens. Powerless to do anything more about the debts, she clung to what she had and waited for word that David's summer work had ended and he was coming home. September stretched into October with no word from him. Then, in late October, he finally wrote. He was lonely: "I have been Dreaming of you every night most," he admitted. "I have got the blues . . . I will be glad when I can get home for I am sick of this knocking around." If those words were welcome to Emma, what came next was not: "I have not money enough to take me home but will strike something to earn some more they charge more to go back [by rail] than they did to come out I think it is 54 dollars to St Paul."[25]

He still made no specific mention of Emma's impending delivery, but he was clearly concerned: "I am afraid you are sick or you would have written. . . . Now Dear you don't know how anxious I am to hear from you and to know how you are. . . . Oh Darling I hope you are well it troubles me all the time." By the time Emma received that letter, she had already given birth to her fifth son, who would not be named until his father was home. The night his baby was born, David was camped in the Bridger Mountains, "wallowing in snow . . . 2½ feet deep." Feeling "just about played out," he passed on to his brother Sandy news he withheld from his wife. Determined "never to settle in this cursed country where they only have about 3 months of plesant weather," he was considering taking Sandy's advice and traveling farther west, into Washington Territory, though he hardly knew "what to do with everything at home."[26]

Those concerns, in the end, tipped the scales, and in early November 1883, with no prior word to Emma, David arrived home to greet his new son, whom—either out of his own good nature or with uncharacteristic shrewdness—he promptly named in honor of his major creditor, Sarah's husband, William Stevens. Glad as he was to be home with Emma and the boys, David was not especially happy to be back in Minnesota's inhospitable climate. Within days of his arrival home, he was overcome by an asthma attack so severe that he was "hardly able to get a breath." Almost simultaneously, he accepted from "a German man" an offer of two thousand dollars for his farm, exactly what he'd hoped to get for the property. Sensitive to his father's need to hold on to the land, David was equally sensitive to his own need to stay solvent—charged as he was with the care of his aging parents as well as that of his growing family. Both farms were in imminent danger of foreclosure, and he could hardly expect help from his brothers in working the land or in meeting the mortgages on Christie holdings in Blue Earth County. If he tried to hold on to everything, he might well lose everything instead. James, well aware that his son's poor health would never allow him to pay off the debts owed on their land, gave his endorsement to David's plan to sell out his portion of the property and move west. In fact, James himself was giving thought to selling out and following the younger Christies once they got settled.[27]

Heartened, David concluded the sale of the land that had long burdened him and, having no farm work to hold him, accepted an invitation to visit Sandy in Washington, D.C. Returning from that visit, he focused his attention on his prospects in Montana. Joe Dodge had written him that the parcel of land he was most interested in was proving to be "a splendid winter range for stock . . . all bare of snow and the cattle and sheep are doing first rate." David shared that letter with Emma, hoping to convince her that at last he had found the land that would provide them a good living; he assured her that it had "the best of watter and plenty of timber and coal and good grass and shelter for stock" and that her "children [would] not grow up cowboys . . . for it is close to a town and [is] a well settled country."[28]

By spring things had begun to fall into place. In late March, David moved himself, Emma, and the boys—and all their possessions—in with James and Persis Christie, promising her that their time in cramped quarters should be relatively brief, for he had come up with a very practical plan for the move west. According to the rail agent at Mankato, he could take an "emigrant car"—a boxcar loaded with himself, two stoves, whatever household goods Emma could spare, enough provisions for one or two months, up to six head of cattle, plus grain and hay for the livestock—to Miles City for seventy dollars. Once in Montana, he would live in a tent and hire men to help him get out the logs he would need for a house, then send for Emma and the boys as soon as the building was completed.[29]

But by late April, David realized that he had been "greatly . . . misinformed in this buisiness of going out with a carr." With everything all but ready for the trip, the freight agent at Mankato told him that he had been mistaken about the rate; the emigrant car would cost almost two hundred dollars, not seventy. At that rate the plan was hardly feasible; the cows and household goods together were not worth the cost of the ticket.[30]

As disappointed as he was by this turn of events, David was no less determined to get west as quickly and as cheaply as he could. When Sarah's stepson Frank Stevens, who had made the trip to Montana a year earlier, wrote that work was available with his old outfit at Godwin's ranch on Cherry Creek, David seized the opportunity. At forty-five dollars a month plus room and board, he could earn enough to bring the family out by rail the next spring—and still be able to purchase the livestock and household goods they would need in Montana. Of course, with the farmhouse sold, Emma and the boys would have to stay with relatives in the interim, and his first plan was to let them stay on with his parents, even though James and Persis could hardly tolerate having noisy children underfoot for longer than a few weeks at a time.[31]

A better, if bolder, plan then presented itself to David. Emma's brother Fred was building a fourteen- by twenty-foot granary about thirty yards east of his house, close by the Christie farm. Emma and the boys, now seven months to nine years in age, could spend the summer in that structure if David merely added a small shed on the side to hold the cookstove and serve as the kitchen. "They will be very comfortable," David wrote Sandy. "I have put in a patch of potatoes and she can have what garden ground she wants, and I am getting up what wood she needs."[32]

There is no written record of what Emma Christie thought of her husband's plan. Surely she shared his relief at having sold the land and lightened their load and would have agreed that spending a long, hot summer in a granary with five little boys might be preferable to spending it within the cramped confines of the James Christie home. Further, since Fred "would not have it," she would have no rent to worry about in David's absence.[33] Whatever her feelings about the new living arrangements, she had little choice but to make the best of the situation.

On an early May morning, David Christie hugged Emma and the boys in turn, said his farewells to his parents and sister, and set out for the depot, armed with the hearty lunch Emma had prepared for him in the new cookshed of her granary home. After an uneventful trip by rail, he arrived in Bozeman, Montana Territory, on May 15, 1884, and went at once to Godwin's ranch. From the first, he missed his family and wrote Emma frequently, asking for every scrap of news about the boys. He also sent vivid pictures of his life on the ranch:

> I have just got my Team turned out and have cooked my Supper and eat it and got my Dishes washed up and the room swept out and some fruit on the stove to Stew and of course Dear you Know I have got my pipe in my mouth but Just hold on a minute it has gone out and I must get a match and there comes my saddle horse up so I must go and put him in for I want him in the morning to ketch the other horses with so when I come in I will sit down and have a chatt with you. I suppose Dear you would laugh if you could see me liveing this old Batch life. . . . it is very lonesome but I have old Tomy the Cat to talk to and he is always glad to see me when I come in at night.[34]

Amused though she was to hear that David had gotten to be "quite a jolly old batch," Emma was torn by thoughts of his having no one to cook and clean for him: "Now I wish that I could bea with you Dear to take care of you I know that you kned things don for you I know that your cloths need washing and mending." From the relative comfort of her granary home, she wrote to ask whether he had made himself a proper bed from the straw ticking she had sent out with him. "No Dear," he replied, "I have not filled my straw tick yet— but I am going to soon . . . [in the meantime] we have . . . two big Buffaloe Robes under us."[35]

When David reported that he had cut his knee with an axe, Emma worried for weeks before finally hearing that the wound had healed without infection. She upbraided him for acting as if he were invulnerable, noting, "you alwayes think there is nothing can hurt you I know you so well." She longed to be with him so she could nurse him back to health, and was haunted by the thought that he might never come home: "I am so afraid that there will [be] something hapen to you what should we do if you should bea taken away."[36]

Unable to protect her far-distant husband from illness or injury, Emma focused on her sons. "Don he has got a bad cold," she wrote David. "Willie has got won tooth he groes like a weed little G[eorge] wants to see pa . . . he is talking about you so much." David was hungry for such news: "How I would like to see you all. Kiss Willie for pa the little pet and Georgy and all of the Dear little boys I hope they are all learning good. . . . now Darling be sure and get your pictures taken and send to me for I want to have them to look at." He reminded nine-year-old Sandy that he was "the oldest so try and be mas little man and do what she tells you promptly and be kind to your brothers." He described his experiences with mountain sheep and bears, knowing his stories would thrill the boys, and he continually reminded them of his love for them: "Pa thinks of his little boys often and hopes that they are good to one another," he wrote that summer.[37]

Clearly David missed his wife as well as his boys, and he was not unmindful of the sacrifices she was making during his absence: "I think of you every hour Dear and am happy to think I am blessed with such a good wife." He shared recollections of good times they had shared, reminding her once of a shopping trip they had made together and asking, "Did you get that hat Dear you were looking at that day Now Darling fix up and go and have your picture taken and send to me for I want to see you so bad Now do pet like a good girl for I am so lonesome away of[f] here alone."[38]

For Emma's part, loneliness often bordered on despair. "Dear you dont know how lonsome I am i hope that we will get settled so that you can bea with us i hope that i Shall get sum good news from you [of] what we are going to do and then i would have sum hopes of not always [having] to live here without you." Suspended as she was between her old world and the promised new one, she found her faith slipping: "I some times give up all hopes of seeing the time that we [are] ever settled. . . . If it was not for the children i some times feel so that i should rather bea sunk in a well than to live this way." Knowing that David was still "unsettled [on] what to do" about moving the family to Montana did nothing to raise her spirits.[39]

David's indecision was prompted by another disappointment. Shortly after his arrival in Montana, he had discovered that the land on which he had built a year's worth of dreams had been claimed by another settler a few days before he left Minnesota. That land had been near Bozeman, and he despaired of finding anything else he could afford so close to town. From the isolation of Cherry Creek, he now painted a bleak picture of life in Montana, where Emma "would have no neighbors and there would be no school for the children." "It is such a wilderness to bring a family to," he declared, "it is such a hard climate perhaps it would be better to go to the Pacific slope." Noting that the only society was "of the Roughest sort," he asked, "Supose one of the children were taken sick it would take 2 Days to get a doctor and then he would charge thirty or forty dollers for one visit and perhaps he would not want to come atall."[40]

Her husband's allusion to the possibility of going on to "the Pacific slope" was a dead giveaway. David had obviously been hearing from his brother Sandy, who for some time had urged on him the idea of looking on the West Coast, "where there is a better climate and better school privelages." Under Sandy's influence and with his own altered perspective, David urged Emma to consider that "In looking up a place to live we must try and better ourselves or else not come at all." In Montana they would hardly be bettering themselves, since "all the farming lands are taken up and have been for years," crops required irrigation, the winters were too long and harsh for fruit, and a stock ranch would take "lots of money to start . . . and a long time to wait for Returns."[41]

Besides, family life in Montana Territory was nonexistent:

> they are mostly old Batches here that den up in the winter like bears and what people that have familys here are a poor lot and dont care whether they know anything or not the children learn more Deviltry than anything else it makes one sick to see them poor misguided wretches fit for nothing but to fill the states prisons and I cant think of givin our inocent Boys such an Education and if they see evil around them they will fall into it and I will not sacrifice the family for me. . . . the women here are enough to make one sick maried women will Drink Beer play cards and ride around with other men that is a fine example to set for their children who could asociate with such people.

Each such diatribe was set against phrases about better opportunities farther west: "Now in Oregon Washington Ter[ritory] and California they have a good climate plenty of fruit crops do not have to be iregated and it is more sivalized and I think it would pay to look at it." If lands farther west did not suit him, he pronounced himself ready to "go further south and east whare we can at least live a decent life." As if he could read Emma's mind and hear her arguments in favor of his remaining where he was, he summarily dismissed them: "Now Dear dont blame me for thinking this way for I am here and see and know and you are there and can only imagine."[42]

Whatever Emma might have been imagining about the opportunities that awaited them in Montana Territory had come, of course, from David's own glowing accounts throughout the winter months. Faced with his startling change of opinion, she read the situation for what it probably was—an attempt to put off as long as possible making the hard choice necessary to their settling in. Early on she had sensed that Sandy's influence was partly to blame for David's wanderlust, writing, "I hope that you will do what is for the best and not listen to Sandy all togeather if you do we never will get settled." Through David's other absences, Emma had tolerated Sandy's interference and acquiesced to David's every decision. Perhaps life within the confines of the granary pushed her to a new assertiveness. Perhaps the realization that her husband's wandering could go on through many summers to come drove her to take her stand. Whatever the reasons for her change in attitude, she now cut through all David's excuses and got to the heart of the matter: "I can tell you what . . . if you dont settle your mind on what you are going to do you can bea runing about all the rest of your days and never bea settled I think there ought to bea somthing settled upon and when there is i would stick to it."[43]

Concerning his talk of going to the West Coast, she spared no words: "It will take evry cent that you have got for you to get there and look up aplace [to] say nothing about b[u]ying any thing or ever geting your famly there." She also countered his disparaging remarks about living in Montana. "Dont say an[y] thing about [not having] neighbors," she wrote, "for we dont have any here you know that i can get along without them if any wone can if you can bea with us." Although schooling for the children could not be so lightly dismissed, since she was "very much oposed to go whare our children cant go to school," it was clear that they could not aspire to have everything they wanted all at once: "We should stop and think we have not very much and we will hafto commence in a very small way where ever we commence. . . . it is geting about time there was somthing settled upon as to the way that we are living most any way would be a pleasant [life] if we only had a place of ourn and you was with us. . . . i dont think that you know what a unplesant life that i haf to live to live this way." And she issued a quasi-ultimatum: "I never felt as i do this summer about living this way. . . . If you do not make up your mind to settle in montanna that is if you go farther than there [so] we cant bea with you [then] . . . i dont feal that i shall bea willing to live this way much longer and i hope that you will not ask me to."[44]

Her life at home had changed but little in his absence. Relations with Sarah and William Stevens were strained enough to keep her from their door, and though she maintained polite ties with all family members, she kept her own counsel, preferring to write her thoughts to her sister Ellen over in Amboy rather than tell them to less sympathetic ears nearby. She went up to the home of her half-brother Albert for a visit and later took the boys out for a ride with him when he came to borrow her sewing machine for his wife. She maintained a dutiful relationship with the elder Christies, heeding their request "to com up and clean and white wash" for them before Sandy's expected arrival for the harvest.[45]

With harvest approaching, Emma was very aware of a new problem. Her brother would obviously need his granary soon, and she would have to make other living arrangements for herself and the boys. David suggested she might move into town, but she was sure it would "cost . . . [too] much to go to Mankato to live." David, too, was "anxious to get some kind of a home of our own and our own Roof over our heads again where I can be with the Family," but he could not be forced into a premature homecoming: "As I am here [already I] will work about 2 months longer and then go home," he promised her.[46]

With no idea of how or where she was to move now that Fred needed her home to store his summer's crop, Emma was near panic. It was all very well for David to suggest that she take a house in Mankato, but how was she to manage such a move? With no money for rent, she could hardly act on her husband's advice. Giving up any hope of help from David, she devised a plan of her own. If she could live in one granary, why not another? Adept as she had become at make-do housing, she would refit an abandoned granary near James Christie's home, move herself and the children in, and thereby maintain the family's rent-free existence. David agreed that her plan had much to recommend it: "I supose Father would be pleased to have us there and it would be much better for Father and mother for they are to Old to live alone in that cold country." Yet knowing the dilapidated state of the building in which she proposed to live, he wondered whether or not they could survive the winter there and asked who she planned to get to repair it.[47]

Coming home himself to see to the repairs was out of the question, for although he hadn't had any trouble with his asthma all summer, going home in August would surely set off an attack, rendering him virtually worthless to help. However, when David's brother Sandy arrived home in mid-August to help with the harvest, he saw at once the extent of Emma's dilemma and wrote to David, demanding that he come home at once and look after his family. Emma must not move until the old granary was cleaned and repaired, yet she must move soon so that Fred's crop would not be lost.[48]

Uncharacteristically, David ignored Sandy's order and lingered on in Montana, explaining to Emma, "We are not done Haying yet and it will take us 2 weeks yet and I cant go away and leave them in such a fix . . . so you will have to do the best you can Dear." Buying time, he promised to be home "by the first of September or my Birthday at farthest" and advised her to move in with his parents until he got there, apparently forgetting the chaos that ensued the last time she and the boys had tried living under the same roof with James and Persis. In late August he sent her a postal order for one hundred dollars.[49] And a few days later, he himself arrived home—in time to celebrate his thirty-sixth birthday on September 6, 1884.

With Fred's new granary bulging with the summer's harvest, Emma and the children were once again living with relatives. At once David set about fixing up the old granary on his father's property and soon had his family settled in what was to be their home until spring.[50] With his farmland sold, there was little for him to do that winter but plan his move west—and father still another child.

That, baby was not due until August, the very end of the emigration season, a fact that posed problems for David. He had vowed to take his family with him the next time he went west, and going alone meant breaking his word and leaving Emma to birth yet another child without him. Furthermore, he dismissed at once the idea of taking a pregnant wife across the plains. Though delaying would mean lost income, he decided to stay at home until the baby was born. With the coming of spring, he planted his father's acreage, but the onset of summer brought recurrent asthma attacks that kept him out of the fields. Confined to the house, he corresponded with friends and relatives in the West, from whom he learned that the foreman at Cherry Creek was holding a place for him at his old job and that Myron Stratton was working on his homestead claim up Bridger Canyon.[51]

Right up to her due date, Emma continued to handle all her accustomed chores while nursing her ailing husband. On August 4, 1885, she was delivered of her first daughter, a healthy little girl named Eliza. Eight days after his daughter's birth, David boarded the train at Mankato, heading for Montana and the Godwin ranch on Cherry Creek. This time plans were fully in place for his family to follow him as soon as Emma was up to the trip and David had a home for them to come to. On August 15, he wrote from the Saint Paul House in Bozeman, noting that soon after his arrival in Montana, his asthma had left him entirely.[52]

Up Bridger Canyon, he found Myron Stratton doing quite well. Stratton's neighbors, the Proffits, were "one of the finest families" David had met in the territory, and they were most hospitable to him during the days he spent in Myron's homesteader shack. With his neighbors, Stratton had put up about one hundred tons of hay and was looking forward to a good winter. "There is a piece of government land that joins Myrons in the same section which he would like me to take," David wrote, "and perhaps I will." But David had first to "go up Cherry Creek way . . . and see how it is there" before settling upon the Bridger Canyon land.[53]

By the end of August, two weeks after having arrived in Montana, David was once more working at Cherry Creek. Although he enjoyed being with his old friends, he had "about made up [his] mind to settle in Bridger near Myron." The parcel of land he had seen had "plenty of good range for stock good watter and lots of heavy timber." It also had fine fertile ground from which "a good deal of hay can be cutt."[54]

Myron had decided to build a house on the land he had staked, and David planned to go up the canyon, stake his own claim, and "commence cutting logs" for both houses. Working with Myron would be doubly advantageous, for the young man owned a team of horses, a wagon, and all the tools David needed to build their new home. Proclaiming everything "as cheap out here as it is [in Minnesota]," he predicted, "we can live as well here as there." With the prize so near his grasp, he fretted that some harm would befall his family before he could bring them out to the promised land, and he was troubled by nightmares in which Emma, the children, or his father were ill or in need of him. Pushing his anxieties aside, he continued to work for wages for nearly two more weeks, but on September 11 he set out for Bozeman and thence up Bridger Canyon to cut the logs for his house and Myron's, determined to get the two homes up "before snow comes."[55]

With Emma's trip to Montana imminent, her brother-in-law Sandy sent her ten dollars, along with the suggestion that she leave her two oldest, Sandy and Don, with James and Persis Christie for the coming year in order that they might attend school. David, though, wanted to have the family all together and reminded Emma that since their homestead was only ten miles up Bridger Canyon from Bozeman, they could rent a house in town for only "10 or 12 Dollars per month" if she wanted the boys to attend school through the winter. He and Myron were "Batching it" up Bridger Canyon in the little shack Myron had built on his claim a year earlier. Within a mile of the claim they had found "trees Sixty feet high as straight as a gun barrel" from which they were cutting logs for their houses. David planned to "build a house about 16 x 20 inside with a good high chamber in it and then build a kitchen on to it perhaps next summer."[56]

Despite his earlier warning that his wife could expect no fit neighbors in Montana, David promised Emma that she would enjoy Sadie Proffitt, "a good Christian woman" who had been very kind to him. And he told Emma of his second thoughts about their spending the winter down in Bozeman. He was confident they could be quite comfortable up Bridger Canyon. Already his own contentment lacked but one thing: "Dear I would feel hapy if you were here."[57]

By month's end, David and Myron had cut the logs for both houses— 120 in all—and had begun "snaking them out to the road." He expected the hauling to take around two days, during which time he would also be cutting the "sleepers and rafters." He and Myron had already purchased their lumber and hauled all but one load to their building sites. His health was good, with not a symptom of asthma.[58]

Now David turned his attention to a list of instructions for Emma. She should sell the cow to Merrell if he wanted her, but "if you can get more from any body else why take it of course." She was to take the bell off the cow before selling her and to get another one of their bells from a Mr. McDowell. When the hog got fat, she should also sell her, taking care to deal only in cash, since they would need the money for the trip west. She was to be sure to bring with her the two augers, his hand saw, a square, and the ripsaw, "if father will let you have it." Other than that, she was to "sell of[f] everything that [she could] sell" and "pay of[f] those Debts" he had told her about.[59]

His instructions for her packing were detailed and well considered: "You had better buy 2 of the largest trunks you can find something cheap to pack cloths and bedding in." She could keep her knives, forks, and spoons, but not her dishes, since they were heavy and could be replaced quite cheaply in Bozeman. Weight was definitely a consideration, since she would be allowed only 150 pounds for each full ticket—"your ticket is one Sandy and Don will be another which is two Davy will be half of one so that will be 365 pounds of baggage you can bring." Advising her to weigh the trunks on Fred's scales, he urged her to "fill them . . . and no more for if they over weigh they charge 7 cents per pound" for everything above the allotted weight. If necessary, she could leave the sewing machine behind, since she could have it and any other household goods shipped later for only two dollars per hundred.[60]

George, Willie, and the baby could all ride without tickets, though David warned Emma that the agent might well try to make her pay for George, who would turn five in early November. He wanted Sarah to accompany them on the train from Mankato to Saint Paul so that Emma would have help in transferring her baggage to the through train to the West. Knowing that his frugal wife would, if left on her own, choose the cheapest fare, David warned her not to come second class but to invest $56.75 in an adult first-class ticket for herself. By his reckoning, the whole family could make the trip for less than $150, plus another $6.00 or so for Sarah's round-trip ticket from Mankato to Saint Paul. He acknowledged that the money might be hard to come by, but if she could get a good price on the sale of her surplus items and if she collected a payment owed on the farm by the new owner, she should be able to come up with about $200. She should send anything beyond what she needed on to him, since he had only $12.00 left after buying lumber for the house, and he still had to buy the shingles and windows.[61]

David expected to be ready for Emma and the children "any time after the 15 or 20 of October," and he asked that she write to let him know just what day she would leave Saint Paul so that he could be at the depot to meet her. Should something keep him from getting to the station, she and the children were to "take a buss and go to the St Paul house in Bozeman," where H. Schabarker, a former Minnesotan, would put her up for the night. "They dont keep much of a Hotell," he warned, "but then they are pretty good folks." His final set of instructions was easy enough to carry out: "Kiss Willie Georgie and little Emma for pa," David told her. If Emma found it disconcerting that he had already forgotten baby Eliza's name, she likely forgave him his error and concentrated on the promise held in his final lines: "Keep up a good heart Dear we will soon have a good home of our own now good night pet from your loving Husband."[62]

On the afternoon of October 12, 1885, Emma Stratton Christie was seated in a first-class car on the Northern Pacific, surrounded by her children. Filled with excitement, anticipation, and some apprehension, she was, at long last, on her way to begin the new life she and David had been moving toward for five long years. Having put Emma and the children on the train at Saint Paul, Sarah telegrammed David to expect the family on October 14 at about 3 in the afternoon.[63]

The train, predictably, was a few hours late, and it was early evening when Emma and the children finally arrived in Bozeman, where David was greeted by "such a host of little chaps with rolls of Blankets and valises and Baskets and all saying at once oh here is pa." The little family had "got through first rate [with] plenty of lunch and Didies," David noted in his letter to Sarah, thanking her for her help in seeing them off. Rather than make the long journey up Bridger Canyon after dark, David chose to stay overnight in Bozeman at the Saint Paul House.[64]

Perhaps it was best that Emma spent her first night in Montana Territory in a hotel, for quite a surprise awaited her the next morning. By his own report, David was not quite ready for them. In reality, the "house" that awaited them amounted to little more than piles of unpeeled logs and stacks of rough lumber. After a cursory tour of the property surrounding the beginnings of their new home, David drove his wife and children on up Spring Creek to Myron Stratton's claim, where he unloaded their belongings into a one-room shack with a lean-to kitchen.[65]

Despite the disappointments they must have felt at not being able to move into their own house, Emma and the children quickly settled into Stratton's homesteader shack. By mid-November, though he had finally managed to get the cellar dug and the rafters, sleepers, and joists peeled, David was ready to concede that he would not get the house up for them to live in that winter. However, he saw no reason for them to move into town. They would winter over in the homestead shack, despite the housekeeping inconveniences and lack of school.[66]

Fortunately, the winter was a mild one through the Christmas season, and under the watchful eyes of his five little boys, David continued to work on the house, notching the logs and setting them in place, then adding the rafters. Heavy snows early in 1886 slowed but did not stop his work, and by early spring the roof was in place at last. His example was not lost on his sons, for seven-year-old Davy and five-year-old George built a little playhouse of short logs and covered it with boards and deerskins. Finding themselves in a world of cowboys, they galloped on their stick horses across the fields, with little Willie close behind. Sandy and Don helped their mother indoors and tended the livestock—fourteen Plymouth Rock hens and a milk cow—and baby Eliza thrived in her new surroundings. The family as a whole was healthy and happy, and by early summer they were very much at home in their new house, a sixteen- by twenty-foot structure with "a good chamber."[67]

With David's family finally settled in their new home, there remained but one final step in the Christies' emigration to Montana Territory. Seventy-five years old and in failing health, James Christie felt that "the mountain air and change of scene [would] tone him up" and began to make plans for moving west. In June 1886, he and Persis traveled to Saint Paul in the company of William Stevens, who saw them safely onto the Northern Pacific, and two days later they were met in Bozeman by David, who loaded them into his wagon and drove them up Bridger Canyon. When the couple once more showed their inability to tolerate life in his boisterous household, David cut and hauled logs and began construction on a smaller house some thirty yards south of his own. In early October 1886, James and Persis Christie moved into their new mountain home.[68]

Once settled in Montana, Emma, who had long lived in close proximity to her siblings, was linked to them only by mail. Over the next few years, letters exchanged by the families carried news of crops and weather, weddings and births, illnesses and deaths. Emma and her sister Ellen exchanged pictures of themselves and their children, scraps of dress material, and bits of gossip from their respective worlds. Sarah Stevens urged David to "tell Emma I would like to see her ever so much & have a whole day's talk." Letters from the Christie children to relatives back east revealed an almost idyllic farm scene, complete with pet lambs, a new colt, and a steer that could be harnessed and made to pull a sled.[69]

Over the next few years the boys worked side by side with their father in planting, harvesting, and herding, and Emma carried on with housework and the care of her cows and chickens. Although their world in Bridger Canyon was not yet all they wanted it to be, it was a much more comfortable world than the one they had struggled to maintain back in Blue Earth County.[70]

In early fall of 1887, less than a year after her move to Montana Territory, Persis Christie grew ill, and Emma, in the last months of another pregnancy, took on the duties of nurse and companion. On the morning of September 27, the eighty-year-old woman died, and James Christie openly grieved the loss of his companion of thirty-four years.[71]

The burial of one Christie was followed by the birth of another, for on October 7, 1887, nearly three weeks earlier than she had expected, Emma gave birth to her first Montana son. David named the boy James in honor of his own father, grandfather, and little James James, the firstborn son they had buried in Blue Earth County and whose picture Emma had brought with her to their new home. After welcoming his namesake, James Christie the elder boarded the train, bound for Minnesota to spend the winter months with Sarah's family.[72]

The next few years were good ones for the Christies. Completely free of asthma, David felt stronger than ever as he celebrated his fortieth birthday. With the help of a hearty rooster, Emma had increased her flock of Plymouth Rock hens to 125, and the herd of Christie cattle had grown large enough to allow David to give each of his sons one cow apiece so that they could start their own herds. They had a large and bountiful garden, and David hauled Emma's eggs, butter, and vegetables to coal miners in Timberline and Cokedale, some fifteen miles to the southeast.[73]

James Christie the elder watched with satisfaction the mounting evidence that this time his dreams of leaving his descendants a legacy of land seemed destined to come true. Satisfied with the present and optimistic about the future, the seventy-eight-year-old patriarch celebrated Montana's statehood with his family in 1889, then died some two months later in his Bridger Canyon home, eigh-

David and Emma Stratton Christie, about 1895. *(Courtesy David B. Christie Family and Montana Historical Society, Helena)*

teen months before David "proved up" on his homestead.[74] The following year, Emma gave birth to another son, Robert Allen, and in the summer of 1894 the birth of a second daughter, Emma Mary, brought an end to her twenty-three years of childbearing.[75]

In the fall of 1897, more than a decade after her departure from Minnesota, Emma returned to Blue Earth County. She had traveled to Montana Territory as a thirty-one-year-old woman surrounded by five young sons and a newborn daughter. Now forty-three and traveling with Eliza, who had just turned twelve, five-year-old Robert, and three-year-old Emma Mary, she spent a month visiting family and friends.[76]

In 1900, David and Emma celebrated the dawn of the new century by moving into a new home, a two-story house with plenty of room at last for all their children. But within four years of that move, their eldest son, Sandy, had married and moved into a home of his own. Weddings for Eliza, Donald, and Davy took place over the next two years. Still busy with her garden, hens, and butter churn, Emma grew more and more involved in the Happy Days Club, a newly formed women's group in the canyon, and she began to assist in the delivery of babies born to Bridger Canyon mothers, including the delivery of one of her own grandchildren. She and David lived quietly, except when visited by grandchildren, who in time numbered thirty-nine.[77]

In 1913, at age sixty-five, David sold their homestead, and he and Emma retired into a small farmhouse on Brackett Creek, further up the canyon and not far from their son James and his wife Pearl. After 1915, when Davy moved his family to Pasadena to start a dairy, Emma and David spent their winters in California and their summers on Brackett Creek. On July 4, 1920, in the company of most of their children and grandchildren, the couple observed their fiftieth wedding anniversary. Just sixteen days later, on the afternoon of July 20, 1920, David Bertie Christie suffered a violent asthma attack. By evening he was dead.[78]

Lost without him, Emma moved onto the ranch that her daughter and son-in-law Eliza and Jim Camp maintained up Brackett Creek, living in a small house her son-in-law built for her a few yards from his back door. Eight months later, on March 15, 1921, some twenty friends and relatives gathered at the Camp home for a supper in honor of Emma's sixty-seventh birthday. The weather that night was wild, as chinook winds lapped at rapidly melting snow. A relative

The Christie family on the porch of their Bridger Canyon home, 1912: *(seated, left to right)* Eliza, David, Emma, and young Emma; *(standing, left to right)* Alexander, Donald, David, Will, James, Robert, and George. *(Courtesy David B. Christie family and Montana Historical Society, Helena)*

who had come over from Clyde Park for the supper decided to stay the night instead of traveling the ten or so miles home, and after the dishes were done, the two women retired to Emma's little house. About eight the next morning, the visitor ran up to the big house to tell Eliza her mother was ill. A scant half hour later, Emma Stratton Christie was dead of heart failure.[79]

Two days of rain followed the chinook, and swollen streams flooded roads and fields, making it difficult for the hearse to make its way from Bozeman over forty miles of unimproved mountain roads. The long delay meant there was plenty of time for all of Emma's children to assemble for her funeral and for her burial beside David in Bozeman's Sunset Hills Cemetery. On that day friends, as well as family, mourned the passing of "an earnest Christian, a devoted wife and mother, and a sympathetic and hospitable friend and neighbor," a woman who had followed her husband west—and helped him achieve his dream of leaving a legacy of land to their children and to Christie generations to come.[80]

Augusta Perham Shipman

"Do Have Your Visit or Exploration or Whatever You Call It and Come Back"

On February 1, 1882, a disillusioned and impatient Augusta Shipman sat down at her desk in Atlantic City, New Jersey, to write a letter to her husband, Clark, and their fifteen-year-old son, Henry, who had left for Montana Territory some two months earlier. Long tantalized by dreams of fertile, debt-free land, Clark had been so caught up in his homesteading plans that he had given little thought to anything else before his departure, and the few letters he had written since that day were long on descriptions of life in the West and short on suggestions for survival in the East.

For the past six weeks Augusta and six-year-old Maggie had been sharing a small flat with the three older Shipman girls—Winnie, Gertie, and Becky—but this was at best a temporary arrangement. While city life was fine for her adult daughters, Augusta knew that she and Maggie needed to be home on Perham Hill in Vermont, though she hardly knew how she could manage the farm by herself. A morning walk on the beach had not brought any answers. Now, back in the cramped apartment, she was faced with the task of letting Clark know her plans for that part of the Shipman clan left in her care. The chatter around her only worsened her mood. "Mag & the other girls are talking so I cant think," she scribbled. Then it all spilled out: "What are you out there for any way. . . . I hope you will find out soon & make calculations to be back sometime."[1]

"Sometime" was a long time coming, for Augusta Shipman was to spend the next eight years maintaining a home on Perham Hill for family members in the East while Clark worked his homestead on the Judith River and the children moved back and forth between them.

⚜

Fanny Augusta Perham was the first child of John and Sarah Whitney Perham of Bethel, Vermont, a small farming community in the Green Mountains. John Perham's father had died young, and his children and lands had been dispersed, but by the time John married Sarah Whitney in 1830 he had already begun to fulfill his dream of buying back his father's acreage. And by the time of Augusta's birth on May 3, 1831, he had almost completely restored Perham Hill. At four, Augusta welcomed a baby brother, Charles (1835), and soon two sisters, Emeline (1838) and Harriet (1840), were born. Although all John Perham's children roamed the birch and maple woodlands and rolling pastures he had worked so hard to reclaim, it was Gusta who was marked by the land.[2]

Like most of their neighbors, the Perhams cultivated some of their acreage and pastured sheep and cattle on the rest. They spun wool and wove cloth, and in the spring, as the sap rose in the maples, they tapped the trees and made syrup. Their total profits were modest, but their life was secure.[3]

Throughout Augusta's girlhood, the Perham family's closest neighbors were the Shipmans, whose farm bordered Perham Hill, though it lay in Royalton, a township adjoining Bethel. The families shared equipment and labor during the growing season and food and supplies during the long winter months. There was little difference in the value of their holdings, but the Shipmans were of higher social standing, for Harvey and Betsey Shipman were teachers as well as farmers, and they aspired to the best in education for their three boys and two girls.[4]

Clark Bigelow Shipman, the second-born of the surviving Shipman sons, was almost an exact contemporary of Gusta Perham. Born on June 1, 1831, in Rochester, some fifteen miles west of Bethel, he was seven when the family moved to the farm that neighbored Perham Hill.[7] Because they lived in different townships, Clark and Augusta did not go to the same school until early adolescence, when they both attended Royalton Academy. Upon completion of her course of study there, Augusta Perham went on to study briefly at

Thetford Hall, a school of some renown in central Vermont, before returning to teach in the Bethel common school where she had earlier been a student.[5]

By the time Gusta returned to Perham Hill, Clark, too, had completed his formal education, but he had decided to remain for a while at the family home, since the death of his twenty-three-year-old brother, Harvey, had thrust him into the role of eldest son. Easy-going as he was, Clark took the role of big brother seriously and established close ties with his siblings—William Rollin, five years younger than he; Sarah DeEtte, seven years younger; and Louisa Janette, ten years younger. Thus his siblings kept in close touch, even after Clark left home in the fall of 1850 to take a teaching position in a nearby village. Within a year, he had moved even farther from home, following his uncle Lucius Eaton, his mother's brother, to the North American Phalanx near Red Bank, New Jersey, a socialist colony established in the tradition of fabled Brook Farm.[6]

What drew the twenty-year-old Clark Shipman to Red Bank was not so much an intellectual commitment to the communitarian ideal as a strong desire to experience life beyond the confines of Vermont. At the phalanx he shared teaching duties with his uncle and quickly won acceptance in the community. He enjoyed his sojourn in New Jersey, finding the weather and the land superior to that in Vermont and boasting to his father, "It hardly seems that so short a distance could make the difference."[7] As he wrote those words, he could hardly have known how alluring New Jersey would be to him in another decade.

In the spring of 1852, having served out a six-month contract with the North American Phalanx, Clark returned home to Royalton, where he spent the summer working on his father's farm before accepting a teaching position in Salisbury in western Vermont. Through all of Clark's wanderings, Gusta Perham had continued to teach in the Bethel village school, living at home on Perham Hill with her parents, her teenaged brother and sisters, her paternal grandmother, an aunt, and an uncle.[8]

Basically a reclusive individual whose world was bounded largely by her work at school and at home, Gusta Perham was intrigued enough by Clark Shipman's reports of adventures in the outside world to welcome his suggestion in 1854 that she return with him to Monmouth County, New Jersey. There were many attractive openings for teachers in and around Red Bank, and Clark had the contacts through which she could secure a position. It was a radical move for a young unmarried woman of Augusta's era, but it was a way out of the constricting world of Bethel—and into the world of Clark Shipman.[9]

On a March day in 1854, twenty-two-year-old Gusta Perham left Bethel by stage, bound for Woodstock and thence for Boston, to catch a boat for Red Bank. Despite her distance from Perham Hill, Gusta adjusted easily to life in New Jersey. Her Aunt Louisa at home in Vermont wrote to congratulate her for "getting into business" that would suit her temperament and dismissed any possibility of homesickness "when there is one so near that can banish all unpleasant feelings."[10]

There is no doubt that the friendship between Augusta Perham and Clark Shipman had developed romantic overtones. Yet there was an element of competition embedded in the courtship. Clark's situation in Holmdel, five miles from Red Bank, was not as satisfying as Gusta's in Scobeyville, which was south of both Holmdel and Red Bank. She had more "scholars" than he, and Clark was convinced that the superintendent was "better pleased with her school than [his]." Thus, while Gusta enjoyed her situation and was of no mind to leave New Jersey, before the end of the year Clark was back home teaching school in East Bethel.[11]

When Augusta finished out her contract in the spring of 1855 and returned to Perham Hill, the two young people made an announcement that surprised no one, and on November 6, 1855, the marriage of Augusta Perham and Clark Shipman, both twenty-four, united two families that had been neighbors for more than fifteen years. The trip the newlyweds made to visit Clark's uncle, William B. Eaton, in Cedar Rapids, Iowa, was more than a honeymoon; it was a reconnaisance of the West, for Clark was thinking of farming the prairie lands of Iowa rather than the mountain acreage of Vermont. But whether the responsibilities at home or the wife at his side dissuaded him, Clark returned to Royalton, settled in on the farm belonging to his parents, and accepted a position as superintendent of the Royalton school.[12]

On October 11, 1856, some eleven months after their wedding, Clark and Augusta Shipman welcomed their first child, a girl they named Winifred Augusta. Needing roots of his own now, Clark approached his father about the possibility of formalizing part ownership in the Shipman land, and in the early summer of 1857, when little Winnie was nine months old, he and Augusta bought half of the Harvey Shipman farm, including the family home, for fifteen hundred dollars. With their twenty-one-year-old son William now enrolled in Middlebury College, Harvey and Betsey moved to their former home in Rochester, taking DeEtte and Janette with them and leaving their acreage in Clark and Augusta's care.[13]

Since Clark's property adjoined that of her parents, Gusta remained closely involved with her family, and she was brought even closer to the fortunes of Perham Hill by the death of her brother Charles from typhoid fever in mid-February of 1857. Two years later, when little Winnie was just past three, Augusta Shipman gave birth to a second daughter, Gratia, who died barely a week after her birth and was buried beside her Uncle Charles in Cherry Hill Cemetery, not far from Perham Hill.[14]

The year 1859 would bring more tragedy. That fall, seventeen-year-old Janette Shipman followed her brother William, who had just finished his degree at Middlebury, to Green Mountain Institute in South Woodstock, where he took up his position as "teacher of languages" and she began a course of secondary study. In late fall Janette fell suddenly and seriously ill, and on January 18, 1860, having just passed her eighteenth birthday, she died. A month later, Augusta gave birth to another daughter, whom she and Clark named Gertrude Janette.[15]

Shortly thereafter, twenty-two-year-old DeEtte, Clark's only surviving sister, was married in the family home in Rochester to a fellow teacher, Edwin Oscar Lee of Vernon, a small farming community in the southeast corner of Vermont. Coming in the wake of Janette's recent death, the ceremony was a quiet affair. Augusta did not attend the wedding, for although her new baby was strong and healthy, she herself was slow in recovering from her confinement. The exact nature of her weakness was hard to describe—and to diagnose—and late that year, fearing she had cancer of some form, Augusta persuaded Clark to take her to Boston to see a specialist, who allayed her fears about cancer but found nothing to account for her discomfort.[16]

Although she enjoyed less-than-robust health, Augusta did enjoy some degree of financial security. In the fifth year of their marriage she and Clark were operating a sixty-five-acre farm that produced good crops of wheat, Indian corn, oats, peas, beans, and Irish potatoes. They kept three horses, eight milk cows, two working oxen, nine other cattle, three sheep, and eight pigs, and they produced four hundred pounds of butter and five hundred pounds of maple syrup a year. Their only help in managing this highly diversified operation came from the fifteen-year-old Irish-born farmhand who lived in their household. On neighboring Perham Hill, Augusta's parents, sixty-one-year-old John and fifty-four-year-old Sarah, ran a similar operation. Gusta's two sisters, Emeline, twenty-two, and Harriet, twenty, were still at home, though Emeline was teaching school and engaged to be married to Henry Sullivan Marcy, a man destined for a bright future in New England railroading.[17]

In early summer of 1861, shortly after her sister's wedding, life changed abruptly for Augusta when she learned that her household was about to expand to include her in-laws. Having decided to sell their house and land in Rochester and return to Royalton, Harvey and Betsey Shipman announced their intentions of joining Clark, Augusta, four-year-old Winnie, and baby Gertie in the home that had once been theirs. That decision could hardly have pleased Augusta, who had never been fully accepted by the close-knit Shipman clan—perhaps because she did not bend to her father-in-law's harsh rule. And while Clark extended a welcome to his parents, he warned them they would be living "all in a heap."[18]

Augusta was "quite sick" that spring of 1861 as she attempted to fit her in-laws into her house and her routine. She was, in fact, in the midst of her fourth pregnancy, though she eventually miscarried. And as war news swept the state, she fretted over Clark's status in the pending draft. In Vernon, some ninety miles to the southeast, DeEtte was not only worried about the draft status of her brothers and husband, but was also concerned about the less-than-ideal situation up in Royalton. She pressed her parents to consider moving down to share the home she and Oscar were building for themselves on the Lee homestead.[19]

In early March 1862, Augusta attended another wedding on Perham Hill as her twenty-one-year-old sister, Harriet, married Charles Whitney. Soon thereafter, tensions in the Shipman household eased somewhat when Harvey and Betsey Shipman moved down to Vernon to help DeEtte and Oscar settle into their new home and to see DeEtte through her first pregnancy. Her in-laws were still in Vernon on December 20, 1862, when Augusta gave birth to a third daughter, Rebecca Maria, and Clark described the delivery in a letter to his father:

Early Fri eve there began to be slight indications of a "good time com-ing" like small thunder a good way off as Augusta called it. But we did not think it necessary to send for reinforcements until about 12 o'clock. At which hour I went over & alarmed Mrs & Mr Dutton, the former of whom came home with me on the double quick and the other volun-teered to go at the same pace for the indispensable Surgeon Danforth. The forces were all on the ground before 2 o'clock and shortly after we held a council of war and decided to encamp until morn, which we all did & slept soundly. The battle was renewed at the first indication of daylight & continued without intermission or accident until about 10 A.M. when a new member . . . was added to the family. She is an 8½ pounder. . . . So far both Mother & child appear to be all right.

Augusta's mother, Sarah Perham, came over to help with the house-hold chores, and baby Rebecca was quickly assimilated into the family routine.[20]

In the fall of 1863, seven-year-old Winnie began school in the little red schoolhouse about a mile from the farm, and by the following spring, four-year-old Gertie was accompanying her sister to school. Because their mother believed in the benefits of fresh air and bare feet—along with "plain food, . . . warm clean clothes, and baths enough"—the two little girls walked to school barefoot each day, though during the winter months they were sometimes carried to school in their father's sleigh.[21]

While the little Shipmans prospered under their mother's care, Augusta's own health continued to be poor. Recurring dental prob-lems caused her to have so many teeth pulled that, by the summer of 1864, although she was only in her early thirties, she looked "very old grannyish." That fall Harvey and Betsey Shipman returned to Royalton, where Augusta turned her parlor into a bedroom for the elder couple while Clark helped build a small house for his parents on two acres they purchased from him.[22] By early summer of 1865, with the elder Shipmans settled in their own home right next door, life resumed some semblance of routine for Clark and Augusta.

The following fall, on November 24, 1866, Augusta gave birth to her first son, who was named Henry Eaton for a cousin of Clark's who had died in the Civil War. With the baby's birth, ten-year-old Winnie assumed some of Augusta's household chores and also looked after Gertie, six, and Becky, not quite four. Any help Gusta received from her mother-in-law, Betsey, was given grudgingly. Clark now began to "fix up" the family home, work he'd been planning to do ever since he and Augusta had taken possession of the house five years earlier. Even as he immersed himself in the long-delayed home improvements, Clark was considering an option that would transport his family from the harsh realities of Vermont farming to the easier life of a New Jersey truck farm, an idea that had been festering in his imagination for at least a dozen years and that became even more tempting as he read the handbills and advertisements that now flooded New England, touting the newly established town of Vineland, New Jersey, where one would find "Rare Opportunity in the best Market and most delightful and healthy Climate in the Union."[23]

Unable to shake the promise of southern New Jersey, Clark Shipman weighed the merits of such a major move. While he was holding his own, he was essentially no better off than his father, Harvey, had been when he'd acquired the land more than twenty-five years earlier. New Jersey offered him a chance to improve his situation, and though he came from a long line of rock-ribbed Vermonters, loyalty had its limits. He had Augusta's support, for her earlier experiences in New Jersey had left her with nothing but good memories of the state. Perhaps its more hospitable climate might improve her health. A move would at least put some distance between the younger and elder Shipmans.

By early fall of 1867, Clark and Augusta had made their decision. That October, Clark sold the farm to their neighbor, John Fales, for forty-five hundred dollars, reserving the right to winter over in the farmhouse. The family spent Christmas together, celebrating with the elder Shipmans, but a day or so after the holiday, Clark set out alone for New Jersey to find a home in Vineland. In his absence, Gusta had to deal with the disparaging remarks other members of the Shipman clan made about the move. But whatever the family's opinion, Clark and Augusta received support from others who dreamt of new worlds themselves.[24]

Inured to his family's comments, Clark returned from New Jersey to describe to his wife and children the small home he had bought in Vineland and to help pack the household belongings. Sometime in late March 1868, he and Augusta and their four children—Winnie, twelve; Gertie, eight; Becky, five; and Henry, fifteen months—bid goodbye to family and friends and took the stage out of Royalton. A day later, having traveled by stage, train, and ferry, they debarked in Vineland.[25]

Originally intending to return to teaching for a year or so or perhaps to take a factory position in one of Vineland's fledgling industries, all the while saving money toward a farm, Clark began to have other thoughts soon after his family's arrival in New Jersey. As the children explored the neighborhood and began school, he and Augusta found themselves more and more uneasy about living in a community that was already twice the size of Bethel and Royalton. In hopes of finding reasonably priced farmland, Clark began to make forays into the surrounding countryside.[26]

By July he had found the ideal place: a fifty-six-acre farm some six miles north of Vineland and two and a half miles east of Malaga, a small farm and factory village that predated Vineland by forty years. It was the best section he had yet seen, and he had "been <u>swinging round</u> the <u>circle</u> a good deal." Thirty of the fifty-six acres were cultivated, and the rest were in "fine timber & wood." There was "considerable saw timber . . . [and] a pretty good old [apple] orchard." The house itself was "not much," but it had five large shade trees around it. Augusta was especially eager to move, for the children had not been healthy since coming to New Jersey, and she feared they were particularly vulnerable to the whooping cough that was rife in Vineland.[27]

In the beginning there was not much to recommend life in Malaga, either. The mosquitoes were "tremendous thick" that hot summer of 1868; eighteen-month-old Henry, called "Bub" within the family circle, came down with whooping cough in spite of their move to the country; and Becky grew "very poor and light," though her parents had hoped that she would grow stronger once they "got out on the farm & had a cow." They were "not yet in paradise," Clark wrote to William, a major admission to make to a brother who still had so little understanding of the motives that had prompted the move to New Jersey.[28]

But as Augusta turned the old house into a home and Winnie and Gertie started school, the family began to be caught up in the rhythms of New Jersey farm life. In addition to a summer harvest of cabbages, sweet potatoes, corn, and wheat, Clark harvested some of his "fine timber" that fall, making $150 off his pine logs, cutting thirty or forty cords of oak, and selling "50 ties to the R.R." to earn "perhaps 150 [dollars] more." Having begun with only a milk cow, over the winter the Shipmans increased their livestock, adding four pigs destined to "take a trip to Vineland or Phil[adelphia]" and one good horse, complete with harness and wagon. Augusta bought 130 chickens—and did daily battle with a hawk that threatened her investment. As Clark put the plow to the ground in mid-March of 1869, his first planting season, he had high hopes for a good year. It would be a critical year, for he had pledged to himself and to Augusta that he was "going to work this year & see if it will pay & if it will not [I] shall never do it again."[29]

Despite his high hopes for a good season, a drought reduced the yields from the fields of sweet potatoes, cabbages, corn, wheat, and "round potatoes." Even the melons, peaches, and apples, highly touted products of the Malaga area, were disappointing. The children were homesick for Vermont and "will not be reconsiled to living here," Clark wrote to his parents, and Augusta fretted over Becky's health, for the six-year-old was doing no better than she had been upon their arrival. Her thoughts were drawn even more frequently to Vermont when a letter came from Perham Hill informing her that her father was "quite unwell."[30]

Within weeks of that letter, Gusta received word of his death. As seventy-year-old John Perham was buried in Cherry Hill Cemetery in October 1869, Augusta made plans to return to Vermont, at least for the winter. There she would be close to her mother, Becky could regain her strength, and Winnie and Gertie would have access to better schooling. The education of their daughters was a paramount consideration now for both Clark and Augusta, and thirteen-year-old Winnie was talking of teaching, a career for which she could not prepare herself in the Malaga school district.[31]

Ultimately, the entire family packed up and went home to Perham Hill that winter, an event marked with some interest by those who saw the return as an admission of defeat in New Jersey, especially on Augusta's part. "I should think that Gusta must have humbled herself a little to come back so soon," a niece wrote to Harvey and Betsey Shipman. "Is [she] any better contented?" Contented or not, Augusta was again at home, where she helped her mother settle her father's affairs and enrolled Winnie in the state normal school in Randolph Center, some ten miles north of Bethel.[32]

With the coming of spring 1870, Augusta and Clark Shipman returned to their New Jersey farm. With them were Becky, Bub, and Grandma Sarah Perham. Left behind were Winnie, who was still in school at Randolph Center, and Gertie, who was living with her paternal grandparents and attending school in Royalton.[33] Despite his earlier pledge to turn to something else if he could not make farming pay during their first full season in New Jersey, Clark Shipman planted his fields for another year in Malaga. In the midst of the growing season, he and Augusta and the two little ones returned briefly to Vermont to visit Winnie and Gertie and to take Sarah Perham home, though their thoughts remained focused on New Jersey, where their fields suffered first from drought, then from flooding in torrential late-season storms. Even though their farm was one of Franklin Township's most productive that year, Clark and Augusta were discouraged, and late that summer, as Augusta canned peaches and pears, pickled watermelons, and made apple cider and vinegar by the barrelsful for sale in Vineland and Hammonton, she made plans to return again to Vermont for the winter to be with the girls and her mother.[34] In early September, taking Becky and Bub with her and leaving Clark to finish the harvest, she set out for New England.

While Augusta was up in Vermont, DeEtte and Oscar Lee, finally swayed by Clark's enthusiasm, were down in New Jersey making arrangements to buy a farm almost directly across the road from the Clark Shipman place. As Augusta busied herself with the children at her mother's house, DeEtte and Oscar prepared themselves and eight-year-old Eddie, six-year-old William, and four-year-old Bertha for the move to New Jersey.[35]

Clark stayed south that winter, except for a brief trip home over the holidays. Returning to New Jersey, he brought Gertie, Becky, and Bub home with him, and he and the three children were all there to greet Augusta and the five Lees when they arrived in mid-March 1871. While waiting to take occupancy of Oak Grove Farm, the Lees moved in with the Shipmans. The little Lees enjoyed the company of their cousins, Oscar did what he could "to get things along," and DeEtte helped Gusta with the management of the house, writing her mother that she and Augusta were "get[ting] along splendidly so far" and that Augusta "acted almost homesick [for Perham Hill] at first, but . . . on the whole she [was] glad to get back [here] and Clark [was] glad to have her."[36]

If Augusta was homesick, it was not only that she missed Winnie, who had stayed on in Vermont to attend school in Royalton but also that she had been newly reminded of the beauty of the hills, brooks, and grassy fields that were so much a part of Perham Hill and so lacking in Malaga. For a while she was comforted by the presence of the Lees. She and Clark had long felt that Jerseyites were prejudiced against "Yankees," and with the exception of their good neighbors and friends, the John Irish family, they had felt somewhat isolated. Now Oscar and Clark dropped in on each other when out on their appointed rounds, and the couples shared babysitting chores so that husband and wife could go together to weekly market in Vineland. And the Lees were there to commiserate with the Shipmans when a late frost nipped Clark's newly planted grapes.[37]

The Thanksgiving holiday was shared by the two families, including Winnie and Grandma Perham, newly arrived from Vermont. The Lees hosted the event; DeEtte served the traditional chicken pie, and, with a fire roaring in the fireplace, Clark played the fiddle, always a sign of high spirits. Right after the holiday, Grandma Perham returned to Vermont, but Winnie stayed on to help teach her younger siblings and cousins, who were schooled at home that term because the Malaga district school was so poor. The situation improved early in 1872 when Oscar Lee, long retired from the classroom, was persuaded to teach in the district school. With their uncle as their teacher, Winnie, Gertie, Becky, and Bub Shipman all enjoyed the session in the Malaga school, as did Eddie and Willie Lee. According to their Aunt DeEtte, Winnie, now fifteen, and Gertie, almost twelve, were "perfectly lady like and scholarly" and along with Eddie were "as oases in the desert" for their teacher.[38]

Life in New Jersey was definitely going well, and Clark and DeEtte were anxious to share it with their parents. Early in 1872, DeEtte began trying to coax Harvey and Betsey to consider coming to New Jersey to celebrate their fiftieth wedding anniversary in late May. William, now teaching at Tufts, at one time planned to join them all in Malaga, but the much-discussed trip was aborted by the onset of "hard measles" in Clark's family. All the children, with the exception of Winnie, were extremely sick, although the greatest fears were, as always, for Becky.[39]

An exceptionally cold winter followed by a cold spring had Clark discouraged again, and he was looking for a chance to sell. Farming in New Jersey had not been "very remunerative . . . for 2 or 3 years & that seems to be the general complaint all about." He was ready to go home to Vermont, but until he had a buyer for his place, he would farm it. Once again he plowed and planted—clover, potatoes, corn, cabbages.[40]

After harvesting the crop that fall of 1872, Clark Shipman took up a new business: selling Howe sewing machines. A personable man, he did quite well in the new business, though he was necessarily on the road with his horse and wagon quite often. Left at home with the children, Augusta became more and more isolated as the strain between her and DeEtte resurfaced. "I do not enjoy going [to the Shipmans]," DeEtte wrote her parents, "& do not go very often Gusta has not been here for a long time. The little ones come a good deal & Winnie runs in quite often I think a great deal of all the children." She thought less of Gusta, with whom there was always the danger of getting "into a muss."[41]

DeEtte invited the Shipmans over for the holidays, as she had the year before, but Winnie declined for the family, explaining that they "were not prepared to contribute presents except for their own folks." Because the New Year's celebration did not call for an exchange of gifts, the Shipmans did agree to spend the first day of 1873 with the Lees at Oak Grove Farm. Once again the fire roared in the fireplace, Clark played the fiddle, and the families shared the traditional chicken pie and plum pudding. Augusta had been "more agreeable than usual of late," DeEtte reported to her mother, and she could only surmise that that meant "that things are working to her [liking]." All she knew was that Clark's new business was proving "thus far to be more lucrative" than farming, and DeEtte imagined that Clark did not "calculate to carry on his farm" that coming year.[42]

In the fall of 1873, Harvey and Betsey Shipman finally visited the Lees and the Shipmans in Malaga, then made a trip to Vineland, where Winnie and Gertie were now boarding while Winnie pursued an interest in the piano and Gertie attended a city school, since her uncle was no longer teaching at Malaga. During their visit, the Shipmans saw the effects of another severe drought that had created "a sorry looking country."[43]

That drought was, perhaps, the reason Clark finally abandoned all thought of farming in New Jersey. In the spring of 1875, rather than planting another crop, he and Augusta went north to Vermont again, leaving their older girls in Vineland to finish out the school term. It was more than a visit home; it was also a business trip, for Clark intended to introduce the Howe sewing machine to the people of central Vermont. Besides canvassing his old neighbors, Clark conducted one other piece of business in Vermont that spring: he and Augusta bought Perham Hill from Sarah Perham.[44]

With the signing of that deed, Clark, Augusta, eleven-year-old

Becky, and seven-year-old Bub moved in at Perham Hill, though Clark made frequent trips to New Jersey to oversee their property and to sell sewing machines. When Winnie and Gertie finished the term in Vineland, they joined the family at Perham Hill, where, on August 25, 1875, Augusta gave birth to her fifth and last child, a girl named Margaret Maud. Shortly afterward Winnie and Gertie set out for Randolph Center to complete their "second course."[45]

In the fall of 1876, twenty-year-old Winnie secured a teaching position at Pittsfield, New Hampshire, while Gertie, now sixteen, went home to Perham Hill. Without her sister's company, Winnie was homesick that school term, and Augusta worried about her oldest daughter even as she weaned her youngest. As Winnie's unhappiness became more evident, Clark began to look around for positions in local schools for her and for Gertie. Missing Winnie as much as she missed all of them, Clark invited her to "come home & run business & I can go in pursuit of script, which I have not done much since you went away, or if worse comes to worst (& I almost hope it will) we can elope & go to keeping house in Jersey."[46]

Despite his offhanded reference to a lack of income, Clark Shipman was in fact making enough off his farms in Vermont and New Jersey and his sewing machine business to turn an adequate profit, for on July 31, 1877, he paid off the thirty-two-hundred-dollar note he'd taken out almost exactly nine years earlier on the fifty-six-acre farm in Malaga. And he succeeded in his other endeavor as well, eventually finding a teaching job for Winnie in Royalton and one for Gertie in Rochester.[47]

But the girls were not satisfied back in Vermont, and within two years both of them had secured teaching positions in New Jersey. Clark's parents had already made a permanent move to New Jersey, settling at Oak Grove Farm with the Lees in 1877. With both his daughters and his parents now in New Jersey, Clark persuaded Augusta to give over the care of Perham Hill to her sister and brother-in-law, Harriet and Charles Whitney, and the Shipmans returned to Malaga.[48]

With the coming of the new decade, Clark Shipman again became restive. Now forty-nine, he was in no better position on his farm in New Jersey than he had been twenty years earlier on the farm in Royalton.[49] Uncles on both sides of the family had pioneered in the Midwest and West, thereby setting a family precedent.[50] Promotional literature of the late 1870s touted the opportunities made available by the Homestead Act of 1862 and its subsequent extensions. But growing discord in the Shipman household likely had as much to do with Clark's interest in going west as did the lure of free land.

Augusta Perham Shipman had never been an easy person to live with. Distant with outsiders and domineering within her own family, she was beset by apprehensions—about her own health, about that of her children, and about the outcome of every venture undertaken by her husband. That anxious personality contrasted with Clark's carefree, adventuresome nature, and the contrast led to tensions that their now adult offspring did not fail to notice. Thus, when Clark first proposed that he and fourteen-year-old Henry explore homesteading possibilites in Montana Territory, there would have been little opposition to the plan from any of the other family members. Indeed, by the fall of 1881, the three oldest daughters had already removed themselves from the fray. Winifred and Rebecca were living in Atlantic City, with Winnie teaching at Atlantic City High, where Becky was finishing her senior year; Gertie was still living and teaching in Hammonton, not far from the Malaga farm. No one questioned Clark's reasons for going west without Augusta, who would remain at home with six-year-old Maggie and maintain an eastern base for the family. Even if Clark was successful in establishing a homestead in Montana, the family might or might not ever be reunited—on that homestead or elsewhere.[51]

In October 1881, in preparing for the separation, Clark and Augusta sold the fifty-six-acre Malaga farm at a loss. At the same time that Augusta was concluding that deal in New Jersey, Clark made one more trip north to Massachusetts and Vermont to see his brother and put to rest what matters he could in Royalton. For a dollar, he surrendered to his mother-in-law, Sarah Perham, all his rights to the eighty-five acres that composed Perham Hill, so that she and Augusta became coowners of the property. He then returned to New Jersey to help Augusta sift through their household belongings. Storing some of their goods at DeEtte's home, they packed the rest to be driven to Atlantic City for temporary storage with Winnie.[52]

Then on Friday morning, December 9, 1881, Clark and Henry, newly turned fifteen, left for Boston, there to spend the night with William before boarding the train for Chicago. They lingered for a month in the Midwest, enjoying the holidays with the Eatons clustered in Illinois and Kansas. In mid-January, father and son boarded the train at

The Shipman family, about 1878: *(seated, left to right)* Augusta, Gertrude, Clark, with Margaret on his lap, Winifred; *(standing, left to right)* Henry and Rebecca. *(Courtesy Susan Shipman Burnham and Montana Historical Society, Helena)*

Salina, Kansas, holding "emigrant" tickets that had cost them ninety-five dollars each and would carry them through to Silver Bow, Montana Territory.[53]

Soon after Clark's departure, Augusta and Maggie—along with Salt, the family's ancient dog, and ten hens—left Malaga for Winnie and Becky's flat in Atlantic City, where Augusta intended to spend the holidays deciding exactly what she would do in Clark's absence. Gertie came over from Hammonton to join them over her two-week vacation. Becky fashioned a Christmas tree from a lamp and a table, she and her mother made gifts, and Augusta baked the traditional chicken pie. Mother and daughters walked the beach several times over the holidays, and their loneliness was tangible: "It seems so strange to think of you out there," Augusta wrote her husband and son on New Year's Day, "I only hope you are safe & not hungry . . . I should feel better if I knew where you were." Intending to overcome some of her uncertainty simply by orienting herself to their route west, she told them she planned to "buy a map & Mag & I shall study your course as we would the march of Napoleon to Moscow."[54]

Gathered in the small quarters in Atlantic City, the five Shipmans talked mostly of the two who were missing. "I fear that bread and butter is a dollar a slice [out there]," Winnie wrote, "and that the people are nearly savage and drink lots of bad whiskey." Noting that she could almost hear her brother's "Bosh!" she conceded that her "imagination [could be] worse than the facts." Uncharacteristically nostalgic, Augusta reminisced with her daughters about her honeymoon trip to the Midwest some twenty-five years earlier. The memories and the loneliness had their effect. Within a week of the holidays, Augusta had "one of her spells," becoming "depressed in spirits."[55]

Soon after her return to Hammonton, Gertrude came back to Atlantic City in need of "doctoring." She suffered from "extreme nervousness" and a "female complaint" the doctor felt was exacerbated "by standing in school and the excitement of teaching." She returned to Hammonton only long enough to resign her position and collect her salary. Once back in the crowded little flat in Atlantic City, the normally reticent Gertie took an apprenticeship at a typesetting shop, becoming "the only girl who has ever tried the business in Atlantic City." Gusta's spirits rose with Gertie's homecoming—and with her own return to health. "When I am sick it <u>does</u> seem as tho I never could go to Vt & see to things," she wrote Clark in mid-January, "but when I get better my courage rises." So did her concerns for her husband and son: "Take care of yourselves first anyhow," she admonished them, "and let the money go. . . . We hope for no accidents but it does seem like tempting providence."[56]

Such worries sent her into another depression. Now fifty years old and all but immobilized by physical and psychological problems, she was sure that she must be starting through "her change." Her physician was treating her for scrofula, but he also mentioned a "thickened" transverse colon, rousing her old fears of cancer and leading her to ask Clark to "pray for [her] if nothing else." Viewing her mother's illness with some skepticism, Winifred informed her father that Augusta had found a very "accommodating doctor who makes no objection to her taking anything she wants . . . [and] she thinks of a good many things to take."[57]

As Augusta suffered in New Jersey, Clark and Henry arrived in Montana Territory and established themselves in a camp three miles east of Helena on the eastern slopes of the Rockies, where they chopped wood for a man who bought and processed hogs "into bacon sausage lard and headcheese." Father and son shared a log cabin that had no floor and cooked their own "vitules." Even so, Henry liked the life "first rate" and assured his mother that he was studying nights with the aid of an arithmetic text and a slate he had bought on the trip out.[58]

Despite her son's enthusiasm for life in the West, Gusta found little solace in the thought that her husband was "way out there chopping for a living." Still rankled at his decision to go west in the first place, she made that fact readily known, informing him that she had a standard response to six-year-old Maggie's persistent questions as to why her father had left them: "To get rid of us I suppose." In turn she urged her husband, "Do have your visit or exploration or whatever you call it & come back."[59]

But as her health improved, her mood—and her letters—mellowed: "I feel a little more natural today & hope I shall get better now," she wrote her husband. "It was so sunny [today] it made me think of sugaring & made me wish so much that you fellows were not in Montana." It also made her know that it was time for her to go home to Vermont to see to things and to allow Maggie "more freedom." In February, as Augusta killed and stewed the last of the hens that had accompanied her from the farm, she was also finalizing arrangements for the trip to Bethel, though she dreaded going north into such cold weather. And she was worried about the status of the note she held on the Malaga farm. The new owner, John Ellis, had had a fatal heart attack shortly after Christmas, and Augusta had no way of knowing whether the man's widow would be able to pay the eight hundred dollars left owing on the note.[60]

Even as Augusta prepared herself and her youngest daughter for the trip to Vermont, her oldest daughter was thinking of a trip to Montana, an idea that had been casually discussed before her father's departure. As the oldest child, Winifred had at first felt some responsibility for keeping the eastern wing of the family together, but in the brief time that her father and brother had been gone, she had come to see that as an impossibility and had allowed her thoughts to wander west. "It would be a lie to say I have never built air castles . . . upon coming to you," she wrote her father. And she was not inclined to come alone, since she was convinced that Gertie and Becky would not do well in Atlantic City without her and would certainly not wish to return to Vermont with their mother.[61]

Their mother—there lay Winnie's biggest problem. If all three girls went to Montana, then surely Augusta would be tempted to come along, and there was the rub. At twenty-four, Winnie knew that she and her mother "would differ as to who was 'boss.'" But her fears went farther than a simple mother-daughter conflict. Tension in the Shipman household had been high before her father's departure, and as much as she missed him, she knew that "Anything is better than the old arrangement." With her parents' growing estrangement, Winnie had fallen easily into the role of her father's surrogate companion, and she confided to him, "I can never give up the idea that you and I shall have a home together; that is the final aim of all my plans and always has been." Even if she stayed on in the East, "it would be with the expectation" that her father would sometime get his fortune "sufficiently repaired to come back." But even as she hoped for his return, she was realistic enough about his reasons for leaving to admit, "It seems foolish to say that when I might know you could not do that without bringing about the old arrangement of affairs. Let anything be done but that!"[62]

Other considerations aside, the very practical Winnie would, in the end, base her decision on simple economics: "Can I make money by going to Montana?" she asked her father. "Answer that question, and we'll see about the rest."[63] With that left hanging between them, she postponed her decision until the end of the school term.

If Winifred remained undecided about her plans, Augusta was firm in hers. On Friday, February 24, 1882, she and six-year-old Maggie started for Vermont, eager to be back at Perham Hill, which was to be her headquarters—and her responsibility—for the duration of her husband's stay in the West.[64] For the first time since Perham Hill had legally become hers, she would be home to work the land, and she intended to take full charge of the farm herself.

With Augusta and Maggie settled in Vermont, the talk in the flat in Atlantic City focused more and more frequently upon plans to go to Montana. As Gertie improved in her typesetting skills, she wrote her father to ask about the possibilities for employment as a compositor out west, since she would prefer that work to "teaching or doing house-work." Winnie, on the other hand, was eager to teach in Montana, and Becky, who would have her high school diploma in May, proposed to run a boardinghouse in which Winnie and Gertie would take their rooms. Gertie was set in the plan to go west, while Winnie and Becky vacillated, "considering the pro's and con's." "What will ma do if I go?" Winnie wrote her father, "And what on earth shall I do for her if I stay?"[65]

In Montana, Clark Shipman himself was on the move. Chopping wood and cleaning pig's feet was not what he had gone west to do. By spring he and Henry had gained enough pocket money to sustain themselves, and they had their eye on the plains to the east, where the better homesteading lands were reported to be. Buying a wagon and a team of horses, Clark and Henry loaded all their possessions— some small tools, some seeds and seed potatoes, and their few personal articles—and headed for the very center of the territory. There, on the Judith River, Clark took up a claim, choosing a site where river water could be easily diverted onto a good number of acres. Within three weeks of their arrival, father and son had placed their "sticks," posted a notice of preemption, plowed two acres, and planted potatoes, beans, corn, and turnips. Having accomplished that, they cut and hauled in logs and laid a foundation for their house, choosing a site in a cottonwood grove by the side of the Judith River. The house, a one-room affair, twelve by sixteen feet, was described quite carefully in Clark's next letter home, a letter that was passed along to various family members in New Jersey and Vermont.[66]

Now that their father had established a base of operations, the young Shipman women began to discuss their plans in earnest. Just a month from her high school graduation, Becky was not yet twenty and could not file on a homestead for at least another year. Since she could "not see the use of going till she [could] do something to earn money," she hoped to stay east and learn a profitable trade, preferably one in which she could use her artistic talents. Her dream was to study at Cooper Union in New York City, which offered tuition-free courses to those talented enough to be accepted. She had only to gain admission—and to find room and board cheap enough for Winnie to support her.[67]

Gertie doubted that she could finish her apprenticeship in the typesetting shop in time to earn the funds she would need for the trip to Montana, "to say nothing of enough [money] to preempt with after [she] got there," but Winnie went so far as to send her father a packet of teaching certificates and recommendations so that he might begin a job search for her in local school districts.[68]

Late in May 1882, with neither her father nor her mother present, but with her older sisters there to celebrate with her, Rebecca Maria Shipman graduated from Atlantic City High School. All the young women's thoughts were on the adventure ahead, for Winnie and Gertie had bought their tickets west. Becky would travel with them as far as Bethel, where she would be staying until she heard the results of her application to Cooper Union.[69]

Winnie had already tendered her resignation, and upon Becky's graduation Gertie left the print shop a month shy of having finished her apprenticeship. Packing up all the belongings accumulated in the flat, the three sisters left Atlantic City and headed for Vermont. After spending a few days in Boston with their Uncle William and Aunt Mattie, they arrived home in Bethel on June 27.[70] Although it was good to be at Perham Hill once more, the two-week visit was not an easy one for Winnie and Gertie. Augusta was harried and made no attempt to hide her feelings. "Mother's business distresses her so that I have offered to stay here and let her go to M.T.," Winnie wrote her father a week after her arrival in Bethel. But the responsibilities of overseeing the farm and caring for her seventy-seven-year-old mother and her seven-year-old daughter were easier for Augusta to consider than life with Clark in Montana Territory, and she refused Winnie's offer—as Winnie had known she would. To her daughters, Augusta's health seemed better than it had been in New Jersey, though she tired easily. She had "a very nice old man" working for her, "but of course some things go cross-grained and there is always something to do." She talked of selling Perham Hill, but Winnie doubted she could get the price she wanted for the farm. And what would she do if she were to sell it?[71]

Those questions she would soon be left to ponder on her own, for early on the afternoon of July 17, three trunks addressed to Montana Territory were hauled to the Bethel stage station, and after a late evening meal, Augusta, Winnie, and Gertie started down the hill to the village in the wagon. When the old mare proved unable to pick her way in the dark, the girls climbed down and bid their mother goodbye. As Augusta turned the rig toward home, they continued on foot into town. Arriving at the station with no time to spare, they boarded the midnight stage and began the long-anticipated journey from Bethel to Ogdensburg, New York; by boat up the Saint Lawrence River to Lake Ontario and on to Toronto; by train across Ontario to Collingwood; by boat across Lake Huron through the Mackinac Straits to Lake Michigan and on to Milwaukee; and finally by train from Milwaukee to Bismarck. There they telegraphed their father to meet them in Fort Benton, at the head of navigation on the Missouri, "several days into August." Boarding the river steamer *Butte*, they began the last leg of their westward journey. The Missouri was low, and the men on board were frequently pressed into service as "donkey engines," pulling the boat over the shallows. Winnie and Gertie used such opportunities to scavenge for geologic specimens and walk among the remnants of Indian encampments on shore.[72]

Alerted by the telegram from Bismarck, Clark and Henry set out from the homestead by the Judith River to meet the girls at Claggett, where the Judith flows into the Missouri, some fifty miles shy of Fort Benton and some fifty miles north of the Shipman cabin. It was late in the afternoon of August 19, 1882, just over a month after the girls had left home, when the *Butte* pulled up to the landing at Clagget. The newly reunited family spent the night at a nearby ranchhouse and early the next morning started south to the Shipman homestead, covering the distance in three days. Arriving a "short time before night," Winnie and Gertie had a chance to survey their new home before falling exhausted into one of the two straw beds that served as the cabin's only furniture.[73]

Over the course of the next few days, the two young women were introduced to life on the homestead, where they prepared their meals in an open-air kitchen; dined on buffalo meat, trout, rabbit, and potatoes; and "craved for something sour." Within two weeks of their arrival, their father installed a stove in the house, and meal preparation became a more civilized affair. He also obtained a cow, which provided milk and butter and fostered larger dreams. Soon Clark Shipman was writing his brother, William, in Boston that he planned to invest in cattle, and he was telling his brother-in-law Henry Marcy in New York that he planned to invest in brood mares.[74]

In early September, Clark helped Winnie choose a homestead site on bottomland two miles south of his own, on the west side of the Judith below Ross Fork. Almost immediately thereafter, he filed for Gertie on 160 acres adjoining Winnie's land.[75] Those claims marked the beginning of the legacy of land that Clark had dreamed of for almost thirty years.

In October, less than two months after her arrival in Montana Territory, Winnie moved to Philbrook, the settlement nearest her father's homestead, and opened the town's first school. Although Philbrook had but one house, one hotel, one store, one saloon, and one blacksmith shop, Winnie enjoyed her life there, finding the mountains "a never failing source of delight," since they, like the ocean, "never seem[ed] twice the same."[76]

Taking advantage of an open winter, Clark, Henry, and Gertrude worked not only on the "home place," but also on the "girls' ranches." On the line between Gertie's and Winnie's land they began to build a log house, with the same twelve- by sixteen-foot floor plan that had served as the basis for Clark's home. But this dwelling differed from the other in one important respect: it was built on skids for ease of transport to future claims. Having finished her school term in March, Winnie took up residence with Gertie in the newly completed one-room house that straddled their property line.[77]

At home in Vermont, Rebecca had spent the fall studying with, and working for, a milliner in Bethel, but she returned to Perham Hill five days before Christmas to celebrate her twentieth birthday with her mother and little sister. The mood was heavy that holiday season. Burdened with both work and worry, Augusta did not hesitate to blame her husband—and her older children—for her situation, noting, "[All of] you seem to be very easy in your minds about the hard things I have to do & as any one of [you] . . . are more able bodied than I am I should not think you would feel like complaining of me." And though widow Lavinia Ellis had managed to make the mortgage payment on the New Jersey farm, Augusta had no intention of forwarding any of the money to Clark to invest in livestock, as he had asked. "You had better help me get to a place where the childre[n] who want to can be schooled sufficiently to do some kind of good business & then you may have the $800," she wrote her husband. "I can not do all the hard work & then hand over the money."[78]

Clark put little store in his wife's complaints, but her refusal to send the money he had requested did put a crimp in his plans. With the coming of spring and Winnie's return to Philbrook, Clark, Gertie, and Henry set aside dreams of a cattle ranch and turned their attention to the realities of truck farming, planting both the home place and Gertie's homestead in onions and potatoes and hoping for better prices than last season's. Early that summer, Clark also went to the two "upper ranches & took down the house in which G & W resided & drew a portion of it to [his] preemption," a 340-acre lot in bottomland at the mouth of Lone Tree Coulee. At about the same time, he filed his "first proof" on his own homestead claim, some fifteen months after having arrived in the Judith Basin.[79]

As the Shipmans worked their lands in the West, Augusta, unbidden, was giving some thought to joining them. She wished she could know her husband's mind, since if he was planning to come home after the next summer's harvest, she would simply lease Perham Hill out for a year and set out to join him immediately. But when she talked the idea over with her brother-in-law William Shipman, he advised against it, since if Clark and the children were, indeed, planning to return to Vermont sometime during the next year, she would have gone all the way out to Montana only to spend the "long cold winter." William's advice made sense; she would much rather have Clark come home to Vermont. "Why can't you pay for your land & so come home for a while before setting up your cattle business?" she queried. His return to the East would give Henry a chance to have the same kind of schooling his older sisters had had. It would also bring the family together again, and, she confessed, "If you were all here I should like it." Nonetheless, she carried on as if reunion were not a possibility and she would remain in sole charge of family business in the East. As 1883 drew to an end, she closed out their New Jersey dealings by accepting the final payment from the widow Ellis and canceling the note on the Malaga property.[80]

Out in Montana, Winnie and Gertie started 1884 with new teaching positions—Winifred in Lewistown, some twenty miles to the east of her father's place, and Gertie in Martinsdale, fifty miles to the southwest. Their departure meant that Clark was left alone on the home ranch that spring, for seventeen-year-old Henry hired himself out as a sheepherder to neighbor John Huson, determined to earn the cash he would need to help carry out a plan that was heartily endorsed by Augusta. In the fall he would return to Vermont, where his Uncle William would place him at Goddard Seminary in Barre until he could qualify for the engineering curriculum at Tufts. Even though his uncle had agreed to subsidize his education, Henry had to earn enough for his train ticket home and the incidentals he would need at school.[81]

Toward that end, Augusta sent him sixty dollars of the Malaga farm mortgage payment she had received that winter. From that same source she drew twenty dollars to invest in more land, buying the acreage that lay across the road from Perham Hill and thus making a further commitment to Vermont at a time when she was ostensibly ambivalent about her future there. As she had for the two previous summers, she rented out the farm to a sharecropper and filled her days caring for her milk cow, pigs, and hens—and teaching lessons to Maggie, now nine. Although Becky was still at home to help her mother with the chores, her thoughts were not on chickens and eggs, but on the excitement that lay ahead, for she had been accepted at Cooper Union for wood engraving classes in the fall.[82] Predictably, Augusta viewed Becky's plans with mixed emotions, for she was less than eager to send her twenty-one-year-old daughter off to the big city by herself.

In early August, Henry closed out his sheepherding contract and came home to the Judith, having earned a hundred dollars toward his impending expenses. After spending a month helping his father work the gardens, he left from Helena for the East. As long as she had anticipated her son's homecoming, Augusta was hardly prepared for his arrival at Perham Hill: "I was washing out in the yard and looked to see Curly barking at a tramp with a trunk on a stick . . . but as he came up I saw it was . . . Henry look[ing] as tho he was 20 years old. . . . he is so strong & broad it does beat all.[83]

As jubilant as Augusta was to welcome her son, she was still in the doldrums over Becky's departure for New York City a day earlier. "It is a venture to send her from me," she wrote to Clark, "but she wanted to go so much that I ventured to risk it." Aunt Em—Emeline Marcy—who lived in Green Island, just north of Albany, had gone down to New York City to help Becky get settled in her quarters at the Home for Destitute Children, and upon her aunt's departure Becky was overwhelmed with homesickness and filled with doubts about her work at Cooper Union.[84]

From the homestead, Clark encouraged Augusta to do all in her power to help both Henry and Becky to take advantage of the educational opportunities available to them. "What money you spend for any of the children will not be lost," he promised. "What W & G had that way is helping them now. I know it is a pity I am not able to do something myself . . . [but] there is no ready money in what we have here now. . . . my faith is unshaken that something will come of it in time."[85]

With no "ready money" of his own that fall of 1884, Clark borrowed "a little money of Win" in order to buy some hogs. Soon thereafter he filed on 160 acres of "timber culture" land on which he planted "balm of gilead & cottonwood sprouts . . . , putting them out in rows a rod apart & about a foot apart in the rows." And he was looking around for a homestead for Becky, now twenty-one years old and eligible to file—were it not for the fact that she was two thousand miles removed from the land her father intended to claim in her name. Gusta was as anxious as her husband to add to the family's holdings, and she had the necessary cash because of her careful management of the small inheritance she had received after her father's death and the lump sum she had received from Widow Ellis for the final Malaga mortgage payment. That fall she wrote Clark that if he were able "to prove up & pay on that Thompson ranch," his original homestead, she would send him $225 toward a preemption claim in Becky's name.[86]

As fall moved on, Henry exchanged labor with his mother's neighbor, Mr. Maxham, and readied himself for school, reviewing algebra and geometry at night. Augusta spent her days at the sewing machine, preparing a full wardrobe of shirts, breeches, and underwear for Henry's first term at Goddard. She also started nine-year-old Maggie, a very willing scholar, in the district school at Christian Hill, a short walk from the farm. And she sent apple seeds from the fruit of her own orchard out to Montana, knowing Clark's special love for the autumn apples of Perham Hill. Tucked in with the apple seeds was a box of Hill's Rheumatic Pills to relieve the hip pain that plagued Clark every winter.[87]

Augusta was increasingly convinced that Gertie should come

home and pursue another career beside teaching, which was not "a congenial work" for her. Clark did not belittle her concern, but he felt that teaching was "as congenial as any work would be" for Gertie. Thus, the young woman became a pawn between her parents—her mother wanting her to come home, and her father insisting that both she and her sister were where they should be, doing what they should be doing, and that "their coming out here was [no] misfortune." Assessing their two-year stay in Montana, he declared, "They are in better health than they were & the chance for them to do something for themselves has been better . . . than it was there. . . . You can write [Gertie] as many letters as you like & try to persuade her that it is best to start out on some new plan . . . & I shall [not] stand in the way but I do not think you will meet with much success."[88]

Despite the press of her responsibilities on Perham Hill, Gusta's thoughts remained centered on her children, far-flung now and out of her control. While trying to entice Gertie to return to school, she turned her energies to keeping Becky there, writing, at first every other day and then almost weekly, with advice as to how to deal with homesickness, bedbugs, a recalcitrant matron who would not send heat to her room, competition in the classroom, and the risk of illness in the big city.[89]

Even as she advised Becky to be vigilant of her health, Gusta herself had a "sick spell." It was hard to keep up with everything. Her house looked "like fury & cleaning is to be done . . . & all the time the corns on my feet ache. . . . [and] getting something to eat & seeing to the farm business makes a lot to do." She would just as soon be rid of the worry of Perham Hill, but she was "getting too old to start off any where without some extra pushing." Perhaps when Henry moved on to Tufts, she and Maggie should consider setting up housekeeping in Boston, so Henry could board with them and Becky could "live at home & work at her trade." Keenly aware of the broken circle, she lamented, "My children are scattered as bad as any family I know of."[90]

Clark dissented: "I do not think we are so much scattered as some families that all live in the same town," he told her. Even as he took issue with her view of things, he had to convey some disheartening news: his preemption claim had been reviewed and denied on the basis of his failure to prove residence.[91] The verdict should not have surprised him; besides his "home ranch," he had the "girls' ranches" *and* the preemption claim to tend to. And he had no help in any of these endeavors—nor could he count on any in the near future with his daughters away teaching school and Henry not scheduled to return to Montana for at least another four years.

On December 1, 1884, after a little more than two months at Perham Hill, Henry Shipman set out for Barre and a term at Goddard Seminary in hopes of qualifying for admission to the engineering program at Tufts by the fall. In the wake of her son's departure, Augusta hired her neighbor Maxham to help with the chores she and Maggie could not see to. She was "repairing the farm some," and the care of her newly calved milk cow, her hens, and some turkeys all kept her busy. After an extended visit with the Marcys in New York, her mother was back at Perham Hill, a mixed blessing since the woman was "fussy" and her presence served to "stir" Augusta. Money—or the lack of it—also had Augusta in a stir. With Henry now in school, she was committed to paying $2.50 a week for his board, though he was on a tuition-free scholarship arranged by his Uncle William. She was also sending money to Becky at Cooper Union. The struggle was worthwhile. "If ever I get rested, I shall appreciate the priveleges that the children are getting & there will be enough left for you to come east & get an education [too]," she wrote Gertie.[92]

More and more frequently, Augusta thought of closing out her interests in Vermont and going west, though Montana weather was less than inviting that winter of 1884–85. Record-setting temperatures of fifty degrees below zero kept Gertrude from getting home from Martinsdale for Christmas, and Winnie barely made it home from Lewistown, arriving in a blizzard in the company of Nicholas Erickson, a young Lewistown merchant. Alone with his thoughts in the postholiday season, Clark Shipman assessed his future in the West. A major part of his plans from the beginning had involved his son, now distant in the East and apparently set upon a new course. "As fast as you get any new idea into your head about what you shall want to do in the future you must let me know," he wrote eighteen-year-old Henry. "If you conclude you shall not want to be a rancher or that you shall rather ranch some where else than on the Judith I shall want to know it for I shall not want to be drawing plans for any big thing & then do it alone."[93]

It was a nostalgic period for Clark, and in a rare letter written directly to Augusta, he reminded her of the dreams they had fashioned on their honeymoon in the Midwest some thirty years before:

A very different condition of things you see [here] from what was ever to be found on the Illinois or Iowa prairies. If it were 1855 instead of 1885 I think the prospect would appear far more encouraging to me here than it did to me there then, & you know what we could have done if we had staid there. . . . But it is not '55 . . . now & never will be again & I begin to have visions of some small sunny corner (in the winter but cool & shady in the summer) where I or we could keep a horse one cow & a pig & four hens & a rooster (no turkeys in mine thank you) & take life easy. . . . Do you ever think that in 16 years more we shall be 70 years old?[94]

Acknowledging that "one old man can't do much any more than one old woman, especially if he has no old woman to cook his grub & mend his stockings," he noted that he could nonetheless stay on in Montana "as well as any where" and was not persuaded by her accounts of the success others had in Vermont:

You are constantly repeating that every body is prospering & getting rich in Vt but it never looked that way to me. . . . Whatever others can do in Bethel & vicinity it did not seem to me that I could do more than get a bare living there. . . . I consider [the land here] worth a good deal more. Tho it might be hard to realize it . . . at present. . . . Of course I should like to see Vt again or even Jersey sand for a change, but . . . if all were here & liked to stay I presume I should be as contented here as I ever expect to be any where.[95]

Lest Augusta construe these comments as an invitation to join him in Montana Territory, Clark hastened to say, "I don't see how you can come here now if you wanted. . . . It is about as necessary for you to keep some kind of a home for the children there as it is for me to do so for the ones here." And an old issue loomed in the foreground: "You ask if I have found out if I can 'make money.' Now ma perhaps I am not & never have been so 'struck' after making money as you think . . . or at least as you would have liked to have had me. I should have liked to have had a plenty of money 'to spend' but I think there are some other things to be thought of for money does not always produce pleasure or comfort." Admitting that he could have "staid right there [in Vermont] & done tread mill work all our lives," he added a telling conditional clause—"provided we could have lived as folks should"—followed by a parenthesized aside indicating the nature and extent of their earlier estrangement and hinting at the conditions under which he would consider reunion: "Having written that last sentence here I will not write it any more, but you may know that I always mean it to be understood, whether the tense is past, present or future."[96]

Returning to the question of profits, he admitted, "No I haven't made any money but I will tell you what I think could be done right here on this ranch & about the same that could be done here could be done on Henry's or on the girls' both together," and he then set forth his plans for plowing and planting all the bottomland to potatoes, grain, and hay and investing in benchland on which to run one hundred head of cattle and one hundred hogs.[97]

While Clark dreamt his dreams in Montana, Augusta was facing reality in Vermont. A prospective buyer for Perham Hill had balked at her asking price, and her mother's rheumatism made her so miserable and testy that just being in the house with her took "the grit all out of" Augusta. Even so, spring had her laying plans again. She, too, wanted to invest in calves, although her dreams of a "cow business" were not as grandiose as those of her husband. She grafted her apple trees and brought bees to Perham Hill. And all the while her poultry business was flourishing: the turkeys were "tame" and the hens were laying well. In early spring, the Maxhams moved, but Maxham had never been a reliable hand anyway, and Henry, home on break from Goddard, helped her with the heavy chores.[98]

In Montana the coming of spring moved Clark into the fields again. As he planted peas, potatoes, onions, wheat, oats, and timothy, his thoughts were in Vermont—on the sugaring season and on his wife's struggles with the farm. Upon Henry's return to school after the spring break, he had described for his father the situation he had found on Perham Hill, where Augusta had "got it into her head that she will raise a lot of calves." Knowing the futility of trying to change his mother's mind about anything, he had concluded it would be "about as well for all concerned to let her run her own ranch and try to help a little in the way she is going." Clark passed this assessment on to his daughters, both of whom had new teaching situations closer to home, Winnie in Philbrook and Gertie in Stanford.[99]

As Winnie and Gertie began their summer sessions, their siblings in the East were finishing up their course work and returning to Perham Hill. Becky came through Barre on her way home from New York City and stopped at Goddard to visit with Henry for a few days in early May of 1885. A month later, her brother followed her home to Bethel, having completed his preparatory course work and qualified for enrollment at Tufts in the fall. Home at Perham Hill, he took over the summer chores, mowing the oats planted months earlier for his mother by his cousin, Willie Whitney, and fencing the brook pasture so that she could turn out her six cows and their calves. And he exchanged labor with a neighbor, haying the man's fields and building "credit" for his mother to use once he returned to school in the fall.[100]

As he worked, Henry became more and more convinced that farming on the Judith was far preferable to farming in Vermont. "I shall come out when I get through with college," he promised his father, "unless things look a good deal better [then] to me in the east." Augusta's plans were no more definite than his. "Mother is very anxious to know if you are coming back in three years," he wrote, "[but she] says she shall never go west even if you do not come back." Although she was again denying any plan to go west, Augusta still had Perham Hill on the market, hoping to sell it for a reasonable price and then settle wherever it would be possible for Maggie to get a good education. To date, the child's schooling had been limited to lessons taught at home or learned in the small district school at Christian Hill.[101]

With the coming of fall 1885, Becky returned for a second year at Cooper Union, and Henry traveled to Boston to live with his Uncle William and Aunt Mattie at College Hill while attending Tufts. He was working for his board and room, but Augusta periodically sent him money, and she wrote asking Clark to pick up some of Becky's expenses in New York City. In response to Gusta's "urgent demands," Clark wrote not to Bethel but directly to New York, informing Becky:

> We have just got a letter from [Ma] in which she says she will take care of Henry but she advises me to send you some money. . . . I have sold some pigs and potatoes & have some more to sell but the trouble is I have not got much money for them yet & it is not very certain how soon I shall. [Perhaps] I can get it of Win or some other rich school marm & she can wait until I get my pay. . . . I am not getting rich very fast but I guess full as fast as I could on P. Hill. . . . Ma is very much disgusted because I have not become as rich as a nabob long before this time but she has not much of an idea what it is to get rooted in a new country.[102]

Clark eventually found cash to send to Becky, and as she acknowledged her father's generosity, she apologized for causing such expense. "I have undertaken to learn a long and costly art," she wrote her father, "and I am afraid it will be quite a while before I can practice it and turn the cost in my favor." Meantime, she wanted him to understand the situation at home:

> Mother . . . has been very generous with me. I think if any of us are really in need out this way it is mother and Maggie. . . . I don't think mother could get along at all with out Mag nor Mag with out mother. I know that you have had a hard time to get started in a new country. . . . [But] it has been hard for mother too. There are two or three mean despicable men in Bethel and Royalton, but they have not succeeded in doing us much harm so far but they failed principally from lack of brains. There are also a great many good people who have been very kind to us.[103]

Clark was willing to concede that his wife had to struggle to carry on alone, but he was by no means ready to think of returning to Vermont. He set forth his reasons in a letter to Becky, asking that she forward it to Henry: "Ma has written a good deal lately nearly all in the same old strain convincing me if I have ever doubted that if we lived in the same house it would be the same old pandemonium & I think you will agree with all the rest of us that it is far better as it is. She has declared in strong terms that she shall never come west & has demanded that [I] 'speak out' as whether I am coming back etc. & decide matters without further delay." Forced to give an answer, he had "with very little . . . feeling" written Augusta "that hereafter we will travel different roads & that I will & she may commence at once to plan accordingly." Despite his disclaimer, Clark was, in fact, deeply moved by his forthright admission of the failure of his marriage, conceding, "It is hard work for me even now after I have been away 4 years to realize that this must be so but I know in all reason there is nothing better to be done. We might try it over again but I do not see the slightest reason to hope that the trial would be anything but short and unsatisfactory. . . . But it does not by any means follow that we will not all continue to have a care for each other."[104]

Although adamant as ever that she would never go west, Augusta continued to look for a way to dispose of Perham Hill and was contemplating selling it to her nephew Willie Whitney for fifteen hundred dollars. Removed though he was from the scene, Clark endorsed the plan. "I think it would be the best thing she could do," he wrote to Becky. "It is probably as much as it is worth now & I know it is as much as he could afford to pay." He wanted his children to understand that if Augusta had "stuck to [the farm] because she was full in the faith that I would come back again & run things according to her own plans it has been her own fault for I have declared to the contrary first & last."[105]

If Augusta was aware that her husband was writing to their children about a permanent separation, if not a divorce, she never betrayed that awareness, concentrating instead on descriptions of her problems in finding a hired hand to help her and of a recurring inflammation of the bowel. She had Gertie's sympathy: "Ma does seem to be in a hard place sure enough," she wrote Becky that winter. "The idea of her and Maggie trying to do the chores in the winter time and wading through the snow to the village every time anything is wanted. She must get off the old place somehow and go somewhere where schooling and company that Maggie needs will come easier. Of course, it must be dreadful for M[aggie] to stay there all alone with ma and grandma. She might just as well be in Montana as on Perham Hill."[106]

Indeed, all the Shipmans in Montana had now begun to press Maggie and Becky to join them, even though life in the West was not without its problems. They had been quite anxious about a complaint filed against Winifred's and Gertrude's homestead claims—which went largely unlived on, although Clark used Gertie's land year after year for growing his produce—and they were relieved when the land inspector's investigation led him to rule in their favor. As Winnie went back to her school in Philbrook, she polled her younger siblings about their financial needs. "I think you had better get what money you want of Win," Henry advised Becky as they settled into another school year that fall. "She would rather you had it than not and if she keeps it she would not get but 5% on it. I am taking mothers money under the same circumstances."[107]

Augusta was feeling especially magnanimous, because she was now fairly certain that she had a buyer for the farm. A Mr. Howe had written that he was coming to look at Perham Hill. But when he offered only $1,350 for the eighty-five acres and demanded that the mown hay and the cut wood be a part of the deal, she "told him to go." Her inability to find anyone to buy or lease the farm scuttled her half-formed plan to move to Randolph Center so eleven-year-old Maggie could be enrolled in school there. Maggie's disappointment matched her mother's, and she spent that winter studying her lessons at home and brooding over her lost opportunities.[108]

Meantime, her father was once again worrying over the family's land claims. It had been almost five years since they had filed their original claims, and Clark was concerned that their patents would all be denied because of irregularities. As he saw it, the irregularities stemmed not from the manner in which he himself was following the guidelines of the Homestead Act, but from the manner in which William Sparks, the commissioner of public lands in Washington, was interpreting that act: "Sparks . . . did his best to make out [that] one could not use both preemption & homestead rights. Then . . . he ruled that a crop must be put in the 2nd year on timber culture tho the law says . . . otherwise & he has ruled that a crop must be raised on desert land when the law says . . . nothing about a crop etc."[109]

However the law was read, Clark Shipman would have difficulty proving his claim and he knew it, though he could easily rationalize his position. "Of course we did not do a great deal of residing & improving but we did as much as thousands of others & have bought the land & paid for it & are paying taxes on it & are genuine settlers of the country," he wrote to his son: "Of course G & I could not be expected to reside on our preemptions after making proof for we filed on homesteads. Win has been in other busines & it is none of Sparks or anybody else's business. I do not reside on my homestead much it seems next to impossible for me to do so. If any body was really bound to jump it I presume they might succeed in doing so."[110]

While Clark worried over the legitimacy of his claims, his daughters were once again living away from their homesteads, further endangering their claims. Winnie spent the winter of 1886–87 at Chestnut, a small settlement not far from the Judith, while Gertie continued on at a "family school" at Stanford. In Vermont, Augusta was well aware of the tenuous situation: "Did you notice that pop said they had not got their title to their land yet?" she gloated to Becky. "I think that is enough to sicken me of the west."[111]

Despite her disappointment at being unable to sell the farm, Augusta enjoyed her easiest winter at Perham Hill since her return to Vermont. Noting his mother's mellow mood, Henry was glad he had chosen to come home for the two-week Christmas holiday to give her a brief respite from the full weight of her responsibilities. As he returned to College Hill in January 1887, his future was heavy in his thoughts. He would be finished with his schooling in another year, and he still did not know what he would do thereafter. "The chances seem to be in favor of my going to work in some place that Uncle Henry [Marcy] will get me," he wrote to Winifred. "You can bet I shall not work on the farm. Mother is losing more dollars than she makes cents on the farm." Such feelings were tempered by his awareness that "Mother will never get off the place until Grandma does not want to stay there any longer, and you know when that will be." Although Henry's graduation was still over a year away, Clark Shipman was also thinking a good deal about his son's future. He had long counted on Henry to ranch with him in Montana, but if "choice or some sense of duty" impelled the young man "to remain with or near ma," Clark assured him he would "try to be content."[112]

By early May, Henry had finished his exams at Tufts and was home working the fields for his mother. Becky was also home that summer of 1887. This time she brought her materials and tools with her, and Augusta fixed up the parlor as her studio. That spring she had sold her first piece of art for $3.50, and now she began to pick up commissions from buyers in New York, Boston, and even Bethel. At almost the same time that her sister and brother returned to Perham Hill, Maggie began school down in Bethel, walking to and from the village each morning and afternoon, a distance of some three miles. Maggie wished she could go to a better school. Augusta reported that Maggie was "very like Win in getting up enthusiasm" for her studies, but she was "more saucy & harder to manage."[113]

It was a good growing season in the Judith Basin, and Clark Shipman had an abundant crop that summer, but he had to "spend a good deal of time peddling" in order to sell his produce. Weekly he hitched his horses to the wagon and made the circuit of Philbrook, Lewistown, Maiden, Stanford, and Utica, selling his vegetables door to door.[114]

As her father harvested his crops and carried the produce into town, Maggie abandoned all hope of getting out west to help him. With the coming of fall, she was still in place on Perham Hill, trudging daily to school in Bethel village. It had been five years now since Gertie and Winnie had seen their little sister, and Henry's and Becky's letters had convinced them that they would not know her. "I can't manage to think of Mag as a big girl," Gertie wrote to her mother. "Whenever I think of [her] coming out here to live it seems as though we should have to build a fence along the Judith the first thing to keep her from tumbling into a deep hole and getting drowned."[115]

That fall, Gertie herself, now twenty-seven, was teaching in Ubet, about twenty miles below the homestead, and Winnie was back in Lewistown. After a long courtship, she was making plans to marry Nicholas Erickson. A year younger than she, the handsome young man had come to Montana Territory from Chicago as a banker some five years earlier but had soon thereafter joined T. C. Power in establishing one of Lewistown's finest stores, the Power Mercantile Company. Winnie had hopes that her mother would be able to come out to her wedding in the spring, and Clark himself was again entertaining the idea of reunion, writing to Maggie, "If the 'fambly' all or nearly all ever gets together again in this world I think it is more likely to do so in the Judith Basin than any where else."[116]

Even Henry was taken with the possibilities. The fact that the railroad was going "up the branch" and would be finished within the year gave him cause to think that Perham Hill would increase in value—and in its attractiveness to a buyer. Before the year was out, Augusta did have an interested buyer, but once again she refused what she felt was a poor offer.[117] Much as she talked of selling out, she might well have had difficulty entertaining even the most generous offer, for her son had been right: the land still had its hold on Augusta, and as long as her mother was alive, Perham Hill provided her with ample reason not to join her husband in Montana.

Meantime, Clark continued to feed his son's dreams of ranching in the West. "You speak of looking for a job," he wrote as Henry started his last term of college. "I shall not feel bad if you find jobs so scarce that you can do no better than come back here . . . to engineer ditches & fences, new houses & obvious other things which I never shall do alone." Becky, who had begun her last year at Cooper Union, was less inclined to look west, filled as she was with high hopes of finding a place in the art world when she finished her degree at Cooper Union.[118]

Winnie's thoughts were on the future too. During the holidays, she and Nicholas had set their wedding date for March 5, and she wrote her mother of the plans, but she had little hope that Augusta would be pleased with her arrangements or that any of her family in the East would be able to attend. Predictably disgruntled with the wedding plan, Augusta complained to Becky, "I lose heart about them out there if they are going to get married and don't care enough for us to come and see us." Despite, or perhaps because of, Augusta's absence, the wedding in the cabin on the Judith was a light-hearted affair. The day after the ceremony, the newlyweds took the train out of Billings for the East, combining a honeymoon with a business trip for Nicholas and a trip home for Winnie. It was a grand tour in which Winnie and Nicholas touched all bases, visiting the Lees in New

Jersey; Becky in New York City; Aunt Em and Uncle Henry in Green Island; Henry, Uncle William, and Aunt Mattie in College Hill; and Ma and Maggie on Perham Hill.[119]

Clark hoped that Maggie would consider coming west with Winnie and Nicholas, though he offered no funds for travel and supposed that "Ma will think it is awful mean for me to want to get them all [out here with me]." Then he added a line, well aware that Maggie would share the letter with her mother: "I wonder," he mused, "if she has any suspicion that I want her too _____ if _____," the unfinished expression conveying his mood more graphically than any words.[120]

With such thoughts in his head, Clark busied himself with the chores of the new season. He plowed, harrowed, and planted; he put in an acre of potatoes; he baked bread and made mince pies; he tended his flock of chickens and his pen full of hogs. And he went about such chores with a lighter heart, for that spring he gained title to 120 acres of his preemption land. A few months later, he had title in Gertie's name to another 160 acres of preemption land. His carefully laid plans were beginning to pay off.[121]

When Winnie and Nicholas Erickson started west in late April 1888, Maggie was not with them. Augusta had not felt she could spare her youngest child, though her own chores were lighter since she had not planted "much of a crop" that spring—only potatoes and sweet corn in her garden. She had sold off "$100 worth of stock" and intended to "sell more as soon as [she could] get her price." She continued to drive her mare back and forth to the village as needed, and those trips were more and more frequent now that Maggie was in school in Bethel. At fifty-seven and in poor health, she was not inclined to travel far from home, and in June she went to neither Becky's nor Henry's commencement because her "nerves" were not "equal to the occasion." It was a disappointment not only to her children, but to Uncle William, too, who had wanted "all the family" to come to College Hill for Henry's graduation. In the end, twelve-year-old Maggie Shipman was the only member of Henry's immediate family to see him receive his diploma.[122]

After the ceremonies, Henry returned to Bethel, still undecided as to what to do. Although he thought his "best chance for an engineering job" lay in Montana, he knew he was in no position "to leave the east until mother is fixed better than she is." His Perham Hill chores were light, since his mother had not planted many acres, and most of his days were spent in haying on the home place and for neighbors. Waiting for Becky's arrival home in midsummer, he did what he could to encourage Maggie to persevere in her work at the village school in Bethel. She wanted desperately to go away to school, but her mother had made it clear that she wouldn't pay out "another single cent" for her education, a statement that Maggie repeated in a letter to her father, adding, "Things are about as mixed up as ever. Mother has not yet decided what to do or where to go."[123]

After a brief visit at Perham Hill, Becky returned to New York, where she had joined a society of women engravers. Now living in Harlem, she was selling more and more of her work to such clients as *Scribner's Magazine* and several children's book publishers. Henry did not linger long at Perham Hill either, for by Thanksgiving he was on his way to Lima, Ohio, to take up a railroad position that his uncle Henry Marcy had secured for him.[124]

Out in Montana, Winnie was settled in an elegant new home on Washington Street in Lewistown, where she had frequent visits from her father and from Gertie, who was teaching in Maiden, a small mining camp just north of Lewistown. On December 9, 1888, the first Shipman grandchild, Anna Margaret Erickson, was born. Clark was elated. Nicholas had gone to the homestead to fetch him at daybreak that morning, and father and grandfather arrived in town within minutes of the baby's birth. When Winnie sent the news to Perham Hill, she admitted that the only thing she wished for now was that her mother and Grandma Perham could "look [the baby] over for [them]selves."[125]

That Christmas, as Clark and Gertie gathered around the tree in the Erickson living room with Winnie, Nicholas, and two-week-old Anna, their celebration was but a prelude to one destined to take place a month later when Henry arrived in Montana after an absence of more than four years.[126] It had taken him less than two months in the railroad office in Ohio to decide that he belonged on the homestead in Montana Territory.

Knowing that Henry was in the West had Augusta considering the move once again. But she was as ambivalent as ever, and this time with cause. Clark had begun to write of making a trip home to Vermont in 1890. Maggie, desperate now to get to Montana, encouraged the plan on both sides and informed her father, "Mother seems quite pleased at the idea of going back with you." The Shipman girls in Montana were optimistic: "They are coming west in a body if father goes after them next winter and succeeds in straightening out matters, selling farms, etc.," Winnie wrote to Gertie, who was now teaching in Grassrange, thirty miles east of Lewistown. Gertie herself saw all kinds of prospects in Augusta's move west: "I wish we could sell some of our ranches at a good price but I don't want to throw them away. If ma were here I think she would see lots of ways of making money that she would want us to go into."[127]

Gertie's wishes aside, Clark was not currently looking to sell any of his land, though he *was* trading it around within the family. Having secured the patent to Gertie's 160 acres in the summer of 1889, he now deeded his own preemption claim to Henry and transferred Gertie's homestead deed to himself. Then, true to his word, after the fall harvest of 1889, he turned the winter operations over to Henry and boarded the train for the East. That long-postponed trip might well have been prompted by his growing suspicions that the General Land Office planned to use his unorthodox living arrangements as the basis for denying his homestead patent. Sure enough, shortly after his departure for Vermont, the Land Office sent a formal denial of his patent, calling the case "very unsatisfactory as to residence and improvements," suspending his entry "until such time as [he should] . . . show satisfactory residence and improvements," and raising a bothersome question: "You testify that your wife is living in Vermont and has never been on the land but no reason is given why she does not live on the land."[128]

Whether or not he realized in advance that his claim was threatened, Clark proceeded eastward, bent on rectifying at least one of the grounds for denial: his wife's absence from the homestead. Arriving in Bethel on November 20, 1889, he was reunited with Augusta after a separation of almost eight years. He found the farm on Perham Hill in excellent shape and had only to convince his wife that she really wanted to sell, even if she could not hope to get what she wanted for the property. Within three months, Gusta had agreed, accepting one thousand dollars for the acreage and house, a price considerably lower than several she had rejected earlier.[129]

Having sold the farm, the stock, and the equipment; "having got all business matters as well arranged as could be expected"; and having settled eighty-four-year-old Sarah Perham at the Marcys' in Green Island, New York, Clark, Augusta, Rebecca, and Maggie Shipman started for Montana on March 27, 1890. They stopped en route at Vernon, Vermont, to visit DeEtte and Oscar Lee, who had sold

Oak Grove Farm down in Malaga the previous year and returned north to the senior Lees' place. After a brief visit in Vernon, Clark, Augusta, and the girls went on to College Hill to visit William and Mattie Shipman. Leaving Boston on April 7, they arrived in Great Falls, Montana, a week later, taking the stage to Utica, where a neighbor, Theo Gray, met them in his wagon and brought them to the homestead on the Judith.[130]

No record remains of Augusta's first impression of her husband's homestead cabin, but shortly after her arrival work began on an impressive two-story structure, twenty-two feet by thirty-four feet. And all through the winter of 1890–91, as construction on the new home continued "piecemeal," Maggie and Augusta slept out in the kitchen and "the rest where they [could] while they waited for doors and windows to arrive." Even under those less-than-optimum circumstances, Augusta seemed a little lighter of spirit. At fifty-nine, bowed by osteoporosis and still bothered by various and sundry other ailments, she remained extremely active, working in the fields as well as in the house.[131]

As the new house was being built, Becky filed on her own homestead, though she had no intentions of living there, and Henry took up residence on his own ranch, the preemption claim that his father had deeded him, not far from the homestead by the Judith. While Becky did her share of farm and housework, she also continued her engraving, winning first prize in the wood engraving exhibit at the Chicago World's Fair in 1893. The year Maggie turned seventeen, she secured a teaching position at Warm Springs Creek, close by the Judith homestead but far enough away that she had to board out. Augusta worked on at the farm but made increasingly frequent trips into Lewistown to visit Winnie, who eventually had two more daughters, Gracia (1891) and Gertrude (1892).[132]

As Gertie had once predicted, her mother did indeed see many financial opportunities that her father had overlooked. Winifred, too, understood that her mother "could always see farther ahead" than her father, and the two watched with interest as Augusta, seeing "nothing but land out here," prodded Clark to buy up more and more of it until in all "some 7 thousand acres were obtained."[133]

Unorthodox as their situation had long been, the family seemed to become a cohesive whole in those early Montana years. "I think we children think more of each other than the majority of families," Becky wrote to Gertrude in the fall of 1892, "and that makes up for some of the failings." Augusta and Clark seemed more at ease with one another, and despite Augusta's inherent reclusivity, the new house on the Judith became the scene of many social gatherings. Fifty neighbors came for a Valentine's celebration and danced until daylight. The Fourth of July was also observed with a dance at the Shipmans', complete with fireworks at midnight, a supper with strawberries and cream at 2 A.M., and more dancing until dawn.[134]

In August 1893, Maggie returned to Vermont to spend a year at Goddard. Now in a better position to support his children than he had been when Henry and Becky were in school, Clark frequently sent spending money to his youngest daughter. He also began to build the herd of cattle he had long dreamed of. In the winter of 1893–94 he and Gertie, in full partnership, invested in thirty steers, hoping to winter them over successfully and sell them at a hundred dollars a head in Chicago the next fall.[135]

While Clark and Henry worked the ranches, Gusta and Becky tended house and garden, Gertie continued her teaching, and Winnie devoted herself to her family in Lewistown, making frequent trips out to the homestead with the three little girls, particularly when her husband was away on buying trips. It was on one such trip, in the spring of 1894, that thirty-seven-year-old Nicholas Erickson was taken suddenly and seriously ill. Leaving the little ones with her mother, Winnie took the train to Saint Paul, where she sat helplessly at her husband's bedside as he died. At home, Augusta did what she could to maintain some normalcy for the little girls, ages five, three, and not quite two, while Winnie buried her husband in Chicago.[136]

As the decade wore on, Clark continued to work on the house on the Judith "piecemeal." He hardly needed the new rooms he had constructed, for all of the children were essentially on their own now, though they were still in Montana—with the exception of Maggie, who had gone on to Tufts after finishing her course at Goddard and was now teaching science in a high school in Minnesota. Clark and Augusta were alone in the big house, and neither had any complaints. "Ma and I have got along very comfortably alone," Clark wrote Gertie, who was teaching school in the Cottonwood district.[137]

Late in the decade, Winifred, who had maintained her husband's part ownership in the Power Mercantile Company, bought a second home in Evanston, Illinois. Living part of the year in Illinois so her daughters could have the advantage of better schooling, she continued to spend summers and holidays in Montana. Periodically, Au-

Augusta Perham Shipman at about sixty-four, about 1895. *(Courtesy Susan Shipman Burnham and Montana Historical Society, Helena)*

gusta accompanied Winnie and her girls on trips to Florida, southern California, and the Southwest, seeking a cure for young Anna's tuberculosis, and Clark dropped in on his granddaughters each fall when he traveled to Chicago to sell his steers.[138]

Shortly after the turn of the century, Clark Shipman observed the twentieth anniversary of his arrival in Montana. At seventy-one, he was an active man, still plowing, planting, and harvesting his fields.

In the winter of 1902–1903 he left Augusta in Montana and took a four-month tour of the East Coast, returning to New Jersey, Massachusetts, and Vermont to visit friends and family.[139]

In 1904, thirty-eight-year-old Henry Shipman married Grace Martin, a second cousin eleven years younger than he who had come out from Rochester, Vermont, to teach school. The wedding was held at the ranch house on a beautiful October day, but without two of the groom's sisters. Winnie was hospitalized in Evanston with typhoid fever, and Gertie had gone east to take care of her three little nieces. The newlyweds settled into the four-room, two-story home Henry had built on his homestead just two miles from his parents' place, and in midsummer of 1905, Grace gave birth to Clark and Augusta's first grandson, Henry Nicholas Shipman.[140]

Both now seventy-four years old, with Clark bothered by rheumatism and cataracts and Augusta by osteoporosis, the couple began to think in terms of returning to the milder climate and easier life of New England. When in March 1906 the Enterprise Land & Improvement Company, a subsidiary of the Great Northern Railroad, offered ten dollars an acre for the 6,364 acres of land the Shipmans had acquired in the Judith Basin, Clark quickly accepted, though he requested a one-year leaseback of his land, buildings, and equipment.[141]

That fall, he accompanied the last of his livestock—eight carloads of cattle—to Chicago, and at the end of their year's lease he and Augusta left the ranch for Lewistown, where they planned to reside only briefly while deciding where to settle on the East Coast. At about the same time, Henry and Grace left the Judith Basin for Vermont to take up residence near her family in Rochester. It was from Rochester in May 1907 that Augusta and Clark received word of the birth of another grandson, Richard.[142]

That July, while Augusta sought treatment for her osteoporosis at Hunter's Hot Springs, a spa some eighty miles south of Lewistown, Clark once again toured the East Coast, this time looking for a place for himself and his wife to live out the rest of their years. Deciding against New Jersey, he turned his sights toward Vermont. There he bought Oscar and DeEtte Lee's farm, the original Chester Lee place, for sixteen hundred dollars, but a month later he turned that deed over to Henry.[143]

He spent that Christmas with his brother, William, and sister, DeEtte, at the Lees' new home in Northfield, Massachusetts. It was a festive reunion for the Shipman siblings, and it was to be their last.

Less than a month later, William died quite suddenly. Clark was one of the hundreds in attendance at his funeral in the chapel at Tufts.[144]

That spring of 1908, Clark returned to Montana, where he and Augusta were to spend the next three years. They traveled extensively—sometimes together, sometimes separately. Invariably they spent the holidays in Evanston with Winnie and the girls, and Augusta sometimes joined Winnie and Anna on trips to the south for treatment of the child's tuberculosis. She also continued her periodic visits to Hunter's Hot Springs, seeking treatment for her osteoporosis and arthritis.[145]

In August 1911, Clark and Augusta took final leave of the Judith Basin and moved to the village of Lee in western Massachusetts, where they were soon joined by Gertie, Becky, and Maggie. There Clark spent hours in his garden, and Augusta, though crippled with osteoporosis, worked beside him, tending her potatoes, corn, tomatoes, beets, carrots, parsnips, squash—and her chickens. Henry made freqent visits from Brattleboro, where he and Grace and the two boys now lived.[146]

Augusta's declining years would perhaps have been the easiest of her life had it not been for her concerns for her second daughter. From childhood Gertie had been marked by "an unhappy nature," and throughout adulthood she had struggled with "nervousness" induced by the stresses of teaching, even though she had given more than thirty years of her life to the profession. Now in her early fifties and beset by "nervous ailments," she had been spending more and more of her time with Winnie in Evanston, where she consulted several doctors. There was some improvement. "Gertrude seems to fit in with us better than I expected," Clark wrote to Winifred a year after the family had settled in Lee, "[though] she has ideas in her head that I fear can never be got out without a surgical operation but she does not harp on them much & seems quite content to do some things much as she has done for years."[147]

Early in 1913, Clark developed pneumonia. Augusta wrote to Winifred in Illinois that although her father was ill, it was not serious and she need not come, since "it would be more to feed." But the congestion in Clark's lungs could not be reversed, and he grew increasingly weaker. He died on February 5, 1913, at eighty-one years of age, survived by his widow, five children, and five grandchildren. The body was returned to the Cherry Hill Cemetery in Bethel, Vermont, for burial.[148]

Augusta lived on with her daughters in Lee for another four years, during which time she continued to work in her garden, putter in the kitchen, and keep abreast of the war news, observing that the troubles in Europe could be laid to "what fools power makes of folks." A lonely woman in age, as perhaps she had been throughout her life, she wrote her children letters that were reminiscent of those written decades earlier: "I want to be with you . . . [but] when shall we be together?" She aged quickly in the few years remaining to her, which were difficult in other ways. In 1916, fifty-six-year-old Gertrude Shipman was committed to the state hospital for the insane at Northampton, Massachusetts, then transferred to a private hospital in Wellesley. Gertie's mental problems and Augusta's own osteoporosis and rheumatism all weighed heavily on the older woman, and she grew more and more irritable and distracted. In a probate report filed with his father's estate in 1917, Henry noted that his mother was "so old and broken that she can neither sign or properly comprehend what is wanted her to sign." Augusta Perham Shipman did not survive that statement more than a few weeks, dying on July 7, 1917. She was buried a few days later beside her husband, Clark, at Cherry Hill Cemetery near Perham Hill. In time three of her children would be buried there as well. Ironically, the headstone that marks the family plot carries the names of *all* the Shipman offspring, giving the illusion that the members of the family that Augusta herself had once described as "scattered as bad as any family I know of" had, at last, all come home to Perham Hill.[149]

Notes

I
Families in Flux

1. James Fergus to Pamelia Fergus, Oct. 10, 1860. The Fergus letters reside in the James Fergus Papers, Mansfield Library Archives, University of Montana, Missoula. For the Fergus story, see Linda Peavy and Ursula Smith, *The Gold Rush Widows of Little Falls* (St. Paul: Minnesota Historical Society Press, 1990). In quoting these and other letters, the authors have chosen to retain the spelling, capitalization, and punctuation found in the original sources.

2. J. S. Holliday's *The World Rushed In: The California Gold Rush Experience* (New York: Simon and Schuster, 1981) is one of the few works that considers letters from women in the East aside from the authors' own work, *Gold Rush Widows,* which was published nearly a decade after Holliday's.

3. For scholarship on women in the West, see, in particular, Susan Armitage and Elizabeth Jameson, eds., *The Women's West* (Norman: University of Oklahoma Press, 1987); John Mack Faragher, *Women and Men on the Overland Trail* (New Haven, Conn.: Yale University Press, 1979); Joan Jensen and Darlis Miller, eds., *New Mexico Women: Intercultural Perspectives* (Albuquerque: University of New Mexico Press, 1986); Sandra Myres, *Westering Women and the Frontier Experience, 1800–1915* (Albuquerque: University of New Mexico Press, 1982); Peggy Pascoe, *Relations of Rescue: The Search for Female Moral Authority in the American West, 1874–1939* (New York: Oxford University Press, 1990); Glenda Riley, *The Female Frontier: A Comparative View of Women on the Prairie and the Plains* (Lawrence: University of Kansas Press, 1988); Glenda Riley, *Women and Indians on the Frontier, 1825–1915* (Albuquerque: University of New Mexico Press, 1984); Lillian Schlissel, *Women's Diaries of the Westward Journey* (New York: Schocken Books, 1982); Lillian Schlissel, Byrd Gibbens, and Elizabeth Hampsten, *Far from Home: Families of the Westward Journey* (New York: Schocken Books, 1989); and Lillian Schlissel, Vicki Ruiz, and Janice Monk, *Western Women: Their Land, Their Lives* (Albuquerque: University of New Mexico Press, 1988).

4. For an overview of this ideology, see Linda Kerber, "Separate Spheres, Female Worlds, Woman's Place: The Rhetoric of Women's History," *Journal of American History* 75 (June 1988): 9–39.

5. While the women of the home frontier were understandably invisible to historians concerned with the westward movement per se, historians of states contributing large numbers of men to that movement have tended to take for granted the existence of women in waiting. In an early history of Illinois, Arthur C. Cole noted that between ten thousand and fifteen thousand men from that state joined the gold rush in 1849, and that in some areas "a majority of the

males," including "the older generations," went west, leaving nearly as many wives behind. Cole also notes that the "dismal complaints of the 'California widows'" may have played a part in slowing the mad dash to California (Arthur C. Cole, *The Era of the Civil War, 1849–1870*, vol. 3, *Centennial History of Illinois*, ed. Clarence Alvord [Springfield, Ill.: Centennial Commission, 1919], 9–12).

6. Almost our sole source of knowledge of the separated family during the westward movement, the letters of stay-at-home wives, a part of the body of what John Mack Faragher has called "the history of the inarticulate," are relatively rare and extremely difficult to find (Faragher, *Women and Men*, 1). They are, of course, still problematic in that they speak directly only for the literate class, though they contain references to many women who left no written records of their own. For any number of reasons, the letters of westering men tended to be preserved and cherished by their families, while letters from back east, valued as they were at the moment they were received, were not always saved. Even when the men did save and bring home the letters sent by their wives, those families that have preserved them have generally done so for their sentimental value rather than their historical value and so have been far less inclined to include such letters in archival donations of papers pertaining to the settling of the West.

7. Andrew Rotter, "'Matilda for Gods Sake Write': Women and Families on the Argonaut Mind," *California Historical Quarterly* 58, no. 2 (Summer 1979): 128–41. The perception of the westward movement as one of single young males had its roots largely in contemporary observations of the makeup of California boomtowns and in early census records that show those towns to be populated by large numbers of men dwelling in houses with no women. This is hardly a valid basis for concluding that such men were single, for no census before 1880 specifically records marital status, except for those married within the past year. Nor are census records helpful in determining the last community in which a person resided, where researchers might find public and private records containing definitive data on their marital status. Even when community of origin can be ascertained by other means, proving a male's absence from or presence in the home community can be difficult, even for census years. For example, although James Fergus left Minnesota for Pikes Peak in April 1860 and did not return for eighteen months, the June census notation shows him to be living in Little Falls alongside his wife and children. The same is true for other Morrison County, Minnesota, men who are known to have been in the West in June 1860.

8. John Marsh Smith to Elizabeth Tyson Smith, Feb. 28, 1850. The Smith letters reside in the John Marsh Smith Collection, Oregon Historical Society, Portland.

Research into the marital status of the group of men who went west with James Fergus from in and around Morrison County, Minnesota, between 1860 and 1864 suggests that, on the average, the westering males of the 1860s were older by five to ten years than those of the 1850s, that at least one-third to one-half of them were married, and that very few of those who were married took their wives and children with them when they first went west (Peavy and Smith, *Gold Rush Widows*).

The Almira Stearns story is told and referenced in chapter 3.

9. Mahala Rayner to Henry Rayner, Oct. 29, 1852. The Rayner letters reside in Collection 777, Merrill G. Burlingame Special Collections, Montana State University Libraries, Bozeman.

10.   Faragher, *Women and Men,* 36. Schlissel, *Women's Diaries,* 13. As Carl Degler has noted, "Marriage has been many things, but at all times it has been a relationship of power, however muted or disguised it may be in any partucular case. . . . Certainly in the 19th century when a husband was acknowledged by all to be the head of the family, there can be no doubt that power or the making of decisions was unequally distributed" (*At Odds: Women and Family in America from the Revolution to the Present* [New York: Oxford University Press, 1980], 29)

11.   Henry Jenkins to Abigail Jenkins, Mar. 21, 1851. The Jenkins letters reside in the C. J. Brosnan Papers, University of Idaho Library, Moscow. Henry Jenkins was operating out of the implicit terms of the nineteenth-century marriage contract. Husbands, the designated breadwinners, were to act as buffers between their wives and the harsh business world; wives, in turn, were to avoid all contact with that world, eschew activities associated with "lay[ing] up property," and devote their energies to creating a space in which values threatened by the rise of industralism and capitalism could be reaffirmed and nurtured. For a discussion of women's work in the context of separate spheres, see Jeanne Boydston, *Home and Work: Housework, Wages, and the Ideology of Labor in the Early Republic* (New York: Oxford University Press, 1990), 144–45.

12.   Cress had already followed her husband from North Carolina to Illinois but had refused to go as far as California. (Elizabeth Cress quoted by Annette Kolodny in *The Land before Her: Fantasy and Experience of the American Frontiers, 1630–1860,* [Chapel Hill: University of North Carolina Press, 1984], 234–35. Augusta Perham Shipman to Clark B. Shipman, Feb. 1, 1882, Clark Bigelow Shipman Family Papers, Montana Historical Society, Helena [the Shipman story is told and referenced in chapter 7]; Leroy Warner to Mary Warner, May 28 and Oct. 5, 1898.) The Warner letters are a part of the Warner family papers held by Dr. Dick Warner of Montana City, Mont., great-grandson of Mary and Leroy Warner.

13.   The authors have based this current study on the papers of fifty-three families separated when the men went west alone. Only in three of those cases were the women invited to accompany their husbands. Two of the three who declined the invitation had already made one move west and could see no reason to go farther, and the third was dissuaded from going west by her parents. For more on family disputes over whether a wife should accompany her husband west, see Robert Griswold, *Family and Divorce in California, 1850–1890: Victorian Illusion and Everyday Realities* (Albany: State University of New York Press, 1982), 85–87.

14.   John Mack Faragher's study of women and men on the frontier led him to conclude that 78 percent of the male heads of household who crossed the plains had already made at least one previous move as an adult (Faragher, *Women and Men,* 18). The authors' own research into the experiences of women in waiting supports the idea that, for most families, moving west was but an extension of an ongoing personal pattern of migration; all six of the men whose family stories are recounted in the chapters that follow—William Hiller, Daniel Stearns, Henry Yesler, Ard Godfrey, David Christie, and Clark Shipman—made more than one exploratory trip westward without the company of their wives.

Harriet Godfrey's story is told and referenced in chapter 5. Agnes Russell's is in *A Genealogical Register of the Descendants of Robert and Agnes (Leitch) Russell* (Saint Paul: Nelson and Robert Flint, 1923; copy in the Morrison County Historical

Society, Little Falls, Minn.). Being left to operate in an unfamiliar culture exacerbated the problems faced by Agnes Russell and other immigrant wives.

15.   John Bozeman to "Mother & Brother & Sisters," Dec. 4, 1866, reprinted with the permission of the Museum of the Rockies, Montana State University, Bozeman. The Emma Christie story is told and referenced in chapter 6. The Bozeman story is found in Merrill Burlingame, *John Bozeman, Montana Trailmaker* (Bozeman, Mont.: Museum of the Rockies, 1983), 7. The wedding license (File 694b, Merrill G. Burlingame Special Collections, Montana State University Libraries, Bozeman) lists Bozeman's wife as Lucinda C. Ingram, but John referred to her as Catharine.

16.   James Fergus to Pamelia Fergus, July 8, 1860; James Fergus to E. A. Wood, Dec. 25, 1886; Joseph Kenney to Susan Kenney, Mar. 2, 1866; Joseph Kenney to Alexander Rhoten, Aug. 26, 1868. The Kenney letters reside in the Joseph Kenney File, Gallatin County Historical Society Museum, Bozeman, Mont. Because the few men who did make money in the West—James Fergus, William Hiller, Henry Yesler, and Ard Godfrey, among them—deliberately avoided setting down specific amounts in their letters and cautioned their wives not to discuss their success back home, it has been difficult to establish with accuracy the degree of financial gain of the westering men. Typical of the men pressing their wives not to divulge such information is Newton Chandler, who wrote Jane of his success in the silver mines of Virginia City, Nevada, but cautioned her, "I wish you to keep my good fortunes within your Self pleas" (Newton Chandler to Jane Chandler, June 28, 1860, Rare Book Room Collection, Ella Strong Denison Library, Scripps College, Claremont, Calif.). Fergus made enough money during his first season of mining in Montana to interest the U.S. government in his tax position (see Peavy and Smith, *Gold Rush Widows,* 272 n. 181).

17.   Joseph Kenney to Susan Kenney, July 13, 1868; Henry Rayner to Mahala Rayner, Nov. 4, 1852; and Mar. 8, 1853.

18.   James Henry Morley Diary, SC 533, Montana Historical Society, Helena; "Luzena Wallace," in Robert Bennett, *Small World of Our Own*, (Walla Walla, Wash: Pioneer Press, 1985), 251–62; Byrd Gibbens, *"This Is a Strange Country": Letters of a Westering Family, 1880–1906* (Albuquerque: University of New Mexico Press, 1988). Stearns story, chapter 3. The Sarah Yesler story is told and referenced in chapter 4.

19.   Godfrey story, chapter 5. Kiser family records are held by Melba Wickes of Kalispell, Mont., the great-granddaughter of Ambrose and Sarah Kiser.

20.   According to Faragher, the homestead—"a highly self-sufficient farm, autonomously owned, operated, and sustained by a husband, wife, and children"—was the major goal of many nineteenth-century American families (Faragher, *Women and Men,* 134). According to the Homestead Act of 1862, anyone who was twenty-one years of age (or the head of a family) and a citizen of the United States could claim of up to 160 acres by filing for a patent on that land and paying a filing fee (usually twenty dollars). After that initial filing of intention, the homesteader had five years to "prove up"—that is, establish residence on and cultivate the land claimed—before the final patent was granted (Paul Gates, *History of Public Land Law Development* [Washington, D.C.: Public Land Law Review Commission, 1968], 245).

For the Shipmans' story, see chapter 7.

21.   Franklin Kirkaldie to Elizabeth Kirkaldie, Aug. 11, 1867, as quoted in Dorothy M. Johnson, "The Patience of Frank Kirkaldie," *Montana the Magazine of Western History,* Winter 1971, p. 23. The Kirkaldie letters reside in Ms File 43, Merrill G. Burlingame Special Collections, Montana State University Libraries, Bozeman.

22.   Joseph Kenney to Folks, May 25, 1865; Joseph Kenney to Susan Kenney, Dec. 23, 1865, and July 4, 1866.

23.   Farming and ranching required a larger cash outlay than did most mining enterprises. Even on free homesteads, a claimant would need from five hundred to one thousand dollars in cash to start up a farming operation that had any chance of success. Consequently, many families failed to prosper and eventually gave up their claims (Faragher, *Women and Men,* 20–21).

24.   Emma Christie to David Christie, June 20, 1884. The Christie letters reside in the David B. Christie and Family Papers, Minnesota Historical Society, Saint Paul; see chapter 6.

25.   James Fergus to Pamelia Fergus, July 8, 1860; Jack Swilling to Mary Jane Swilling, Nov. 15, 1858. The Swilling letters reside in the Salt River Project Museum, Phoenix, Ariz.; photocopies of the letters are held in the Jack Swilling File, Arizona Historical Society, Tucson. "To have seen the elephant," a phrase first used by Forty-niners, meant to have seen it all and was often used by those who had given up and gone home.

26.   Pioneer memoirs and reminiscences may or may not reveal the extent to which such "push" factors played a role in the settling of the West, since not all settlers were candid about the reasons they left home. As one woman whose grandparents moved to Montana from Missouri about 1870 put it, many descendants of early pioneers have been reluctant to look too closely at family history, since "everybody who came out here was probably running from something" (response from audience member to presentation by Peavy, Denton, Mont., Feb. 1985).

27.   See chapter 5.

28.   Joseph Kenney to Susan Kenney, Mar. 2, 1866. Most married men who went west had probably faced setbacks of some sort already, since the well-to-do seldom made the journey. But none of them had yet failed utterly, since making the trip west required resources of some kind.

29.   Godfrey story, chapter 5; "William Z. Jenkins," *History of Jay and Blackford Counties, Indiana* (Chicago: Lewis Publishing Co., 1887), 396–97.

30.   Robert Russell to James Fergus, Jan. 26, 1862, James Fergus Papers, Mansfield Library Archives, University of Montana, Missoula.

31.   Granberry Rose to Mary Elizabeth Rose, Dec. 28, 1850, and Feb. 8, 1854, quoted in Beverly Jensen, "The California Letters of Granberry Rose, 1850–1855" (English seminar paper, University of North Dakota, 1987), 6, 9.

32.   Alonzo Boardman to Nancy Boardman, July 28, 1863. The Boardman letters reside in the Alonzo Boardman Collection, MS 68, Colorado Historical Society, Denver.

33.   Paul Rodman Wilson, *Mining Frontiers of the Far West, 1848–1880* (New York: Holt, Rinehart, and Winston, 1963), 26.

34.   Isabell Leaver of Birmingham, Alabama, great-granddaughter of Jack and Mary Jane Swilling, to Lori Davisson, Arizona Historical Society, Dec. 21,

1984. In a subsequent interview with Earl Zarbin, Leaver shared a family legend that Swilling "was supposed to have killed a man in Wetumpka and left [Alabama]" (Earl Zarbin "Founder of Phoenix Nearly Wasn't," *Arizona Republic* [Tucson], Jan. 27, 1985). However, since the time of that interview, Leaver and other family members have searched extensively in newspapers and court records and have "found nothing on J. W. Swilling being in trouble with the law" (Leaver to Peavy, Aug. 21, 1992). For an overview of the Swilling story, see Earl Zarbin, "The Swilling Legacy," serialized in the *Arizona Republic,* Aug. 13–30, 1978, and reprinted in monograph form by the Salt River Project, Phoenix, 1981.

35.   Mollie Kelley to Robert Kelley, March 1858. The Kelley letters and family records are held by Rivé N. Talbott Hoover of Lebanon, Ore., the Kelleys' great-granddaughter. Background information on Kelley's proslavery activities was found in records held by Hoover, including an article appearing in the *Kansas Chief* (Troy), June 25, 1885.

36.   The Levengood story is told in full in a family history compiled by Edna Levengood Head and currently in the possession of Shirley Levengood Bachini of Havre, Mont. Shortly after Levengood's arrival, Idaho Territory was divided, with the eastern portion becoming Montana Territory in May 1864.

37.   Franklin Friend to Martha Friend, Nov. 11, 1864, and Jan. 31, 1865. The Friend letters reside with Joel Overholser in the Fort Benton Files, River Press, Fort Benton, Mont. The sketchy story of the Friend brothers is told in Henry Pope's "Researching the Ophir Massacre 122 Years Later" and "Ophir Metropolis: A Dream with a Tragic Ending," both in the Fort Benton Files, and Joel Overholser, *Fort Benton in Territorial Days* (Fort Benton, Mont.: River Press, 1987).

38.   Joseph Kenney to Susan Kenney, Sept. 23, 1864; James Fergus to Pamelia Fergus, Nov. 2, 1862.

39.   Augusta Shipman to Clark Shipman, undated, ca. early 1882. The Shipman letters are found in the Clark Bigelow Shipman Family Papers, Montana Historical Society, Helena; see also chapter 7.

40.   John Bozeman to Mother & Brother & Sisters, Dec. 4, 1866, reprinted with permission of the Museum of the Rockies, Montana State University, Bozeman.

41.   That division of labor was inplicit in the unwritten terms of the nineteenth-century marriage contract. As John Mack Faragher has argued, understanding nineteenth-century marriages requires analyzing "work and the division of labor, attitudes and beliefs about the proper roles for men and women, and those social groupings, including the family, that mediated the participation of women and men in the social order" (Faragher, *Women and Men,* 4)

42.   Pamelia Fergus to James Fergus, July 4, 1860; Samuel Bassett, *Buffalo County Nebraska and Its People* (Chicago: Clarke Publishing Company, 1916), 1: 71; Augusta Shipman to Rebecca Shipman, Dec. 22, 1886; see also chapter 7. In the absence of their husbands, who would normally have taken their products to market, Augusta Shipman and Sarah Oliver could cross gender boundaries and undertake business ventures that might have brought them scorn under other circumstances. Laurel Thatcher Ulrich has described the situations in which colonial women acted as "deputy husbands" in her *Good Wives.* "Should fate or circumstance prevent the husband from fulfilling his role," Ulrich points out, almost any task was considered suitable for a woman, "as long as it furthered

the good of her family and was acceptable to her husband" (*Good Wives: Image and Reality in the Lives of Women in Northern New England, 1650–1750* [New York: Knopf, 1982], 36, 38).

43. Isabell Leaver of Birmingham, Ala., great-granddaughter of Jack and Mary Jane Swilling, to Peavy, May 13, 1985; Bassett, *Buffalo County,* 71.

44. Margaretha Ault to Robert and Mary Fergus Hamilton, Jan. 29, 1872, James Fergus Papers, Mansfield Library Archives, University of Montana, Missoula. See also Peavy and Smith, *Gold Rush Windows,* 212–13.

45. Peavy and Smith, *Gold Rush Windows,* 95.

46. Jane Chandler to Newton Chandler, Feb. 27, 1859; Newton Chandler to Jane Chandler, Mar. 17, 1859, and Mar. 1, 1860.

47. Abigail Jenkins to Henry Jenkins, June 26, 1852.

48. *Genealogical Register;* Peavy and Smith, *Gold Rush Widows,* 64, 95; see also chapters 3 and 5.

49. Alonzo Boardman to Nancy Boardman, Aug. 1, 1863; Pamelia Fergus to James Fergus, May 8, 1860; James Fergus to Pamelia Fergus, Sept. 28, 1860. Pamelia held a seat on the board of directors of the Little Falls Manufacturing Company by virtue of the power of attorney James gave her on his departure for the West (Power of Attorney, Mar. 22, 1860, Legal Documents, 1851–1900, James Fergus Papers, Mansfield Library Archives, University of Montana, Missoula).

50. Pamelia Fergus to James Fergus, Feb. 11, 1861, and Oct. 23, 1860; Rebecca Shipman to Clark Shipman, Dec. 13, 1885.

51. See chapters 2 and 3.

52. Pamelia Fergus to James Fergus, Apr. 14 and 23, 1861.

53. Godfrey story, chapter 5. Almira Stearns to Daniel Stearns, Mar. 3, 1862; see also chapter 3.

54. Granberry Rose to Mary Elizabeth Rose, June 5 and 25, 1853, as quoted in Jensen, "California Letters," 9, 11.

55. Alonzo Boardman to Nancy Boardman, June 10 and Nov. 1, 1863; Joseph Kenney to Susan Kenney, July 13, 1868.

56. Edward Oliver to Sarah Oliver, Aug. 25, no year, Edward Oliver File, Buffalo County Historical Society, Kearney, Nebr.; Leroy Warner to Mary Warner, June 11, 1898, and Feb. 10, 1901; Mary Warner Account Books, 1901–1911, in possession of Norma Telford, Eau Claire, Wis.; Dr. Dick Warner interviews with Peavy, spring and fall, 1987.

57. David DeWolf, "Diary of the Overland Trial and Letters of Captain David DeWolf," *Transactions of the Illinois State Historical Society, 1925,* 185, as quoted in Rotter, "Matilda," 136; Henry Rayner to Mahala Rayner, Jan. 7, 1853; Joseph Kenney to Susan Kenney, June 26, 1868.

58. Henry Shipman to Winnie Shipman, Jan. 21, 1887; Clark Shipman to Augusta Shipman, Dec. 25, 1882; Augusta Shipman to Clark Shipman, Dec. 25, 1882; see also chapter 7.

59. See Peavy and Smith, *Gold Rush Windows,* 69–70.

60. Pamelia Fergus to James Fergus, Oct. 1862, and Dec. 18, 1862; June 14 and Jan. 25, 1863; and Feb. 1864. The "Indian excitement" refers to the Dakota Conflict of 1862. The Abiah Hiller story is told and referenced in chapter 2.

61. Emma Christie to Alexander Christie, June 4, 1883; Abigail Jenkins to Henry Jenkins, Sept. 10 and June 11, 1853.

62. Rotter, "Matilda," 132–34; Granberry Rose to Mary Elizabeth Rose, May 31, 1850, as quoted in Jensen, "California Letters," 5. Rose's reference to women as "property" here is all the more interesting in light of the fact that his professed goal out west was to earn enough money "to be able to buy two black boys and two girls and a farm that suits me" (Granberry Rose to Mary Elizabeth Rose, Aug. 16, 1853, as quoted in Jensen, "California Letters," 9).

63. James Fergus to Pamelia Fergus, undated, ca. spring 1860; Pamelia Fergus to James Fergus, Aug. 28, 1860. Jeanne Boydston has called this attitude toward women's work the "pastoralization of housework," which devalued the work of women by viewing it as "a way of being rather than . . . a conscious form of labor" (Boydston, *Home and Work,* 145).

64. Bassett, *Buffalo County,* 71; *Genealogical Register.*

65. Yesler story, chapter 4; Maggie Brown to Charles Brown, June 6, 1880, as quoted in Byrd Gibbens, "Impact of the Western Frontier on Family Configuration: The Charles Albert Brown Collection of Letters (1874–1930), a Study in Literary Analysis of Correspondence" (Ph.D. diss., University of New Mexico, 1983), 75; Schlissel, Gibbens, and Hampsten, *Far from Home,* 114.

66. Joseph Kenney to Susan Kenney, July 4, 1866.

67. Stearns story, chapter 3; Emma Christie to David Christie, June 20, 1884.

68. Hiller story, chapter 2; Jane Chandler to Newton Chandler, Feb. 27, 1859.

69. Kiser family records; Peavy interviews with Dr. Dick Warner, spring and fall, 1987.

70. Cole, *Era of the Civil War,* 9; Henry Jenkins to Abby Jenkins, Mar. 21, 1851.

71. See Peavy and Smith, *Gold Rush Widows,* 70, 86–87.

72. Mollie Kelley to Robert Kelley, Mar. 1858.

73. Abby Jenkins to William Jenkins, Oct. 7, 1856. Concerning Warner's ties with his children, see Leroy Warner to Mary Warner, Mar. 28, Oct. 5, and Oct. 31, 1898, and May 17, 1900; Leroy Warner to children, June 3 and June 11, 1898; see also chapter 6. Kirkaldie's interest in his children is expressed in Franklin Kirkaldie to Elizabeth Kirkaldie, May 1 and May 29, 1864, as quoted in Johnson, "Patience," 13 and 14.

74. Granberry Rose to Mary Elizabeth Rose, May 31, 1850, as quoted in Jensen, "California Letters," 6; Alonzo Boardman to Nancy Boardman, June 10 and Aug. 2, 1863; Joseph Kenney to Susan Kenney, June 8 and Oct. 16, 1864.

75. Newton Chandler to Jane Chandler, March 17, 1859; May 30, June 29, and August 19, 1860.

76. Hiller story, chapter 2; Rosanna Sturgis to William Sturgis, Oct. 8, 1862, William Sturgis Family Papers, SC 809, Montana Historical Society, Helena.

77. Abby Jenkins to Henry Jenkins, Sept. 10, 1853; Alonzo Boardman to Nancy Boardman, Aug. 16, 1863; James Fergus to Pamelia Fergus, Nov. 23, 1860.

78. Although the goldfields of Bannack and Virginia City were a part of Washington Territory when James Fergus first arrived there in the summer of 1862, they became a part of Idaho Territory in the spring of 1863 and a part of Montana Territory a year later. Pamelia was understandably confused by such shifting boundaries, but James had little sympathy, scolding, "Be particular about your address" (James Fergus to Pamelia Fergus, May 10, 1863).

79. David Christie letter in possession of his grandson, Lawrence Christie, of Bozeman, Mont.; Booklet in Collection 777, Merrill G. Burlingame Special Col-

lections, Montana State University Libraries, Bozeman. In the early 1850s mail could be sent as cheaply as three cents, "guaranteed delivery in thirty days to California" (Henry Rayner pocket letter book, Merrill G. Burlingame Special Collections, Montana State University Libraries, Bozeman). A letter could be sent to Alaska in 1898 for two cents (Leroy Warner to Mary Warner, Jan. 24, 1898). In the territories miners were sometimes assessed a twenty-five cent surcharge per letter (Peavy and Smith, *Gold Rush Windows*, 43–44, 130).

80. Mahala Rayner to Henry Rayner, Oct. 29, 1852; James Fergus to Pamelia Fergus, undated.

81. Pamelia Fergus to James Fergus, May 20, 1861; see also chapters 2 and 3.

82. David Christie to Emma Christie, Oct. 25, 1883; Leroy Warner to Mary Warner, June 11, 1898.

83. Joseph Kenney to Susan Kenney, June 25, 1865. Born July 8, 1898, four months after Leroy's departure for Alaska, the boy was not referred to by name in a letter until March 1902. Before then, his father called him "that other little one," "the baby," "Pub," and "Muggins." Mary Warner finally named the child Don (Leroy Warner to Mary Warner, Feb. 19, 1899; Apr. 30, July 5, and Sept. 11, 1900; June 11, 1901; Mar. 24, 1902).

84. Henry Rayner to Mahala Rayner, Nov. 4, 1852; Henry Jenkins to Abby Jenkins, Aug. 31, 1851.

85. Abby Jenkins to Henry Jenkins, Feb. 6, 1853.

86. Charles Brown to Maggie Brown, July 19, 1881; Gibbens, "Impact of the Western Frontier," 157–60; Henry Jenkins to Abby Jenkins, Mar. 21, 1851.

87. Augusta Shipman to Clark Shipman, Jan. 1 and 16 and Feb. 1, 1882; see also chapter 7.

88. Mary Jane Colburn to Pamelia Fergus, Apr. 22, 1860; Pamelia Fergus to James Fergus, Apr. 30 and July 4, 1860; chapters 2 and 6. See also Elizabeth Hampsten, *Read This Only to Yourself: The Private Writings of Midwestern Women, 1880–1910*, (Bloomington: Indiana University Press, 1982), especially 96–121. As Hampsten notes, "For day-to-day emotional sustenance as well as remedies for aches and pains, women turned to other women, companionable mothers, aunts, sisters, cousins, friends—allies of a lifetime" (p. 111). Pamelia Fergus is the rare exception, in the authors' readings, of a woman who writes of intimate health problems in detail to her husband. Perhaps it was James's interest in medicine and Pamelia's own experience as a midwife and physician's assistant that made such discussions acceptable in the Fergus household. See Peavy and Smith, *Gold Rush Widows*.

89. Granberry Rose to Mary Elizabeth Rose, Sept. 19, 1852, as quoted in Jensen, "California Letters," 8; Henry Jenkins to Abby Jenkins, Aug. 31, 1851; Mollie Kelley to Robert Kelley, Mar. 1858.

90. Henry Rayner to Mahala Rayner, Jan. 23 and Feb. 7, 1853; Mahala Rayner to Henry Rayner, Oct. 29, 1852. Up in Alaska, Leroy Warner had dreams of a stronger sort, writing his wife, Mary, "I dreamed about you last night—and you can imagine the result" (Leroy Warner to Mary Warner, Nov. 13, 1898).

91. Charles Brown to Maggie Brown, Feb. 16 and Apr. 16, 1881; Maggie Brown to Charles Brown, June 6, 1880, and Mar. 23, 1881, all quoted in Schlissel, Gibbens, and Hampsten, *Far from Home*, 115, 126, 128. Charles and Maggie were unusually frank in their discussion of sexual feelings and actions. Comments in

their letters stand in contrast to those in the letters of other separated couples and to those found in the Forty-niner diaries studied by Andrew Rotter, who noted that "sex was not often discussed in print in mid-nineteenth century America" and warned that "the researcher will look in vain for information concerning the diarists' sex lives" (Rotter, "Matilda," 130).

92. *Weekly Independent* (Helena, Mont.), Nov. 2, 1867, p. 1; William Butler to James Fergus, Oct. 20, 1867; James Fergus to William Butler, Mar. 20, 1875; John Ault obituary, *Bozeman Avant Courier,* Jan. 1, 1875, p. 3.

93. Jack Swilling to Mary Jane Swilling, Jan. 6, 1861; Marriage Register of Saint Augustine's Cathedral, Tucson, Ariz., 1:3.

94. Joseph Kenney to Susan Kenney, Jan. 31 and Aug. 26, 1868; William Hiller to Abiah Hiller, Apr. 30, 1851; Leroy Warner to Mary Warner, May 24, 1898. The Hiller letters reside in the C. B. Dunning Papers, Cheney Cowles Museum, Eastern Washington State Historical Society, Spokane.

95. Melba Wickes to Catherine Armitage, Oct. 25, 1980. According to Wickes, although Ambrose Kiser's second wife, Elizabeth, knew of his first wife and children, the couple apparently chose not to tell the Montana children of their half-siblings in Indiana. Through the years Ambrose did maintain contact with relatives in the Midwest, and for the last decade of his life he corresponded with his and Sarah's youngest daughter, Frances (Wickes to Peavy and Smith, Aug. 21, 1992).

96. Helen Stauffer of Kearney State College, Kearney, Nebr., to Peavy and Smith, Sept. 6, 1985.

97. Abby Jenkins to Henry Jenkins, Mar. 2 and June 26, 1852; Henry Jenkins to Abby Jenkins, Nov. 19, 1851.

98. Granberry Rose to Mary Elizabeth Rose, Aug. 1, 1854, as quoted in Jensen, "California Letters," 8. Alonzo Boardman to Nancy Boardman, July 28, 1863.

99. See also chapter 5. For an excellent treatment of frontier women in relationship to native Americans, see Riley, *Women and Indians.*

100. Newton Chandler to Jane Chandler, Jan. 12, 1860. Newton was writing from an area just east of the California line, around Virginia City, Utah Territory, soon to become Nevada Territory.

101. John Marsh Smith to Elizabeth Smith, Feb. 28, 1850; Franklin Friend to Martha Friend, July 9, 1864; Moses Clark to the wives of Franklin and George Friend, July 28, 1865; Pope, "Researching the Ophir Massacre"; Overholser, *Fort Benton,* 51; clipping from the *Weekly Montana Democrat,* Joseph Kenney File, Gallatin County Historical Society, Bozeman, Mont.

102. "Commonwealth Reporter Features," Nov. 8, 1968, clipping in the Samuel Beall File, Fond du Lac County Historical Society, Fond du Lac, Wis; Peavy and Smith, *Gold Rush Widows,* 209.

103. Isabell Leaver to Peavy, May 30, 1985; Granberry Rose to Mary Elizabeth Rose, Aug. 1, 1854, as quoted in Jensen, "California Letters," 13–14.

104. Peavy and Smith, *Gold Rush Widows,* 119; Microfilm 73b, Mrs. James C. Day Papers, Montana Historical Society, Helena; *History of Jay and Blackford Counties,* 307; Abby Jenkins to Henry Jenkins, Sept. 10, 1853.

105. Newton Chandler to Jane Chandler, Dec. 22, 1869. Newton's last extant letter was dated 1872, and the rest of their story has not yet been ascertained.

106.   Leroy Warner to Mary Warner, May 24, 1898, and Sept. 10, 1905; Dr. Dick Warner interviews, spring and fall 1987.

107.   Henry Rayner to Mahala Rayner, Dec. 8, 1852; Henry Jenkins to Abby Jenkins, Oct. 18, 1851; Cornelius Hedges Family Papers, MC 33, Montana Historical Society, Helena; 1870 U.S. Manuscript Census.

108.   "Steamboating in Early Days: Captain Massie Tells about His Experiences on the Upper Missouri," in "Items of Long Ago" column, *Saint Louis Globe-Democrat,* 1899, Fort Benton File, River Press, Fort Benton, Mont.

109.   Peavy and Smith, *Gold Rush Widows,* 208.

110.   Abby Jenkins to Henry Jenkins, Feb. 6, 1853 (see also chapter 4); Elizabeth Tyson Smith to John Marsh Smith, Feb. 8, 1850.

111.   J. C. Avery biography, in *Willamette Valley Oregon* (Portland: Chapman Publishing Company, 1903), 869; Mrs. J. R. Russell to Mollie Kelley, Nov. 1911.

112.   James Fergus to Pamelia Fergus, Oct. 10, 1860. James had asked his mining partner, O. J. Rockwell, to assist Pamelia in her journey to Montana, a situation she described as "the awfless mess I ever was in" (Pamelia Fergus to James Fergus, May 13, 1864; see also Peavy and Smith, *Gold Rush Widows,* 178–90).

113.   James Fergus to Pamelia Fergus, undated, ca. fall 1864. This letter offers a rare bit of concrete evidence of the adjustment problems faced by those couples who were eventually reunited. In most cases, the letters that provide glimpses of the dynamics of separation ceased to be written once the couple was back together, making it all but impossible to determine the long-term repercussions of the separation of families in the westward movement.

114.   James Fergus to Robert Hamilton, May 13, 1899; James Fergus to Daughter, undated, ca. 1887.

115.   Abby Jenkins to Henry Jenkins, Feb. 6 and June 11, 1853. Although Pamelia Fergus did apparently enjoy the independence she achieved as a gold rush widow and later as a westering wife, some scholars, notably Julie Roy Jeffrey (*Frontier Women: The Trans-Mississippi West, 1840–1880* [New York: Hill and Wang, 1979]), have concluded that the frontier experience itself was not usually liberating for women (pp. xv–xvi). Paula Petrik's examination of the experiences of women in Helena, Montana, during the late nineteenth century led her to a more complex interpretation: "On the one hand, it seems clear that first-generation westering women did not use the frontier as a springboard to self-fulfillment; on the other hand, it is evident that the frontier thrust these women into situations that fundamentally altered their lives. Frontier women, in short, redefined womanhood, but they did it reluctantly and only when confronted with an environment antithetical to their sensibilities. To look for liberation is to look to the second generation on the frontier" (*No Step Backward: Women and Family on the Rocky Mountain Mining Frontier, Helena, Montana, 1865–1900,* [Helena: Montana Historical Society Press, 1987], 96)

116.   Abby Jenkins to Henry Jenkins, Feb. 6, 1853.

II
Abiah Warren Hiller

1.   Abiah Hiller to William Hiller, Apr. 10, 1851, Charles B. Dunning Papers, Cheney Cowles Memorial Museum, Eastern Washington State Historical Society

(hereafter cited as EWSHS), Spokane. The Abiah Hiller story has been largely based on materials in that collection, and unless otherwise indicated, all letters, diaries, and journals quoted hereafter in this chapter are from that collection. In addition to several diaries, daybooks, and account books, the Dunning collection contains letters from Hiller and Warren family members and friends plus sixteen letters from William to Abiah and nine from Abiah to William during his California sojourn and three letters from William to Abiah and two from Abiah to William during his Illinois and Virginia adventures. The Dunning Papers were donated to EWSHS by Jane Dunning Baldwin, great-granddaughter of Abiah and William Hiller. In quoting these materials, the authors have chosen to retain the spelling, capitalization, and punctuation found in the original sources. In the following notes to this chapter Abiah Hiller is referenced as AH and William Hiller as WH.

2. AH to WH, December 5, 1851.

3. Albert Annett and Alice E. E. Lehtinen, *The Generations of Jaffrey, New Hampshire* (Jaffrey: n.p., 1934), 833–34; Daniel B. Cutter, *History of the Town of Jaffrey, New Hampshire, 1749–1880* (Concord, N.H.: Republican Press Association, 1881), 38, 512; Marie Elsbree Dunning (Abiah and William Hiller's granddaughter), "Notes," now in the possession of Virginia Ashlock, widow of Dunning's great-nephew Peter Aslock. Abiah also had a sister, Almeda Lois Warren, born September 16 and died October 8, 1811 (Annett and Lehtinen, *Generations* 834). In "'Not Gainfully Employed': Women on the Iowa Frontier, 1833–1870," *Pacific Historical Review,* May 1980, p. 240, Glenda Riley discusses the economic aspects of the domestic arts and notes that "the skills . . . needed in [a woman's] life's work were of such great consequence that she spent a good portion of her girlhood in apprenticeship to her mother or another woman to learn them thoroughly."

4. Monadnock Moment #299, "Chesterfield Academy"; clipping from the *Keene* (N.H.) *Sentinel,* 1903; *Sentinel Answer Book,* March 28, 1990, p. 8; Dunning "Notes." Established in 1794, Chesterfield Academy was considered one of the best schools in New Hampshire at a time when twelve private academies provided that state's students with their only chance for secondary education.

5. William Hayden III, town historian of McDonough, N.Y., noted Abiah Hiller's skills in Latin and Greek in a Nov. 8, 1985, letter to Peavy and Smith; Sophia L. Whitmore to Abiah S. Warren, Nov. 5, 1826; June 6, 1823, entry in Abiah Warren's diary, 1831–32; Dunning, "Notes"; May 17, 1838, entry and Library List in Abiah Warren's diary, 1836–38; Abiah S. Warren essay in Dunning Papers, EWSHS. Abiah concluded the essay: "We cannot believe that the Diety has employed his creative power in peopling our little globe only, which is nothing but a speck in the universe in comparison with others, but that there is an order of beings on every planet & that the wants of each is suited to its situation."

6. Andrew Warren eulogy of Abiah Hiller, 1873, Dunning Papers, EWSHS; Abiah Warren's musical notebooks and diaries, 1831–32. The notebooks and diaries were themselves of Abiah's own handbound devising. Most of the songs in the copybooks were hymns, and some were likely of her own composition.

7. Invitations for "Mr. F. Wheelock & Lady" to a Thanksgiving Ball at New Ipswich, Nov. 24, 1831, and a Citizens Union Ball at Groton, Feb. 27, 1833; Abiah Warren's diary, 1831–33. Abiah's diary entries are peppered with references to the many church services she attended, and in most cases, she noted the minis-

ter and his text, sometimes critiquing both. It was the time of the Second Great Awakening, and for Abiah, as for many other unmarried working women of the time, attendance at church services provided an acceptable social framework in which to meet new friends and embrace new causes. It provided, as well, an atmosphere in which some of her many questions concerning spiritual matters could be addressed by various authorities.

8. Abiah Warren's diary, 1836–38, Sept. 1838.

9. Andrew Oliver Warren obituary, *Independent Republican* (Montrose, Pa.), May 4, 1895. Abiah Warren's diary, 1836–38. Abiah found painting death portraits "a very unpleasant task indeed." One assignment necessitated her making several visits to the tomb of a woman who had been dead for six weeks.

10. Abiah Warren's diary, 1836–38, May 8, 1836 entry; July 17, 1837 entry; Oliver Warren and Lawrence Brooks of Jaffrey, Cheshire County, N.H., purchased two hundred acres of Lot 64 on Oct. 15, 1838 (Deed Book 57(2), p. 289, Chenango County Courthouse, Norwich, N.Y.; Hayden to Peavy and Smith, Nov. 8, 1985).

11. Abiah Warren's first meeting with William Hiller, the man she would later marry, has been reconstructed from several sources. A letter from Alan F. Rumrill of Historical Society of Cheshire County, Keene, New Hampshire, to Peavy and Smith suggests a possible connection between the Hiller family and a Towne family that later settled in Jaffrey. John Towne, master carpenter, moved to Jaffrey about 1833, and during his days in the goldfields, William Hiller corresponded with a George Towne (Sophia Underwood to Abiah Warren, May 27, 1839; Alan F. Rumrill to Peavy and Smith, Aug. 7, 1985; George Towne to William Hiller, Jan. 15, 1851; Annett and Lehtinen, *Generations,* vol. 2, p. 807).

12. Oliver Warren to Abiah Warren, Apr. 8, 1839.

13. The letter Brooks wrote to Abiah Hiller is not extant, but its approximate contents can be readily deduced from the comments her parents made about it (Oliver and Abiah Warren to Abiah Stanley Warren, Apr. 8, 1839).

14. Abiah Stanley Warren to Abiah Warren, Apr. 8, 1839.

15. Oliver Warren to Abiah Warren, June 1839. Lawrence Brooks sold eighty-nine and one-half acres of Lot 64 to Oliver Warren for five hundred dollars on May 27, 1839 (Deed Book 75, p. 7, Chenango County Courthouse, Norwich, N.Y.).

16. Sophia Underwood to Abiah Warren, May 27, 1839; Andrew Warren to Abiah Warren, May 30, 1839. It is unclear whether Abiah was teaching for a neighborhood school or had opened her own school, although the former seems more likely.

17. Oliver Warren to Abiah Warren, June 1839; certificate addressed "To Miss A. S. Warren," McDonough, Mar. 6, 1840. While the exact date of Abiah's departure from New York City is not known, she must have remained in the city through early 1840. Sarah Cutter of Jaffrey addressed a letter to her in New York City in April of that year, not realizing that she had already moved to McDonough (Sarah Cutter to Abiah Warren, Apr. 20, 1840).

18. Quakers from Rhode Island, Wing Hiller's family had immigrated to Duchess County in southeastern New York in the late 1770s, and it was there he and Mary Elsbree met and married. According to Dunning, William Hiller claimed to have been born in Rhode Island, so his parents may well have met and married there and later moved to Duchess County, where many of Mary

Elsbree's relatives lived, or his mother might have been on a visit to Rhode Island at the time of his birth (Dunning, "Notes").

19.   Sophia Underwood, born Feb. 19, 1811, was the daughter of Jereme and Nabby (Gage) Underwood of Jaffrey (Annett and Lehtinen, *Generations*, vol. 2, p. 821; Cutter, *History of the Town*, 513). At twenty-nine, Sophia was nearly six years older than Andrew. Over the first years of his marriage, Andrew Warren held pastorates in Smithville Flats and Upper Lisle, both of which were within ten miles of McDonough (*Universalist Register*, 1896, p. 103; Cutter, *History of the Town*, 513).

According to Helen Hill Tuttle's history of McDonough, Abiah was "a great botonist [*sic*] and every flower, weed, and shrub were known to her" (Helen Hill, "History of McDonough," Tuttle, unpublished manuscript, McDonough, N.Y., 141, 163). The letters Hiller wrote during his voyage to California are filled with references to the stars in the southern hemisphere.

20.   Ella S. Warren was born Apr. 14, 1841; Jane M. Warren was born Feb. 26, 1842; Oliver Warren died Apr. 12, 1842 (Cutter, *History of the Town*, 513).

21.   Andrew Warren was executor of the estate, which included two spinning wheels; six plates; six teacups and saucers; six knives, forks, and spoons; one cow; two swine; one family Bible and several other books; eight cotton sheets; eight pillow cases; assorted carpenter's tools; a grindstone; and lumber from the sawmill (Oliver Warren Probate, Case 2472A, Probate Records, Chenango County Courthouse, Norwich, N.Y.).

22.   Cutter, *History of the Town*, 512.

23.   Although Tuttle notes that "Phebe Anna" was the child's given name, Dunning, a closer family source, cites "Phebe Amna." The infant was named for her paternal aunt, Phebe Hiller Wilcox. One of William's three older sisters, Phebe Hiller, was born Oct. 29, 1809, and married Tyler Wilcox of McDonough. While Dunning notes "Tyler" as the given name of Phebe's husband, Tuttle lists "Philo" (Dunning, "Notes"; Tuttle, "History of McDonough," 2, 3, 4). Josephine's birth is recorded in Dunning "Notes." Born June 17, 1815, William's sister Mary is listed by Dunning as "Mary Elsbree Kenyon" and by Tuttle as "Mary Jane Kenyon" (Dunning, "Notes"; Tuttle, "History of McDonough," Hiller family entries, p. 2.). After William Hiller's father, Wing Hiller, died Apr. 3, 1844, his widow lived with Mary Jane and Singleton Kenyon (Dunning, "Notes"). In 1845, McDonough had three private schools, one of them run by Abiah Hiller (Hiram Clark, *History of Chenango County* [Norwich, N.Y.: Thompson and Pratt, 1850], 85).

24.   Deed Book 75, p. 13, Chenango County Courthouse, Norwich, N.Y.; Hiller Journal & Cash Account Book, 1846–49, 1854–67; Deed Book 75, Sept. 1, 1847, William and Abiah Hiller to Lyman Isbell of McDonough, Chenango County Courthouse, Norwich, N.Y.

25.   Hiller Journal & Cash Account Book, 1846–49, 1854–67.

26.   Tuttle, "History, of McDonough," 2. According to Tuttle's history, "at that time driving a team to mill was deemed rather unusual for a woman" (ibid., 163). However, Abiah's own mother had once driven a team from Jaffrey, New Hampshire, to McDonough, New York, so she had precedent in flaunting convention.

27.   WH to Nelson Campbell, Jan. 16, 1848; WH to AH, Jan. 2, 1848. Apparently William Hiller wrote at least two letters home during his trip to Illinois, for

in a the Jan. 2, 1848, letter he implies that by Dec. 10 Abiah had received only the first of two letters he had written after leaving home.

28. Abiah's letter is not extant; its contents were surmised from William's reply of Jan. 2, 1848. That reply was written right after he received her letter—written two months earlier and declared by William to have been "on a pilgrimage to Jamaca or some other place." (WH to AH, Jan. 2, 1848) In response to Abiah's question, William wrote that weaving was "midling" at best, with "plain cloth" bringing only eight cents a yard in northern Illinois and twelve cents to the south.

29. WH to AH, Jan. 2, 1848; E. Blodgett to AH, Apr. 16, 1848.

30. Hiller left his journal and cash account book in Abiah's hands when he left in October 1847, and his first entry upon his return to McDonough was made on Apr. 24, 1848. His last McDonough journal entry was made on June 15, 1848 (Hiller Journal & Cash Account Book, 1846–49, 1854–67).

31. WH to AH, July 30, 1848. Hiller went by stage, boat, and rail to Baltimore, there boarding a steamer for passage down Chesapeake Bay to Norfolk, where he booked passage up the York River, noting only primitive piers and "near chant[ies]" along that isolated stretch. His water route ended some eighteen miles shy of Richmond, and he completed his journey by rail, arriving in Richmond on July 20, his trip having cost him $22.05. The McDonough-to-Baltimore portion of his journey was deduced from his later instructions for Abiah's trip to Richmond. (WH to AH, Aug. 29, 1848). Although Hiller notes only that he did not come up the James River but "another of the name I do not remember," the York seems his most likely route (WH to AH, July 30, 1848; Hiller Journal & Cash Account Book, 1846–49, 1854–67).

32. WH to AH, July 30, 1848.

33. Hiller Journal & Cash Account Book, 1846–49; WH to AH, July 30, 1848.

34. Letter of Recommendation from Ephraim K. Frost et al., 1848, Dunning Papers, EWSHS. Information on Abiah's preparations for the move is derived from William's response to a letter from Abiah (WH to AH, Aug. 20, 1848).

35. WH to AH, Aug. 20, 1848. The house stood on Franklin Street between 22nd and 23rd avenues.

36. Ibid. Born Aug. 26, 1807, eleven years before William, Ira Hiller married Celinda Dalton of McDonough (Tuttle, "History of McDonough," 2). John Hiller, born Mar. 3, 1805, almost thirteen years before William, married a widow with several children and eventually settled in New Bedford, Illinois (Dunning, "Notes").

37. WH to AH, Aug. 20, 1848. William knew money would be "verry scarce" and asked Abiah to bring all she could "conveniently acquire." Martin Daniels himself would be "obliged to depend on [Hiller] for money for the company until [the] fore part of winter," when his own notes were expected to come in and would be forwarded to them in Richmond (Martin Daniels to WH, Aug. 29, 1848).

38. WH to AH, Aug. 29, 1848.

39. AH to WH, Aug. 29, 1848.

40. AH trip diary, Sept. 10, 1848. William's letter of Aug. 20, 1848, indicates that they would go as far east as Catskill before turning south, from which point it is likely they took the steamer down the Hudson to New York City.

41. Hiller Journal & Cash Account Book, 1846–49, 1854–67. The family paid

ten dollars a week for their room and board at Mrs. Daws's. William Hiller's journal entries during the family's Richmond sojourn are dotted with "gave wife" entries, although there had been virtually no such entries during their earlier years together in McDonough, and the only such entries in the years after his return from California were for special expenses, such as money for a trip or cloth for a sewing project. In late November, Abiah and William spent twenty-five cents to hear a lecture on "Pecology." On Nov. 16, William Hiller gave Phebe eight cents to buy a book of her own.

42. Hiller Journal & Cash Account Book, 1846–49, 1854–67; *Philadelphia North American*, Sept. 14, 1848, as noted in William S. Greever, *The Bonanza West: The Story of the Western Mining Rushes, 1848–1900* (Norman: University of Oklahoma Press, 1963). Publishers rushed to bring out such guidebooks as *The Emigrant's Guide*, which was published in 1848 (and reprinted in 1978 by Headframe Publishing Company, Haverford, Penn.). Some twenty-five to thirty guidebooks of this type were published in 1848 and 1849. Although guidebooks and media reports such as those Hiller read may have been worthy of skepticism, Americans had less cause to doubt President James K. Polk's address to Congress on December 7, 1848, in which he asserted that "the accounts of the abundance of gold in that territory are of such an extraordinary character as would scarcely command belief were they not corroborated by the authentic reports of officers in the public service." Those officers insisted that a man in the mines could earn in one day a soldier's wages for a month (Greever, *Bonanza West*, 11).

43. For an excellent treatment of emigration companies, see Greever, *Bonanza West*, 25–26, and Oscar Lewis, *Sea Routes to the Gold Fields: The Migration by Water to California in 1849–1852* (New York: Knopf, 1949), 23.

44. Greever, *Bonanza West*, 23. As the company's name implies, the interests of the Pacific Mining and Trading Company went beyond gold mining. They may even have taken a shipment of goods to California, in hopes of selling it at boom-town prices.

45. Hiller Journal & Cash Account Book, 1846–49, 1854–67. Hiller paid $1.00 for the Bible, $2.50 for the millwright's guide, and $.70 for the book on astronomy. He paid $.24 for the blank book and pen points.

46. Hiller Journal & Cash Account Book, 1846–49, 1854–67. Apparently, the *Mariana* departed from Richmond and took on still more expedition members in Hampton Roads, leaving that city on March 24, 1849 (William Hiller biographical statement on envelope in Dunning Papers, EWSHS; WH to AH, Mar. 18 and May 21, 1849). During the month of February 1849 about two hundred ships had sailed from three major ports—sixty from New York City, seventy from Philadelphia, and seventy from Boston. Over 15,500 persons, almost all of them men and many of them married, sailed to San Francisco in 1849 by way of Cape Horn, with another 6,500 making their way west via the isthmus of Panama (Greever, *Bonanza West*, 21–22, 34).

47. WH to AH, Mar. 18, 1849. The man who served as steward with Hiller was a Mr. Vaugh. Although it was a far cry from the good cooking he had enjoyed in Richmond, the food Hiller and Vaugh prepared was well received, going over "first rate" with the twenty men of the company, or "so they all sed." Having lived so recently in a world where slaves did most of the cooking, Hiller confes-

sed that "the way we do it up is a sin to Niggers," doubtless meant as a compliment. Hiller, though antislavery in his sentiments, was given to using such terms as "darkies" and "Niggers."

48. WH to AH, May 21, 1849; WH to AH, Sept. 4, 1849; WH to Singleton Kenyon, May 24, 1849. "Seeing the Elephant" was a common nineteenth-century phrase implying that one had seen all there was to see. The phrase was often associated with miners and homesteaders who gave up and returned home after trying their luck in the West (WH to AH, Oct. 7, 1849).

49. Between 1850 and 1860, the amount of trackage in the United States tripled, with the Northeast developing the most comprehensive rail system (Richard N. Current, et al., *American History: A Survey* [New York: Knopf, 1987], 307). Information on Abiah's trip to Montrose and her return to McDonough was derived from a letter written by Martin Daniels to William Hiller, Aug. 21, 1849. The entire family had made the trip home for only forty-four dollars, thanks, in part, to Martin Daniels's having charged them only for the lumber and other materials needed to crate their goods and not for his labor or that of his crew.

50. Mary Kenyon to WH, Aug. 19, 1849; Martin Daniels to WH, Aug. 21, 1849; AH to WH, Oct. 14, 1849.

51. WH to AH, May 21, 1849. William was confident that the ship could have withstood even "a much harder storm" than that they endured, although he confessed, "i do not care to try it" (WH to AH, June 3, 1849).

52. WH to AH, May 21 and May 22, 1849; WH to Singleton Kenyon, May 24, 1849. The roofing was evidently similar to the Spanish-style tile roofing common in the southwestern United States.

53. WH to Singleton Kenyon, May 24, 1849; WH to AH, May 21 and June 3, 1849. While he found the banana and coconut trees "most beautiful," Hiller was especially intrigued with the palm tree, which he pronounced "one of the most singula[r] trees" he had ever seen.

54. WH to AH, June 3, 1849; WH to AH, May 21, 1849.

55. WH to AH, May 21 and June 3, 1849. The *Mariana* was only one of 110 ships that had been moored in Rio's busy harbor "since the run commenced," and a good many more had sailed past without putting in for repairs or supplies.

56. Martin Daniels to WH, Aug. 21, 1849; WH to AH, Mar. 22, 1849. California was organized as a territory in the fall of 1849 and became the thirty-first state a year later, on Sept. 9, 1850, coming into the Union as a free state.

57. Mary Jane Kenyon to WH, Aug. 19 and Oct. 7, 1849. Born Mar. 5, 1813, Susan Hiller Barrows married Orlando Emmet Barrows (Josephine Chapin Dunning Ashlock Pettyman, "Notes," held by Virginia Ashlock; Mary Jane Kenyon to WH, Aug. 19, 1849; AH to WH, Oct. 14, 1849).

58. AH to WH, Oct. 14, 1849. The lawsuit involved Singleton Kenyon and a Mr. Campbell; Burdick charged Abiah seven dollars to handle the case (AH to WH, Oct. 14, 1849; Lewis Burdick to WH, Oct. 15, 1849).

59. AH to WH, Oct. 14, 1849. Abiah eventually realized that Phebe had whooping cough (AH to WH, Dec. 11, 1850).

60. AH to WH, October 14, 1849. Diaper, a soft, white, distinctly patterned linen or cotton fabric, was used primarily for tablecloths or towels.

61. After rounding the Horn, the company had enjoyed a brief respite from the rhythms of the sea during a layover in Concepción, a Chilean port city of

some twenty-five hundred people. Reporting that many of the men of Concepción had "gone to California," he pronounced the women "with but few exceptions" to be "ignorent and of bad carictor." William was so aware that the region was prone to "the shakes" that he was glad to move back out to sea as soon as repairs had been made and supplies had been taken on board. Hiller identified the "dark spot to the left of the cross" in his sketch as the darkest one of the Magellan clouds and the star below the cross as one "of the first magnitude but . . . said to be changable" (WH to AH, Sept. 4 and Sept. 9, 1849).

62.   Hiller had little time to write, but he did manage to convey to Abiah the picture of San Francisco as a wide-open city where "almost every thing that is wanted is plenty and . . . money [is] very plent[iful]," with "the most gambling that you ever heard of." Some two hundred vessels were in port—"from all nations and more acomeing every day" (WH to AH, Oct. 7, 1849).

63.   WH to AH, Feb. 6 and 28, 1850.

64.   WH to AH, Feb. 28 and Mar. 11, 1850. Hiller reported having made and left eighty-two dollars in Stockton without explaining how or why he left the money. He also pronounced himself in good health, proudly reporting a weight of 173, although it is not known whether this represented a gain or a loss after a year away from home.

65.   WH to AH, Feb. 6, 1850.

66.   WH to AH, Feb. 28, 1850. William was headed for Trinidad Bay because early miners erroneously thought the Trinity flowed into the Pacific and that they could reach gold country by sailing inland from Trinidad Bay (Clarence Pearsall, *The Quest for Qual-A-Wa-Loo* [Oakland: The Holmes Book Company, 1966], 189).

67.   WH to AH, Mar. 11, 1850. Fare from San Francisco to Trinidad Bay was fifty dollars. Hiller also put two dollars into the purchase of a "Tin pan to wash gold in" and another two dollars into a pick. Besides that, fifty pounds of flour, ten pounds of rice, ten pounds of beans, ten pounds of sugar, seventeen pounds of "sea bread," and one-half pound of "Saleraetus," a leavening agent consisting primarily of sodium bicarbonate, had cost him a total of $10.88.

68.   Bill of passage for William Hiller, ten dollars for passage from Smith's River to Trinidad Bay, April 9, 1850 (WH to AH, July 6, 1850). A man named Marsh captained the *Paragon* (WH to AH, Mar. 11, 1850). There are varying descriptions of the shipwreck. According to Phebe Hiller, the *Paragon* wrecked on Mar. 31, 1850 (Phebe Hiller to Josephine Hiller Dunning, Mar. 10, 1884). According to Don Marshall, *California Shipwrecks: Footsteps in the Sea* (Chicago: Binfords & Mort, 1978), the wreck occurred on Mar. 23, 1850, off Point Saint George, less than twenty miles from the Oregon border and seventy miles north of Humboldt Bay. Wallace E. Martin, *Sail and Steam, 1850–1859* (San Francisco: National Maritime Museum, 1983), 52, notes that Crescent City was first called Paragon City "as a remembrance of the first boat to be wrecked there."

Nineteenth-century Union Town on Humboldt Bay is not to be confused with present-day Union City in the San Franscisco Bay area. Union Town is no longer on the map; Arcata occupies the site of the 1850s gold camp (Glen Mason of Eastern Washington State Historical Society to Peavy and Smith, Aug. 20, 1991).

69.   WH to AH, July 6, 1850.

70.   The *Alta California* of May 25, 1850, noted a population of 260 in Union

Town, attributing the town's rapid growth to the road its founders had built directly to the Trinity mines (Chad Hoopes, *The Lure of the Humboldt Bay Region*, [Dubuque, Iowa: Kendall/Hunt Publishing Co., 1966], 49). Hiller's daybook notes that he worked from June 19 to August 30, 1850, while in a letter to Abiah he writes June 23 as his starting date (William Hiller Daybook, 1850, Union Town; WH to AH, Oct. 18, 1850). Hiller worked for Benjamin Kelsey from Sept. 4 to Nov. 3, 1850, at a rate that varied from ten to twelve dollars a day (Hiller Daybook, 1850, Union Town). Letters Hiller received from a friend in Stockton confirmed the fact that he was doing far better in the northern gold camp than he would have done in the south (George Towne to WH, Oct. 14, 1850).

71. AH to WH, Oct. 10, 1850.

72. Ibid.; WH to AH, Oct. 18, 1850. Abiah did not complete the letter begun Oct. 10, 1850, until Dec. 12.

73. WH to AH, Oct. 18 and July 6, 1850.

74. WH to AH, Oct. 18, 1850.

75. Ibid.

76. Ibid.

77. AH to WH, Dec. 11, 1850. "Daguerian apparatus" refers to equipment for producing a daguerreotype, a photograph on a silver or silver-coated copper plate.

78. AH to WH, Dec. 11, 1850. Dr. Frost, Abiah's neighbor, was also superintendent of common schools in the McDonough area at that time and in that position had signed the letter of recommendation in 1848 for Abiah's proposed teaching venture in Richmond.

79. AH to WH, Dec. 11, 1850.

80. Hiller worked for Benjamin Kelsey from Nov. 10, 1850, to Jan. 25, 1851, at ten dollars per day. Kelsey furnished all materials, provided Hiller with room and board, and paid him three hundred dollars for his work (Hiller Daybook, 1850–51, Union Town).

81. AH to WH, Jan. 5, 1851.

82. AH to WH, Jan. 5, 1851. This letter, Abiah noted, was her tenth to William since his departure some twenty-one months earlier.

83. AH to WH, Apr. 10, 1851.

84. Ibid. After the fire, Abiah never again mentioned her "Dagerreotype apparatus." She identified the Kings "and their hired hands" as the neighbors who helped her save the furniture.

85. Ibid.

86. Ibid.

87. Hiller Daybook, 1850–51, Mar. 4 and May 15, 1851, entries; George Towne to WH, Jan. 15, 1851; AH to WH, Apr. 10, 1851. By February 1851, Union Town's population was around five hundred, nearly double what it had been the previous summer (Hoopes, *Lure*, 49). Hiller charged twenty-five dollars for an adult's coffin, four dollars for a child's.

88. *Alta California*, May 25, 1850; Hiller Daybook, 1850–51, May, June, and July 1850 entries.

89. Dunning Notes; AH to WH, Aug. 19, 1851, and Mar. 21, 1852; June 21, 1851, handbill in Dunning Papers, EWSHS. Frugal as always, Abiah left the exact day and year blank on the handbill—"on Monday, Sept.   185"—so she could use the leftovers season after season by simply filling in the appropriate dates.

90.   AH to WH, Aug. 19 and Dec. 5, 1851. Gold had been slow in coming: Abiah had had but two pieces from William in the course of the last two years, not counting the tiny bits he had sent to the children. News had been slow in coming, too. Although she often read newspaper accounts of activities in other California gold towns, she had heard "nothing from Humboldt Bay" since December. Brooks's farm was bought by E. W. Barrows; a year earlier, Abiah could have had the property for fifteen hundred dollars.

91.   AH to WH, Aug. 19, 1851. John Hiller had sold off his paper mill in McDonough and gone to Illinois to "keep sheep" (AH to WH, Dec. 15, 1851).

92.   WH to AH, Sept. 30, 1851; AH to WH, Mar. 21, 1852.

93.   WH to AH, Sept. 30, 1851.

94.   Ibid.

95.   Martin Daniels to WH, Nov. 9, 1851; AH to WH, Dec. 5, 1851.

96.   AH to WH, Dec. 25, 1851.

97.   Abiah had ultimately decided on a house twenty-eight feet square, "with 17 feet posts, 8 feet between joints, and 18 feet rafters" (AH to WH, Dec. 5, 1851). The schoolroom was sixteen feet by twenty feet with eight-foot ceilings (AH to WH, Dec. 25, 1851). The blackboard in the classroom bore a motto on its border that was to become the byword of Abiah's students for decades to come: "What Man has done, Man may do." (Tuttle, "History of McDonough," 22).

98.   AH to WH, Dec. 5, 1851.

99.   AH to WH, Dec. 25, 1851.

100.   Ibid.

101.   Hiller Daybook, 1850–51; WH to AH, Jan. 20, 1852.

102.   WH to AH, Jan. 20, 1852. Abiah herself had not stayed up to watch the eclipse in McDonough, since for her its occurrence came three hours later than it had for William and she could not afford to sit up into the early hours of the morning to see it (AH to WH, Mar. 21, 1852).

103.   WH to AH, Jan. 20 and 25, 1852; William Hiller Daybook, 1850–51.

104.   WH to AH, Mar. 7, 1851.

105.   WH to AH, Mar. 9, 1851. Hiller's reference to "old Tip's" log cabin harked back to the successful 1840 presidential campaign of William Henry Harrison, the hero of the battle of Tippecanoe.

106.   Abiah had managed to get one coat of paint on the outside before winter set in. She had thought the paint was fireproof when she bought it, only to discover later that it was not. Nevertheless, it was cheap and would "lay a good foundation for some handsomer color," whenever she had the funds to put on another coat (AH to WH, Mar. 21, 1852).

107.   AH to WH, Mar. 21, 1852.

108.   Ibid. Still a bachelor, Ira Hiller was thirty-five that spring of 1852. His mother, Mary, was sixty-four. (1860 U.S. Manuscript Census).

109.   AH to WH, December 25, 1851, and Mar. 21, 1852.

110.   AH to WH, Mar. 21, 1852.

111.   WH to AH, April 26 and 30, 1852.

112.   AH to WH, May 30, 1852. A Mr. Crenshaw, who originally had been part-owner with Daniels, was the ill-fated businessman who lost the mill to bankruptcy. In the end, Martin Daniels settled with his family in Canada (Martin

Daniels to H, Apr. 13, 1853). Orondo Beardsly of McDonough was cited as the organizer of the "company" leaving for Oregon.

113.   AH to WH, May 30, 1852.

114.   WH to AH, March 7 and Aug. 22, 1852.

115.   WH to AH, Aug. 22 and 31, 1852.

116.   Andrew Warren eulogy; WH to AH, Mar. 7, 1852.

117.   William Hiller Travel Notebook from Union to McDonough, Dunning Collection, EWSHS; H. V. Bereau to WH, Mar. 24, 1853.

118.   Oct. 24, 1852 entry in Hiller Travel Notebook begun Oct. 23, 1852. The figures Hiller gave show that California gold was selling at about sixteen dollars an ounce in the fall of 1852.

119.   Hiller Travel Notebook. The passage on the *Arnold* from Humboldt Bay to San Francisco took a week's time. Hiller left San Francisco on Nov. 15. His trip home across the isthmus was accomplished in almost one-third the time consumed by his earlier trip west via the Horn.

120.   Ibid. Clara Barton, who rose to fame during the Civil War, studied at the Liberal Institute in Clinton, New York, in 1851 and went to Bordentown shortly thereafter. Dates and details concerning William Hiller's passage to Bordentown were derived from his travel diary; details concerning his land journey and Clara Barton's feelings toward "Friend E." were derived from her letter of thanks to William Hiller (Clara H. Barton to WH, Apr. 8, 1853).

121.   Hiller Travel Notebook; Clara H. Barton to WH, Apr. 8, 1853.

122.   Hiller Travel Notebook; A. H. Murdock to WH, July 11, 1853.

123.   H. V. Bereau to WH, Mar. 24, 1853; Sam Clark to WH, Mar. 3, 1853; John Preston to WH, Apr. 14, May 4, July 3, and Oct. 9, 1853. In an election held in Union Town in the summer of 1854, a total of 673 citizens voted, and with more and more families arriving, sixty women attended the Fourth of July ball that year (John Preston to WH, June 11, 1854; A. H. Murdock to WH, July 11, 1853).

124.   William Hiller Account Book, 1853–54; Hiller Journal & Cash Account Book, 1846–49, 1854–67; William Hiller Journal, Jan. 1 to June 18, 1855.

125.   Olive Burpee to AH, June 9 and Mar. 10, 1855.

126.   Teaching certificates of Phebe A. Hiller, 1858; Tuttle, "History of McDonough," 93; entry in Hiller Cash Account Book, Mar. 16, 1859; Hiller Journal & Cash Account Book, 1846–49, 1854–67. For the next fifteen years, Phebe continued to teach in "common schools" in Chenango County. William Hiller served as a county commissioner for twenty-five years, from 1854 to 1879, and he also served as town clerk and railroad commissioner (Tuttle, "History of McDonough," 93).

127.   A. B. Northrup to Phebe and Josephine Hiller, Nov. 26, 1862; patriotic poem composed by Enf. Burdick, Dunning Papers, EWSHS.

128.   Hiller Journal & Cash Account Book, 1846–49, 1854–63, Oct. 28, 1863, entry; William Hiller Journal of Liquors Bought and Sold, Nov. 16 entry.

129.   Hiller Journal of Liquors Bought & Sold, Nov. 16, 1863 entry; Hiller Journal & Cash Account Book, 1846–49, 1854–67. Hiller paid V. C. Emerson & Company $2.79 for the shroud, but his meticulous account books contain no record of the purchase of a coffin, perhaps because he himself built his wife's coffin, having learned the craft well during his days in California (Hiller Journal & Cash

Account Book, 1846–49, 1854–67, Nov. 16, 1863; A. O. Warren to WH, Nov. 17, 1863).

130.   Andrew Warren to WH, Nov. 17, 1863.

131.   Andrew Warren to Phebe and Josephine Hiller, Nov. 17, 1863; Andrew Warren to Abiah Stanley Warren, Nov. 16, 1863.

132.   Hiller's Journal & Cash Account Book, 1846–49, 1854–67. William Hiller paid Elder Smith five dollars to perform his marriage service (Tuttle, "History of McDonough," 93–94; Hiller Journal & Cash Account Book, 1846–49, 1854–67, Apr. 27, 1867, entry). At thirty-six, William Hiller's new wife was almost exactly the same age Abiah Warren had been when he married her.

A comparison of letters by William Hiller's two wives reveals the difference in their intellects and educations, and William's account books show that his new wife depended upon him for her support (Abigail Roe Hiller to C. B. and Josephine Dunning, undated, ca. 1880s; Hiller Journal & Cash Account Book, 1846–49, 1854–67).

133.   Annett and Lehtinen, *Generations*, 512; Andrew Warren eulogy of Abiah Hiller, Dunning Papers, EWSHS. Andrew himself died on Apr. 28, 1895 (*Universalist Register*, 1896, p. 103).

134.   Josephine Hiller and Charles Dunning, a native of nearby Smithville Flats, were married on Apr. 22, 1868, a year after her father's marriage to Abigail Roe (Dunning, "Notes"). The four Dunning children were William, born Apr. 20, 1869; Amata Abiah, born Feb. 25, 1872; Joseph Warren, born July 18, 1873; and Mary Elsbree, born Oct. 12, 1876 (Dunning, "Notes"; N. A. Durham, *Spokane and the Inland Empire*, 2:621). On Jan. 28, 1880, plagued by ill health and seeking a better climate, Charles Dunning set out for Walla Walla, Washington Territory, accompanied by his wife and four children, ages three to ten (Dunning, "Notes"; Durham, *Spokane*, 621).

135.   Apparently William Hiller's illness began as dysentery (Andrew Warren to Josephine Hiller Dunning, Sept. 7, 1884). Being the businesswoman that she was, Phebe was careful to add to the note of his death: "He wishes this house & lot to be his wifes her lifetime then to come to me as an offset for the money CB Dunning has had which he would only have had by being Joe's husband."

Hard feelings arose between the two sisters shortly after their father's death, and in the lengthy probate battle that ensued, Phebe and her stepmother carried on as joint administrators of William Hiller's estate, finally completing the settlement in February 1891, nearly seven years after his death. According to probate records, Hiller's assets were about twenty-six thousand dollars, a considerable sum for that era (William Hiller Probate Record 328, Chenango County Courthouse, Norwich, N.Y.).

Abigail Roe Hiller died on Nov. 8, 1893. By Abigail's last will and testament, Phebe inherited all her property, but by the time of her own death just seven years later, Phebe's entire estate had mysteriously dwindled to some two thousand dollars (Abigail Hiller Last Will and Testament, Book 191, p. 523, Aug. 8, 1888, and Phebe Hiller Probate Record 1820, Chenango County Courthouse Records, Norwich, N.Y.; Dunning, "Notes"). A four-year probate investigation did not solve the mystery of the missing money and real estate. Josephine outlived Phebe by nearly thirty years, dying in Spokane, Washington, on Dec. 18, 1929 (Dunning, "Notes").

III
Almira Fay Stearns

1. Daniel W. Stearns, "Some Recollections of Early Days," 1911, Daniel Stearns Papers, Special Collections, University of Oregon, Eugene. All letters in this chapter are from this collection unless otherwise stated. The Almira Stearns story has been reconstructed largely on the basis of letters and materials in the Stearns Papers and in the Stearns and Chenoweth Papers housed in the archives of the University of Oregon at Eugene. In quoting these materials, the authors have chosen to retain the spelling, capitalization, and punctuation found in the original sources. In the following notes to this chapter we refer to Almira Fay Stearns as AF or AS and Daniel Stearns as DS.

2. Rolstyn Bridges Notebooks, No. 2, Douglas County Historical Society, Roseburg, Ore. (hereafter cited as DCHS); Stearns, "Some Recollections," 3, 6. Almira Fay Stearns wrote no memoirs of her journey west. In fact, we have little in the way of a written record of her life, other than a series of thirty-nine letters she wrote to her husband from 1861 to 1865 while he was in the Salmon River country of what was then Washington Territory and she was in the frontier town of Roseburg, Oregon, caring for their five sons and Daniel's assorted properties. Although there is internal evidence that Almira received at least twenty-five letters from Daniel between 1861 and 1865, none of his letters are found in the Stearns collections at the University of Oregon. Survival of the wife's letters and the loss of those of the absent husband is most unusual, and this case is singular in our experience. In the absence of copies of his letters, Daniel Stearns's activities have been deduced from Almira's responses to his news from the mines and from details given in his reminiscences and in Alonzo Brown's comprehensive autobiography, written in 1922 and housed in the University of Idaho archives in Moscow.

3. Almira Fay Stearns obituary, Oregon Historical Society, Portland (hereafter cited as OHS); Simeon Fay Probate 7162, Book B, p. 35, Probate Court, Hampshire County Courthouse, Northampton, Mass.; Deed Book, vol. 107, p. 487, Hampden County Courthouse, Springfield, Mass. Whether taught at home or educated at school, Almira must have received more than a minimum of formal schooling, for the letters she wrote in later life are those of an educated woman.

4. Cabotville, today called Chicopee, is a part of Springfield, Mass. (Helen Lister, Belchertown Historical Association, to Peavy and Smith, Aug. 9, 1985). All through the first half of the nineteenth century, young women left rural homes for nearby cities, looking for factory work that would help them contribute to family finances at home, accumulate a dowry, or gain some measure of independence (Vera Shlakman, "Economic History of a Factory Town: A Study of Chicopee, Massachusetts," *Smith College Studies in History* 22:50). See also Thomas Dublin, ed., *Farm to Factory: Women's Letters, 1830–1860,* (New York: Columbia University Press, 1981), for an excellent treatment of the lives of the mill workers.

An incomplete entry in the Palmer (Massachusetts) Vital Records to 1850 lists the death of a Mrs. Fay in 1840, when Almira would have been fifteen years old. If that Mrs. Fay was Almira's mother, then Desire Fay, listed in Simeon's probate as his wife, would be Almira's stepmother.

5. "History of Cabotville," *1846 Directory, Town & Country Register*, 34; Shlak-

man, "Economic History," 58. Almira boarded in a house owned by a Mr. Abbott, who either already was or was soon to become her brother-in-law (DS to AF, Dec. 12, 1854). Sally Abbott, a widow of Springfield, is listed as a sibling of Almira's in Simeon Fay's probate (Simeon Fay Probate 7162, Book B, p. 35, Probate Court, Hampshire County Courthouse). The figures concerning wages represent extrapolations from data found in Shlakman, "Economic History," 50, 53, 56.

6. Glimpses of Almira Fay's life in Cabotville were gleaned from eleven courtship letters written to her over a fifteen-month period (1845–46) by Daniel Stearns and residing now in the Daniel Stearns Papers, University of Oregon.

7. Frank Hodgkins and J. J. Galvin, eds., *Pen Pictures of Representative Men of Oregon* (Portland, Ore.: Farmer and Harriman Publishing House, 1882), 21; Stearns, "Some Recollections," 3; *Portrait and Biographical Record of Western Oregon* (Chicago: Chapman, 1904), 757; DS to AF, Aug. 31, 1845.

Although Daniel's reminiscences attribute only seven children to his parents, two boys and five girls, there were actually six daughters born to Arba and Harriet Stearns (Benjamin Read, *The History of Swanzey, New Hampshire, from 1734 to 1890* [Salem, Mass.: Salem Press, 1892], 456–57; Oran E. Randall, *History of Chesterfield, Cheshire County, N.H.* [Brattleboro, Vt.: D. Leonard, 1882], 449; Stearns Family Book, in possession of Robert and Louise Stearns, Oakland, Ore.).

8. DS to AF, Oct. 26, 1845, and Feb. 16, 1846. Daniel's letters give evidence of almost monthly visits to Cabotville. Nathaniel Pomeroy was the husband of Daniel's oldest sister, Emily, born Mar. 10, 1820 (Read, *History of Swanzey*, 456; DS to AF, May 17, 1846).

9. DS to AF, May 17 and Nov. 1, 1846.

10. DS to AF, Nov. 1, 1846; Births, Marriages, Deaths, 1843–1857, vol. A, p. 48, Belchertown Town Hall, Belchertown, Mass.; Hodgkins and Galvin, *Pen Pictures*, 21. George Jones Stearns was born Oct. 26, 1847 (Read, *History of Swanzey*, 457).

11. Stearns, "Some Recollections," 1; Oscar Lewis, *Sea Routes to the Gold Fields: The Migration by Water to California in 1849–1852* (New York: Knopf, 1949), 7–8. A letter to the editor of a Philadelphia paper in September 1848 first turned the attention of the eastern seaboard to what was going on in California, but President Polk's message to Congress in December of that year was the true impetus of the gold fever in the East. Shortly thereafter, "guidebooks" became readily available to all who were planning to make a speedy departure for the goldfields of the West. (William S. Greever, *The Bonanza West: The Story of Western Mining Rushes, 1848–1900* [Norman: University of Oklahoma Press, 1963], 10, 11).

12. Alonzo Brown, Autobiography [1922], typescript, University of Idaho Library, Moscow. As was usually the case in "companies" formed in the mid-nineteenth century for the purpose of emigration westward, the Massasoit Company had an organizational structure that included a president, a clerk, and a treasurer (Stearns, "Some Recollections," 3). The Massasoit Company was one of 102 such companies chartered in Massachusetts in 1849 (Lewis, *Sea Routes*, 22).

13. Stearns, "Some Recollections," 3. The *Harriet Neal* arrived in Chagres on Apr. 11, 1849 (*Portrait and Biographical Record*, 757). Poled by three or four natives, each bungo, approximately twenty-five feet by two and one-half feet, carried two to four passengers and their baggage. Average cost per person for

passage on the river jumped from ten dollars in 1848 to as high as fifty dollars in 1849, though prices were back to normal in a year or so (Stearns, "Some Recollections," 3–5; Greever, *Bonanza West*, 32–33). Although Stearns rented bulls at Gorgona, most travelers used mules for this purpose (Stearns, "Some Recollections," 5).

14. Stearns, "Some Recollections," 6–7. It is unclear from his reminiscences whether Stearns reached San Francisco on July 3 or 4, 1849. While he did not specify that the twenty-nine-ton vessel he took out of Panama City was a sailing vessel, both the length of time adrift at sea and the size of the boat would indicate that the ship was not a steamer (see Greever, *Bonanza West*, 29).

15. Stearns, "Some Recollections," 8; *Portrait and Biographical Record*, 757.

16. Alonzo Brown, Autobiography. The northern California Salmon River country where Daniel Stearns spent the summer of 1851 is not to be confused with the Salmon River country of Idaho, the center of great mining activity a decade later.

Henry Gardner Brown crossed the isthmus in 1852, having come to California at his brother Loyal's urging shortly after Loyal himself was established in the western mines (Brown obituary, Scrapbook 36, p. 227, OHS; 1860 census; Stearns, "Some Recollections," 10). Situated as it was at the head of navigation of the Umpqua estuary, Scottsburg was larger and busier at this time than Portland (Stephen Beckham, *Land of the Umpqua* [Roseburg, Ore.: Douglas County Commission, 1986], 140).

17. Stearns Family Book. Almira and George also visited periodically with Daniel's oldest sister, Emily, and her husband Nathaniel Pomeroy, who were living in nearby Keene.

18. Stearns, "Some Recollections," 11; Fred Lockley, *History of the Columbia River Valley from The Dalles to the Sea* (Chicago: Clarke, 1928), 2:158.

19. Grace Brown Agee, Memoirs, DCHS; Read, *History of Swanzey*, 456.

The cost of the voyage, Boston to San Francisco, including the land passage, was likely not much over a hundred dollars a person because of competition that had developed between shipping lines in the 1850s (Earnest Wiltsee, *Gold Rush Steamers [of the Pacific]* [San Francisco: Grabhorn Press, 1938; reprint, 1976], 92, 50, 51). The passage via the Isthmus of Panama, although some seven hundred miles longer than the Nicaragna route, was the quickest and most traveled route to California during the gold rush. It was not, however, one taken very often by families. Glenda Riley notes that "because of the arduous nature of the crossing, female emigrants along the isthmus route were probably not very numerous. The journey was not only marked by seasickness, overcrowding, bad food, and boredom while on shipboard, but during the Panama crossing it was characterized by disease, terrible accommodations, a hot and steamy jungle climate, and resentful natives" (Glenda Riley, *Women and Indians on the Frontier, 1825–1915* [Albuquerque: University of New Mexico Press, 1984], 240–41). Although Riley was speaking here specifically of the Panama route, the description, with the lessened possibility of disease, would characterize as well the Nicaragua route.

20. Stearns, "Some Recollections," 11, 12; Wiltsee, *Gold Rush Steamers*, 53; Lewis, *Sea Routes*, 201–202, 221; Arba Fay Stearns "Reminiscences of Southern Oregon Pioneers," in possession of Opal and Jim Stearns, Oakland, Ore.; Bridges, Notebooks, No. 2, DCHS.

21. Stearns, "Some Recollections," 12; A. G. Walling, *History of Southern Oregon* (Portland, Ore.: A. G. Walling Lithography House, 1884), 540; Harold Avery Minter, *Umpqua Valley, Oregon, and Its Pioneers* (Portland: Binfords & Mort, 1967), 113.

22. Stearns, "Some Recollections," 12; Fannie Dimmick to AS, May 11, 1905; *Portrait and Biographical Record*, 757.

23. Arba Stearns, "Reminiscences"; Stearns, "Some Recollections," 12; Account of Goods Burnt and Destroyed by Indians, Stearns and Chenoweth Papers, Special Collections, University of Oregon, Eugene; Beckham, *Land of the Umpqua,* 138. For a good treatment of the Rogue River War, see Stephen Beckham, *Requiem for a People: The Rogue Indians and the Frontiersmen* (Norman: University of Oklahoma Press, 1971). Although the "Indian War" of Oregon Territory is usually dated as 1855–56, tensions between whites and natives that had existed from the beginning of the decade were not relieved until 1859, when on March 8 the federal government ratified the Indian treaties that brought an official end to hostilities and, in effect, threw open the southeastern lands to settlement (Charles Henry Carey, *History of Oregon* [Chicago: Pioneer History Publishing Company, 1922], 1:624).

24. Priscilla and Henry were married on Sept. 15, 1856 (Agee, Memoirs). Henry's obituary gives the wedding date as Sept. 15, 1855 (Scrapbook 36, p. 227, OHS). At twenty-four, Henry was eight years younger than his bride (1860 U.S. Manuscript Census).

Daniel paid thirty-five hundred dollars for the 640 acres of bottomland, using his newly acquired livestock as collateral (Stearns, "Some Recollections," 12; Deed Book B, p. 27, Feb. 20, 1857, Douglas County Courthouse, Roseberg, Ore.).

25. John Warren Stearns was born Mar. 11, 1857 (Cedar Hill Cemetery headstone, Oakland, Ore.); Stearns, "Some Recollections," 12; Bridges, Notebooks, No. 2; *Portrait and Biographical Record*, 758.

26. William Robbins, "The Far Western Frontier: Economic Opportunity and Social Democracy in Early Roseburg, Oregon" (doctoral thesis, University of Oregon, 1968), 42, 47; Walling, *History*, 10; Douglas Robertson, Roseburg Chamber of Commerce pamphlet, DCHS; Beckham, *Land of the Umpqua*, 77; Captain John Mullan, "From Walla Walla to San Francisco," *Oregon Historical Society Quarterly* 4 (1903): 217–18. Loyal was the oldest of the Brown brothers; John was a year younger than he, Henry two years younger, and Alonzo, who would eventually come west as well, was six years younger (Bridges, Notebooks, File A-25; Brown, "Autobiography"; 1860 U.S. Manuscript Census).

Roseburg's name was officially spelled "Roseburgh" until the weight of custom brought about a legal change in 1894 (Beckham, *Land of the Umpqua*, 138).

27. Although A. C. Gibbs, soon to become governor of Oregon, managed the business at the time of the sale, the property was owned by Stephen Chadwick (Sept. 12, 1859, Deed Book 2, p. 93, Douglas County Courthouse). John Brown was Daniel's comanager and cohabitant in the American Hotel venture, but Loyal and Sarah Brown ultimately held the mortgage on the Brown half of the enterprise, as noted by the sale of their portion exactly one year later (Sept. 12, 1860, Deed Book 2, p. 821, Douglas County Courthouse).

Alexander Brown had been uncle to the Brown brothers long before his marriage to his brother's widow made him their stepfather as well. The elder Browns had a sixteen-year-old daughter of their own, Emma (Brown, Autobiography).

The Biography Index (Vital Statistics), OHS, indicates that Martha arrived in Oregon on Aug. 10, 1859. One history notes that Martha came west with a brother; perhaps John Stearns went home to New Hampshire while Daniel and Almira were at Elkton (*A Brief History of Seventy Years: Grace Church, Astoria, Oregon* [Astoria: Grace Church, 1939], 5; copy in OHS).

The Douglas County census records of 1860 list as residents not only the Stearns family—Daniel, thirty-eight; Almira, thirty-five; George, twelve; Laurial *[sic]*, seven; Arbia *[sic]*, five; John, three; Ralph, one; and Martha, twenty-one—but fourteen others as well, including five farm laborers, a blacksmith, a minister, a cook, three male "servants," and the four members of the John Brown family (1860 U.S. Manuscript Census; Bridges, Notebooks, No. 3. The census mistakenly lists Daniel Stearns as Dale Stevens and also lists the third Stearns child, Arba, as a female).

28. Bridges, Notebooks, No. 4; Deed Book 2, Sept. 12, 1860, p. 281, Douglas County Courthouse, Roseburg, Ore.; Lillie Lila Moore, "Roseburg, 1851–1929," manuscript, DCHS; Brown, Autobiography; Stearns, "Some Recollections," 12. The 1860 U.S. Manuscript Census assesses the value of Stearns's real and personal property at eighty-five hundred dollars, more than double the value Stearns himself claimed.

29. Dorothy Povey, *Ghost Mining Camps of Idaho: Their History and How to Find Them* (Boise, Idaho: Golden West, 1984), 6. In the summer of 1860 gold was found at Pierce, and in the spring of 1861 another strike was reported at Elk City. The Salmon River mines were within Washington Territory until Mar. 1863, when Idaho Territory was established (Greever, *Bonanza West*, 259–60).

John Stearns bought the saloon and all fixtures and stock from John Party, a French immigrant, for thirty-five hundred dollars on Jan. 16, 1860, just months after his brother had bought the American Hotel (Deed Book 2, p. 154, Douglas County Courthouse, Roseburg; 1860 U.S. Manuscript Census). John Brown had married Clara Smith of San Francisco in 1851. At the time they bought the Eagle Hotel, they had two children: Charles, age three, and Ella Louise, two (Bridges, Notebook, File A-25; Brown, Autobiography; 1860 U.S. Manuscript Census). Loyal Brown had married Sarah Cruzan, a Scottsburg woman, in 1854, and they had sometime thereafter settled on ranchland near Roseburg that was owned by her parents. They, too, had two small children: Roland and Betty (Bridges, Notebooks, No. 4; 1860 U.S. Manuscript Census; Brown, Autobiography; *Portrait and Biographical Record*, 665). Alonzo Brown had married Adaline Lamkin of Boston in 1854. They crossed the plains in 1860 with two small children, three-year-old Minnie and three-month-old Edgar (Brown, Autobiography).

30. Bridges, Notebooks, No. 4. Hyland had arrived in Roseburg, newly immigrated from Ireland, in May 1860, to serve in Roseburg's mission church in the diocese of Bishop Thomas Scott (*Brief History of Seventy Years*, 7–8; Arba Stearns, Reminiscences). The 1860 U.S. Manuscript Census mistakenly lists a Tremond Hyland, forty, a minister born in England, as a resident of the American Hotel. The Hyland-Stearns wedding took place on June 23, 1861, likely the first such ceremony performed in Roseburg's new church.

31. 1860 U.S. Manuscript Census; AS to DS, July 20, 1862.

32. *Oregonian,* Oct. 21, 1861, as quoted in "The Salmon River Mines," *Idaho Yesterdays,* Spring 1962, p. 42. With the discovery of gold at Oro Fino in 1860, the Nez Percés had renegotiated their treaty with the federal government. It was agreed that miners could work north of the Clearwater River but not south. That agreement, signed on Apr. 11, 1861, like all others, was short-lived (Greever, *Bonanza West,* 258; F. Ross Peterson, *Idaho: A Bicentennial History* [New York: Norton, 1976], 56). Within a month, prospectors had moved south of the Clearwater, and the claims at Elk City, Florence, and Warren were clearly in violation of the Indian treaties. Although the Nez Percés initially threatened the invaders with expulsion, they finally relented and agreed to the illegal intrusion. In fact, had the Indians not been willing to provide food and supplies in the devastating winter of 1861–62, many of the miners would have perished (Peterson, *Idaho,* 57).

33. Donald C. Miller, *Ghost Towns of Idaho* (Boulder: Prescott, 1976), 52. Dr. Baker was probably Dr. Dorsey Baker, who had been engaged in various enterprises in the Umpaqua Valley in the mid-1850s and who was by now established in Walla Walla (W. D. Lyman, *History of Walla Walla* [n.p., 1901], 288).

34. Stearns, "Some Recollections," 13.

35. AS to DS, Sept. 27, 1861. John Floed was a prosperous merchant, and his wife was the daughter of Joseph Lane, the first territorial governor of Oregon as well as the state's first U.S. senator (1860 U.S. Manuscript Census; Sister Margaret Jean Kelly, *The Career of Joseph Lane, Frontier Politician* [Washington, D.C.: Catholic University of America Press, 1942], 13).

36. AS to DS, Sept. 27, 1861.

37. AS to DS, Apr. 8, 1862. Crane paid twenty-eight hundred dollars for the Eagle Hotel, one hundred dollars down and the balance in six months (AS to DS, Feb. 16, 1862). In the way of commerce of the day the proposed purchase of the American by Nancy Kent was discussed by Almira Stearns's brother-in-law, John, and Nancy Kent's son, though the two women were the primary parties to the transaction. Over the course of the next two years, Nancy Kent continued to manifest a periodic interest in the American, but that interest never turned into ownership (AS to DS, Feb. 16, 1862 and Apr. 10 and May 3, 1863).

38. Brown, Autobiography; AS to DS, Feb. 16 and 26, 1862; 1860 U.S. Manuscript Census; Robertson, Roseburg Chamber of Commerce pamphlet. June Underwood treats of this situation in the lives of nineteenth-century western women in her article "Western Women and True Womanhood," noting that western women invariably "modeled their prescriptive roles to suit the needs, personal and public, that they perceived around them" ("Western Woman and True Womanhood: Culture and Symbol in History and Literature," *Great Plains Quarterly* 5 (Spring 1985): 95).

39. Stearns, "Some Recollections," 13; C. J. Brosnan, *History of the State of Idaho* (New York: Scribners, 1948), 140. For six of his seventeen days on the trail, Daniel Stearns did not see another human being.

40. Stearns, "Some Recollections," 14.

41. AS to DS, Feb. 16, 1862. Having lost all his livestock in the harsh winter, Alonzo had moved his family into town, but he felt there was little to hold him there (*Portrait and Biographical Record,* 665).

42. AS to DS, Feb. 16 and Mar. 3, 1862.

43. AS to DS, Mar. 3, 1862.

44. Ibid.; AS to DS, Mar. 16, 1862.

45. AS to DS, Mar. 16, 1862.

46. 1860 U.S. Manuscript Census; AS to DS, Mar. 16, 1862.

47. AS to DS, Mar. 16, 1862; Brown, Autobiography.

48. Brown, Autobiography; Povey, *Ghost Mining Camps*, 6.

49. Brown, Autobiography; AS to DS, Apr. 8, 16, and 23, 1862.

50. AS to DS, Apr. 8, 1862.

51. AS to DS, Apr. 16 and June 1, 1862. Particularly helpful in assessing Almira's statement is Glenda Riley's study of women's contributions to family economy in "'Not Gainfully Employed': Women on the Iowa Frontier 1833–1870," *Pacific Historical Review*, May 1980, pp. 237–64. "Western women still produced . . . foodstuffs, soap, lighting facilities, clothing in their own homes. Frontier women manufactured many items and purchased little . . . . The woman and her home, like the worker and the workplace, were the key link in turning unusable raw materials into consumable finished goods. She was to the family what the factory was to industrialized society. . . . Women's diaries, memoirs, and correspondence indicate that [a woman] was a full economic producer in her own right," though her activities were not equated with gainful employment (Riley, "Not Gainfully Employed," 240–42).

52. AS to DS, Sept. 27, 1861; Apr. 23, 1862; and Mar. 3, 1863. The Hyland baby was named Edward Arthur. The extent of the alienation of the Fay family is evidenced by the fact that Polly, who was eight months late in sending the news to Almira, had not herself heard of her father's illness until one-half hour before his funeral. When Almira received another letter from Polly, telling her that she had inherited something from her father's estate, she forwarded the letter to Daniel, seeking his advice: "It is so little that it seems hardly worth while to trouble about it but still I suppose it belongs to me" (AS to DS, Oct. 8, 1862). Her father's probate showed an estate having a net value of $105. Almira's share, at best one-ninth of that amount, was indeed small (Simeon Fay Probate 7162, Book B, p. 35, Probate Court, Hampshire County Courthouse, Northampton, Mass.).

53. AS to DS, June 1, 1862.

54. AS to DS, Apr. 23, 1862.

55. AS to DS, June 1, 1862. In May 1862, Daniel also shipped $913.90 in gold bullion directly to San Francisco (Invoices and Receipts, Stearns Papers).

56. AS to DS, June 1, 1862. When Almira was unable to convert her newly acquired gold dust to greenbacks in Roseburg, John Floed helped her send it on to San Francisco. That decision cost her dearly, since "Northern dust" was selling for only $12.00 an ounce, in contrast to the $20.00 an ounce California gold had brought a decade earlier, and simply sending it to San Francisco entailed $6.50 in postage (Greever, *Bonanza West*, 74). Even so, Almira realized $201.60 in the transaction.

57. AS to DS, June 1 and 28, 1862, Stearns and Chenoweth Papers. Bishop Thomas Scott held services in the church that had been built while Thomas Hyland served Roseburg (*History of Grace Church*).

58. AS to DS, June 1, 1862.

59. AS to DS, June 28, 1862, Sterns and Chenoweth Papers.

60. AS to DS, Apr. 23, 1862, Stearns Papers, and June 28, 1862, Stearns and Chenoweth Papers, 1860 U.S. Manuscript Census. "Blistering" was the application of a hot-mustard plaster or some other medicated plaster to the chest.

61. AS to DS, July 18, 1862, Stearns and Chenoweth Papers.

62. Ibid.

63. AS to DS, June 1 and Sept. 11, 1862. Almira was never again to comment on the rapidity of the delivery of the mail.

64. AS to DS, Sept. 11, Oct. 8, and Oct. 20, 1862; Brown, Autobiography. There is no evidence of what might have prompted Daniel's hasty and unanticipated trip home. In order to settle George in school, he may have timed his return to coincide with the opening of the fall term at Bishop Scott Academy in Portland, which later became Hill Academy.

65. AS to DS, Oct. 8, Oct. 20, and Nov. 1862.

66. AS to DS, Oct. 8, 1862. The buyer of the Hudson ranch was a blacksmith from Roseburg, a Mr. Buell (1860 U.S. Manuscript Census).

67. AS to DS, Nov., Dec. 10, 1862. Daniel Stearns in his late-life memoirs recalled the days when the Salmon River country was "full of robbers and highwaymen." During the winter of 1862–63, he reported that "over twenty of these robbers had been hung at the Blackfoot mines in thirty days" (Stearns, "Some Recollections," 14).

68. AS to DS, Nov. 1862.

69. AS to DS, Dec. 10, 1862.

70. Ibid., Joseph Lane had run unsuccessfully as the Democratic candidate for the vice-presidency of the United States on the Breckenridge ticket in 1860. Winifred Lane was most likely the daughter of Rev. Jesse Lane, Joseph Lane's brother. (Loisa Kendall Rogers, "The Lanes: Cavaliers of the South in the Early Wars of Early America," typescript, File G-21, DCHS; Stearns, "Some Recollections," 15).

71. AS to DS, Nov. 1862; Jan. 1 and Feb. 24, 1863.

72. AS to DS, Jan. 1, 1863; Loyal Stearns to DS, Jan. 1, 1863. The teenager with whom John Stearns danced was Sarah Stevenson.

73. AS to DS, Nov. 1862, and Jan. 1, 1863.

74. AS to DS, Jan. 18, 1863.

75. Brown, Autobiography; Miller, *Ghost Towns*, 59. Warren was at various times called Warren's, Warrens, and Warren's Diggins (Povey, *Ghost Mining Camps*, 17). For consistency, it will hereafter be referred to as Warren.

76. AS to DS, Jan. 18, Feb. 7, 1863; Brown, Autobiography. John Stearns rented his saloon to John Hulse, a carpenter (1860 U.S. Manuscript Census; AS to DS, Nov. 1862). Loyal Brown eventually bought the Milner Trail from its original developer, Moses Milner (Brown, Autobiography).

77. AS to DS, Feb. 24, 1863.

78. AS to DS, Feb. 7 and 24, 1863. The youngest of ten children of former Territorial Governor Joseph Lane and his wife, Mary, Emma (or Emily) Lane Floed (wife of Almira's landlord, John Floed) and Winifred Lane Mosher (wife of Roseburg attorney Lafayette Mosher) were likely cousins of schoolteacher Winifred Lane Barton (1860 U.S. Manuscript Census; Kelly, *Career*, 13).

79. AS to DS, Feb. 24, Mar. 25, Apr. 10 and 16, 1863. George Stearns was not

the only student to leave Bishop Scott Academy that term. In 1862–63 the school was under the leadership of a Reverend Facker, who did not seem to get on well with his charges—thirteen day scholars and ten boarding students. By the end of the school year only five of those students remained at the school (Charles Lewis, "The History of the Educational Activities of the Protestant Episcopal Church in Oregon," *Quarterly of the Oregon Historical Society* 25, no. 2 [June 1924]: 106).

Almira Stearns, of course, was not an enfranchised citizen and could not vote on the free school question, although she was vitally interested in the outcome (AS to DS, Apr. 16, 1863). Apparently Roseburg schools before 1863 had been private institutions run by teachers who charged tuition for their services.

80. AS to DS, Mar. 25 and May 3, 1863; Brown, Autobiography.

81. AS to DS, Sept. 21 and 27, 1861; May 3, 1863. Jane Chadwick was the wife of Stephen Chadwick, the attorney who took sometime care of the Stearns legal matters (1860 U.S. Manuscript Census; Stephen Chadwick to DS, June 12, 1864; AS to DS, May 3, 1863). No evidence can be found to substantiate or explain Almira's reference to Morgan's still-living wife.

The Dearborns figured prominently in Almira's letters to Daniel. Richard, a merchant, was often away from home, either seeking treatment for various health problems or looking for better business opportunities (1860 U.S. Manuscript Census; AS to DS, Sept. 21, 1861; Feb. 16, 1862; May 3, 1863).

A year earlier, Almira had teased Emma Floed that she intended to steal her "beautiful babe" and wrote to Daniel that she had "got a daughter" (AS to DS, June 28, 1862, Stearns and Chenoweth Papers).

82. AS to DS, May 3 and June 12 and 24, 1863. Benjamin Heineberg was a forty-one-year-old merchant. Both he and his wife, Sarah, who was fourteen years younger than he, had been born in Prussia (1860 U.S. Manuscript Census). As abruptly as they had left, both Richard Dearborn and Benjamin Heineberg returned to resume life in Roseburg (AS to DS, June 24, 1863). John Stearns filed bankruptcy in Douglas County on Sept. 20, 1870 (Deed Book 4, p. 795, Douglas County Courthouse, Roseburg, Ore.).

83. AS to DS, April 16, May 3, June 24, and July 12, 1863.

84. AS to DS, June 24, 1863.

85. AS to DS, June 12 and 24 and May 3 and 21, 1863; Loyal Stearns to DS, May 21, 1863.

86. AS to DS, July 26, 1863; Brown, Autobiography.

87. Brown, Autobiography. For a good description of the rhythm of commerce in the Idaho gold camps, see Sister M. Alfreda Elsensohn, O.S.B., *Pioneer Days in Idaho County*, vol. 2, (Caldwell, Idaho: Caxton, 1951).

88. AS to DS, July 26 and Aug. 12, 1863.

89. Ibid.

90. AS to DS, July 26, 1863.

91. George and Loyal helped Almira and Ada by carting firewood from the house to the hotel (George Stearns to DS, July 26, 1863).

92. AS to DS, Aug. 12, 1863.

93. Ibid. and AS to DS, Aug. 26, 1863.

94. Ibid. and Sept. 13, 1863. Almira had at first attached a fifty dollar value to her room and board.

95. AS to DS, Sept. 13, 1863. Ada and the children took their room for twenty dollars a month.

96. AS to DS, Oct. and Nov. 16, 1863. Homeopathy was a popular nineteenth-century branch of medicine characterized by treatment of illness with small doses of drugs that, in a healthy person, produced symptoms similar to the illness being treated. Almira was probably using the term loosely, since there is no evidence in her letters that she was reading homeopathy literature or dealing with homeopathic physicians.

97. AS to DS, Sept. 13 and Oct. 1863. The 1860 census records of Roseburg do not list a Mrs. Gaddis, but show a Crawford Gaddis, a sixteen-year-old male, a carpenter by trade, as the head of a household that included three other males, all carpenters, all older than he. It could be that Crawford Gaddis's mother was the "crazy Mrs. Gaddis," and not listed by the census taker. Mrs. Abraham, whom Almira refers to only by her surname, would have been the wife of either Solomon or Hyman Abraham, young Polish-born brothers who had a dry goods store in Roseburg (1860 U.S. Manuscript Census).

98. AS to DS, Oct. and Nov. 16, 1863. The poem contained in that letter has not survived, and there is no way of knowing its nature or authorship.

99. AS to DS, Oct. and Nov. 16, 1863.

100. AS to DS, Nov. 16, 1863.

101. AS to DS, Nov. 28, 1863, Stearns and Chenoweth Papers.

102. AS to DS, Nov. 16, 1863; Brown, Autobiography.

103. AS to DS, Sept. 13 and Nov. 16, 1863.

104. Loyal Stearns to DS, Nov. 28, 1863 and Jan. 31, 1864; AS to DS, Nov. 28, 1863, Stearns and Chenoweth Papers; AS to DS, Aug. 2 and Nov. 16, 1863, and Jan. 16 and Apr. 18, 1864. In the Stearns Papers and the Stearns and Chenoweth Papers are nine letters to Daniel written by Loyal and four written by George.

105. AS to DS, Nov. 28, 1863, Stearns and Chenoweth Papers.

106. Ibid. and AS to DS, Nov. 16, 1863.

107. Brown, Autobiography; Greever, *Bonanza West*, 262–64.

108. AS to DS, Jan. 16, 1864.

109. AS to DS, Feb. 3, 1864, Stearns and Chenoweth Papers; AS to DS, Jan. 16, 1864.

110. AS to DS, Feb. 3, 1864, Stearns and Chenoweth Papers. Bannock, the first name given to a settlement that would later be known as Idaho City, should not be confused with Bannack, the gold camp established almost simultaneously in that part of Washington Territory that would soon become Montana Territory (Greever, *Bonanza West*, 204).

111. There is no record that Daniel left Almira with power of attorney, and this incident would suggest that he had not done so (AS to DS, Apr. 18, 1864).

112. AS to DS, May 15, 1864.

113. Ibid.

114. Ibid. and AS to DS, June 11, 1864. Before going into the mercantile business, John Fitzhugh had been an editor of the *Roseburgh Express*, the town's first paper (Moore, "Roseburg," 116).

115. AS to DS, May 27, 1864; Moore, "Roseburg," 118.

116. AS to DS, Jan. 16, Apr. 7, and May 15 and 29, 1864.

117. AS to DS, June 11, 1864; S. T. Chadwick to DS, June 12, 1864.

118. Brown, Autobiography; AS to DS, July 27, 1864. "Gallop and Rheubarb" was evidently a purgative, since Almira reported it "operated powerfully" and produced "a bad diarrhaea."

119. AS to DS, May 27 and July 27, 1864. This is Almira's last extant letter from Daniel's time in the mines of Idaho, though she had another year of "widow-hood" to live through.

120. Brown, Autobiography; Arba Stearns, "Reminiscences." Daniel Stearns's journal of 1864 bears a last entry of Dec. 5, 1864, at Warren.

121. Brown, Autobiography.

122. Ibid.; Daniel Stearns daybook, Warren, Washington, 1865, July 3–12, 1865, Stearns and Chenoweth Papers; Arba Stearns, "Reminiscences." A receipt dated Sept. 7, 1865, in Portland, credited Daniel Stearns with $751.59 in gold bullion (Stearns and Chenoweth Papers).

123. Stearns, "Some Recollections," 15. The American Hotel was not sold until Feb. 2, 1872, to D. C. McClallan for three thousand dollars (Deed Book V, p. 427, Douglas County Courthouse). How the hotel was managed between the Stearnses' move to Elkton in 1865 and the sale in 1872 has not been determined.

124. Robbins, "Far Western Frontier," 57; Arba Stearns, "Reminiscences"; Stearns, "Some Recollections," 15.

125. In mid-November 1865, perhaps about the same time that the Stearnses were settling themselves on the ranch in Elkton, Alonzo, Ada, Minnie, and Freddy Brown took up life as a family on their Oakland farm (Brown, Autobiography).

126. Iris Hancock of Lincoln City, Ore., to Peavy and Smith, Apr. 4, 1988; Marietta Ransome to grandfather, Apr. 20, 1868. Only "short-term schooling" was pro-vided in the small schoolhouse on the western border of the Stearns ranch, since there were only four families living in the area. Loyal and Arba, and eventually Johnny and Ralph, were sent away to Umpqua Academy in Wilbur and to Bishop Scott Academy in Portland (Arba Stearns, "Reminiscences"; Portrait and Biographi-cal Record, 757; L. B. Stearns obituary, Oregonian, June 3, 1936, p. 5).

127. Hancock to Peavy and Smith, Apr. 4, 1988; Stearns family interview with Peavy and Smith, Oct. 1988; Ransom to grandfather, Apr. 20, 1868. According to Iris Hancock, granddaughter of Marietta Ransom, the young girl who had come over from Scottsburg to help Almira at Elkton, "It was surprising the [number of] women . . . from Coos and Curry counties . . . who lost their minds," including several "out by way of Scottsburg." According to Hancock, "the trouble may have been boredom," since "many [women were] taken . . . back in the hills. The men went to town once in a while to get supplies. [The] women stayed home and most had a big family. They broke down" (Hancock to Peavy and Smith, Apr. 4, 1988). Coos and Curry counties are neighboring counties on the southern coast of Oregon; Elkton is in Douglas County, just north and east of Coos County.

128. Brown, Autobiography. Although Brown's memoirs state that he left his family in a rented house in Oakland during his 1869 season in the mines, the census puts them in Elkton (1870 U.S. Manuscript Census).

129. Hancock to Peavy and Smith, Apr. 4, 1988; Stearns, "Some Recollec-tions," 16.

130. Arba Stearns, "Reminiscences." George Stearns married Mary (Nettie) Young, daughter of an Oakland merchant, on Oct. 1, 1876 (Marriage Records, June 24, 1863, vol. 2, p. 337, Douglas County Courthouse).

Home to stay after Minnie's death, Alonzo invested in a general store in Oakland with Silas Crane. In 1872, on a tip that a railroad would soon be coming through, Alonzo bought 736 acres close to the proposed lines and about a mile southwest of the old town. When the railroad forced the relocation of Oakland, Alonzo realized "enormous profits" from the sale of lots (Brown, Autobiography; Agee, Memoirs; *Portrait and Biographical Record*, 665).

131. *Historic Douglas County*; L. B. Stearns obituary, *Oregonian*, June 3, 1936, p. 5; AS to DS, Sept. 4, 1880. George and Nettie Stearns eventually had three children: Jeanette, Roy, and Ellen May (George Stearns Probate, 1908, Box 150, Douglas County Courthouse, Roseburg, Ore.).

132. *Roseburg News Review*, Jan. 4, 1897, DCHS. In 1895, George Stearns had 130 workers in his hop fields, and his father employed 75 workers in the twelve acres he had planted in hops (Beckham, *Land of the Umpquas*, 213). George was also a partner in his father-in-law's Oakland hardware business, E. C. Young and Company (Bridges, Notebook, File E-84; Rolstyn Bridges, "Daniel W. Stearns, Oregon Argonaut," *Umpqua Trapper* 3 [Winter 1967]: 3–7).

Loyal married a widow, Mary Frances Carr, nee Hoyt, in June 1883, and his seven-year-old stepdaughter, Ethel Carr Stearns, took his name (Biographical Index, Vital Statistics, OHS, and *Oregonian*, June 29, 1883, p. 2). Arba married Nancy Chenoweth on Oct. 2, 1881 (Marriage Record, vol 3, p. 234, Douglas County Courthouse, Roseburg, Ore.). They had four children: Harry, James Edwin, Fay, and Esther Stearns Peeler (Nancy Chenoweth Stearns Probate 2060, Box 193, Douglas County Courthouse, Roseburg, Ore.). Ralph married Mary Harvey on June 26, 1881 (Marriage Record vol. 3, p. 204, Douglas County Courthouse, Roseburg, Ore.). They also had four children: Merle, Martha, Loyal, and Ralph (D. W. Stearns Probate 712, Box 118, Douglas County Courthouse, Roseburg, Ore.).

133. Loyal Brown to DS and AS, July 27, 1905.

134. AS obituary, *Daily Review*, Feb. 6, 1911. Ada Brown died in 1888; Alonzo, who remarried, lived well into the next century, dying in 1937 (Scrapbook 36, p. 79, OHS). John Stearns died at Astoria in 1891 (Stearns Family Book). Thomas Hyland also died there on Dec. 11, 1904, at age seventy. (*History of Grace Church*, 8). Martha Hyland died on June 25, 1925, leaving Grace Church an estate of ten thousand dollars (*History of Grace Church*, 8). Priscilla and Henry Brown both passed away in 1902 (Bridges, Notebooks, No. 3).

135. Stearns, "Some Recollections," 16. D. W. Stearns Probate 712, Box 118, Douglas County Courthouse, Roseburg, Ore., showed that Daniel left $12,500 in real estate and $2,500 in personal property. John Warren Stearns died a bachelor in San Francisco on Jan. 27, 1919, the first of the Stearns brothers to die. George died next, on Oct. 20, 1923; Loyal died in Portland on June 2, 1936; Ralph died in 1943; and Arba died in 1955 at the age of 101 (Stearns Family Book).

IV
Sarah Burgert Yesler

1. The Sarah Yesler story has been reconstructed largely on the basis of letters and papers collected in the Henry Leiter Yesler Papers, University of Washington Libraries, Seattle (hereafter cited as HLY/UW); the Henry Yesler Collection, Washington State Historical Society, Tacoma (hereafter cited as WHS); the Henry Yesler Papers, Museum of History and Industry, Seattle (hereafter cited as

MHI); and the George Plummer Papers, Clarence Bagley Collection, University of Washington Libraries, Seattle. (In quoting these materials, the authors have chosen to retain the spelling, capitalization, and punctuation found in the original sources.) Also useful were John Robert Finger's Ph.D. dissertation, "Henry L. Yesler's Seattle Years, 1852–1892," University of Washington, 1968, and Henry L. Yesler's own statement as sent by him to H. H. Bancroft in 1878 for use in *History of the Pacific Northwest* and later published in full under Henry L. Yesler's name as "Henry Yesler and the Founding of Seattle," *Pacific Northwest Quarterly* 42 (Oct. 1951): 271–76 (hereafter referred to as Yesler Article). In the following notes to this chapter Sarah Yesler is abbreviated as SY and Henry Leiter Yesler as HLY.

2. *Daily Post Intelligencer*, Aug. 30, 1887; 1820 U.S. Manuscript Census. David and Elenor Burgert were married in March 1820 (Marriage Records, Stark County Courthouse, Canton, Ohio; David Burgert to SY, Jan. 5, 1858, WHS). Names and birth dates of Sarah Burgert Yesler's siblings were derived from Probate 628, Estate of Sarah B. Yesler, King County Courthouse, Seattle, Wash.

3. Probate 628, Estate of Sarah B. Yesler, King County Courthouse, Seattle, Wash.; SY to HLY, July 4, 1852, WHS. On July 14, 1828, David Burgert and Elenor Burgert, whose mark rather than signature is on the deed, had sold their land in Stark County to Peter Tecker and Francis Rimrey (Land Records, vol. G, p. 498, Stark County Courthouse, Canton, Ohio).

4. A goodly number of Burgert kin were scattered throughout Stark County in the early 1800s (William Perrin, ed., *History of Stark County* [n.p.: Baskins and Battey, 1881], 314, 507; E. T. Heald, *The Stark County Story* [Canton, Ohio: Stark County Historical Society, 1949], 56; H. T. O. Blue, *History of Stark County, Ohio* [Chicago: S. J. Clarke Publishing Company, 1828], 42). The George Zieglers, who owned 128 acres northeast of Paris, were related to close friends of Henry Yesler: Louis, Barbara, and Magdeline Ziegler of Leitersberg, Ohio (Ben F. Thomas map of Paris Township, Township XVII, Range VI, ca. 1830). Henry's first year in Massillon is described in Finger, "Seattle Years," 6.

5. Finger, "Seattle Years," 1–4. Joseph Leiter, Henry's great-grandfather, was the first settler in Leitersburg, Md., although Herbert C. Bell's *History of the Leitersburg District* (Leitersburg: n.p., 1898), 305, notes that Henry Yesler was "grandson of Andrew Leiter, the founder of Leitersburg." Yesler's home in Leitersburg was described in a *Daily Post-Intelligencer* article of Nov. 29, 1887. Finger's discussion of the confusion surrounding Yesler's birthdate notes that his obituary in the Dec. 19, 1892, *Daily Post-Intelligencer* gives the date as Dec. 31, 1810, as do other sources thereafter. However, Yesler's 1890 certificate of marriage to Minnie Gagle gives Dec. 4, 1810 (Marriage Certificate 36516, Clerk of Orphan's Court, Philadelphia, Pa.).

The complexities surrounding the "marriage" and subsequent divorce and remarriages of Henry Yesler's parents are outlined by Finger, who cites, among other sources, *Daily Post-Intelligencer* articles of Feb. 10 and 12, 1893. In addition, see *Marriages of Washington County, Maryland, 1799–1860; Wills of Washington County, Maryland, an Index: 1776–1880*; and J. Thomas Scharf's *History of Western Maryland* (Philadelphia: n.p., 1882), 2:1305, in the Simms A. Jameson Memorial Library of the Washington County Historical Society, Hagerstown, Md. Dates and names from these references were supplied to Peavy and Smith in a letter sent by personnel at the Washington County Historical Society, July 28, 1985. The sources cited above indicate that in 1810 Henry Yesler the elder married a woman named Catherine Slater, by whom he had five children, three of whom survived to adulthood. No record of his marriage to Catherine Leiter has been found. Although it is possible that the "Catherine Slater" he married in 1810 was actually Catherine Leiter, this seems unlikely, since he was later buried beside this woman.

In his later years, Henry Yesler turned over the management of his financial affairs to James D. Lowman, son of his favorite stepbrother, Daniel S. Lowman (Finger, "Seattle Years," 349).

6. *Daily Post-Intelligencer*, Nov. 29, 1887; Harvey K. Hines, *History of the State of Washington* (Chicago: n.p., 1893), 252; *Northwest Magazine*, Apr. 1888, sec. 6, pp. 18–19.

7. Finger, "Seattle Years," 3–4, 5. Located just east of the Allegheny range, Leitersburg had, for a century, been a pass-through point for German immigrants on their way to Pennsylvania, Ohio, and beyond. For the early history of Massillon, see Bessie V. R. Skinner, *Massillon Once upon a Time* (Massillon, Ohio: The Independent Publishing Company, 1928), and Mrs. Barton E. Smith, *Upon These Hills: Massillon's Beginnings and Early Days* (Massillon, Ohio: DAR Chapter, 1962).

8. Louis Ziegler to HLY, June 14, 1835, MHI; Finger, "Seattle Years," 6; *Daily Post-Intelligencer*, Nov. 11, 1887; Christian Welty to HLY, Nov. 25, 1851, MHI; Hines, *History of the State*, 252; Josiah Harris to HLY, Dec. 14, 1836, WHS. Henry's transfer of affections for Barbara perhaps stemmed from his relationship with Louis Ziegler, who once remarked that he held Henry "in so high estimation" that "were the same [feeling] implanted for a female it should no doubt terminate in what is termed love" (Louis Zeigler to HLY, July 27, 1834, and June 18, 1836, MHI).

9. Josiah Harris and Tim Roath to HLY, May 8, 1837, MHI; Tim Roath to HLY, Jan. 20, 1840, MHI; and Tim Roath to HLY, May 27, 1840, WHS. None of Henry's old crowd had yet married, though they were all approaching thirty. In their letters to each other, the strength of their enduring ties is made apparent by the use of nicknames, inside jokes, and other such familiarities (Josiah Harris to HLY, Aug. 26, 1837, WHS; "Tim" and "Sophet" to HLY, May 8, 1837, MHI).

The books Tim shared with Sarah included *Don Sebastian, Sallas Rook, Romance of the Forest*, and *The Antiquary* (Tim Roath to HLY, Feb. 5, 1839, MHI).

Rev. Orrin N. Sage conducted the service (Marriage Records B124, p. 326, Stark County Courthouse, Canton, Ohio).

10. Heald, *Stark County*, 361, 419; Finger, "Seattle Years," 7, citing Hines, *History of the State*, 252; *Northwest Magazine*, Apr. 1888, sect. 6, p. 19; *John Ross vs. Henry Yesler*, Civil Cause 2103, Testimony, 138–39, Civil Cases, Stark County Courthouse, Canton, Ohio; Horace G. Brown, "History of the Charity School of Kendall, Massillon," May 13, 1905, in First Minute Book of Charity School of Kendall, 4, 6. The old Leitersburg circle was prematurely broken in 1843 when Louis Ziegler, still in his midthirties, died. Josiah attended him in his last illness, and Henry provided the funds for the quinine that proved ineffective against the fatal fever (Josiah Harris to HLY, Oct. 9, 1843, MHI).

11. Perrin, *Stark County*, 680–81. A native of Pennsylvania, McLain had been orphaned soon after his family emigrated to Ohio. He began as a blacksmith, later purchased a threshing machine company, then succeeded at several enterprises—from livery and carriages to drugs and dry goods—before becoming in-

volved in the laying of rails and the building of carshops for the Ohio & Pennsylvania Railroad, later to become the Pittsburgh, Ft. Wayne & Chicago. In the mid-1840s the McLains and the Yeslers acquired joint interest in a lot just south of the Yesler home on Muskingum and Charles streets. At most, the two families lived six blocks apart. The location of the Yesler and McLain homes is based on a letter in which Harper Partridge notes that he had moved into the Yesler home on Muskingum and Charles streets and on an 1850s map of Massillon (H. Partridge to HLY, Apr. 3, 1852, WHS; map of Massillon by F. Krause, civil engineer, published by German Deposit Bank of Massillon, ca. 1855). John McLain and Henry Yesler were never partners, either in Massillon dealings or in Henry's sawmill out west. McLain simply loaned Henry the money with which to purchase, repair, and operate his mills. See Finger's dissertation for a fuller discussion of the business dealings of these two men.

12. Harriet McLain was born in 1839, James in 1842, and Charles in 1844 (1860 U.S. Manuscript Census; Perrin, *Stark County*, 680–81; Betty [Mrs. Robert P. L.] McLain, telephone conversation with Peavy and Smith, summer 1987). No public or private records exist concerning the Yesler's infant daughter; not even a name can be found. Indeed, it is hard to establish the birth order of this baby girl and the boy, Henry George. Because Sarah Yesler's obituary implies that the girl was her firstborn, that birth order has been assumed in this chapter (Finger, "Seattle Years," 7).

The probable year of George's birth is based on cemetery records that give his death date as June 1859 and his age at that time as thirteen. Records were searched by Larry C. Steffee, superintendent of Massillon Cemetery, in 1971 at the request of John Robert Finger. No stone marks the grave, but Steffee's notes from handwritten cemetery records identify the boy buried there as Henry S. Yesler (Margy Vogt, Registrar, Massillon Museum, to Peavy and Smith, Sept. 11, 1985). The "S" cited by Steffee was likely a scripted "G," since the boy was always referred to as George and was apparently named for Sarah's brother, George Burgert (SY to HLY, Apr. 21 and July 4, 1852; HLY to SY, Jan. 8, 1858; Adam Burgert to SY and HLY, May 15, 1860; David Burgert to SY, Oct. 1, 1858, WHS).

The sawmill purchase is recorded in Henry and Sarah Yesler to Mary D. Upham, Sept. 30, 1850, Mortgage and Deed Records, vol. 46, p. 141, Stark County Courthouse, Canton, Ohio.

13. Henry and Sarah B. Yesler to Mary D. Upham, Sept. 30, 1850, Mortgage and Deed Records, vol. 46, p. 141, Stark County Courthouse, Canton, Ohio. Concerning the town lots, see the following in Mortgage and Deed Records, Stark County Courthouse: Henry and Sarah B. Yesler from Sheriff Brandon, Sept. 13, 1843, vol. 31, p. 138; Henry and Sarah B. Yesler from James and Eliza Duncan, Apr. 24, 1846, vol. 35, p. 316; Henry and Sarah B. Yesler to John Lowe, Feb. 22, 1849, vol. 44, p. 120; Henry and Sarah B. Yesler to Michael Kister, Jan. 18, 1850, vol. 45, p. 11; Henry and Sarah B. Yesler from T. R. and Jane Richmond, Oct. 22, 1845, vol. 34, p. 366.

14. Power of Attorney Citation, Apr. 1, 1851, Mortgage and Deed Records, vol. 48, p. 189, Stark County Courthouse, Canton, Ohio; J. E. McLain to HLY, Aug. 23, 1851, HLY/UW; SY to HYL, Apr. 21, 1852, MHI. As Finger ("Seattle Years," 8) has noted, Hines (*History of the State*, 252) cites New York City as Yesler's point of

departure, while A. E. Schades's "Denkschrift über Henry L. Yesler," in the *Seventh Annual Report of the Society for the History of the German in Maryland* (Baltimore: the society, 1893), 29, cites Baltimore. Wherever his point of departure, Yesler visited his mother and half-siblings in Maryland while on the East Coast (Annie B. Lowman and B. Lowman to HLY, Feb. 22, 1853, MHI).

15.   William S. Greever, *The Bonanza West: The Story of the Western Mining Rushes, 1848–1900* (Norman: University of Oklahoma Press, 1963), 30, 32.

16.   Ibid.

17.   Finger "Seattle Years," 8; *Northwest Magazine*, Apr. 1888, p. 19; see also Hines, *History of the State*, 252; Yesler Article, 271. Although Finger noted that Henry Yesler was already in Portland by April 1851, that date seems suspect, since Yesler and his wife did not sign the power of attorney document with McLain until Apr. 1, 1851. Considering that the best time for the journey from New York City to San Francisco in those days was thirty-three to thirty-five days, it is more likely that Yesler did not arrive in Portland until May 1851 (Greever, *Bonanza West*, 30).

18.   J. E. McLain to HLY, Aug. 12, 1851, HLY/UW. At one time McLain wrote that he himself was willing to invest "from three to four thousand dollars" in any project Henry thought worth the risk (J. E. McLain to HLY, Aug. 23, 1851, HLY/UW). The bids were for a twelve-horsepower engine, saw, portable mill equipment, carriage irons, extra fifty-four-inch saw, and such other incidentals as canthooks, files, wrenches, and a punch. Ultimately, the boiler came from Pittsburg, the engine from Massillon, and the mill itself from Baltimore (J. E. McLain to HYL, Aug. 23, 1851, HLY/UW; George Page & Company, Baltimore, to J. E. McLain, Aug. 11, 1851, MHI; Yesler Article, 271). McLain was largely self-educated, as the spelling, punctuation, and tone of his letters would suggest.

19.   J. E. McLain to HLY, Aug. 12, 1851, HLY/UW.

20.   Sarah's preoccupation with the possibility of going west can only be known through John McLain's letters to Henry. Only three of Sarah's letters to Henry survive from their period of separation; four letters from Henry to her are extant.

One inquirer about the West, a bachelor, noted, "Most of us are single yet but think of getting married before we go. There are more young ladies here ready to go than men to take them" (F. C. Miller to HLY, Mar. 22, 1852, WHS).

McLain refers to the Buckinses as "S. and Henrietta"; the Canes are never referred to by given names (J. E. McLain to HLY, Feb. 6 and 18, 1852, WHS).

21.   J. E. McLain to HLY, Feb. 18, 1852, WHS; SY to HLY, Apr. 21, 1852, MHI; SY to HLY, July 4, 1852, WHS.

22.   J. E. McLain, Feb. 18, 1852, WHS; SY to HLY, Apr. 21, 1852, MHI.

23.   SY to HLY, Apr. 21, 1852, MHI.

24.   Ibid.; H. Partridge to HLY, Apr. 3, 1852, WHS. Harper Partridge specialized in foundry work and wrote to ask Henry what opportunities might be available for such work in Oregon Territory.

25.   SY to HLY, Apr. 21, 1852, MHI; H. Partridge to HLY, Apr. 3, 1852, WHS.

26.   SY to HLY, Apr. 21, 1852, MHI.

27.   Yesler Article, 271.

28.   Warren H. Smith to HLY, Sept. 25, 1852, MHI; *Daily Post-Intelligencer,*

June 7, 1888; Yesler Article, 272; Finger, "Seattle Years," 11; SY to HLY, July 4, 1852, WHS.

29. SY to HLY, July 4, 1952, WHS. The four McLain children included Harriet, thirteen; James, ten; Charles, eight; and Clarence, three. In 1854, the McLains had another daughter, Mary (1860 U.S. Manuscript Census).

30. Hydropathy, or the water cure, was widely practiced in the nineteenth century, and the wet-sheet pack was the most popular water-cure process. The patient was placed on a sheet that had been dipped in cold water, wrung out, and spread over four blankets. The sheet, and each blanket in turn, was then wrapped tightly around the patient, leaving only the face exposed (Susan E. Cayleff, *Wash and Be Healed: The Water-Cure Movement and Women's Health* [Philadelphia: Temple University Press, 1987], 38; SY to HLY, July 4, 1852, WHS).

31. SY to HLY, July 4, 1852, WHS.

32. Ibid.; S. Underhill to HLY, Jan. 29, 1852, MHI; Finger, "Seattle Years," 284–85. Howard Kerr estimates that in the 1850s, one million of the nation's twenty-five million people "owed allegiance" to spiritualism (Howard Kerr, *Mediums and Spirit-Rappers and Roaring Radicals: Spiritualism in American Literature, 1850–1900* [Champaign: University of Illinois Press, 1972], 9). Noting that the spiritualist aversion to organization makes an enumeration of followers extremely difficult and that "enthusiastic supporters and alarmed detractors proposed alarming figures, all equally without basis," Ann Braude cites estimates ranging from a few hundred thousand to eleven million by the early 1890s, a time when spiritualism was on the decline (Ann Braude, *Radical Spirits: Spiritualism and Women's Rights in Nineteenth-Century America* [Boston: Beacon Press, 1989], 25).

33. SY to HLY, July 4, 1852, WHS.

34. Yesler Article, 272.

35. Hines, *History of the State*, 253; Yesler Article, 272, 275; Finger, "Seattle Years," 12–13; Annemarie Sauerlander, "Henry L. Yesler in Early Seattle," *American German Review* 26 (Feb.–Mar. 1960): 7. Although the village on Alki Point was first called New York, it later became simply Alki, an Indian word meaning "by and by"—implying that there would be a village there by and by.

36. Yesler Article, 275.

37. Ibid.; Finger, "Seattle Years," 13–15.

38. Finger, "Seattle Years," 13–15 and 22 n. 53; Thomas Stowell Phelps, "The Indian Attack on Seattle, January 26, 1856," as reprinted from "Reminiscences of Seattle, Washington Territory," *United Service Magazine* 5 (Dec. 1881): 14–15, and especially 32 for an excellent map of early Seattle.

39. SY to HLY, July 4, 1852, WHS

40. Ibid.

41. Ibid.

42. SY to HLY, Nov. 8, 1852, WHS.

43. Ibid. It is possible that most of the letters sent to Henry from Massillon during his first eighteen months in the West might have gone unclaimed at the various addresses he sent to his wife. Receiving letters from home could mean standing in long lines for several hours after the arrival of a mail shipment, and Yesler had complained that because his name began with Y he was always the

last to be called. Then, too, the vagaries of the mail often meant standing in line only to be disappointed. Impatient as he was by nature, Henry might well have neglected to take the time to wait for his mail as he moved up and down the coast (SY to HLY, July 4, 1852, WHS).

44. George Burgert to HLY, Feb. 15, 1853, MHI.

45. Once Henry began his Seattle milling venture in earnest, his letters home were infrequent and consisted mostly of notes covering pressing business matters. He was even more remiss in writing to his mother back in Maryland, not having sent her a single line since he had visited her in Leitersburg on his way to California. All her news of his travels had been secondhand, and at one point she had written Sarah to check out a rumor that Henry was dead (Annie B. and D. B. Lowman to HLY, Feb. 2, 1853, MHI).

About the time of the mill's arrival, Seattle was named the county seat of newly designated King County, and Henry Yesler was named probate clerk. Washington became a territory shortly thereafter, in March 1853 (Finger, "Seattle Years," 16; Minutes of King County Commission, Jan. 6, 1853, WHS). It was midspring before the first steam-powered mill on Puget Sound began sawing timbers (Finger, "Seattle Years," 16). Sources vary concerning the exact date on which the mill began its operation. Clarence Booth Bagley, *History of Seattle from the Earliest Settlement to the Present Time* (Chicago: n.p., 1916), 1:223; Hines, *History of the State*, 253; and Yesler Article, 273, give March as the opening date, but the *Olympia Columbian* of Apr. 9, 1853, notes that the mill was not yet operational.

46. Finger, "Seattle Years," 17, 24–25.

47. Sauerlander, "Henry L. Yesler," 7; Finger, "Seattle Years," 25; Yesler Article, 275.

48. Sauerlander, "Henry L. Yesler," 8; Finger, "Seattle Years," 17. The population figure took into account only nonnative residents.

49. Finger, "Seattle Years," 26–27. Besides developing the wharf, Yesler also established the city's first water supply system . To feed his steam-operated sawmill, he built a long, V-shaped trough from the spring-fed streams that laced the hills above the village down to his mill, cookhouse, and wharf (Finger, "Seattle Years," 134–35).

In actuality, the transcontinental railroad was not to reach Seattle for another thirty years.

50. *Olympia Pioneer and Democrat*, Feb. 17, 1855; Finger, "Seattle Years," 63.

51. Finger, "Seattle Years," 28–37; Sauerlander, "Henry L. Yesler," 9. The friendly Duwamish were among the tribes referred to as "canoe Indians" because of their marine-based culture.

52. HLY to SY, fragment ca. Jan. 1856, MHI.

53. Ibid.

54. Yesler Article, 274–76; Finger, "Seattle Years," 31–37. The stockade was one-half mile in length.

55. Finger, "Seattle Years," 37; *Pioneer and Democrat*, Sept. 5, 1856; Yesler Article, 274.

56. Sauerlander, "Henry L. Yesler," 9; *Pioneer and Democrat*, Sept. 5, 1856; Finger, "Seattle Years," 40.

57. Sauerlander, "Henry L. Yesler," 9; Finger, "Seattle Years," 192–96.

58.   Sarah's sentiments have been deduced from Henry's answer to her letter of this period. See especially HLY to SY, Aug. 22, 1857, WHS.

59.   Ibid.

60.   HLY to SY, Aug. 22, 1857, WHS. Mr. Meigs is likely G. A. Meigs, who bought out a large mill in Port Madison on the north end of Bainbridge Island (Yesler Article, 273).

61.   The contents of Sarah's letter of Nov. 14, 1857, have been deduced from Henry's letter of Jan. 8, 1858 (WHS).

62.   HLY to SY, Jan. 8, 1858, WHS. Although not all of Henry Yesler's letters to Sarah and others have been preserved, none of the extant letters approaches this one in expressing tenderness toward his son.

63.   Ibid. In allowing Sarah to have the final word on whether George would go to Seattle, Henry Yesler set himself apart from most of his contemporaries, since most men of his era headed their households in all matters—and particularly in regards to their children. For a further discussion of the authority of nineteenth-century fathers, see Carl Degler's *At Odds: Women and the Family in America From the Revolution to the Present* (New York: Oxford University Press, 1980), 78–79.

64.   HLY to SY, Jan. 8, 1858, WHS. Mr. Blinn was most likely Samuel P. Blinn, a member of the San Francisco–based firm of Adams, Blinn, & Company, parent firm to the Washington Mill Company with which Henry had entered into a loose partnership late in 1857 (Finger, "Seattle Years," 64–65, 86–88).

65.   HLY to SY, Jan. 8, 1858, WHS.

66.   HLY to SY, Jan. 22, 1858, WHS.

67.   Ibid.

68.   The presumed delay in Sarah's departure is based on the fact that she did not send a single note to her relatives back east until mid-July, yet their replies would indicate that she had written shortly after her arrival in Seattle (David Burgert to SY, Oct. 1, 1858, WHS; Amanda Burgert to SY, Oct. 3, 1858, MHI).

69.   This description of the Yesler home was based on a photo taken in 1859 (MHI, photo 1323). Regarded as the first Seattle house "of any importance," the Yesler home was located at the intersection of present-day First and James (Finger, "Seattle Years," 43; *Daily Post-Intelligencer*, Mar. 15, 1889).

70.   Greever, *Bonanza West*, 31. Aspinwall later became Colon. Begun shortly after 1849, the Panama Railroad was finished in 1855 at a cost of $6.5 million (Greever, *Bonanza West*, 34). The pleasantness of Sarah's journey was relayed in the letters she sent back east from Seattle, notably her letter of July 15, 1858, to her sister Amanda, who was spending the summer in Cleveland with Adam and Lizzie (Amanda Burgert to SY, Oct. 3, 1858, WHS). Six years earlier Henry's Pacific passage alone had consumed three weeks, the duration of Sarah's entire journey. Sarah Yesler observed her thirty-sixth birthday on the ocean somewhere between Panama and California.

71.   Louisa Goodwin to SY, Aug. 11, 1858, WHS.

72.   Dubuar Scrapbook, No. 86, Pacific Northwest Collection, University of Washington, Libraries, Seattle, p. 9; "The Mercer Expeditions" in Bagley, *History of Seattle*, 407.

73.   SY to HLY, Apr. 21, 1852, MHI. Details concerning Sarah's improvements

have been drawn from study of the 1859 photograph of Sarah and Henry on the porch of their new home.

74. Finger, "Seattle Years," 44, 89, 233; 1860 U.S. Manuscript Census.

75. Dates and contents of Sarah's letters east have been deduced from comments made by those who received them (Amanda Burgert to SY, Oct. 3, 1858, WHS; David Burgert to SY, Oct. 1, 1858, WHS).

76. Louisa M. Goodwin to SY, Aug. 29, 1858, WHS; Amanda Burgert to SY, Oct. 3, 1858, WHS.

77. David Burgert to SY, Oct. 1, 1858, WHS; Amanda Burgert to SY, Oct. 3, 1858, WHS.

78. M. A. DeVotre to SY, Apr. 8, 1859, WHS. Although only a few of Sarah Yesler's own letters are housed in the three collections upon which this chapter is based, internal evidence in the letters of her father, siblings, and friends substantiates the fact that she wrote copious letters to those from whom she was separated.

79. Elizabeth Wilson's situation has been reconstructed from a letter she wrote to Sarah in 1860; the nature of Horace's "sickliness" was revealed by his mother in a letter written early in 1861 (Elizabeth B. Wilson to SY, Mar. 29, 1860, and Jan. 28, 1861, WHS).

80. George Burgert to SY, July 18, 1858, MHI, and June 1, 1859, WHS. Lucinda Burgert, twelve years younger than Sarah, had married Jacob Hockstetter a few years earlier, and shortly after the wedding the young couple had settled in Nebraska City (David Burgert to SY, Oct. 1, 1858, WHS).

81. The date of George's death was obtained from cemetery records in Massillon. See note 12, above, this chapter (Margy Vogt, Registrar, Massillon Museum, to Peavy and Smith, Sept. 11, 1985). The details of George's final hours were written nearly a year after the fact by Adam Burgert to the Yeslers (Adam Burgert to HLY and SY, May 15, 1860, WHS). The cause of the boy's death has not been established; the illness could have been any one of the many maladies of the time.

Although the Yesler collections contain no letters from Ohio between June 1, 1859, and the following spring, speculation based on a study of Burgert family dynamics has led to the conclusion that, as patriarch of the family, David Burgert was most likely the one who first broke the news of George's death to the Yeslers. Adam's letter of May 5, 1860, makes it clear that neither he nor his wife had discussed the death before that time.

82. Sarah's sister, Amanda, who was easily seasick and terrified of water, noted she would almost brave the ocean if Sarah thought she might "stand a slim chance among so many [men]" (Amanda Burgert to SY, Oct. 3, 1858, MHI).

83. 1860 U.S. Manuscript Census; Rosa Bushnell to SY, May 12, 1861, WHS; HLY to SY, Mar. 14, 1860. Rosa Bushnell is variously referred to as both Rose and Rosa; aside from direct quotations, the authors refer to her here as Rosa.

Eliza A. Hurd married James K. Hurd on June 13, 1855; two years later, on Sept. 11, 1857, Hurd was gored to death by a wild ox (Genealogy Index, Seattle Public Library; Mrs. George E. Blankenship, ed., *Early History of Thurston County* [Olympia: n.p., 1914], 24, 28, 209, 380, 382; 1860 U.S. Manuscript Census, Thurston County, Washington Territory; Salome Woodard to SY, Mar. 17, 1860, WHS).

84. Salome Woodard to SY, Mar. 17, 1860, WHS. Salome (Mrs. H. R.) Wood-

ard is identified as Eliza Hurd DeWolf's mother in a transcript reprinted in "A Reluctant Bridegroom," Blankenship, *Early History*, 291. The psychological benefits of "the baths" often equaled or excelled their physical benefits, since water-cure establishments provided an unrestricted environment in which to meet and mingle with women friends. See Cayleff's *Wash and Be Healed*; Kathryn Kish Sklar's "All Hail to Pure Cold Water," in *Women and Health in America*, ed. Judith Leavitt (Madison: University of Wisconsin Press, 1984); and Sklar's *Catharine Beecher: A Study in American Domesticity* (New Haven, Conn.: Yale University Press, 1973), for discussion of this aspect of hydropathy establishments.

85. Elizabeth B. Wilson to SY, Mar. 29, 1860, WHS.

86. Ibid.; George Burgert to SY and HLY, May 10, 1860, WHS.

87. Adam Burgert to SY and HLY, May 15, 1860, WHS.

88. Ibid.

89. Eliza Hurd to SY, July 29, 1860, MHI.

90. Eliza Hurd to SY, July 23 and 29 and Oct. 1, 1860, MHI. To most readers in the twentieth century, Eliza Hurd's wish to "sleep with" Sarah Yesler would suggest at least latent homosexuality, but the implications of Eliza's ardent outpourings should be considered in the context of the times in which the two women lived and loved, since, as Carroll Smith-Rosenberg has observed in "The Female World of Love and Ritual," "a different kind of emotional landscape existed in the nineteenth century." Speculation on the exact nature of physical expressions of love between women is, by and large, a post-Freudian phenomenon, and written declarations of love in the diaries and letters of nineteenth-century women were apt to be less guarded than those of today. While noting that bonds between women of that era "were often physical as well as emotional" and that an "undeniably romantic and even sensual note frequently marked female relationships," Smith-Rosenberg suggests that such expressions of affection could be viewed as part of a "continuum or spectrum of affect gradations strongly affected by cultural norms and arrangements . . . . At one end of the continuum lies committed heterosexuality, at the other uncompromising homosexuality; between, a wide latitude of emotions and sexual feelings." In view of the fact that nineteenth-century culture permitted "individuals a great deal of freedom in moving across this spectrum," Smith-Rosenberg speculates that "the supposedly repressive and destructive Victorian sexual ethos may have been more flexible and responsive to the needs of particular individuals than those of the mid-twentieth century." While it is impossible to determine exactly where Sarah Yesler and Eliza Hurd would fall on the Smith-Rosenberg continuum, Eliza's letters leave no doubt about her passionate devotion and physical attraction to Sarah (Carroll Smith-Rosenberg, "The Female World of Love and Ritual" in *Disorderly Conduct: Visions of Gender in Victorian America* [New York: Alfred A. Knopf, 1985], 74, 71, 75, 76). For a fuller discussion of passionate friendships between nineteenth-century women, see not only Smith-Rosenberg but also Lillian Faderman, *Surpassing the Love of Men: Romantic Friendship and Love Between Women from the Renaissance to the Present* (New York: Morrow, 1981); Leila J. Rupp, "'Imagine My Surprise': Women's Relationships in Historical Perspective," in *Women and Health in America*, ed. Judith W. Leavitt (Madison: University of Wisconsin Press, 1984); and Blanche W. Cook, "The Historical Denial of Lesbianism," *Radical History Review* 20 (1979): 60–65. Lillian Faderman

contrasts nineteenth- and twentieth-century attitudes toward intimate friendships between women; she notes that only in the late nineteenth and early
twentieth centuries were women who loved women given the label of "female
sexual invert," a label imposing on them a set of concepts "by which they had to
scrutinize feelings that would have been seen as natural and even admirable in
earlier days" (Faderman, *Odd Girls and Twilight Lovers: A History of Lesbian Life in
Twentieth-Century America* [New York: Columbia University Press, 1991], 2).

Like other couples of their day, the Yeslers operated in separate spheres, with
Henry moving in a predominately male world of sea captains and businessmen
while Sarah made her way among her women friends. While he was quite content to allow female friends to relieve him of the responsibility of being all things
to the woman he had married and evidently found it not at all remarkable that
Sarah sought and enjoyed intimate friendships with women, he would hardly
have countenanced her seeking equally intimate friendships with men. As
Smith-Rosenberg has observed, although nineteenth-century women "wrote
unself-consciously of their passion for other women . . . [and] showed their
letters to husbands, daughters, and friends, neither they nor their families de-
fined their emotions as sexually 'unnatural'" (Smith-Rosenberg, *Disorderly Conduct*, 36).

91. Eliza Hurd to SY, July 29 and Aug. 16, 1860, MHI; Eliza Hurd and Rosa
Bushnell to SY, Aug. 19, 1860, MHI. Eliza's caretaking of Rosa is typical of that
observed in many close friendships of the era, and Smith-Rosenberg has noted
that when friends were far from their extended families, "one woman might
routinely assume the nurturing role of pseudo-mother, the other the depending
role of daughter" (Smith-Rosenberg, *Disorderly Conduct*, 67).

92. Rosa Bushnell to SY, undated (ca. Sept. 1860), MHI; Eliza Hurd to SY,
Oct. 1, 1860, WHS. Eliza Hurd was not totally dependent upon her skills as dress-
maker. According to the 1860 U.S. Manuscript Census, she had real estate and
personal property worth four thousand dollars. This wealth could have come
from an inheritance from her late husband; she was apparently also liberally
supported by her parents, with whom she maintained close ties. In any event,
she was able to travel freely, and income does not seem to have been a problem
for her.

93. 1860 U.S. Manuscript Census; Eliza Hurd to SY, July 23 and Aug. 26,
1860, MHI, and Oct. 1, 1860, WHS.

94. For seventeen years—beginning in 1872—Henry Yesler, Bailey Gatzert,
and M. R. Maddocks made New Year's Day calls on the ladies of Seattle (*Daily
Post-Intelligencer*, Dec. 18, 1892, and Jan. 27 and Apr. 20, 1893).

95. Mary Ann Burgert to SY, Aug. 12, 1860; Amanda Burgert to SY, Oct. 3,
1858; and Jan. 27, 1861, WHS.

96. Elizabeth B. Wilson to SY, Jan. 28, 1861, WHS.

97. Eliza Hurd to SY, Mar. 11, 1861, MHI; Mrs. W. D. Adams to SY, Mar. 11,
1861, MHI; G. M. Bourne to SY, Apr. 29 and May 3, 1861, MHI.

98. Sarah informed Eliza Hurd of the attacks on her character in a letter
mailed in late February (Eliza Hurd to SY, Mar. 11, 1861, MHI). While Sarah Yesler's appearance might have suggested good health, her recurrent depression
and sheer exhaustion from her civic duties made a visit to the spa an attractive
prospect. As Susan E. Cayleff notes in *Wash and Be Healed*, "For reform activists

and professional women, the live-in cures offered freedom from public scrutiny and demands, a legitimate focus on oneself as opposed to one's labors and relationships, the opportunity to commune with like-minded residents, the respite from the isolation and demands of home, the prospect of companionship and new or rejuvenated relationships, and genuine physical restoration." Further, Cayleff cites "the precious salve of female companionship" as one of the more important healing attributes of water-cure establishments (Cayleff, *Wash*, 157, 158).

While it is unlikely that any criticism noting Sarah's preference for the company of women would have carried with it the idea of sexual infidelity, lesbian activity may well have been a part of the water-cure scene. According to Cayleff, "The supportive, nurturant, and homosocial nature of the [water] cures was further enhanced by the overtly sensual and possibly sexual experiences that women encountered at the cures" (Cayleff, *Wash*, 145). While acknowledging the possibility of sexual intimacy among women who frequented water-cure establishments, Cayleff follows the lead of Leila J. Rupp, who cautions against "labeling women [as] lesbians who might violently reject the label, or, on the other hand, glossing over the significance of women's relationships by labeling them Victorian" (Rupp, "Imagine," 90–91).

Concerning Sarah's depression, see Eliza Hurd to SY, Mar. 11, 1861, MHI.

99. Eliza Hurd to SY, Mar. 11, 1861, MHI.

100. Ibid.

101. Eliza McLain to SY, May 8, 1861, WHS.

102. Ibid. Lovina "Hat" to SY, undated. Although the letter was signed "Lovina Hat," the surname is undoubtedly a contraction of Hatmaker.

103. Dr. G. M. Bourne to SY, Apr. 29 and May 3, 1861, MHI. Dr. Bourne's warnings were not without basis, for as Susan E. Cayleff has noted, traditional medicine tended to view many normal aspects of female physiology as "sickness" that warranted harsh and potentially harmful medications and treatments (See R. T. Trall, *Pathology of the Reproductive Organs: Embracing All Forms of Sexual Disorders* [Boston: Leverett Emerson, 1863], 169–70). In contrast, hydropathy stressed noninvasive treatments and urged women to become the guardians of their own health, rather than relying so heavily on physicians (see "Hydropathy, Woman's Physiology, and Her Role" in Cayleff, *Wash*, 49–74).

104. Mrs. W. P. Adams to SY, Mar. 11 (likely 1861), MHI; Rosa Bushnell to SY, May 12, 1861, MHI; W. E. Bushnell to HLY, May 12, 1861, MHI.

105. Eliza Hurd to SY, Mar. 11 and Oct. 6, 1861, MHI.

106. Mrs. O. Evans to SY, Sept. 9, 1861, WHS. The original Yesler Hall, a two-story frame building, was located on the southwest corner of Mill and Commercial Streets, present-day Yesler Way and First Avenue (Finger, "Seattle Years," 272).

107. Eliza Hurd to SY, Oct. 6, 1861, MHI. Charles DeWolf's advocation of free love was in keeping with the philosophy of many spiritualists of the time. According to Ann Braude, "Free love in the nineteenth century did not imply the principle of sexual permissiveness that the phrase suggests to the twentieth-century reader. Rather, it referred to the belief that the morality of sexual intercourse depended on freely experienced compelling mutual desire—that is, love—*not* on whether the parties were married" (Braude, *Radical Spirits*, 128).

108. Blankenship, *Early History*, 191–93; Eliza Hurd to SY, Oct. 6, 1861, MHI.

The ceremony was held on May 20, 1862, at the home of the bride's parents, and the newlyweds spent their first night there. The next morning, just as the couple was about to embark on a honeymoon cruise, the sheriff arrested them for having violated "the matrimonial law." Summarily brought before a judge, they were interrogated on all aspects of the purported marriage. When the judge asked the accused whether or not they had, indeed, consented to take each other as man and wife, they both answered in the affirmative. Triumphantly, the judge declared that their answer constituted legal vows before a legally constituted authority, and they were therefore now legally married—much to the consternation of the bride and groom themselves.

109.   Eliza Hurd DeWolf to SY, June 11, 1862, MHI. Eliza Hurd's attachments were as ephemeral as they were intense, and from the moment she met Charles DeWolfe, though she continued to avow her devotion to Sarah, her actions made it clear that her love for him had become her primary focus.

110.   Among the items Sarah Yesler ordered from George Plummer was a lady's riding saddle for herself (SY to George Plummer, Mar. 24, 1864, George Plummer Papers, Clarence Bagley Collection, University of Washington Libraries, Seattle; Sarah Yesler to George Plummer, July 27, 1865, Sarah Burgert Yesler Papers, Clarence Bagley Collection, University of Washington Libraries, Seattle; Finger, "Seattle Years," 90–95).

111.   Arriving in Seattle on May 16, 1864, the first Mercer expedition brought eleven young women to Puget Sound. The second, arriving a year later, brought several hundred women to the area (Bagley, *History of Seattle*, 1:407–18) The expeditions met with many obstacles and were only partially successful in achieving their goals.

112.   *Seattle Weekly Intelligencer*, Nov. 7, 1870; Finger, "Seattle Years," 272–75.

113.   Finger, "Seattle Years," 69–70, 146, 155, 159; *Seattle Weekly Intelligencer*, July 3, 1875.

114.   Finger, "Seattle Years," 26, 114, 275, 283.

115.   Bagley, *History of Seattle*, 2:487–88; *Olympia Transcript*, Oct. 21, 1871. See also T. A. Larson, "The Woman Suffrage Movement in Washington," *Pacific Northwest Quarterly* 67, no. 2 (Apr. 1976): 49ff. On Nov. 19, 1883, when Abigail Scott Duniway, then vice-president of the National Woman Suffrage Association, presided at a meeting in Olympia, she read a letter of support from Sarah B. Yesler, whom she identified as one of Washington Territory's largest taxpayers (*Seattle Post Intelligencer*, Nov. 21, 1883).

116.   Finger, "Seattle Years," 278–80; MHI File 115; *Seattle Times Pacific* (insert), July 25, 1982. In subsequent years, Henry Yesler continued to support Seattle's library effort, donating both land and money to the cause. In 1899, six years after Henry's death the Seattle Library rented the Yesler Mansion, from which it operated until the mansion was destroyed by fire on January 1, 1900, and twenty-five thousand volumes were lost. In 1912, the Yesler Branch of the Seattle Library Association was established at 23rd Avenue and Yesler Way (Finger, "Seattle Years," 279–82; MHI File 115).

117.   Finger, "Seattle Years," 283–84. Among those men involved in the whittling brigade were Yesler's old buddies Maddocks and Gatzert (Thomas E. Jessett, "Bishop Scott and the Episcopal Church in Washington," *Pacific Northwest Quarterly* 38 [Jan. 1947]: 16).

118.   Finger, "Seattle Years," 235–39, 284–85. About 1871, when Flora Well-man, a young piano teacher who shared the Yeslers' spiritualist leanings, sought refuge in Seattle after a quarrel with her parents back home in Massillon, the couple took her into their home and soon thereafter introduced her to Cheney. When he moved down to San Francisco, Flora followed him as lover and fellow medium, actions that gave the Yeslers no particular cause for alarm until they learned that Flora had been deserted after Cheney learned that she was expect-ing his child. Shortly after the birth of her son, Flora married widower John London, who gave the boy his name. Neither Sarah nor Henry could have guessed that a chance meeting of spiritualists gathered in their home in Seattle could have led to the liaison that resulted in the birth of novelist Jack London. For a fuller discussion of the Cheney-Wellman liaison, see *Irving Stone's Jack London* (Garden City, N.J.: Doubleday, 1977).

119.   Finger, "Seattle Years," 161–63. As part of the settlement in the lottery trial, Yesler was ordered to donate all the ticket sales to the construction of the Snoqualmie Road (ibid., 164–70; Indictment of *Territory of Washington* vs *Henry Lieter Yesler*, Grand Jury, Apr. 30, 1876, MHI File 221). According to Sarah Yesler's obituary, she made a trip back to Ohio in 1876, a crucial time in the Yesler-McLain dealings. Perhaps she went as ambassador for her husband in an attempt to stave off the lawsuit that McLain ultimately brought against Henry (Finger, "Seat-tle Years," 173; *Seattle Post-Intelligencer*, Aug. 30, 1887). In 1881, after three years of complex negotiation, Henry Yesler was able to clear the balance of his McLain debt, at that time something over fifty thousand dollars (Finger, "Seattle Years," 173–81).

120.   *Weekly Intelligencer*, Sept. 15, 1877; Finger, "Seattle Years," 35.

121.   MHI File 221, receipt from the American Hotel for month's rent of "Ho-tel's Water," Sept. 1, 1877, MHI; Finger, "Seattle Years," 343, 346. Many of Henry's legal problems stemmed from his generosity and/or naïveté. He frequently co-signed notes for friends and acquaintances less solvent than he (Finger, "Seattle Years," 287–88, 347–48).

122.   Finger, "Seattle Years," 240–41; 246–47. Yesler's law-and-order and business loyalties were mixed. When a lynch mob hanged three suspects from a board suspended between two trees in Sarah Yesler's front yard, she objected to the "desecration" of her yard, but Henry sided with the lynch mob as having struck a blow for law and order (ibid., 240–41).

123.   Ibid., 247–48.

124.   Ibid., 255–56, 259; *Seattle Post Intellingencer*, Feb. 19, 1886. The "Chinese question" was a cause of continuing tension and violence for months to come. Seattle was placed under martial law for almost two weeks in February 1886, and federal troops remained in the city until August of that year. By then almost five hundred Chinese had been forced to leave the city (ibid., 247–59).

125.   Bagley, *History of Seattle*, 2:488–89; *Seattle Times*, Dec. 18, 1950; Dec. 13, 1959; and Jan. 17, 1964; *Seattle Children's Home Yearbook*, 1927, pp. 7–8. Sarah's obituary praises her as always "thrifty," and her business dealings showed her to be one who sought earnestly to dispel the cloud of debt under which she and Henry seemed doomed to live (Finger, "Seattle Years," 346–47; *Seattle Post-In-telligencer*, Aug. 30, 1887; Dubuar Scrapbook, 7–10, Pacific Northwest Collection, University of Washington Libraries, Seattle).

Filling an entire city block, the mansion was bordered by present-day James and Jefferson streets and stood between Second and Third avenues (Richard Cardwell, MHI, to Peavy and Smith, Oct. 21, 1988; Finger, "Seattle Years," 346–47)

126. *Seattle Post-Intelligencer*, Aug. 30 and 31, 1887.

127. Ibid.

128. *Seattle Post-Intelligencer*, Aug. 30, 1887; "Seattle Years," 352–54, 358–59. J. D. Lowman, a native of Leitersburg, was the son of Henry Yesler's half-brother, Daniel S. Lowman. James Lowman defended his uncle's right to inherit all of Sarah's property and eventually succeeded in gaining for Henry all properties except for half-interest in those real estate holdings that were indisuptably in Sarah's name (Finger "Seattle Years," 352).

In addition to Henry L. Yesler, Sarah's probate listed as her survivors Elizabeth Burgert Wilson, sixty-seven, of Massillon; Adam Burgert, sixty-three, of Toledo; Catherine Burgert, sixty-one, of Toledo; Mary Ann Burgert, fifty-nine, of Toledo; George Burgert, fifty-seven, of Nebraska City; James Burgert, fifty-five, of Cleveland; Lucinda Burgert Hockstetter, fifty-three, of Nebraska City; Amos Burgert, fifty-one, of Seattle; and Amanda Burgert Hart, forty-eight, of Toledo (SY Probate 628, Abstract of Title Book, p. 33, King County Courthouse, Seattle).

129. The Pioneer Building has been restored and is today a feature of Seattle's historic Pioneer Square (Finger, "Seattle Years," 359–62).

130. Finger, "Seattle Years," 363. An "anonymous friend" wrote Henry that "the story that is going round is that you sleep with that girl you have at your house and that she has been with child by you several times and you have had it doctered away" (Anonymous Friend to HLY, Nov. 10, 1890, WHS). Whatever Seattle's opinion of Minnie Gagle before Yesler's marriage to her, his obituary treated his young widow kindly enough, describing her as one who had been "a faithful and attentive companion of his declining years" (*Seattle Post-Intelligencer*, Dec. 18, 1892).

131. Bagley, *History of Seattle*, 490–92; Finger, "Seattle Years," 289. Henry's New Year's Day outings with Bailey Gatzert and M. R. Maddocks had already ceased before his marriage to Minnie. However, up until Bailey Gatzert's death in 1893 they continued to send around calling cards containing a photograph of the three of them (Finger, "Seattle Years," 363; *Daily Post-Intelligencer*, Dec. 18, 1892, and Jan. 27 and Apr. 20, 1893).

132. *Seattle Post-Intelligencer*, Dec. 16 and 17, 1892; Finger, "Seattle Years," 364–65. According to Henry Yesler's probate, he owned $60,000 in personal property and another $60,000 in real estate. Total value of the estate was listed as greater than $500,000, with $350,000 in liabilities. His widow, Minnie G. Yesler, claimed the estate was actually worth $1.5 million and that Henry's debts amounted to only $300,000. Her estimate was borne out in an 1894 assessment of his assets (HLY Probate 1633, Henry Leiter Yesler Court Papers, University of Washington Libraries, Seattle).

133. *Seattle Post-Intelligencer*, Dec. 18, 1892; Lake View Cemetery site visit by Dr. Clarann Weinert, Oct. 29, 1992; George Nemeth, Jr., Lake View Cemetery manager, to Peavy and Smith, Oct. 9, 1992. Finger describes in some detail the litigation that followed Yesler's death, much of it centered upon whether or not there might have been a will leaving properties to the city, a plan Henry Yesler discussed quite frequently in his final years. Minnie Gagle Yesler lived on in the

Yesler mansion until 1899, when it was taken over by the Seattle Public Library (Finger, "Seattle Years," 364–69).

V
Harriet Burr Godfrey

1. Harriet Burr Godfrey (hereafter abbreviated as HG) to Ard Godfrey (hereafter abbreviated as AG), Sept. 11, 1862; Abner Godfrey to AG, Sept. 11, 1862. The Harriet Godfrey story has been reconstructed largely on the basis of letters, diaries, reminiscences, and other materials collected in the Ard Godfrey Papers that reside in the Minnesota Historical Society, Saint Paul (hereafter cited as MHS), and in the Ard Godfrey File at the Hennepin History Museum, Minneapolis (hereafter cited as HHM). In quoting these materials, the authors have chosen to retain the spelling, capitalization, and punctuation found in the original sources. Unless otherwise specified, the letters cited are found in the MHS.

2. HG to AG, Sept. 11, 1862.

3. "Brewer and Holden Families," *Bangor Historical Magazine* 6:80–81; Bangor Historical Society to Mrs. Carter Delaettre, Sept. 1, 1977; Mildred Thayer, *Brewer: Orrington Holden and Eddington History and Families* (Brewer, Maine: 150th Anniversary Committee, 1962, 51, 107; Godfrey Family Records kept by Harriet Razada Godfrey, daughter of Harriet B. and Ard Godfrey, and currently in possession of Gretchen Palen Peterson, great-granddaughter of the Godfreys. The other ten children of Joseph and Sally Proctor Burr were Joseph B., born 1798; Jonathan, 1799; Polly, 1801; William, 1804; Ann Elizabeth, 1805; Mary Eleanor, 1808; Hiram, 1810; Martha, 1813; Martha Bates, 1814; and Benjamin, 1820 (Godfrey Family Records).

Although there is no way to verify the extent of Harriet's schooling, it is likely that she had formal education at least through her midteens, since the letters that survive from her adulthood are those of a well-educated woman.

4. Georgia Ray, "Two Yankees on the Minnesota Frontier: The Shared Destiny of Ard Godfrey and John Harrington Stevens," *Hennepin County History,* Fall 1986, p. 4; Harriet Razada Godfrey, "The Diary of the First White Child Born in Minneapolis," *Minneapolis Journal,* Feb. 20, 1927, Godfrey Papers, MHS (the first of a five-part series commissioned by the *Journal* for which Harriet Razada Godfrey received four hundred dollars). The other twelve children of Ard Godfrey, Sr., and Catherine Reed Ganbert Godfrey were Cynthia, born 1802; John Reid, 1804; Diana, 1805; Covina, 1807; Louisa, 1809; Adeline, 1811; Chandler, 1815; Margaret, 1817; Alfred, 1819; Nancy, 1820; Harriet, 1822; and Esther, 1824 (Godfrey Family Records).

It is not likely that Ard Godfrey, Jr., spent many years in a classroom, for the letters he wrote in later life reveal a barely literate man.

5. Penobscot County Courthouse Records, 1834–48, Bangor, Maine. Ard was often joined in his dealings by his brothers-in-law: Temple Emery, John Jameson, Alexander Gordon, and Benjamin Burr.

6. Thayer, *Brewer,* appendix p. 139; Godfrey Family Records. Joseph Burr died on Apr. 7, 1837. Harriet's oldest brother, Joseph, Jr., almost forty, had assumed the family homestead (Bangor Historical Society to Mrs. Carter Delaettre, Sept. 1, 1977).

7. Contract between Shaw and Earle and Godfrey, Providence, Nov. 2, 1839,

Godfrey Papers, MHS; AG to HG, Oct. 12, 1839. The baby was born on Feb. 2, 1839 (Godfrey Family Records).

8. AG to HG, Oct. 12, 1839; HRG, "Diary of the First White Child," Feb. 20, 1927; AG to HG, Oct. 12, 1839.

9. Contract, Godfrey Papers, MHS; Godfrey Family Records. John Reid was born Sept. 17, 1840. Four of Ard Godfrey's siblings died in infancy or early childhood—two brothers, John Reid and Chandler, and two sisters, Covina and Esther.

10. Samuel Valentine–Ard Godfrey contracts and legal papers, Feb. 22, May 6, and Dec. 2, 1841, and Mar. 4, May 31, and June 7, 1842, Maine State Archives. Legal action included a two-thousand-dollar breach-of-contract suit brought against Ard, and the real estate attached included three lots assessed at over eleven hundred dollars; personal property was not inventoried (Record of Deeds, vol. 143, p. 68, June 7, 1842, Penobscot County Courthouse, Bangor, Maine).

11. The cause of John Reid Godfrey's death is not known. Born on Aug. 21, Laura Godfrey died on Sept. 29, 1842 (Godfrey Family Records).

12. Bankruptcy petition, Godfrey Papers; Record of Deeds, vol. 143, p. 68, Penobscot County Courthouse. Ard, Sr., died on June 13, 1843 (Godfrey Family Records). The probate of Ard Godfrey, Sr., listed thirteen pieces of real estate, including the 113-acre family homestead, with a total value of $4,000.55. The probate also listed $3,242.28 in collectible debts and $7,531.50 in personal property. The estate was left to his heirs, who, by a will drawn just two and a half weeks before his death, included his wife, his nine surviving children, and one grandchild (Ard Godfrey Probate, filed July 25, 1843, Penobscot County Courthouse, and Ard Godfrey will, dated May 27, 1843, and contained in the probate papers). Leaving their mother the 113-acre homestead, Ard and his siblings each redeemed various parcels of land from his father's estate (Record of Deeds, vol. 149, pp. 19, 39, 283, 405; vol. 150, p. 467; vol. 159, p. 43; vol. 162, p. 214, all Apr. 24, 1844, Penobscot County Courthouse).

While the records in the Bangor courthouse give the fourth Tuesday of June 1843 as the date of judgment, the archivist at the Maine State Archives, in a letter of Aug. 11, 1987, to Peavy and Smith, cited the documents for the case of *Valentine* vs. *Godfrey* as coming from the June term of 1842.

13. Godfrey Family Records; Record of Deeds, vol. 162, p. 214, and vol. 150, p. 27, Penobscot County Courthouse). Four days after her son's birth, Harriet's forty-three-year-old brother, Johnathan, a state legislator, died (Brewer and Holden Families, p. 80).

In none of Ard's fifty-nine separate land transactions at this time—from 1834 until a power of attorney filing in 1850—does Harriet's name appear on a document. Ard paid $250 for the Bradley land (Record of Deeds, vol. 170, p. 261, Penobscot County Courthouse; HG to AG, Apr. 2, 1848).

Sarah Catherine was born on June 24, 1847 (Godfrey Family Records).

14. Lucile Kane, *The Falls of St. Anthony: The Waterfall That Built Minneapolis* (Saint Paul: Minnesota Historical Society, 1987), 13–15.

15. Ibid., 16–20. Steele most likely heard of Ard through Daniel Stanchfield of Maine, who had surveyed local timber prospects for Steele (ibid., 17).

16. Helen Godfrey Berry, Reminiscences, Godfrey Papers, MHS; James Sasevich, "Godfrey House Research Summary," June 1983; Kane, *Falls*, 18, 28. The

unidentified woman died the following spring (HRG, "Diary of the First White Child," Feb. 29, 1927).

17. Berry, Reminiscences; Sasevich, "Godfrey House"; Kane, *Falls*, 18; AG to HG, Mar. 12, 1848. Located a short distance above the edge of the falls, the dam crossed the east channel of the river, running from the shore to a point twenty feet above the head of Hennepin Island and then to the foot of Nicollet Island. Approximately seven hundred feet long, sixteen feet high, forty feet wide at the base, and twelve feet wide at the top, the structure was anchored to the riverbed, and flumes were placed at intervals to admit water. Upstream behind the dam was a millpond where logs were floated until they could be sawed (Kane, *Falls*, 18).

18. HG to AG, Apr. 2, 1848; AG to HG, Mar. 12, 1848. The new Minnesota Territory was created on Mar. 3, 1849.

19. AG to HG, Mar. 12, 1848.

20. HG to AG, Apr. 2, 1848.

21. HRG, "Diary of the First White Child," Feb. 27, 1927. Helen Berry in her reminiscences says that her father had "not over one-seventh and not less than one-tenth interest in the Mill Co. business," but the terms on paper indicate a one-eighteenth interest. The firm is known both as Steele and Godfrey and the Saint Anthony Mill Company (Sasevich, "Godfrey House").

22. HRG, "Diary of the First White Child," Feb. 20, 1927. In her reminiscences, Helen Berry praised carpenters Charles Merceau and James Brisette for their diligence and craftsmanship. It is not known whether Harriet knew ahead of time of Ard's plans for the house and participated in its design or whether the house was a surprise to her when she arrived in Saint Anthony (Sasevich, "Godfrey House"). The house was never actually owned by the Godfreys; it belonged to the Saint Anthony Mill Company and was simply used by the Godfreys.

23. Steele paid Godfrey for 195 days of work, beginning on Oct. 1, 1847, and ending on Apr. 30, 1848, at five dollars per day (Sasevich, "Godfrey House"). Sarah Catherine died on Sept. 10, 1848 (Godfrey Family Records).

24. Ann Eliza Chamberlain to HG, Jan. 2, 1848.

25. Franklin Steele to AG, Oct. 11, 1848; HRG, "Diary of the First White Child," Feb. 27, 1927; Berry, Reminiscences. Harriet, Ard's youngest surviving sister, was married to Hiram Emery (Godfrey Family Records).

26. HRG, "Diary of the First White Child," Feb. 20, 1927.

27. Colonel John Rollins, another millwright, accompanied Ard on the long, arduous ride from Beloit to Saint Anthony (Berry, Reminiscences; HRG, "Diary of the First White Child," Feb. 20, 1927; Abner Godfrey, "Journey from Maine to St. Anthony in 1848," Ard Godfrey file, HHM).

28. AG to HG, Feb. 7, 1849.

29. HRG, "Diary of the First White Child," Feb. 20, 1927.

30. Ibid.; Berry, Reminiscences; HG to AG, Mar. 2, 1849; Godfrey, "Journey."

31. HRG, "Diary of the First White Child," Feb. 20, 1927. The exact date of the family's arrival has been debated. Abner's reminiscences indicate that the stage left Saint Paul at 8:30 A.M. on a Sunday in "the Latter Part of April 1849," arriving in Saint Anthony "about 2-P.M . . . Rather late for the Salt Pork and Boiled Potatoes." His sister Harriet Razada Godfrey's 1930 reminiscence claims that the family arrived in Saint Paul on Monday, Apr. 9. The *Minnesota Territorial Pioneers,*

Souvenir No. 2, 1901, p. 118, claims that the Godfreys arrived in Saint Anthony on Thursday, Apr. 12, 1849 (Godfrey, "Journey"; HRG, "Diary of the First White Child," Feb. 20, 1927; Berry, Reminiscences).

32.   The chest was alternately referred to as "the old green chest" (by Helen) and "the old blue chest" (by Harriet) in the children's later reminiscences. Helen tells the story of the contraband doll in her memoirs. Other furnishings brought by the family from Maine included an "art rug" braided by Harriet herself and a bureau made by Grandfather Burr and containing Harriet's and Ard's "love letters" (Berry, Reminiscences).

33.   Abner Godfrey to Edwin Clark, May 11, 1905, Ard Godfery File, HHM; Godfrey House tour notes; HRG, "Diary of the First White Child," Feb. 20, 1927.

34.   Ardis MacGregor, "Restoration of the Godfrey House," Part III, *Hennepin County History,* Winter 1979–80, p. 14. The crush of people arriving daily was such that a territorial census taken in mid-1849 listed 50 people—43 males and 7 females—in residence in the Godfrey's two-story, nine-room house (Sasevich, "Godfrey House"). Those 50 people represented almost one-tenth the population of Saint Anthony itself (Ray, "Two Yankees," 9). The 1849 territorial census, taken on June 11, less than two months after Harriet's arrival, showed 571 people (352 males and 219 females) in Saint Anthony.

35.   Godfrey Family Records. Supposedly, once he doffed his overalls, Zachariah Jodon never again appeared in anything but a fine suit, silk hat, and walking stick (HRG, "Diary of the First White Child," Feb. 20, 1927). Helen Berry's reminiscences list a Dr. Kingsley of Nicollet Island as attending physician, not Dr. Jodon.

36.   Berry, Reminiscences.

37.   Ibid.; HRG, "Diary of the First White Child," Feb. 27, 1927; *Minnesota Territorial Pioneers,* 118; Abner Godfrey obituary, Nov. 5, 1928, Godfrey Papers, MHS. In her reminiscences, Harriet Razada Godfrey credits schoolteacher Elizabeth Backus as having assisted Dr. Jodon in her delivery.

At one point Ard returned from his mail run to Saint Paul deathly ill with what was diagnosed as cholera, which Helen Berry later surmised to be a generic name for the prevalent fever and intestinal upset of the day.

38.   Berry, Reminiscences.

39.   Ibid. Helen Berry identifies the family only as the Slaymakers.

40.   Ibid.; Carlton Qualey, "John Wesley North and the Minnesota Frontier," *Minnesota History* 35, no. 3 (Sept. 1956): 103–104.

41.   1850 U.S. Manuscript Census (Sept. 5); Hiram Emery to AG, Oct. 20, 1851; HRG, "Diary of the First White Child," Feb. 20, 1927; Berry, Reminiscences. Helen mistakenly identifies Nicollet Island as Hennepin Island in her reminiscences. Ann Loomis North, Helen's piano teacher, was the wife of attorney John Wesley North, a prominent figure in early Minnesota politics. By the end of 1850, the Norths had moved from their Nicollet Island home to Saint Anthony proper, and Helen's piano lessons became a less adventuresome undertaking (Qualey, "John Wesley North," 101–16).

42.   Ray, "Two Yankees," 9; Berry, Reminiscences. The meeting was held on Feb. 14, 1851 (Ard Godfrey obituary, Godfrey scrapbook, MHS). HRG, "Diary of the First White Child," Feb. 27, 1927, dates it a year later, on Feb. 14, 1852. Although Harriet was later to join Eastern Star, she was never fully active in the

organization, according to her daughter's reminiscences, simply because her life was too busy to allow her to enjoy the organization's many activities (Harriet Razada Godfrey, Reminiscences, Godfrey Papers, MHS). The cost for shipping the piano from Boston to Saint Paul was twenty-seven dollars. (Berry, Reminiscences; *Minneapolis Morning Tribune,* Feb. 15, 1927, Scrapbook, Godfrey Papers, MHS; MacGregor, "Restoration," Part III, p. 15).

43. Godfrey Family Records; Kane, *Falls,* 21–24. For Mattie's birth, Harriet was tended not by Dr. Jodon or Dr. Kingsley but by Dr. John H. Murphy, who, with his young wife, had stayed briefly with the Godfreys when they first arrived in Saint Anthony (Berry, Reminiscences).

According to Berry, Reminiscences, the Godfreys held ten thousand dollars in bags of gold in the family's old green chest at one point during the negotiations for the buyout. Harriet Razada Godfrey also mentions this ten thousand dollars in gold in the chest, but she recalls that the gold was put up against the day the federal government would make the Fort Snelling land available to settlers, since it was her father's plan to buy land on the west side of the river (HRG, "Diary of the First White Child," Feb. 27, 1927).

44. Ray, "Two Yankees," 10, 12; Sasevich, "Godfrey House"; HRG, Reminiscences; *Minneapolis Journal,* Feb. 15, 1927. Although Alcy Barlow Nordeen in her article on the restoration of the Godfrey House (*Hennepin County History,* Spring-Summer 1977, p. 8) notes that Godfrey claimed 90 acres, Ray confirms 160 acres. Minnehaha Falls (*Minnehaha* means "laughing waters" in the Dakota language) were high but narrow and not always a reliable source of power, as Ard would discover (Kane, *Falls,* 38, 9).

Ard Godfrey entered into business with Charles W. Borup on June 14, 1852, renting four saws and "pond for floating logs" from Franklin Steele (Articles of Agreement between Ard Godfrey and C. W. Borup, July 14, 1852, Godfrey Papers, MHS). According to Ray, Ard Godfrey had withdrawn from his partnership with Steele in 1850 and with five other men had formed the Saint Anthony Boom Company, a rival sawmill operation that continued in business until 1856 (Ray, "Two Yankees," 10). Godfrey House Research Summary seconds the information, claiming that on Feb. 3, 1851, Ard Godfrey and five others from Saint Anthony organized the Saint Anthony Boom Company. Neither source mentions dissolution of the Steele and Godfrey entity.

45. Berry, Reminiscences; HRG, "Diary of the First White Child," Feb. 27, 1927; *Minneapolis Journal,* Feb. 15, 1927. Minneapolis at that point had a population of about three hundred people (Kane, *Falls,* 38).

46. Godfrey Family Records; HRG, "Diary of the First White Child," Feb. 20 and 27, 1927; HRG, Reminiscences; HG, Diary, Jan. 1858; Berry, Reminiscences; HG to AG, Jan. 29 and Apr. 21, 1863. Helen traveled to Bangor with her aunt, Margaret Fuller, Ard's recently widowed sister who had been visiting at Minnehaha (A. E. Chamberlain to HG, Mar. 20, 1854; HG to AG, Mar. 2, 1849). Helen was home by October 1854, according to a letter from H. B. Morgan to AG, Oct. 1, 1854. Kittie, the second Sarah Catherine Godfrey, was born Mar. 19, 1854.

47. HRG, *Minneapolis Journal,* Feb. 15, 1927.

48. 1857 Minnesota Territorial Census; HRG, "Diary of the First White Child," Feb. 27, 1927; HG, Diary, Feb., Mar., and Aug. 1858 and Apr. 1863; A. E. Chamberlain to HG, Mar. 20, 1854; Ray, "Two Yankees," 10.

Both John, who was caretaker for the mill property, and Mary Kernon were natives of Ireland; the couple had two little girls. Reuben Robinson was head millhand (1857 Minnesota Territorial Census; HRG, "Diary of the First White Child," Feb. 27, 1927).

Although Harriet generally had great fear of and antipathy toward Indians, particularly after the uprising of 1862, she found Delia Pettijohn a woman of "estimable character" (HRG, "Diary of the First White Child," Feb. 27, 1927).

Ray cites only a sawmill at Elk River, but a gristmill was also in operation (Ray, "Two Yankees," 10; Agreement, Godfrey, McMullen, and Turner, Sept. 28, 1852, Godfrey Papers, MHS).

49. Berry, Reminiscences.

50. Undated letter from A. E. Chamberlain to AG; "Brewer and Holden Families," 80; HG to A. E. Chamberlain, Jan. 17, 1858; HRG, "Diary of the First White Child," Mar. 27, 1927; HG to A. E. Chamberlain, Apr. 17, 1861. The size of the twins is especially remarkable because Harriet was a small, fine-boned woman. Harriet nursed the twins for five and a half months, weaning them on Apr. 17, 1858 (HG, Diary, Apr. 17, 1858). The housegirls are identified only as Hannah and Julia. The exact identity of "Cousin Martha" has not been established (HRG, "Diary of the First White Child," Feb. 27, 1927).

51. HRG, "Diary of the First White Child," Feb. 20, 1927; MacGregor, "Restoration," Part III, p. 16.

52. HG to A. E. Chamberlain, Jan. 17, 1858. A letter from an associate notes that Ard had heretofore accumulated a "fortune . . . [he had] a right to exult over" (Joseph Alpin to AG, July 10, 1853).

53. HG to A. E. Chamberlain, Apr. 17, 1861. The laborers living in the Godfrey household were Lewis Meeker, twenty-seven, of Ohio; Henry Curry, twenty-five, a British immigrant; John Hanson, twenty-one, a millman from Nova Scotia; and Peter Hadenburg, twenty-seven, a teamster from Germany (1860 U.S. Manuscript Census). Louis Meeker (although he appears as "Lewis" on the census, Meeker always signed himself "Louis") became a close family friend, and his Civil War letters are included in the Godfrey Papers.

54. HRG, "Diary of the First White Child," Feb. 27, 1927; Ard Godfrey obituary, Godfrey Papers.

55. Ard Godfrey obituary, Godfrey Papers; HRG, "Diary of the First White Child," Feb. 27 and Mar. 30, 1927; AG to HG, July 5, 1862. The Salmon River strikes were in the panhandle of present-day Idaho; the region became a part of Idaho Territory on Mar. 3, 1863, nearly a year after Ard Godfrey left Minnesota.

56. HRG, "Diary of the First White Child," Feb. 27 and Mar. 30, 1927. In January 1862 Congress approved the expenditure of $25,000 for the protection of emigration to California, Oregon, and Washington. The 130 members of the 1862 expedition—117 men and 13 women—traveled in a total of fifty-three wagons (Helen McCann White, ed., *Ho! For the Gold Fields: Northern Overland Wagon Trains of the 1860s* [Saint Paul: Minnesota Historical Society Press, 1966], 26, 31).

57. Helen Godfrey to AG, June 6, 1862. According to Harriet R. Godfrey's reminiscences, her mother was left with sixty dollars in cash (HRG, "Diary of the First White Child," Feb. 27, 1927). Helen had taught the previous term in "Mr. Bartlett's district," according to a letter from a niece of Ard's (Niece Emery to AG, July 12, 1861).

58. AG to HG, July 5, 1862. An excellent treatment of the Fisk Expedition of 1862 is found in White, *Ho! For the Gold Fields.*

59. Abner Godfrey to AG, Sept. 11, 1862; Helen Godfrey to AG, June 29, Sept. 1, and Oct. 26, 1862, and Jan. 28, 1863.

60. AG to HG, Aug. 10 and Sept. 8, 1862. The uprising has become known as the Dakota Conflict of 1862. Total fatalities during the uprising amounted to somewhere between 457 and 500 whites, both civilian and military. The number of Dakota lives lost is harder to determine, though later testimony by Indians themselves put the number at twenty-one. To that number must be added the lives of the thirty-eight Indians who were hanged at Mankato on Dec. 26, 1862, by order of President Lincoln (Kenneth Carley, *The Sioux Uprising of 1862* [Saint Paul: Minnesota Historical Society Press, 1979], 1–5, 68–75).

61. HG to AG, Sept. 11, 1862; Abner Godfrey to AG, Sept. 11, 1862; AG to HG, Aug. 10, 1862. Harriet's old neighbors, the Pettijohns, lost almost all their possessions in the wake of the uprising (HG to AG, undated; Helen Godfrey to AG, Jan. 28, 1863). By Ard's account, they had seen a total of twenty-six Indians, who, had they been "all together wod have be[en] ugly if thay daired to . . . try to steal from us."

62. AG to HG, Aug. 10, 1862.

63. HG to AG, June 29, 1862; Helen Godfrey to AG, Oct. 14, 1862. A Mr. Woodbridge held the Minnehaha mortgage (HG to AG, Sept. 11, 1862; Helen Godfrey to AG, Oct. 14, 1862, and Jan. 28, 1863).

64. Helen Godfrey to AG, Oct. 14 and Dec. 20, 1862. Having been promised $81.00 for "five or six days" work, Abner received only $24.50.

65. Helen Godfrey to AG, Oct. 26 and Dec. 20, 1862; Louis Meeker to Godfrey Family, Dec. 20, 1861, and Jan. 17, Feb. 20, Apr. 14, May 12, and June 29, 1862; HG to AG, Oct. 26, 1862. On Sept. 22, after the Union victory at Antietam, Abraham Lincoln issued the preliminary version of the Emancipation Proclamation (Richard T. Current, T. Harry Williams, Frank Freidel, and Alan Brinbley, *American History: A Survey*, 7th ed. [New York: Knopf, 1862], 410).

66. Helen Godfrey to AG, Oct. 14, 1862. Over the fourteen months of Ard's absence, the Godfrey family was kept in tenuous touch through the exchange of letters, none of which ever reached their destination in less than six weeks and some of which never reached their destination at all. The letters from Minnehaha that carried family news out to the frontier were generally written on a Sunday afternoon and sent off about every two weeks (Helen Godfrey to AG, Oct. 16 and Dec. 20, 1862). Twelve of Harriet's and eleven of the children's letters to Ard survive. Helen's letters contain even more details on business and family affairs than do her mother's. Abner, Hattie, and Mattie usually added notes to the back pages of their mother's letters, though sometimes Harriet finished a letter one of her younger children had started. The family recorded the arrival of each of Ard's letters, and the eleven extant letters represent the sum total of his correspondence with his family during the fourteen months of his absence. Ard's letters are those of a taciturn man, brief but warm and filled as often with questions about things at home as with descriptions of the scenes in which he moved. All letters cited here reside in the Godfrey Papers, MHS.

67. HG to AG, Oct. 26, 1862. A part of Washington Territory at the time Ard Godfrey arrived there in 1862, the Beaverhead Mining District became a part of

Idaho Territory on Mar. 3, 1863, and a part of newly designated Montana Territory on May 26, 1864.

68.   Helen Godfrey to AG, Oct. 27, 1862, and Jan. 28, 1863.

69.   AG to HG, Nov. 3, 1862. Bannack was, by Ard's reckoning, some 300 miles from Salt Lake City and about the same distance from Fort Benton, the head of Missouri River navigation. In actuality, Bannack was about 250 miles from Fort Benton and about 360 from Salt Lake. Now a ghost town, Bannack is located just southwest of Dillon, Mont.

70.   AG to HG, Dec. 13, 1862.

71.   Helen Godfrey to AG, Jan. 28, 1863; HG to AG, undated.

72.   AG to HG, Dec. 13, 1862.

73.   Helen Godfrey to AG, Oct. 14 and Dec. 20, 1862; 1860 U.S. Manuscript Census.

74.   Helen Godfrey to AG, Dec. 20, 1862, and Jan. 28, 1863; HG to AG, undated.

75.   Ibid.; Helen Godfrey to AG, Jan. 25, 1863; HG to AG, Feb. 15, 1863. Although there is no record of the dissolution of Borup & Godfrey, in 1853, a year after the formation of the firm, Ard Godfrey was already negotiating to sell a half-interest in the dam and the sawmill on Minnehaha Creek to William Sibley for four thousand dollars. The Sibley venture fell through, but it probably marks the beginning of the end of Borup & Godfrey (Articles of Agreement between AG and William C. Sibley, July 20, 1853; Sibley to AG, Aug. 3, 1853). There is no record of the exact date when the suit against Charles Borup was brought or of what was at issue in the suit.

76.   HG to AG, undated; Helen Godfrey to AG, Jan. 25, 1863.

77.   Mattie Godfrey to AG, undated; Helen Godfrey to AG, Jan. 28, 1863; HG to AG, Jan. 29, 1863; Abner Godfrey to AG, Jan. 25, 1863. Abner's own letters to his father never mention his dream of going west. Ard noted that "it was all a divine Providane" that he had left home when he did, since Abner might otherwise have been drafted and "wee wood have had moor to worrey about then wee now have . . . wee had beter be sepperate a short time then risk the loss of our only son that appears so prommising to us" (AG to HG, Mar. 22, 1863).

Helen too wrote her father that business had "never been so brisk as now since 1856. . . . Merchants are prospering" (Helen Godfrey to AG, Jan. 28, 1863).

78.   HG to AG, undated, but confirmed from Helen's letter to be written on Jan. 25, 1863.

79.   Helen Godfrey to AG, Jan. 28, 1863; Abner Godfrey to AG, Jan. 25, 1863; HG to AG, Mar. 22, 1863.

80.   HG to AG, undated; HG to AG, Mar. 22, 1863.

81.   HG to AG, Mar. 8 and Apr. 12, 1863.

82.   HG to AG, Mar. 22 and Apr. 12, 1863.

83.   AG to HG, Mar. 21 and 22, 1863. Godfrey felled the timbers for the mill on the neighboring mountainsides and dragged them to the mill site. His circular saw, a saw that would have cost him about six dollars at home in Minnesota, had been packed by train from Salt Lake City at a total cost of fifty dollars (HRG, "Diary of the First White Child," Mar. 6, 1927).

84.   Helen Godfrey to AG, Jan. 28, 1863; HG to AG, Jan. 29, 1863. Little Crow was a leader of the Dakota Sioux.

85.   HG to AG, Feb. 15, 1863. Harriet's letters are filled with references to God as guardian of all.

86.   HRG, "Diary of the First White Child," Mar. 13, 1927.

87.   AG to HG, May 10 and 26, 1863. Harriet had done her part in reducing the mortgage on the Minnehaha property by applying to that debt the five hundred dollars she had obtained from the sale of the Elk River mill (AG to HG, May 10, 1863). Although it is not known exactly how much Ard brought home from his trip to the gold country, his fellow miners obviously perceived him to be a success. In a letter written shortly after Ard's departure from Montana, a friend wrote him: "You were fortunate in selling out your mill interest as you did as the water is again as low as ever it was" (N. P. Langford to AG, June 16, 1863).

88.   HRG, "Diary of the First White Child," Mar. 13 and 20, 1927. The wisdom of Ard's decision to return to Fort Benton with the riverboat was confirmed when on the trip back downriver, members of the ship's company who had been sent ashore to gather fuel were waylaid by a party of Indians very near the spot where Ard had abandoned his flatboat. In the two-hour battle that followed, one of the ship's company fell to Indian arrows, and seventy-five Indians were reportedly killed or injured (HRG, "Diary of the First White Child," Mar. 13, 1927).

89.   HRG, "Diary of the First White Child," Mar. 20, 1927. Ard and Harriet journeyed to Industriana, present-day Brooklyn Center, to find a Mrs. Dumply, whose husband had sent money home from Bannack. "Dumply" may be a miswriting of "Dunphy," since an Elijah Dunphy of Saint Anthony had gone west with Ard on the 1862 Fisk expedition (White, *Ho! For the Gold Fields*, 265).

90.   Ray, "Two Yankees," 12–14; HRG, "Diary of the First White Child," Mar. 20, 1927.

91.   HRG, "Diary of the First White Child," Mar. 20, 1927. New Orleans was actually captured by Union forces in April 1862 and held securely through the end of the war (Current et al., *American History*, 422–23).

92.   The Godfrey girls attended Union School (HRG, "Diary of the First White Child," Mar. 20, 1927).

93.   Godfrey Family Records; HRG, "Diary of the First White Child," Mar. 20, 1927; "To Preserve Ard Godfrey House," *Minneapolis Times*, July 1, 1905. The child was born on Feb. 3, 1866 (Godfrey Family Records).

94.   HRG, "Diary of the First White Child," Mar. 20, 1927; Godfrey Family Records.

95.   HRG, "Diary of the First White Child," Mar. 20, 1927. Horace Shepley Godfrey was born on July 15, 1867, and Eugene Harlan Godfrey on Sept. 4, 1869 (Godfrey Family Records). In the next four years, Abner and Viola had two more children, a daughter and son, both of whom died in infancy. Hiram Godfrey Berry was born on Jan. 29, 1869, and died in August 1869.(Godfrey Family History, Ard Godfrey File, HHM). In the course of the next seven years, Helen had two more children, David Mark, born in Feb. 1872, and Vida Helen, born in Jan. 1876.

96.   HRG, "Diary of the First White Child," Mar. 20 and 27, 1927; Ray, "Two Yankees," 14.

97.   Ray, "Two Yankees," 13; Scrapbook, Martha Annie Godfrey obituary, Nov. 13, 1919, Godfrey Papers; HRG, "Diary of the First White Child," Mar. 27, 1927. Minneapolis and Saint Anthony were consolidated on April 9, 1872 (Kane, *Falls*, 77). Mattie's obituary identifies the buyer of the mills only as a man from

New Jersey; the sale price is not known. Simultaneous with the sale of the mills, Harriet and Ard also sold twenty of the Minnehaha acres to Gidron and Margaret Walker of Hennepin County for five thousand dollars (Deed Book 30, p. 315, Hennepin County Courthouse, Minneapolis, Minn.; It is not known what use the Godfreys made of the house or who managed the farm once they moved to town. Ard Godfrey's obituary (1894) lists 3247 Chicago Avenue as his home address.

    98.   Kittie married John Osborne on Mar. 30, 1880, at age twenty-nine, and a year later she gave birth to a son, John Godfrey Osborne (Godfrey Family Records). At twenty-five, twin Mary Godfrey married Charles Parsons on May 9, 1883, and moved with him to Milwaukee, where they raised four children (Godfrey Family Records). Thirty-three-year-old Mattie wed Jotham P. Bonnell on June 3, 1885, in a marriage her parents disapproved of. Mattie had no children and divorced Bonnell in 1891, resuming her family name. The basis of the Godfreys' objections to the marriage is not known, but a codicil in Ard Godfrey's will specified that in the event that Mattie survived both her parents, she was not to claim her inheritance until the death or divorce of her husband (Probate File 4730, Hennepin County Courthouse, *Martha Annie Bonnell* vs. *Jotham Bonnell*, Hennepin County District Court File 50022). In the last of the Godfrey weddings, twin Minnie married Daniel Webster Ham on July 28, 1886. Remaining in Minneapolis, the Hams had three children: Newell, Helen, and Marguerite (Godfrey Family Records).

    Abner and Viola Godfrey lost three of their five children: Ardie, who died of diphtheria at age six in the summer of 1872; Robin, the Godfreys' first granddaughter, who died at age four months in 1872; and Guy, who died at eleven months of age in 1873. Helen and Mark Berry lost their first-born, Hiram, at age seven months in 1869; and Minnie and Daniel Ham lost four-year-old Newell in 1892. All the Godfrey granchildren were buried in the family plot in Lakewood Cemetery, Minneapolis (Godfrey Family Records; Lakewood Cemetery Records).

    Although Kittie's husband, John Osborne, eventually remarried, he is buried alongside Kittie at Lakewood Cemetery (Lakewood Cemetery Records; Ard Godfrey will, Godfrey Papers; Gretchen Palen Peterson to Peavy and Smith, July 11, 1991).

    99.   Deed Records, Bk. 246, p. 543, Hennepin County Courthouse. Harriet Godfrey's trip east in the summer of 1872 was her first visit to Maine since she had moved to Minnesota Territory twenty-three years earlier (HG, Diary, June–Sept. 1872). It was during that sojourn that Harriet and Ard heard of the death of Ardie Godfrey, their six-year-old grandson. While it is not known exactly when Helen and Mark Berry moved to California, their letters from the West Coast date from the 1880s.

    The Godfreys donated ten thousand dollars of the sixty-thousand-dollar selling price for the Minnehaha house to the Soldier's Home fund. Today Minnehaha Park is located on the site of the family homestead (Nordeen, "Restoration," Part I, p. 8).

    100.   HG, Diary, Feb. 17 and Sept. 20, 1890.

    101.   According to probate papers, Ard held real estate valued at $20,000, mortages and notes worth $22,025, and personal property valued at $300 (Probate File 4730, Hennepin County Courthouse).

    102.   HRG, Diary, May 8, 1896. The City Directory of Minneapolis, 1895, shows

Harriet still living at 3247 Chicago Avenue, with Hattie and Mattie also residing in the home. Abner and Viola and the boys lived at 2623 Chicago Avenue in 1895.

103. HRG, Diary, June 24, 26, and 29, 1896. As he had for his grandfather, Eugene Godfrey served as the executor of Harriet's estate, in which her six surviving children and John Osborne, Kittie's fifteen-year-old son, shared equally. Valued at $33,520, the estate consisted almost entirely of real estate. Household goods and furniture were valued at $100; the balance of the personal goods comprised a canopy-top carriage, a jump-seat cutter, and an upright piano and stool. Eugene Godfrey was named guardian for John Osborne, a minor (Harriet N. Godfrey Probate File 5276, Hennepin County Courthouse).

Helen Godfrey Berry died at age sixty-three on March 27, 1902, in Los Angeles (Godfrey Family Records). On Nov. 13, 1919, after an eleven-month illness, sixty-eight-year-old Martha Annie died at 3045 Harriet Avenue, where she lived with her sister Harriet and brother Abner (Godfrey Family Records). Her obituary referred to her only as Godfrey and made no mention of the marriage to Bonnell. She was interred in the family plot at Lakewood Cemetery (Scrapbook, Godfrey Papers). Abner Godfrey, beloved great-uncle to a new generation of Godfrey children, died on Nov. 5, 1928, at age eighty-five. (Palen interview, HHM; scrapbook, Godfrey Papers; Godfrey Family Record). Mary Godfrey Parsons, age seventy-five years, died on Mar. 22, 1932. Her twin, Minnie Godfrey Ham, died on Tuesday, Apr. 30, 1935, at age seventy-eight. Harriet Razada Godfrey, aged ninety-three years, having survived all her siblings, died in Minneapolis on Feb. 16, 1943.

After a long history of neglect and nebulous plans for restoration, the Godfrey House was finally rescued from decay by the Minneapolis Women's Club, which, in 1975, brought together a coalition of the Minneapolis Building and Trades Council, the Minneapolis Parks and Recreation Board, and the Minnesota Historical Society to restore the old house, which then rested in its fifth location. Originally conceived by the Women's Club as a bicentennial project, the restoration took the major part of four years, with the house opening to the public on Memorial Day, 1979. A kitchen was added in 1985 (Carol McPheeters to Peavy and Smith, Apr. 17, 1991). The Godfrey House is located in Richard Chute Square at the intersection of Central Avenue and University Avenue N.E., Minneapolis, about a block from its original location (see Nordeen, "Restoration," 3–15, and MacGregor, "Restoration," Part III, pp. 13–22, and Part IV, pp. 17–22).

VI
Emma Stratton Christie

1. David B. Christie (hereafter abbreviated as DC) to Emma Stratton Christie (hereafter abbreviated as EC), Sept. 23, 1885. Emma and David's story has been reconstructed largely from letters and other materials in the David B. Christie and Family Papers and the James C. Christie and Family Papers, two collections that comprise more than thirty-five linear feet in the Minnesota Historical Society archives in Saint Paul (hereafter cited as MHS). Unless otherwise noted, all letters cited come from these two collections. In quoting these materials, the authors have chosen to retain the spelling, capitalization, and punctuation found in the original sources.

2. Ibid.

3. Clyman is about forty miles northwest of Milwaukee.

James Stratton also had four children by his first wife, Nancy Lofsee (Christie family records in possession of Ina Christie Denton of Bozeman, Mont., granddaughter of David and Emma Christie).

4. Emma's brothers Martin and John and half-brother Albert also owned property in the township. Ellen, seven years older than Emma, had married Allen Merrell (1865 Minnesota State Census; Christie family records).

5. Eliza Christie died on Aug. 30, 1850, and James Christie married Persis Noyes in 1853, according to Dela Koch Rider and Ina Christie Denton, eds., *History of the Families of David & Emma Christie,* 2. Hereafter referred to as the Christie Family History, this 202-page book was privately published by the Christie family in 1975. A copy resides in the MHS archives. For an overview of James Christie's life, see Bonnie Palmquist, "The Journey to Canaan: Letters of the Christie Family." M.A. thesis, Hamline University, 1990.

6. Alexander Christie (hereafter abbreviated as AC) to Sarah Christie (hereafter abbreviated as SC), July 13, 1870; 1870 U.S. Manuscript Census; 1875 Minnesota State Census.

7. Warranty Deed, Book V, p. 376, Nov. 28, 1870, Blue Earth County Courthouse, Mankato, Minn.; DC to SC, Mar. 25, 1872, and Dec. 6, 1874; Christie Family History, 5; DC to AC, May 15, 1872. The origins of Sarah Christie's financial problems are unknown, though they were to affect her parents' and brothers' financial situation for years to come. Sarah had given up teaching and had set up a dressmaking shop in Beloit, where her brother Tom was studying. Failing at that enterprise, she had resumed her teaching career, yet had fallen even further into debt. Ascribing her great-aunt's financial problems at least in part to "careless management and openhanded ways of living," Jean Christie implies that Tom was prodigal as well and that to some degree Sarah supported him financially during his Beloit days. Even so, Jean Christie concludes that "how [Sarah] came to owe large sums remains mysterious" and does not dismiss Sandy's suspicion that she may have been the victim of blackmail (Jean Christie, "Sarah Christie Stevens, Schoolwoman," in *Minnesota History,* Summer 1983, pp. 247–48).

8. James Christie (hereafter abbreviated as JC) to SC, Aug. 12, 1874; JC to AC, Aug. 16, 1874. Jamie's fatal illness was in all likelihood some form of meningitis.

9. AC to DC, Aug. 23, 1874; DC to SC, Jan. 3, 1872; Sept. 12, 1874; and Mar. 31; Apr. 14, and June 27, 1875; Data sheets from David Christie Papers, MHS. The fraudulent note was in the amount of three hundred dollars (DC to SC, Sept. 27, 1874).

10. DC to AC, Nov. 23, 1876, and Jan. 14, 1877.

11. DC to AC, June 26, 1877; Sarah Christie Stevens (hereafter abbreviated as SCS) to DC, July 10, 1884.

12. DC to AC, July 28 and Oct. 9, 1877, and Jan. 16 and Feb. 26, 1878; AC to DC, Jan. 27, 1878.

13. Christie Family History, 5; DC to AC, Jan. 16, 1881.

14. The scene was described fully by Sarah in a letter to brother Sandy: "Dave's house burned down yesterday—went like a tinder box. . . . Emma saw the fire too late to do ANYTHING toward saving the house . . . roof all aflame

around chimney & spreading in all directions with the greatest rapidity. Thermometer at about 6 above and a north wind. . . . [Had the wind been] from any other direction would have wiped out woodpile, straw, granary, hay & slabling ALL would have gone." The Christies carried insurance and figured to have about $150 to replace their home (SCS to AC, Jan. 29, 1881).

15. DC to AC, Apr. 1, Aug. 14, and Sept. 25, 1881; and Feb. 25, 1882.

16. DC to AC, Sept. 25 and Dec. 21, 1881; DC to SCS, May 15, 1832. Sarah Christie, thirty-five years old, had married William Stevens, age fifty-four, on Jan. 30, 1879 (Christie, "Sarah Christie Stevens," 248).

17. DC to SCS, May 15, 1882.

18. DC to SCS, May 26, 1882; AC to DC, Aug. 29, 1882; DC to AC, Oct. 11 and Nov. 11, 1882. David needed only a small loan, he wrote Sandy, since he still hoped to earn some money before leaving the West. His itinerary for the trip home included plans to stop in Denver to see the "great Exposition" (DC to AC, Aug. 31, 1882).

19. DC to AC, Nov. 11, 1882. At about this same time, David, who had been involved in various ways in board activities for School 79 near the center of Rapidan Township, asked Sandy for a loan of $16.13 to repay money he had borrowed from the school to use on his own debts. He needed to square up his account so he could resign his office as treasurer in good standing before his move to Montana (DC to AC, Feb. 21, 1883).

20. DC to AC, May 4, 1883.

21. Ina Christie Denton and Lawrence G. Christie of Bozeman, Mont., grandchildren of David and Emma Christie, to Peavy and Smith, August 1983.

22. DC to Frank Stevens, Aug. 4, 1883; EC to AC, June 4, 1883. Mail service was highly reliable and relatively prompt; Emma often received letters from Montana within four days of David's having posted them. Although occasional letters were lost or delayed in transit, for the most part correspondence was regular and steady, and the life of the Christie family at home in Blue Earth County was largely orchestrated by David from his distant command post. Twenty-four letters from David to Emma survive in the Christie archival collections, and five of hers to him. Because of the close relationship between David and his brother Sandy, as much of the family situation is revealed in letters exchanged by David and Sandy as in the letters exchanged by David and Emma.

23. EC to AC, June 4, 1883. Glenda Riley's "'Not Gainfully Employed': Women on the Iowa Frontier 1833–1870," *Pacific Historical Review,* May 1980, pp. 237–64, provides an excellent overview of women's use of resources. See note 51 in chapter 3, this volume.

24. DC to AC, Sept. 13, and Oct. 25, 1883; EC to AC, Sept. 30, 1883. At this point Stevens held four separate notes from David, which totaled $470 (AC to DC, Oct. 21, 1883).

25. SCS to AC, Oct. 15, 1883; AC to DC, Oct. 21, 1883; DC to EC, Oct. 25, 1883.

26. DC to EC, Oct. 25, 1883; DC to AC, Oct. 25, 1883. The baby was born on Oct. 25, 1883 (Christie Family History, 5).

27. DC to AC, Nov. 7, 1883, and Mar. 16, 1884; Carl A. Matzke to David Christie and wife, Warranty Deed, Deed Book 28, p. 356, Blue Earth County Courthouse, Mankato, Minn. Despite the honor of having the child named for him, William Stevens chose not to extend the Christies' note that had come due.

Sandy, having finished his education, was working for the U.S. Coastal Survey out of Washington, D.C. Tom, a graduate of Andover Seminary and an ordained Congregationalist minister, was on a mission assignment in Turkey, where he was to live and work for the next forty years, serving part of that time as president of Saint Paul's Insitute in Tarsus (Palmquist, "Journey to Canaan," 66, 69; Thomas Christie to AC, Mar. 9, 1890). A howling March blizzard that spring of 1884 made David and Emma newly mindful of their obligation to his parents. When Blue Earth County became virtually snowbound, David, Emma, and all the boys moved in with the old couple for a while rather than leave them alone during the storm (DC to AC, Mar. 3, 1884).

On Nov. 21, 1883, Carl August Matzke paid David Christie two thousand dollars for David's portion of the Christie quarter section, granting an easement "wide enough for teams" for passage onto James Christie's portion of the land "during [James's] natural life only" (Carl A. Matzke to David Christie and wife, Warranty Deed, Deed Book 28, p. 356 Blue Earth County Courthouse).

28.   DC to Uncle William Christie, Feb. 18, 1884; DC to AC, Feb. 7 and Mar. 3, 1884.

29.   DC to AC, Mar. 28, 1884.

30.   DC to AC, Apr. 21, 1884.

31.   DC to AC, Apr. 18, 1884.

32.   1885 Minnesota State Manuscript Census; DC to AC, May 2, 1884.

33.   DC to AC, May 2, 1884.

34.   DC to EC, May 15 and 21 and June 12, 1884.

35.   EC to DC, July 9, 1884; DC to EC, June 29, 1884.

36.   EC to DC, July 9 and 18, 1884; DC to EC, July 18, 1884.

37.   EC to DC, June 18, 1884; DC to EC, June 18, 1884; DC to son Sandy Christie, July 3, 1884.

38.   DC to EC, June 18 and 29, 1884.

39.   EC to DC, June 18 and 20, 1884.

40.   DC to EC, June 12 and 18, 1884.

41.   Ibid.

42.   DC to EC, June 18, 1884.

43.   EC to DC, June 18 and 20, 1884.

44.   EC to DC, June 20 and 29, 1884.

45.   EC to DC, June 18 and July 9, 1884. Born in 1835, Emma's half-brother, Albert Stratton, was the last child of James Stratton and his first wife, Nancy. Albert had come to Blue Earth County at the same time his father had in the early 1860s (1865 Minnesota State Census).

Emma also did sewing for Persis, making a dress and two aprons for her mother-in-law that summer.

46.   EC to DC, July 9, 1884. Mankato was the county seat and market center some three miles north of the Christie farm. DC to JC, July 28, 1884; DC to EC, Aug. 1, 1884.

47.   DC to EC, Aug. 2, 1884.

48.   AC to DC, Aug. 23, 1884.

49.   DC to EC, Aug. 11 and 25, 1884.

50.   It cannot be known for certain where the Christies spent the fall and winter of 1885–86, but in late August, Emma had noted in a letter to David that

"Will ward is fixing the chimly i shall have the stove set up in here then," phrasing that would tend to indicate that some sort of work was being done to turn the granary into temporary housing (EC to DC, Aug. 22, 1885).

51. DC to AC, June 16, 1885.

52. Christie Family History, 5; DC to EC, Aug. 12 and 15, 1885.

53. DC to EC, Aug. 19, 1885. The James Proffits, members of a nonpolygamous Mormon sect, had moved to Bridger Canyon from Johnson County, Mo. (Ina Christie Denton interview with Peavy, Apr. 1978).

54. DC to EC, Sept. 11 and 16, 1885; DC to SCS, Sept. 13, 1885.

55. DC to EC, Aug. 29 and Sept. 11, 1885.

56. AC to DC, Oct. 8, 1885; DC to EC, Aug. 29 and Sept. 11 and 16, 1885.

57. DC to EC, Sept. 16, 1885.

58. DC to EC, Sept. 23, 1885.

59. Ibid.

60. Ibid. Emma's machine was an "improved" Wheeler and Wilson No. 7 with a straight needle (DC to SCS, Apr. 28, 1887).

61. DC to EC, Sept. 23, 1885. Children aged five to twelve were charged half fare.

62. Ibid.

63. DC to SCS, Oct. 14, 1885.

64. DC to SCS, Oct. 15 and 30, 1885.

65. DC to SCS, Oct. 14, 1885; DC to JC, Nov. 11, 1885. While Stratton's own house may have been far enough along to allow him to move into it and bequeath his homesteader's shack to the Christies, it is equally possible that he and the Christies all spent the winter of 1885–86 in that shack.

66. DC to JC, Nov. 17 and 23, 1885.

67. DC to JC, Nov. 17 and 23 and Dec. 6, 1885; DC to SCS, Apr. 18, 1886. Cattle were scarce and expensive that season, and it was not until December that David found a cow he could afford: she was fourteen years old and cost him sixty dollars (DC to JC, Dec. 6, 1885). The increased dimensions of the new house were cited in a letter from David to his father late in 1885 (DC to JC, Dec. 6, 1885).

68. AC to DC, May 6, 1886; Telegram, SCS to DC, June 3, 1886; DC to SCS, Oct. 4, 1886.

69. A. J. Stratton to DC and EC, Aug. 29, 1886; Ellen Stratton Merrel to EC, Sept. 5, 1886, and undated; SCS to DC, Jan. 27, 1887; Donald Christie to SCS, Jan. 28, 1887.

70. DC to SCS, Sept. 5 and 25, 1887.

71. DC to SCS, Sept. 27, 1887.

72. Christie Family History, 5; SCS to DC, Nov. 5, 1887; JC to DC, Dec. 8, 1887. The glass on little Jamie's picture had broken during the train trip, but the picture itself had been saved (DC to JC, Nov. 10, 1885).

73. DC to SCS, Sept. 16, 1888. David always took along one of the younger boys to open and close all the gates that lay between his home in Bridger Canyon and the mining towns on Trail Creek (DC to SCS, Sept. 16, 1888; Lawrence Christie interview with Peavy, Apr. 1978).

74. James Christie died on Jan. 13, 1890 (Christie Family History, 2). Homestead Certificate 682, Aug. 4, 1891; Marie Christie of Bozeman, Mont., to Peavy and Smith, July 14, 1992).

According to the Homestead Act of 1862, to qualify for a patent that transfered ownership of up to 160 acres for the payment of a filing fee of about twenty dollars, the homesteader had to be twenty-one years of age (or the head of a family) and a citizen of the United States (or in the process of becoming a citizen). After an initial filing of intention, the homesteader had to "prove up" over a five-year period of time—that is, establish residence and cultivate and improve the land claimed—before the final patent was granted (Paul Gates, *History of Public Land Law Development* [Washington, D.C.: Public Land Law Review Commission, 1968], 245).

75.   DC to SCS, Nov. 16, 1890. Robert Allen, a red-haired, blue-eyed baby, weighed eleven pounds at birth on Oct. 19, 1892; Emma Mary was born on Aug. 14, 1894 (DC to AC, Oct. 21, 1891; Christie Family History, 5).

76.   DC to EC, Oct. 18, 1897.

77.   Ina Christie Denton interview with Peavy and Smith, Oct. 1983; Christie Family History, 4. Sandy married Christina Bervin on June 1, 1904; Eliza married James Camp on Dec. 25, 1905; Donald married Lulu Camp on June 7, 1906; and Davy married Elizabeth A. Fields on June 17, 1906 (Christie Family History, 12, 82, 24, and 42). In time, all of the Christie offspring, except George, would marry. Will Christie married Eva Sparr on June 3, 1908; James Christie married Pearl Berryhill on Jan. 1, 1912; Emma Mary Christie married James William Curdy on Nov. 19, 1912; and Robert Allen Christie married Orpha Naomi Montgomery on Dec. 18, 1912 (Christie Family History, 64, 68, 109, 163, 137).

The Happy Days Club, which eventually became the Bridger Canyon Women's Club, remains a vital organization and still boasts Christies on its membership roles.

78.   Ina Christie Denton interview with Peavy and Smith, Oct. 1983; Mabel Curdy reminiscence, Christie family records. David sold his home to W. E. Wicker (D. B. Christie obituary, Christie Family History, 8).

79.   Emma Stratton Christie obituary, Christie Family History, 9; Mabel Curdy reminiscence, Christie family records.

80.   Emma Stratton Christie obituary, Christie Family History, 9. Tom Christie died on May 25, 1921; Sandy on Apr. 5, 1933; and Sarah in Sept. 1919 (Ina Christie Denton interview with Peavy and Smith, Oct. 1983). Most of the Christie children, save little James James, lived into vigorous old age. George was the first to die, on Nov. 30, 1950, at age seventy; Sandy died on Dec. 3, 1953, at age seventy-nine; Robert on Nov. 6, 1954, at a young sixty-three; Donald on Feb. 3, 1955, at age seventy-eight; and Davy on June 26, 1964, at age eighty-five. Will and Eliza both died in 1962, Will on June 14 at age seventy-eight, and Eliza on Sept. 14 at age seventy-seven. James died on Mar. 28, 1968, at age eighty, and Emma, the youngest of the siblings, was the last to die, on Feb. 20, 1974, at age seventy-nine (Christie Family History, 5, 12, 137, 24, 42, 68, 82, 109, 163).

VII
Augusta Perham Shipman

1.   Augusta Perham Shipman (hereafter abbreviated as AP before her marriage and AS after) to Clark B. Shipman (hereafter abbreviated as CBS), Feb. 1, 1882. The Shipman story has been reconstructed largely on the basis of letters and journals found in the Clark Bigelow Shipman Family Papers at the Montana

Historical Society in Helena (hereafter cited as MHS). The collection is a rich one, comprising more than a thousand letters exchanged by four generations of Shipmans from the 1850s to the 1950s. Unless otherwise indicated, all letters cited in this chapter are found in that collection. In quoting these materials, the authors have chosen to retain the spelling, capitalization, and punctuation found in the original sources.

2. Book of Births, Deaths, and Marriages, 1771–1857, Bethel Town Hall, Bethel, Vt. Although her name is recorded as Fanny Augusta at the time of her birth, Augusta used Augusta F. as her legal name throughout her adult life. Augusta Perham's birthplace is listed as Bethel, though technically Perham Hill, the family farm on which she was born, lay in East Bethel, three miles to the northeast.

David Perham had left a widow, Lavinia, and four children. The children were given to court-appointed guardians, and when Lavinia Perham remarried, the land David had purchased in the late eighteenth century was lost to them (Samuel Dudley to David Perham, Mar. 18, 1792, Deed Book 1, p. 139, Bethel Town Hall, Bethel, Vt.; Probate Record Book 3, pp. 204–205, Windsor County Courthouse, Woodstock, Vt.). John Perham began to reclaim his father's land in 1819 (J. Patten Davis to John Perham, June 6, 1819, Deed Book 4, p. 363; Orpha Perham to John Perham, Apr. 4, 1823, Deed Book 5, p. 194; Peter and Daniel Woodbury to John Perham, Oct. 10, 1830, Deed Book 6, p. 233, Bethel Town Hall). He continued to add to his domain until he had acquired 160 acres (on some tax rolls, he is credited with 166) (Jasper Buckman to John Perham, Nov. 8, 1834, Deed Book 6, p. 43; Jasper Buckman to John Perham, Sept. 28, 1835, Deed Book 7, p. 96; Pliny Warren to John Perham, July 13, 1844, Deed Book 9, p. 548; Alonzo Brooks to John Perham, Mar. 26, 1858, Deed Book 14, p. 464, Bethel Town Hall).

Charles Whitney Perham was born on May 14, 1835; Emeline Josephine on Mar. 3, 1838; and Harriet Williamine on July 30, 1840 (Book of Births, Deaths, and Marriages, 1771–1857, Bethel Town Hall).

3. Grand List of Bethel, 1845 and 1855; 1855 tax assessment record, all in Bethel Town Hall, Bethel, Vt.

4. 1850 U.S. Agricultural Census and 1850 U.S. Manuscript Census. By these records, John Perham held 166 acres with a value of twenty-five hundred dollars, and Harvey Shipman held 65 acres with the same value. By the time they moved to Bethel, the Shipmans had already lost two children, William Rollin (1829–31) and Betsey Aurora (1825–33).

5. Augusta F. Shipman obituary, Shipman Family Records, in possession of Susan Shipman Burhnam of Lewistown, Mont., granddaughter of Clark and Augusta Shipman. Both Harvey and Betsey Clark Shipman grew up in Rochester, and there they first settled after their marriage in 1822 (Thomas B. Peck, *Richard Clarke of Rowley, Massachusetts, and His Descendants* . . . , [Boston: Clapp & Son, 1905], 29; Harvey Shipman to William R. Shipman, Mar. 26, 1865; Evelyn Lovejoy, *History of Royalton, Vermont* [Burlington: Free Press, 1911], 955–56; John Brooks to Harvey Shipman, February 14, 1839, Land Records of Royalton, Book I, p. 24, Royalton Town Hall, Royalton, Vt.).

6. Clark Shipman's brother Harvey (1823–46), eight years older than Clark and a schoolteacher, died when Clark was fifteen and still attending Royalton Academy. William Rollin Shipman was born on May 4, 1836; Sarah DeEtte on

May 20, 1838; and Louisa Janette on Jan. 11, 1841. William Rollin was given the same name as the Shipman son who had died at age two in 1830. Both girls were known by their middle rather than their first names (Peck, *Richard Clarke*, 29).

Concerning Clark's leaving home to teach, see Harvey Shipman to CBS, Jan. 10, 1851.

The North American Phalanx, like Brook Farm, was an outgrowth of a movement launched by Charles Fourier, a Frenchman who developed a utopian plan for social reorganization that called for the establishment of rural colonies of four hundred to four thousand people. These "phalanxes" would be self-supporting, growing their own food and making their own clothes, furniture, and other articles. Although Brook Farm was the best known, the New Jersey colony was the longest-lived of the country's nineteenth-century socialist communes. Based on social and economic principles that included profit-sharing, a thirty-hour work week, planned education for workers, religious tolerance, and gender equity, the North American Phalanx numbered about one hundred persons when Clark arrived in 1851 (Robert Van Benthuysen and Audrey Wilson, *Monmouth County: A Pictorial History* [Norfolk, Va.: Donning, n.d.], 44–45). For a good treatment of the colony, see Herman Belz, "The North American Phalanx: Experiment in Socialism," *Proceedings of the New Jersey Historical Society* 81, no. 4 (Oct. 1963): 215–46.

7. CBS to family, Nov. 30, 1851. Lucius Eaton and his wife Lucy had come to North American Phalanx from Brook Farm, arriving in 1846, some three years after the establishment of the New Jersey colony, and investing in twenty-five shares of commune stock at ten dollars a share (New American Phalanx account books, Monmouth County Historical Society, Freehold, N.J.).

8. Lucius Eaton to Bro & sister, Mar. 21, 1852; J. N. Moore to CBS, Nov. 23, 1852; U.S. Manuscript Census, 1850. Augusta's grandmother, Lavinia Perham Matthews by virtue of her remarriage, would die on Feb. 14, 1853, at age eighty-three (Cherry Hill Cemetery Records, Bethel Town Hall, Bethel, Vt.). The uncle was Charles Whitney, her mother's brother; the aunt, her father's half-sister, Louisa Matthews.

9. Louisa Matthews to AP, Apr. 2, 1854; CBS to Betsey Shipman, Aug. 28, 1854.

10. Louisa Matthews to AP, Apr. 2, 1854. Augusta's itinerary has been reconstructed from Walton's *The Vermont Register* (White River Junction, Ut.: White River Paper Co., 1875), 50.

11. CBS to Betsey Shipman, Sept. 28, 1854; CBS, Journal, 1855. In a late-life letter, Clark noted that he had taught at "Edinburgh school house" and Augusta at Scobeyville (CBS to Rebecca Shipman (hereafter abbreviated as RS), Nov. 5, 1884). Clark Shipman's journals are in the possession of his granddaughter, Susan Shipman Burnham; accurate and complete transcriptions of several of the journals are found in the Shipman Family Papers, MHS.

12. William B. Shipman to William R. Shipman, Jan. 8, 1858; CBS to AS, Feb. 5, 1885; Lovejoy, *History of Royalton*, 304. The ceremony took place in Royalton, perhaps at the groom's home, rather than on Perham Hill (Peck, *Richard Clarke*, 53).

13. Peck, *Richard Clarke*, 53; Arthur DeGoosh, *Address at the Unveiling of a Memorial Tablet to William Rollin Shipman . . . ,* 4. The thirty-some acres were

deeded for fifteen hundred dollars "in lieu of any right or interest in the estate of said Harvey and Betsey Eaton Shipman" (Harvey and Betsey Shipman to Clark B. Shipman, June 27, 1857, Book O, p. 356, Land Records of Royalton, Town Hall of Royalton, Royalton, Vt.).

14. Peck, *Richard Clarke*, 53. Charles Perham, twenty-one, died on Feb. 16, 1857, and was buried in Bethel's Cherry Hill cemetery beside his grandmother and grandfather Perham and a brother and sister who had died in infancy (Cherry Hill Cemetery Records, Bethel Town Hall; Book of Births, Deaths, and Marriages, 1857–82, Bethel Town Hall). Born on Mar. 17, 1859, Gratia died Mar. 26, 1859.

15. Janette Shipman to Harvey and Betsey Shipman, Sept. 9, 1859; "Laurie" to Janette Shipman, Dec. 4, 1859; CBS to Harvey Shipman, Jan. 12, 1860; Peck, *Richard Clarke*, 29, 53. DeEtte was also enrolled at Green Mountain at about this time (DeEtte Shipman Lee obituary, 1915, Shipman Family Records).

16. Peck, *Richard Clarke*, 54; DeEtte S. Lee to Harvey and Betsey Shipman, Nov. 24, 1860. The couple was married on Mar. 7, 1860.

17. The Shipmans' land was valued at two thousand dollars and the livestock at eight hundred dollars; their young farmhand was named Patrick Carney (1860 U.S. Agricultural and Manuscript Censuses). The Perham land was valued at three thousand dollars and their livestock at five hundred dollars, and their butter and maple syrup production was fifty pounds less, in each case, than that of the Shipmans (1860 U.S. Agricultural and Manuscript Censuses).

The wedding took place on June 3, 1861, in Bethel. Henry Marcy became the president of the Fitchburg Railroad (Book of Births, Deaths, and Marriages, 1857–82, Bethel Town Hall); Walton's *The Vermont Register;* Lovejoy, *History of Royalton*, 643).

18. CBS to Harvey and Betsey Shipman, Mar. 20, 1861; Winifred Shipman Erickson, "Reminiscences," Shipman Family Papers, MHS. By 1861, William, twenty-five, was principal of Green Mountain Institute as well as a member of the faculty there (Green Mountain Institute handbill, Shipman Family Papers, MHS). Oscar Lee's father, Chester, a well-to-do farmer and surveyor, and his mother, Lydia Crouch Lee, were longstanding residents of Vernon (Peck, *Richard Clarke*, 54).

19. CBS to Harvey and Betsey Shipman, Mar. 20, 1861; CBS to Harvey Shipman, Mar. 27, 1861; DeEtte S. Lee to Betsey Shipman, Apr. 28 and Aug. 5, 1861; Peck, *Richard Clarke*, 54. Oscar Lee was superintendent of the local school district at Vernon. In the end, neither Clark nor his brother-in-law Oscar Lee was called to serve in the Civil War. His brother, William, who had thought his status as educator would exempt him, was drafted but paid the three-hundred-dollar fee and escaped induction (CBS to Harvey and Betsey Shipman, Sept. 7, 1862; CBS to William R. Shipman, July 26, 1863; William R. Shipman to Harvey and Betsey Shipman, Aug. 2, 1864).

20. DeEtte S. Lee to Harvey and Betsey Shipman, Apr. 4, 1862, and Aug. 5, 1861; CBS to Harvey and Betsey Shipman and DeEtte S. Lee, June 19, 1862; CBS to Harvey Shipman, Dec. 21, 1862. Harriet's wedding took place on Mar. 2, 1862 (Lovejoy, *History of Royalton*, 1029). Charles Whitney was likely related in some way to the Perhams, given the fact he bore a family name.

21. Erickson, "Reminiscences."

22. CBS to Harvey and Betsey Shipman, Dec. 29, 1863, and May 8, 1864; CBS

to Harvey Shipman, May 29, 1864. Harvey paid his son two hundred dollars for two acres on which to build the house (Clark B. Shipman to Harvey Shipman, Sept. 5, 1865, Book Q, p. 263, Land Records of Royalton, Royalton Town Hall, Royalton, Vt.). That acreage was bounded on the west by the road "leading to John Perhams's."

23.   William R. Shipman to Betsey Shipman, Apr. 3, 1867. Clark's cousin, Henry Eaton, had been killed in battle just two years earlier at Poplar Grove, Virginia (Peck, *Richard Clarke*, 31, 53). DeEtte Lee wrote her mother from Vernon, cautioning Betsey not to "work too hard" and wondering "if Gusta's conscience smites her any" (DeEtte S. Lee to Harvey and Betsey Shipman, Apr. 28, 1867).

One of the first planned communities in America, Vineland was developed by Charles K. Landis in the early 1860s on one square mile of wilderness that Landis envisioned as supporting a city of broad avenues, comfortable homes, bustling industry, and clean factories and surrounded by fertile orchards, vineyards, and farms. He laid out his city in 1861 and advertised widely in New England and in Italy (See *Vineland: General Information. Reports of Dr. Charles T. Jackson and Solon Robinson* [Vineland, N.J.: Vineland Historical Society, 1869], especially 7–8, and *This Is Vineland* [Vineland, N.J.: League of Women Voters, 1960]; "A New England Settlement [in] Southern New Jersey," broadside in the Newfield file, Gloucester County Historical Society, Woodbury, N.J.).

24.   William R. Shipman to Harvey and Betsey Shipman, Jan. 2, 1868. The deed to the farm also reserved Harvey Shipman's right to draw water for his two acres from the aqueduct running across the land (Clark B. Shipman to John D. Fales, Oct. 11, 1867, Book Q, p. 609, Land Records of Royalton, Royalton Town Hall). Clark and Augusta carried a note on the farm that was paid in full by Fales on Aug. 17, 1872 (Book Q, p. 611, Land Records of Royalton, Royalton Town Hall).

Skeptical of the enthusiastic claims coming out of New Jersey, DeEtte Lee could not imagine what her brother and sister-in-law expected to find there, and William Shipman shocked his parents with an uncharacteristically negative comment about Clark—for which he quickly apologized (DeEtte S. Lee to Harvey and Betsey Shipman, May 9, 1868; William R. Shipman to Betsey Shipman, May 24, 1868) Only William's contrite follow-up letter is extant; the letter conveying the disparaging comment itself has not been located. A single-minded, hard-working scholar, William may well have viewed his brother as somewhat irresponsible. He himself had left the Green Mountain Institute early in 1864 to join the humanities faculty at Tufts College in Boston as professor of rhetoric, logic, and English literature. A year later he was ordained a Universalist minister, and though he was never to have a parish of his own, he preached frequently from pulpits throughout New England (DeGoosh, *Address*, 7) Instrumental in the establishment of Goddard Seminary in Barre, Vermont, in 1870, he sat on its board of directors for the duration of his life. In 1900, William became dean of the College of Letters at Tufts (DeGoosh, *Address*, 8; Peck, *Richard Clarke*, 54).

Augusta received a letter in early March 1868 from a friend who chided her for not taking her south with her, as she had once promised. The friend wished Augusta and her family well in a land that must be "flowing with milk and honey" (E. M. Williams to AS, Mar. 3, 1868).

25.   Connecting with the Boston stage in Woodstock, the family took the train from Boston to New York City, then caught the ferry to Jersey City, where

they took the New Jersey Railroad to Philadelphia and then boarded another ferry to Camden, where they connected with the West Jersey Railroad that took them on to Vineland (*Vineland: General Information*).

26. CBS to Harvey and Betsey Shipman, July 19, 1868. By 1868, Vineland claimed a population of nearly three thousand people (*Vineland: General Information*, 3). Contemporary Bethel had a population of eighteen hundred and Royalton about seventeen hundred. (Walton's *Vermont Register*, 50, 131).

27. CBS to Harvey and Betsey Shipman, July 19, 1868. Clark and Augusta paid forty-two hundred dollars for the fifty-six acres, taking out a thirty-two-hundred-dollar mortgage on the property (Clark and Augusta Shipman to John Vansant, Aug. 5, 1868, Deed Book G5, p. 680, and Mortgage Book HH, p. 352, Gloucester County Courthouse, Woodbury, N.J.). In 1868, when the Shipman family took possession of their farm, Malaga had a population of just over two hundred. (Thomas Cushing and Charles Sheppard, *History of the Counties of Gloucester, Salem, and Cumberland, New Jersey* [Philadelphia: Everts & Peck, 1883], 218). The five shade trees were described as "2 weeping willows, 1 oak, 1 apple, & 1 balm of Gillahead."

One of the children's Vineland playmates died of whooping cough complicated by asthma the day the family moved to Malaga (CBS to William R. Shipman, Aug. 3, 1868).

28. CBS to Harvey and Betsey Shipman, July 19, 1868; CBS to William R. Shipman, Aug. 3, 1868. As Augusta and Clark were in the middle of the move from Vineland to Malaga, William R. Shipman was being married in Somerville, Massachusetts, to Martha Frances Willis, daughter of Rev. John and Charlotte Willis (Peck, *Richard Clarke*, 54).

29. CBS to Harvey Shipman, Mar. 14 and 29, 1869.

30. William R. Shipman to Harvey and Betsey Shipman, Sept. 19 and Oct. 22, 1869; CBS to Harvey and Betsey Shipman, Sept. 26, 1869.

31. Erickson, "Reminiscences." John Perham died on Oct. 10, 1869, of consumption (Book of Births, Deaths, and Marriages, 1857–82, Bethel Town Hall). By the terms of his will, John's widow Sarah was to get all of Perham Hill plus ten acres of woodland in the southwest corner of Jasper Buchman's property plus all household goods. The three surviving children, Fannie Augusta Shipman, Emeline Josephine Marcy, and Harriet Williamine Whitney, were each to get one-third of the "Green lot plus $100" (Last Will and Testament of John Perham of Bethel, Jan. 15, 1869, Legal Documents, Shipman Family Papers, MHS). In accordance with an option outlined in the will, her three daughters sold Sarah Perham their inherited parcels of land for fifteen hundred dollars on Aug. 6, 1870, ten months after their father's death (Book 19, p. 50, Aug. 6, 1870, Land Records of Bethel, Bethel Town Hall; Last Will and Testament of John Perham, Jan. 15, 1869, MHS).

32. Lucy Eaton to Harvey and Betsey Shipman, Jan. 3, 1869; Frank Swasey to Winifred Shipman (hereafter abbreviated as WS), Feb. 21, 1870. According to the U.S. Agricultural and Manuscript censuses of 1870, Charles and Harriet Whitney, Augusta's youngest sister and her brother-in-law, and their two children were living at Perham Hill with Sarah Perham and operating 150 acres of farmland that had a value of $2,500. They kept four horses, five milk cows, three other cattle, and thirty sheep, all the livestock having a value of $700. Their 100 acres of

improved cropland were planted in Indian corn, oats, and Irish potatoes; the farm also produced 120 pounds of wool, 300 pounds of butter, twenty-five tons of hay, and 300 pounds of maple syrup, all of the products having a total estimated value of $750.

33. DeEtte S. Lee to Harvey and Betsey Shipman, Mar. 13, 1870; CBS to Harvey Shipman, Aug. 16, 1870. The 1870 U.S. Manuscript Census, taken Aug. 20, shows Clark Shipman, a thirty-nine-year-old farmer; Augusta Shipman, also thirty-nine; Rebecca, seven, and Henry, three, in residence at Malaga.

34. William R. Shipman to Harvey and Betsey Shipman, July 15, 1870; CBS to Harvey Shipman, Aug. 16, 1870; AS to WS and Gertrude Shipman (hereafter abbreviated as GS), Aug. 29, 1870. This letter of August 1870 is the first letter that survives from Augusta's hand. Although Augusta was a teacher, her handwriting is cramped and her composition is unsophisticated, in stark contrast to the penmanship and content of the letters of her husband and children. Total value of all the products of the Shipman farm that year, including wheat, Indian corn, buckwheat, Irish potatoes, sweet potatoes, orchard products, butter, and hay, was $1,560; the cash value of the land itself was $600, and $150 was counted in equipment and machinery (1870 U.S. Agricultural Census).

35. DeEtte S. Lee to Harvey and Betsey Shipman, Feb. 13 and Nov. 20, 1870, and Mar. 26, 1871. Peck, *Richard Clarke,* 55. Oscar and DeEtte had first considered a move to "the lovely valley of the Salmon River" to partake of "pioneer life, log cabins, etc." before deciding instead on the more settled environment of New Jersey. Whether they spoke of the Salmon River country of northern California or of Idaho cannot be determined (DeEtte S. Lee to Harvey and Betsey Shipman, Nov. 20, 1870). On Jan. 5, 1872, nine months after moving to New Jersey, Oscar Lee gave a mortgage on Oak Grove Farm, Franklin Township, New Jersey, to Chester Lee (S. DeEtta Lee et al. and Chester Lee, January 5, 1872, Deed Book JJ, p. 651, Gloucester County Courthouse, Woodbury, N.J.).

36. CBS to Harvey Shipman, Aug. 16, 1870; DeEtte S. Lee to Harvey and Betsey Shipman, Mar. 26, 1871.

37. DeEtte S. Lee to Harvey and Betsey Shipman, May 7, 1871, and Jan. 12, 1872; WS to Harvey and Betsey Shipman, Dec. 15, 1872.

38. WS to Betsey Shipman, Dec. 3, 1871; CBS to Harvey and Betsey Shipman, Nov. 30, 1871; DeEtte S. Lee to Harvey and Betsey Shipman, Jan. 12, 1872.

39. DeEtte S. Lee to Harvey and Betsey Shipman, Jan. 12, 1872; CBS to Harvey and Betsey Shipman, Apr. 19, 1872.

40. CBS to Harvey and Betsey Shipman, Apr. 19, 1872.

41. DeEtte S. Lee to Harvey and Betsey Shipman, Nov. 21 and Dec. 8, 1872, and Jan. 2, 1873. On Aug. 17, 1872, John Fales paid off the forty-five-hundred-dollar note that Clark and Augusta had carried on the Vermont farm (Book Q, p. 611, Land Records of Royalton, Royalton Town Hall).

42. DeEtte S. Lee to Betsey Shipman, Dec. 22, 1872, and Jan. 12, 1873. The Lees, too, had had a hard year financially (William R. Shipman to Harvey and Betsey Shipman, Dec. 29, 1872). Clark had the farm on the market for five thousand dollars, an equitable sum, he thought, given the value of other local property (CBS to Harvey and Betsey Shipman, Apr. 19, 1872).

43. William R. Shipman to Oscar Lee, Oct. 28, 1873; WS to Betsey Shipman, Feb. 10, 1873, and May 25, 1874; DeEtte S. Lee to Harvey and Betsey Shipman,

July 27, 1873. After one term in the classroom, Oscar Lee retired from teaching in order to devote himself to farming. At one point, Clark wrote his daughters proposing that they find a place to board where the housekeeper would take a sewing machine in lieu of four months' rent (CBS to Daughters, Feb. 25, 1874).

The elder Shipmans were present on Dec. 5, 1873, for the birth of Chester Harvey Lee, their fifth grandson, DeEtte's fourth child (WS to Betsey Shipman, May 23, 1874; Peck, *Richard Clarke*, 55).

44. CBS to Harvey and Betsey Shipman, Feb. 9, 1873. The Shipmans paid Sarah Perham $1,100 for the eighty-five acres left to her by her husband upon his death five years previously, promising not only to assume the land but also "to maintain [Sarah Perham] in the state to which she is accustomed" to the end of her life. At the same time, Augusta bought all the stock, farming tools, and implements on the farm from her mother for $550 (Clark and Augusta Shipman to Sarah Perham, April 22, 1874, Deed Book 20, pp. 129–30, Bethel Town Hall); John Perham Last Will and Testament, Legal Documents, Shipman Family Papers, MHS).

45. DeEtte S. Lee to Harvey and Betsey Shipman, June 5, 1875; Annie [Irish] to WS, July 16, 1874; DeEtte S. Lee to WS and GS, Oct. 18, 1874; Frank Swasey to WS, Mar. 27, 1875; M. C. Wheeler to WS, Oct. 20, 1875; "Tin" to WS, Mar. 3, 1878; Peck, *Richard Clarke*, 53; "Lill" to WS, Feb. 13, 1876; "Lill" to GS, Feb. 13, 1876. Clark may have rented out the Malaga farm over the next few years while he himself lived primarily in Bethel (Junie Woodworth to WS, Sept. 27, 1875).

On Maggie's birth record the father's occupation is listed as "sewing machine agent" and the parents' place of residence is given as Bethel (Book of Births, Deaths, and Marriages, 1857–82, Bethel Town Hall).

46. Annie [Irish] to WS, July 11, 1876; "Tin" to WS, Nov. 5, 1876; GS to WS, Feb. 10, 1876; CBS to WS, Oct. 22, 1876. Clark's closeness to his children is evidenced by the frequency and intimacy of his letters to them during periods of separation, and by the fact that he was integrally involved in childcare, not a typical activity of nineteenth-century fathers. For a good discussion of gender roles in nineteenth-century parenting, see Carl Degler's *At Odds: Women and the Family in America from the Revolution to the Present* (New York: Oxford University Press, 1980).

47. Clark B. and Augusta F. Shipman to John C. Vansant, July 31, 1877, Mortgage Book HH, p. 352, Gloucester County Courthouse, Woodbury, N.J.; WS to GS, Dec. 9, 1877.

48. Having first passed the teachers' exam at Trenton, Winnie was teaching in Hammonton, not far from the Malaga farm, and Gertie in Camden, thirty miles north of Hammonton (Erickson, "Reminiscences"; GS teaching certificate, Shipman Family Papers, MHS; William R. Shipman to WS, May 14, 1879).

The night after his arrival in New Jersey, seventy-seven-year-old Harvey Shipman had "a rather light shock of paralysis, affecting his right side & his speech." Never fully recovering from the effects of the stroke, he died two years later on Aug. 5, 1879 (CBS to GS, Nov. 23, 1877; Peck, *Richard Clarke*, 29).

Sarah Perham lived alone in the farmhouse after the Shipmans left, and though Perham Hill may have been leased out to a neighbor to farm, it is far likelier that Charles Whitney worked the farm for the Shipmans (1880 U.S. Manuscript Census).

49. The 1880 Franklin Township census shows Clark, forty-nine, a farmer; Augusta, forty-nine, keeping house; and Winifred, twenty-three; Gertrude, nineteen; Rebecca, seventeen; Henry, thirteen; and Margaret, four, in residence on the farm. The U.S. Agricultural Census taken in June of that year shows that the family had sold no farm products in 1879, though there were thirty acres under cultivation and three acres given to meadows, orchards, and vineyards, with another twenty in woodland. The land, fences, and house were valued at $1,500, and the livestock—a milk cow, horse, and ten chickens—were valued at $110.

50. William B. Shipman to William R. Shipman, Jan. 8, 1858. William B. Shipman, the uncle Clark had visited on his honeymoon, had pioneered in Iowa. Lucius Eaton, who had first lured Clark Shipman to the North American Phalanx in the early 1850s, moved to Champaign County, Illinois, in 1854, to take up farming and blacksmithing. Clark Eaton, an itinerant preacher, had gone even farther west to Iowa, Kansas, and eventually California (Peck, *Richard Clarke*, 36 and 32).

51. Erickson, "Reminiscences"; DeEtte S. Lee to Betsey and Harvey Shipman, Jan. 2, 1873; Lucy Eaton to Betsey and Harvey Shipman, Jan. 3, 1869; AS to CBS, Feb. 1, 1882; AS to CBS, undated (winter of 1882).

52. William R. Shipman to CBS, Jan. 16, 1882; deed from Clark Shipman to Sarah Perham, Legal Documents, Shipman Family Papers, MHS. John and Lavinia Ellis of Philadelphia bought the farm for twenty-one hundred dollars, exactly half of what the Shipmans had paid for it some thirteen years earlier. The Ellises put thirteen hundred dollars down; Augusta F. Shipman, as her own person, carried a mortgage on the farm for eight hundred dollars (Erickson, "Reminiscences"; Augusta F. Shipman to John Ellis, Oct. 12, 1881, Deed Book RR, p. 377, Gloucester County Courthouse, Woodbury, N.J.).

53. DeEtte S. Lee to CBS, Dec. 7, 1888; CBS, Journal, 1882, MHS; Oscar Lee to CBS, Dec. 18, 1881. Silver Bow is a short distance west of Butte, Montana.

54. CBS, Journal, 1882; AS to CBS, Jan. 1, 1882. The next spring Winnie was obliged to chloroform Salt "to save him from longer suffering" (Rebecca Shipman [hereafter abbreviated as RS] to CBS, Apr. 30, 1882). The hens met an even quicker fate, becoming a dietary staple for the Shipman women over the next two months (WS to CBS, Feb. 12, 1882).

Becky, with Augusta's help, made the Christmas gifts the family exchanged that year. Winnie was given a "wall jacket" and Gertrude a lined work basket, and Augusta herself received a white "neck tie." Maggie's gift was not specified. This New Year's Day letter was the first from Augusta to Clark. Of the more than a thousand letters that compose the Shipman Family Papers in the MHS, only a small fraction—sixty-eight—are from Augusta, and most of those are addressed to Winnie, Gertie, or Becky. No more than three are addressed directly and solely to her husband, although Clark makes reference to at least one more letter from his wife that is not found in the Shipman Family Papers, MHS.

55. WS to CBS, Jan. 1 and 7, 1882; RS to CBS, Jan. 1, 1882.

56. GS to CBS, Jan. 7 and 31, 1882; WS to CBS, Jan. 16, 1882; AS to CBS, Jan. 16, 1882.

57. AS to CBS, undated; WS to CBS, Jan. 31, 1882. The physician who treated both Augusta and Gertrude was a Dr. Wright (AS to CBS, Jan. 29, 1882).

58. CBS, Journal, 1882; Henry Shipman (hereafter abbreviated as HS) to family, Jan. 29, 1882.

59. AS to CBS, undated.

60. Ibid.; WS to CBS, Feb. 12 and 21, 1882; RS to CBS, Feb. 12 and 21, 1882.

61. WS to CBS, Feb. 21, 1882.

62. Ibid.

63. Ibid.

64. AS to CBS, Feb. 26, 1882; Oscar Lee to CBS, Mar. 19, 1882. Although Augusta variously used both Bethel and East Bethel as the dateline on her letters from Perham Hill, and though each community had its own post office, they were never considered separate municipalities (Gladys Ferris, Royalton Town Clerk, Royalton, Vt., to Peavy and Smith, July 22, 1991).

65. GS to CBS, Mar. 5, 1882; WS to CBS, Mar. 3, 1882.

66. CBS, Journal, 1882; WS to CBS, Apr. 16 and 30, 1882; Susan Shipman Burnham, "Fergus County '89ers Centennial Facts," Shipman Family Papers, MHS. Clark and Henry collected seventy dollars for their two months' labor. According to the Homestead Act of 1862, to qualify for a patent that transfered ownership of up to 160 acres for the payment of a filing fee of about twenty dollars, one had only to be twenty-one years of age (or the head of a family) and a citizen of the United States (or in the process of becoming a citizen). After an initial filing of intention, the homesteader had to "prove up" over a five-year period of time—that is, establish residence and cultivate and improve the land claimed—before the final patent was granted (Paul Gates, *History of Public Land Law Development* [Washington, D.C.: Public Land Law Review Commission, 1968], 245).

With the family now existing in three different worlds, letters became round-robin affairs. Written in Montana, they were read in Atlantic City and sent on to Vermont, or read in Vermont and sent on to Atlantic City; written in Vermont, they were sent to Atlantic City to be forwarded to Montana (WS to CBS, Feb. 5 and Mar. 3, 1882; HS to RS, Dec. 14, 1884; CBS to family, Dec. 25, 1884). Clark's letters to his mother and sister at Oak Grove Farm or to William in Boston were also shared around the circuit.

67. WS to CBS, Apr. 9, 1882.

68. GS to CBS, Apr. 23, 1882; WS to CBS, Apr. 22, 1882.

69. Graduation program, third annual commencement, Atlantic City High School, 1882, Shipman Family Papers, MHS; WS to CBS, June 25, 1882. Becky was her high school's senior class prophet. The tickets west had each cost $89.80; they were first class, since safety and comfort seemed well worth the few extra dollars. The itinerary outlined a seven-day trip from Bethel to Bismarck, Dakota Territory, followed by another seven days from Bismarck to Fort Benton, Montana Territory.

70. GS to CBS, undated; WS to CBS, June 25, 1882. In Boston the girls also visited the dentist, "not being suited with the Vineland and Bethel dentists." Gertie had wisdom teeth pulled and three teeth filled (with gold) for sixteen dollars; Becky had one tooth filled for eight dollars; and Winnie had only an examination, for which she paid four dollars.

71. WS to CBS, July 7, 1882. Winnie cautioned her father in her written

report of the situation at Perham Hill "not [to] make much mention of these things when you write and I will tell you the rest when I get there."

72. WS to CBS, July 19, 1882; GS to CBS, July 19, 1882; Erickson, "Reminiscences"; CBS, Journal, 1882. The trip was substantially delayed in Bismarck when the crew of the riverboat that was to take them from Bismarck to Fort Benton deserted the steamer for the higher wages of fieldwork, leaving the Shipman sisters and their fellow passengers to await the arrival of a replacement crew.

73. CBS, Journal, 1882. Winnie's reminiscences, written in later life, conflict with her father's contemporary account; she recalls arriving late at night in a heavy rainstorm (Erickson, "Reminiscences").

74. Erickson, "Reminiscences"; William R. Shipman to CBS, July 7, 1882; H. Marcy to CBS, Aug. 6, 1882.

75. CBS, Journal, 1882; Patent Records, Bureau of Land Management, Billings, Mont.

76. CBS, Journal, 1882; WS to AS, Nov. 26, 1882. Winnie received sixty dollars a month for the three-month term and boarded with the Porter family in Philbrook for forty dollars for the term. The schoolhouse had been a chickenhouse; there were no desks and, for the first six weeks, no books. Winnie wrote out stories on brown paper for reading lessons, drew maps on the floor for geography lessons, and took her students outdoors to study rocks and dissect hawks and rabbits for science lessons. Before long, she had whitewashed the inside of the building, and at the end of the term she invited the families of her four scholars to a Christmas program given in the chickenhouse/classroom (WS to AS, Nov. 4 and 26, 1882; Burnham article, Shipman Family Papers, MHS).

77. CBS, Journal, 1882, 1883. Apparently, moving a house on skids from one homestead claim to another was not an unusual practice in Montana during this era (Richard Roeder to Peavy and Smith, Sept. 1991). Over the course of the next twenty-six years, the Shipman clan was to claim twenty-three different pieces of property in two townships in Fergus County: five homesteads in Clark's, Winifred's, Gertrude's, Rebecca's, and Henry's names; one timber culture claim in Clark's name; seven desert land claims, with three in Clark's name, two in Augusta's, one in Henry's, and one in Gertrude's; and ten cash-entry or preemption claims (Patent Records, Bureau of Land Management, Billings, Mont.).

78. RS to family, Dec. 19, 1882; AS to CBS, Dec. 25, 1882.

79. CBS, Journal, 1883; William R. Shipman to CBS, June 3, 1883; F. Adkinson, U.S. Land Office, Helena, Montana Territory, to CBS, Sept. 12, 1883. Clark filed "first proof" on this preemption late that same year. A preemption claim differed from a homestead claim in that the claimant paid cash for the land, usually at $1.25 an acre plus filing fees, and a final patent could be obtained on a preemption claim much sooner than on a homestead claim, that is, two years after filing "first proof." All other homestead qualifications—citizenship, residency, cultivation, and improvement of the land—pertained (Gates, *History of Public Land Law*, 245).

80. AS to CBS, July 17, 1883; deed canceled, Dec. 22, 1883, Deed Book RR, p. 377, Gloucester County Courthouse, Woodbury, N.J.

81. CBS Journal, 1883; WS to GS, Apr. 24, 1884; CBS to GS, May 7 and June 16, 1884; HS to CBS, Sept. 30, 1884; AS to RS, Sept. 30, 1884. Gertie was earning

sixty-five dollars a month, and Winnie, sixty dollars (DeEtte S. Lee to WS, Oct. 5, 1884).

Cash was not a ready commodity on the Judith; Clark himself worked "for hire" a month or so each year in order to earn money for tobacco and clothes (CBS to HS, Oct. 5, 1884).

82. CBS to GS, June 16, 1884; DeEtte S. Lee to CBS, June 29, 1884; Gardiner Wallace to Augusta Shipman, Aug. 9, 1884, Book 23, p. 13, Land Records of Bethel, Bethel Town Hall); HS to CBS, Sept. 30, 1884; AS to GS, May 21 and July 30, 1884.

83. AS to RS, Sept. 30, 1884.

84. Ibid.; AS to folks, Oct. 1, 1884. Becky paid three dollars a week to board at the home, located at 23 East 11th Street (AS to folks, Oct. 1, 1884).

85. CBS to family, Oct. 5, 1884.

86. CBS to family, Oct. 5, 1884; CBS to HS, n.d., 1884, and May 19, 1887; AS to RS, Nov. 14, [1884]. The Timber Culture Act of 1873 enabled settlers to pick up 160 acres if they planted 40 of those acres in trees. Unlike homestead and cash-entry or preemption land, residency was not required on timber culture land (Gates, *History of Public Land Law*, 399). Balm of Gilead and cottonwood, both species of the poplar and frequently used in windbreaks, are easily planted from switches.

At one time Clark wrote Augusta that it began "to look as tho John Perham's money might do something for his grandchildren through your management after all" (CBS to AS, Oct. 5, 1884).

Augusta referred to Clark's original claim as the "Thompson ranch" because a man named Thompson was working it with Clark and probably because she was running out of ways to refer to the various claims. The $225 would have covered a 160-acre tract.

87. AS to GS, Oct. 16 and 27, 1884; HS to GS, Nov. 30, 1884; AS to RS, Oct. 16 and 24 and Dec. 9, 1884; HS to CBS, Sept. 30, 1884; CBS to family, Oct. 19, 1884; AS to family, undated [autumn 1884]; CBS to HS, undated, 1884.

88. CBS to AS, Oct. 19, 1884.

89. AS to RS, Oct. 21, 1884. Augusta's suggested remedies for any health problems Becky might encounter included lots of rest and daily doses of "Warners Safe Kidney Cure."

90. Ibid.; AS to GS, Oct. 27, 1884.

91. CBS to AS, Nov. 21, 1884; CBS to family, Nov. 8, 1884.

92. AS to RS, Oct. 24 and Dec. 9, 1884, and Jan. 30, 1885; AS to GS, Oct. 27, 1884.

93. AS to RS, Dec. 9, 1884; CBS to HS, Dec. 23, 1884, and Jan. 18, 1885.

94. CBS to AS, Feb. 5, 1885. This is one of only four extant letters that Clark wrote directly and solely to his wife.

95. Ibid.

96. Ibid.

97. Ibid. The reference to "Henry's [ranch]" is unclear, since there was as yet no claim made for Henry, who was still underage. Perhaps Clark intended the preemption claim to be in Henry's name eventually. Clark as yet had no cattle, but he did have "8 respectable young lady pigs [who would] go into business for themselves early in the spring" (CBS to family, Nov. 8, 1884).

98.   AS to CBS, Dec. 26, 1882; AS to RS, Dec. 9, 1884, and Jan. 30, Feb. 22, Mar. 1, and Apr. 22, 1885; HS to family, Mar. 8, 1885.

99.   HS to CBS, Mar. 20, 1885; WS to CBS, Aug. 6, 1885; GS to CBS, Aug. 13, 1885.

100.   HS to CBS, May 5 and Aug. 9, 1885; AS to RS, Apr. 19 and May 4, 1885; HS to CBS, July 5 and Aug. 9, 1885. The neighbor was identified as Ed Morse.

101.   HS to CBS, Aug. 9, 1885; AS to RS, Oct. 3, 1885.

102.   CBS to RS, Nov. 19, 1885. Becky was now living in a boarding house on West 21st Street, about three-fourths of a mile from school.

103.RS to CBS, Dec. 13, 1885.

104.   CBS to RS, Jan. 13, 1886.

105.   AS to RS, Jan. 1, 1886; CBS to RS, Jan. 13, 1886.

106.   AS to RS, Mar. 10, 1886; GS to RS, Mar. 18, 1886.

107.   WS to HS, Apr. 4, 1886; CBS, Journal, 1883; HS to RS, Oct. 13, 1886. The complainant, Winnie was sure, was the Mr. Thompson who had worked with her father in the early days and had "made mischief" ever since a quarrel over claim rights.

108.   AS to RS, Oct. 12 and 20, [1886]; AS to HS, Oct. 21, [1886]; RS to CBS, Oct. 16, 1886.

109.   CBS to HS, Dec. 3, 1886. Commissioner of Public Lands through the 1880s, William Sparks sought to reform the land acquisition process, which many aspiring homesteaders were twisting to their own benefit. Clark Shipman was one of those abusing the spirit of the law, and the fact that he even knew of William Sparks and his administration is proof that he was far more knowledgeable—and interested—in land law than the vast majority of homesteaders.

110.   Ibid. Ken Karsmizki of Western History Research, Bozeman, Mont., reviewed the Shipman case with the authors, noting that Clark Shipman's comments illustrate a common difference of opinion between the homesteader and the federal government. The settlers may not have seen their activities as fraudulent; in many cases they felt the laws as written ensured the failure of an honest person; in some cases they saw a neighbor's creative solution to expanding landholdings as the appropriate course to take in their own situation; and in some cases they were even advised by land agents to engage in activities outside the letter of the law. "These speculations regarding the motivations of the settlers are just that, speculation, in the absence of direct evidence regarding what prompted their actions," Karsmizki cautioned. "Some were consciously engaging in fraud, some were ignorant of the laws, and some were grasping at straws, illegal or otherwise, in an effort to succeed against the odds" (Karsmizki to Peavy and Smith, Oct. 16, 1992).

111.   CBS to HS, Dec. 3, 1886; CBS to RS, Dec. 20, 1886; GS to RS, Jan. 2, 1887; AS to RS, Jan. 22, [1887].

112.   HS to CBS, Jan. 11, 1887; HS to WS, Jan. 21, 1887; CBS to HS, Feb. 22, 1887.

113.   HS to CBS, May 10, 1887; AS to RS, Apr. 28 and May 4, 1887, and Jan. 8, 1888; CBS to RS, Apr. 18, 1887.

114.   GS to family, Sept. 25, 1887. Clark made one hundred dollars selling

vegetables from the back of his wagon that summer of 1887 (CBS, Journal, 1887; CBS to MS, Nov. 27, 1887).

115. GS to AS, Oct. 2, 1887.

116. GS to AS, Sept. 25 and Oct. 2, 1887; WS to RS, Nov. 30, 1887; HS to RS, Jan. 14, 1888; Winifred Shipman Erickson obituary and Gertrude Erickson Loeb obituary, both in Shipman Family Records; CBS to Margaret Shipman (hereafter abbreviated as MS), Nov. 27, 1887. Ubet, like Philbrook, no longer exists.

117. HS to RS, Oct. 24 and Dec. 2, 1887.

118. CBS to HS, Jan. 1, 1888; AS to RS, Jan. 8, 1888; WS to GS, Jan. 18, 1888.

119. AS to RS, Jan. 8, 1888; GS to RS, Mar. 17, 1888; CBS to MS, Apr. 13, 1888; HS to RS, Apr. 2, 1888.

120. CBS to MS, Apr. 13, 1888.

121. CBS to MS, Apr. 13, 1888; Patent for Cash Entry 1456, May 29, 1888, Legal Documents, Shipman Family Papers, MHS; Patent for Cash Entry 1277, Deed Book 11, p. 392, Fergus County Courthouse, Lewistown, Mont. A cash entry was much like a preemption claim; a settler could buy up to 160 acres at $1.25 an acre by filing a declaratory statement and paying the fees after a two-year waiting period (Gates, *History of Public Land Law*, 244, 245, 394). Clark Shipman circumvented the more stringent requirements of the Homestead Act by acquiring much of his land by cash entry or preemption. Ken Karsmizki of Western History Research, Bozeman, Mont., noted that of the twenty-three patents issued over a twenty-year period to Shipman family members, almost half were either cash entries or preemptions, indicating "a level of affluence that is not necessarily typical on the 'homesteading frontier' where land was 'bought by the sweat of the brow.'" Shipman claims were also made using the Homestead Act, Timber and Stone Act, and the Desert Land Act, and Karsmizki has surmised that "the Shipman family was pretty familiar with the various public land laws and used them to their advantage" and that "with that much activity the chance of fraud has increased dramatically. Four homesteads, for instance, by Shipman family members would make me ask what . . . was happening at each claim. . . . The correspondence [between Shipman and the General Land Office] seems to suggest that Clark Shipman was stretching the law quite a bit if not directly trying to defraud the government" (Karsmizki to Peavy and Smith, Sept. 8, 1991).

Winnie's preemption claim would not mature for another two years. The homestead claim filed in Gertrude's name matured in 1889, seven years after her arrival in Montana, and Clark's homestead was patented in 1891, after three years of legal maneuvers. For some reason, Winnie's homestead was not patented until 1902, twenty years after she had filed on it (Gertrude Shipman, July 12, 1889, Deed Book 4, p. 551; Winifred Shipman, June 6, 1890, Deed Book 36, p. 50; Clark B. Shipman, Nov. 23, 1891, Deed Book 21, p. 336; Winlfred Shlpman, Apr. 8, 1902, Deed Book 21, p. 112, all in Fergus County Courthouse, Lewistown, Mont.).

122. AS to RS, May 2 and 13, 1888; MS to CBS, Aug. 14, 1888; Cooper Union Annual Report, 1888; HS to folks, June 27, 1888.

123. HS to folks, May 9 and June 27, 1888; MS to CBS, Aug. 14, 1888.

124. RS to GS, Aug. 20, 1888; RS to CBS, Nov. 25, 1888; WS to RS, Dec. 19, 1888; Rebecca Shipman obituary, Shipman Family Records.

125.   WS to GS, Oct. 7 and Nov. 11, 1888; CBS, Journal, 1888; WS to AS, Jan. 20, 1889.

126.   CBS, Journal, 1888.

127.   AS to RS, Jan. 30, 1889; MS to CBS, Mar. 11 and July 4, 1889; WS to GS, July 29, 1889; GS to AS, RS, and MS, July 27, 1889.

128.   CBS, Journal, 1890; U.S. Land Office to CBS, Nov. 19, 1889.

129.   CBS, Journal, 1890; Book 23, p. 184, and Book 24, p. 187, Feb. 22, 1890, Land Records of Bethel, Bethel Town Hall). Perham Hill was sold to Alonzo Spooner.

130.   WS to GS, Feb. 5, 1892; CBS, Journal, 1890; William R. Shipman to CBS, Jan. 15, 1889. Montana had attained statehood in November of 1889, a few months before Augusta's arrival there.

131.   AS to GS, Feb. 6, [1891], and Apr. 10, undated; CBS to GS, Mar. 26, 1892; RS to GS, Feb. 7, 1892. Gusta's description of sleeping arrangements suggests that she and Clark chose not to share a bed, even after their reunion.

132.   Patent Records, Bureau of Land Management, Billings, Mont.; CBS, Journal, 1891 and 1892; WS to GS, Mar. 26, 1892; Asa Cheffetz to Miss Shipman, Jan. 7, 1938; Rebecca Shipman obituary, Shipman Family Records. Within two years, Becky had commuted the claim to a cash-entry payment. Ironically, as Becky was beginning to receive widespread recognition for her work in wood engraving, that art form was being replaced by metal plate and photo engraving, work in which Becky had little interest and no training.

Gratia Shipman Erickson was born on Apr. 2, 1891; Gertrude Winifred Erickson was born on July 27, 1892 (Peck, *Richard Clarke*, 53).

133.   Erickson, "Reminiscences." Before his wife's arrival, Clark and his adult children had filed on five different pieces; after she came, the family took out eighteen more claims (Patent Records, Bureau of Land Management, Billings, Mont.).

134.   RS to GS, Sept. 1892; CBS, Journals, 1893 and 1895.

135.   CBS to MS, Dec. 31, 1893.

136.   CBS, Journal, 1894; WS to MS, Apr. 7, 1894; WS to William R. Shipman, May 16, 1994. Nicholas Erickson likely died of pneumonia, perhaps with a heart complication (Susan Shipman Burnham to Peavy and Smith, July 8, 1992). The children were not told of their father's death until their mother's return (AS to MS, Apr. 16, 1894).

137.   CBS to GS, Jan. 7, 1898; CBS, Journals, 1895, 1897, 1901; Margaret Shipman obituary, Shipman Family Records. Six years after he had begun the construction of the home, Clark was still in the process of putting up siding and painting. The original cabin was eventually torn down to accommodate an addition to the new house (CBS, Journal, 1896).

138.   CBS, Journals, 1897, 1898, and 1899; Winifred Shipman Erickson obituary and Gertrude Erickson Loeb obituary, both in Shipman Family Records; Erickson, "Reminiscences"; Susan Shipman Burnham to Peavy and Smith, Sept. 9, 1991.

139.   CBS, Journal, 1902–1903.

140.   Because of the age difference, Grace and Henry had not been well acquainted before she came to Montana (Peck, *Richard Clarke*, 53; Grace Martin Shipman, Reminiscences, Shipman Family Papers, MHS). Grace Shipman's reminiscences state that Winifred was hospitalized in Saint Louis while attending the

World's Fair, but Clark's 1904 journal notes that she was hospitalized in Evanston. Although Augusta had insisted that the wedding celebration take a decorous tone, given the seriousness of Winnie's condition, a crowd of friends organized a chivaree for the bridal couple on their wedding night, to which revelry the groom's mother took great exception (Shipman, Reminiscences).

Henry Nicholas Shipman was born on July 27, 1905 (CBS, Journal, 1905).

141. CBS, Journals, 1906 and 1907; Susan Shipman Burnham to Peavy and Smith, Sept. 9, 1991; Agreement between Henry E. Shipman . . . and John Q. Adams. . . , March 28, 1906, Legal Documents, Shipman Family Papers, MHS; news clipping from Shipman Family Records. Although it was clearly Clark who negotiated the sale, the contract was signed by his son, Henry. The various pieces of land sold were held in the names of all the Shipman clan: Clark B., Augusta F., Winifred, Gertrude, Henry, Rebecca, Margaret, and Grace Martin Shipman (CBS, Journal, 1906; Deed Book 5, pp. 376 and 377; Deed Book 23, p. 153; Deed Book 26, pp. 162–65, all in the Fergus County Courthouse, Lewistown, Mont.). Henry held over 4,000 acres, Clark 1,010, Gertrude 870, and the others smaller parcels ("Immense Tract Fergus Land Sold," *News-Argus*, 1905 or 1906, clipping in Shipman Family Records). John Q. Adams of Chicago, Illinois, as agent for the Enterprise Land and Improvement Company, made fifty separate land purchases in Fergus County between 1906 and 1908, when the Great Northern was laying a new road from Billings to Great Falls (Index to Deed Books, Fergus County Courthouse, Lewistown, Mont.; Tawny Killham, "A Century of Pioneering," Shipman Family Papers, MHS).

142. CBS, Journal, 1907; Richard Shipman was born on Apr. 28, 1907 (Shipman Family Records). Clark found it harder to divest himself of his horses than his cattle, especially Old Mag, the mare he had bought in Helena in 1882 to pull his wagon to the Judith Basin. "Sorry to see the old horses go," Clark noted in his journal in the spring of 1907. "But it is best for us & perhaps just as well for them." It cannot be determined from the records where Clark and Augusta lived in Lewistown; quite likely they moved into Winnie's house, since she and the girls were in Illinois a large part of the year.

143. CBS, Journal, 1907; Grace Martin Shipman, Reminiscences.

144. CBS, Journal, 1908. Oscar Lee died in October 1910; DeEtte Shipman Lee died at the home of her daughter Bertha in Northfield in November 1915 (DeEtte S. Lee and Oscar Lee obituaries, both in Shipman Family Records; CBS, Journal, 1910).

145. CBS, Journal, 1910; Susan Shipman Burnham to Peavy and Smith, Oct. 1991.

146. CBS obituary, Shipman Family Records; George W. Leach to Clark B. Shipman, Dec. 14, 1911, Deed Book 367, pp. 156–57, Berkshire County Courthouse, Pittsfield, Mass.; CBS to WS, July 22 and 27, 1912; AS to WS, undated, and June 14, n.y. Since receiving her master's degree from Tufts in 1900, Margaret Shipman had been teaching in various high schools in the Midwest, but at age thirty-six, she gave up her teaching career when she joined her parents in Lee (Margaret Shipman obituary, 1955, Shipman Family Records).

147. CBS to WS, June 24, 1912.

148. AS to WS, Feb. 3, 1913; CBS obituary, Shipman Family Records. The five grandchildren included Winnie's three girls and Henry's two boys. A sixth grand-

child, Susan Shipman, Henry's and Grace's first and only daughter, was born on Apr. 20, 1915 (Shipman Family Records). According to the probate filed two weeks after his death in the Berkshire County Courthouse, Clark Shipman's widow was to receive one-third of his property; three of his daughters—Gertrude, Rebecca, and Margaret—were to get all the rest. Winifred and Henry were not included in the inheritance "for the reason that they are each well provided for" (C. B. Shipman will, Legal Documents, Shipman Family Papers, MHS). Clark's estate at his death was worth close to $20,000, the vast majority of it—. $18,657—being in mortgages; the real property held was only the lot and house on Saint James Avenue, valued at $500 (Clark B. Shipman Probate 27572, Berkshire County Courthouse, Pittsfield, Mass.).

149.   AS to WS, Aug. 19, [1915]; AS to folks, Dec. 20, 1914, and undated; HS to Judge of Probate, Berkshire County, May 29, 1917, Probate 30356, Berkshire County Courthouse, Pittsfield, Mass.; AS obituary, Shipman Family Records; Cherry Hill Cemetery Records, Bethel Town Hall, Bethel, Vt. Augusta suffered rheumatism in addition to osteoporosis, and her late-life letters to Henry and Winifred are written in a large scrawl (AS to WS, undated; AS to folks, Dec. 20, 1914).

According to Gertrude's admission records, Winifred Erickson was her legal guardian in 1916. Notes from the state hospital records indicate a long history of "talking to herself" and note that the "patient persistently gazes at floor" and "sits quiet with head down for long periods." The private hospital was Dr. Edward Wiswall's Wellesley Nervine Hospital (Northhampton State Hospital Records, Massachusetts State Archives, Boston).

According to her probate, Augusta F. Shipman left an estate valued at over $20,000. Her personal property, $20,950, consisted mostly of certificates of deposit held in Lewistown, Mont., banks. Her real property amounted to $1,175, which represented her one-third interest in the house on Saint James Avenue (Augusta F. Shipman Probate 30356, Berkshire County Courthouse, Pittsfield, Mass.). According to their mother's will, Winnie and Henry were given one dollar each, and Margaret was given a life estate in all property, which would pass to Becky, thence to Gertrude, and thence to the three Erickson girls (AS will, Sept. 14, 1912, Probate 30356, Berkshire County Courthouse, Pittsfield, Mass.). Augusta's will is unusual in that it named her youngest daughter, Margaret, her primary heir, with Becky and Gertrude standing in secondary positions. At the time the will was drawn, Gertie had not yet been declared "an insane person."

Winifred Shipman, seventy-four, died at the home of her daughter Gratia in Palo Alto, California, on June 12, 1930 and was buried beside her husband in Chicago. (Winifred Shipman Erickson obituary, Shipman Family Records). Gertrude Shipman, eventually released from Wellesley Nervine Hospital into the care of her sisters Rebecca and Margaret, spent the last fifteen years of her life lying in a darkened room in the family home on Saint James Avenue (Helen Botto, one-time neighbor of the Shipman sisters, Lee, Mass., in a telephone interview with Peavy and Smith, June 1990). She died in Lee, Massachusetts, on Dec. 26, 1936, at seventy-six. (Gertrude Shipman obituary, Shipman Family Records). Henry Shipman, sixty-eight, died on Mar. 26, 1937 (Henry Shipman Probate 65142, Berkshire County Courthouse, Pittsfield, Mass.). Rebecca, eighty-one, died at home in Lee on Nov. 9, 1944 (Rebecca Shipman obituary, Shipman Family Records). Margaret died on Apr. 28, 1955, at age seventy-nine (Margaret Shipman obituary, *Berkshire Eagle,* Apr. 28, 1955, p. 12).

Family records indicate that the ashes of Gertrude, Rebecca, and Margaret were interred in the family plot at Cherry Hill Cemetery. Gratia, the child who died in infancy, was buried beside her Perham grandparents at Cherry Hill, Henry's ashes were scattered on the ranch in Montana, and Winifred was buried beside her husband in Chicago (Susan Burnham telephone interview with Peavy and Smith, July 1993; Cherry Hill Cemetery Records, Bethel Town Hall).

Index

References to illustrations are printed in boldface type.